Proceedings

Fourteenth Workshop on
Parallel and Distributed Simulation

Proceedings

Fourteenth Workshop on
Parallel and Distributed Simulation

PADS 2000

28–31 May 2000
Bologna, Italy

Edited by
David Bruce, Lorenzo Donatiello, and Stephen Turner

Sponsored by
IEEE Computer Society Technical Committee on Simulation (IEEE-TCSIM) Φ
ACM Special Interest Group on Simulation (SIGSIM) acm
Society for Computer Simulation (SCS) scs

IEEE
COMPUTER
SOCIETY

Los Alamitos, California

Washington • Brussels • Tokyo

IEEE Computer Society Order Number PR00667
ISBN 0-7695-0667-1
ISBN 0-7695-0679-8 (microfiche)
ISN Number 1087-4097

Additional copies may be ordered from:

IEEE Computer Society
Customer Service Center
10662 Los Vaqueros Circle
P.O. Box 3014
Los Alamitos, CA 90720-1314
Tel: + 1 714 821 8380
Fax: + 1 714 821 4641
http://computer.org/
csbooks@computer.org

IEEE Service Center
445 Hoes Lane
P.O. Box 1331
Piscataway, NJ 08855-1331
Tel: + 1 732 981 0060
Fax: + 1 732 981 9667
http://shop.ieee.org/store/
customer-service@ieee.org

IEEE Computer Society
Asia/Pacific Office
Watanabe Bldg., 1-4-2
Minami-Aoyama
Minato-ku, Tokyo 107-0062
JAPAN
Tel: + 81 3 3408 3118
Fax: + 81 3 3408 3553
tokyo.ofc@computer.org

Editorial production by Anne Rawlinson

Cover art production by Joe Daigle/Studio Productions

Printed in the United States of America by Technical Communication Services

IEEE
COMPUTER
SOCIETY

Table of Contents

Message from the General Chairs

Welcome to the 14th ACM/IEEE/SCS Workshop on Parallel and Distributed Simulation (PADS 2000). Bologna University is very proud to host such a prominent event in the field of simulation.

Bologna is the seat of one of the most ancient universities in the world. The University of Bologna, in fact, has recently celebrated the ninth century of its life.

The conference is being held in one of the most historic and meaningful places of Bologna: San Giovanni in Monte. Staying in these buildings is a real chance to experience a unique atmosphere, so many different ages having left their mark in this place. The richness of styles that characterizes San Giovanni in Monte reveals a succession of different cultural ages: the Gothic style, the Renaissance style, and the more classical style that is typical of Bologna can be admired one next to the other in these buildings.

The Conference Welcome and the Banquet Dinner are being held in a different site, the dining room of the "Circolo Ufficiali," a private club of the high-ranking officers of the Italian Army. Such a club is situated in Palazzo Grassi, one of the most characteristic buildings in the very centre of Bologna.

Our sincere thanks go to the many individuals who have helped to make PADS 2000 a success. In particular, our acknowledgements must include David Bruce for all his work in putting together such an excellent program, Marco Roccetti and members of the local organizing committee, and Bianca Angeloni for secretarial support.

Lorenzo Donatiello
Stephen Turner

PADS 2000 General Chairs

Message from the Program Chair

Welcome to PADS 2000, the Fourteenth ACM/IEEE/SCS Workshop on Parallel and Distributed Simulation.

Few could have failed to notice how much attention has been turned to matters of time over the past year, culminating in spectacular Millennium celebrations the world over. Although to some this date is just an arbitrary temporal marker, it has nevertheless inspired many to reflect on what has come before. Indeed, if one takes the opportunity to look back over the twenty years or so of research into parallel and distributed simulation, it is clear just how much this community has achieved.

I would rather look forward to the future, however, for it is equally clear that much exciting work remains to be done. It gives me great pleasure, then, to introduce two excellent keynote speakers for PADS 2000, each with a clear vision of the future and a willingness to spark debate.

W. H. (Dell) Lunceford, Jr. is Director of the US Army Model and Simulation Office, and Vice Chair/Secretary of the Simulation Interoperability Standards Organization. His involvement in modelling and simulation spans twenty-five years, and previous rôles (most recently at DARPA) have included being in a position to fund PADS research. Dell will give us his perspective on what actually matters to the simulation community at large, and where the PADS community might be able to make a difference.

Frederick Wieland, from the MITRE Corporation (USA), has been involved in parallel simulation since the early days, and is responsible for one of the most successful applications of parallel simulation to date — a civil aviation model called DPAT. Fred will describe what has made DPAT so successful, and suggest how other researchers might be able to have similar success in their own domain.

Program chair introductions often include gratuitous statistics, and I'm afraid that this is no exception. Thirty-six papers were submitted to PADS 2000, and subjected to an extensive double-blind review process. Over a very short period of time, the seventeen program committee members and fifty-six additional reviewers returned a total of 168 reviews, with most papers receiving five reports (including at least two from program committee members). These informed very good discussions at a productive program committee meeting in Phoenix, Arizona, USA, where twenty papers were selected for publication and presentation. (We also made history, I think, by finishing in good time for dinner!) Unfortunately, one author subsequently had to withdraw his (excellent) paper, after his organization changed their policy on supporting participation in conferences.

As in recent years, the best paper award will be judged on the final versions that appear in these proceedings. As the text of this foreword is due at the publishers at the same time as are the papers, this policy has the side-effect of keeping the candidates in suspense until the award ceremony at the workshop's banquet dinner! Nominations received from the program committee resulted in the following shortlist, to be reviewed again by the award sub-committee:

Parallel Mixed-Technology Simulation
Peter Frey, Radharamanan Radhakrishnan, Harold W. Carter, and Philip A. Wilsey

Repeatability in Real-Time Distributed Simulation Executions
Thom McLean and Richard Fujimoto

Grain Sensitive Event Scheduling in Time Warp Parallel Discrete Event Simulation
Francesco Quaglia and Vittorio Cortellessa

Locality-Preserving Load-Balancing Mechanisms
for Synchronous Simulations on Shared-Memory Multiprocessors
Voon-Yee Vee and Wen-Jing Hsu

The winning paper will also be recorded for posterity in next year's proceedings.

Speaking of which ... on behalf of last year's Program Chair I am delighted to confirm that the PADS'99 best paper award went to:

Efficient Optimistic Parallel Simulations using Reverse Computation
Christopher D. Carothers, Kalyan S. Perumalla, and Richard M. Fujimoto

Congratulations!

It takes a lot of work from a lot of people to organize a workshop like PADS 2000, and I would like to take this opportunity to recognize everyone involved. Lorenzo Donatiello, Marco Roccetti, and their colleagues at Bologna have been involved from the very beginning, and their handling of all the behind-the-scenes activities that make an event like this run smoothly is greatly appreciated.

I must of course thank all of the authors who submitted papers, without which there would be no point having a workshop in the first place. I was especially encouraged by how many of them were new to PADS, which is surely a good sign for the community. I have already mentioned the sterling job done by the program committee and reviewers, for which I thank them all. (Special mentions for Carl Tropper, first to return a review; Richard Meyer, first to return all his reviews; and Lois Ferscha, for brinkmanship to rival mine, his last review arriving just five minutes before I left for my flight to the PC meeting!)

David Nicol's excellent WIMPE system helped me not only to assign, collect, and process the reviews, but also to bombard authors and reviewers with email requests and reminders — at least, it did these things once Peter Hoare and Mark Cusack had helped get me a connection working through our local firewall!

Shirley Mendenhall and her team at the Pointe Hilton at Squaw Peak in Phoenix helped arrange a room for the program committee meeting at short notice, and kept us supplied with coffee. Finally, you wouldn't be reading any of this without the work of the editorial staff at IEEE Computer Society Press, particularly Anne Rawlinson, who produced these proceedings despite my scant regard for almost every deadline they set me!

Personal thanks are due to Richard Fujimoto, for volunteering me as Program Chair, and to Brian Unger, for telling me just how much work I was letting myself in for. (I didn't really believe him, of course, but I know now that he was right! So does my wife, Veronica, who has really been very patient about it all.) As always, it's been fun working with Lois Ferscha and my colleagues on the steering committee. But most of all, Steve Turner has helped me in so many ways — as last year's Program Chair, with some helpful hints and tricks-of-the-trade; as General Co-Chair, gently reminding me when things I should have done became (over)due; and as a friend, through some difficult times. Thanks, Steve.

I'm looking forward to enjoying PADS 2000, and I hope that you do too!

David Bruce

PADS 2000 Program Chair   Malvern, March 2000

Organizing Committees

Steering Committee

Current members

R. L. Bagrodia	University of California at Los Angeles, USA	(elected, 1998–2001)
D. I. Bruce	Defence Evaluation and Research Agency, UK	(ACM SIGSIM)
A. S. Elmaghraby	University of Louisville, USA	(IEEE TC-SIM)
A. Ferscha (chair)	University of Vienna, Austria	(elected, 1997–2000)
B. W. Unger	University of Calgary, Canada	(SCS)
F. P. Wieland	The MITRE Corporation, USA	(elected, 1999–2002)

Past members, whose term included PADS 2000 business

J. G. Cleary	University of Waikato, New Zealand	(elected, 1996–1999)
R. M. Fujimoto	Georgia Institute of Technology, USA	(elected, 1995–1998)

General Chairs

S. J. Turner	University of Exeter, UK
L. Donatiello	University of Bologna, Italy

Local Organizing Committee

M. Roccetti (chair)	University of Bologna, Italy
L. Bononi	University of Bologna, Italy
M. Furini	University of Bologna, Italy

Program Chair

D. I. Bruce	Defence Evaluation and Research Agency, UK

International Program Committee

R. L. Bagrodia	University of California, Los Angeles, USA
W. Cai	Nanyang Technological University, Singapore
C. D. Carothers	Rensselaer Polytechnic Institute, USA
J. G. Cleary	University of Waikato, New Zealand
S. R. Das	University of Texas, San Antonio, USA
L. Donatiello	University of Bologna, Italy
A. Ferscha	University of Vienna, Austria
R. M. Fujimoto	Georgia Institute of Technology, USA
D. M. Nicol	Dartmouth College, USA
E. H. Page	The MITRE Corporation, USA
F. Quaglia	University of Rome, Italy
B. R. Rönngren	Royal Institute of Technology, Sweden
C. Tropper	McGill University, Canada
S. J. Turner	University of Exeter, UK
B. W. Unger	University of Calgary, Canada
F. P. Wieland	The MITRE Corporation, USA
P. A. Wilsey	University of Cincinnati, USA

Reviewers

Rajive Bagrodia
Chris Booth
Azzedine Boukerche
Russell Bradford
Wentong Cai
Christopher Carothers
Roger Chamberlain
Yu-an Chen
Malolan Chetlur
John Cleary
Robert Cubert
Mark Cusack
Samir Das
Ewa Deelman
Lorenzo Donatiello
Alessandro Fabbri
Steve Ferenci
Alois Ferscha
Steve Franks
Richard Fujimoto
Boon-Ping Gan
Vijay Garg
Julian Hsu
Tom Lake
Michael Liljenstam
Jason Liu
Brian Logan
Margaret Loper
Guang Lu
Johannes Luethi
Steve McGough
Thom McLean
Richard Meyer
Farshad Moradi
Katherine Morse
Anand Natrajan
David Neufeld

David Nicol
Bradley Noble
James Nutaro
Ernie Page
Luiz Perrone
Kalyan Perumalla
CongDuc Pham
Anna Poplawski
Sushil Prasad
Brian Premore
Francesco Quaglia
Radharamanan Radhakrishnan
George Riley
Marco Roccetti
Robert Rönngren
David Roberts
Rob Simmonds
Roger Smith
Ha Yoon Song
Boleslaw Szymanski
Ivan Tacic
Mineo Takai
Gary Tan
Simon Taylor
Georgios Theodoropoulos
Carl Tropper
Stephen Turner
Brian Unger
Voon Yee Vee
Fred Wieland
Philip Wilsey
Linda Wilson
Paul Wonnacott
Christopher Young
Xiao Zhonge
Ziayan Zhu

PADS in the 20th Century:
A Brief History of Previous PADS Workshops

The PADS workshops began life as a track at the 1985 SCS MultiConference (now its Western MultiConference). After several meetings, however, the field of parallel and distributed simulation had gathered sufficient momentum that — albeit with some trepidation — the PADS community felt able to stand alone. In 1993, PADS joined several other conferences at the first Federated Computing Research Conference, which proved to be a great success. PADS' FCRC participation was repeated in both 1996 and 1999. In 1994, again with some trepidation, PADS left North America for Europe; once more, this proved highly successful. European venues in 1997 and for 2000 have continued PADS' international adventure.

PADS'99: 13th Workshop on Parallel and Distributed Simulation (part of FCRC'99)
Website • http://www.dcs.exeter.ac.uk/~pads99
Venue • Atlanta, Georgia, USA, 1–4 May 1999
General Chair • Richard Fujimoto
Program Chair • Stephen Turner
Proceedings • published by the IEEE Computer Society

PADS'98: 12th Workshop on Parallel and Distributed Simulation
Website • http://www.wnet.ca/pads98
Venue • Banff, Alberta, Canada, 26–29 May 1998
General Chair • Brian Unger
Program Chair • Alois Ferscha
Proceedings • published by the ACM and IEEE as Simulation Digest, Vol. 28, No. 1, July 1998

PADS'97: 11th Workshop on Parallel and Distributed Simulation
Website • http://www.ani.univie.ac.at/~ferscha/pads97
Venue • Lockenhaus, Austria, 10–13 June 1997
General Chair • Alois Ferscha
Program Co-Chairs • Rassul Ayani and Carl Tropper
Proceedings • published by the ACM and IEEE as Simulation Digest, Vol. 27, No. 1, July 1997

PADS'96: 10th Workshop on Parallel and Distributed Simulation (part of FCRC'96)
Website • http://www.pads.uwaterloo.ca/pads96
Venue • Philadelphia, Pennsylvania, USA, 22–24 May 1996
General Chair • Mary Bailey
Program Co-Chairs • Wayne Loucks and Bruno Preiss
Proceedings • published by the ACM and IEEE as Simulation Digest, Vol. 26, No. 1, July 1996

PADS'95: 9th Workshop on Parallel and Distributed Simulation
Venue • Lake Placid, New York, USA, 14–16 June 1995
General Chair • Jason Yi-Bing Lin
Program Chair • Mary Bailey
Proceedings • published by the ACM and IEEE as Simulation Digest, Vol. 25, No. 1, July 1995

PADS'94: 8th Workshop on Parallel and Distributed Simulation

Venue • Edinburgh, Scotland, UK, 6–8 July 1994
General Chair • Rajive Bagrodia
Program Co-Chairs • Damal Arvind and Jason Yi-Bing Lin
Proceedings • published by the ACM and IEEE as Simulation Digest, Vol. 24, No. 1, July 1994

PADS'93: 7th Workshop on Parallel and Distributed Simulation (part of FCRC'93)

Venue • San Diego, California, USA, 16–19 May 1993
General Co-Chairs • Richard Fujimoto and Brian Unger
Program Co-Chairs • Rajive Bagrodia and David Jefferson
Proceedings • published by the ACM and IEEE as Simulation Digest, Vol. 23, No. 1, July 1993

PADS'92: 6th Workshop on Parallel and Distributed Simulation

Venue • Newport Beach, California, USA, 20–22 January 1992
General Chair • Paul Reynolds
Program Chair • Marc Abrams
Proceedings • published by the SCS as Simulation Series, Vol. 24, No. 3

PADS'91: SCS Multiconference on Advances in Parallel and Distributed Simulation

Venue • Anaheim, California, USA, 23–25 January 1991
General Chair • David Nicol
Program Chair • Vijay Madisetti
Proceedings • published by the SCS as Simulation Series, Vol. 23, No. 1

PADS'90: SCS Multiconference on Distributed Simulation

Venue • San Diego, California, USA, 17–19 January 1990
General and Program Chair • David Nicol
Proceedings • published by the SCS as Simulation Series, Vol. 22, No. 1, January 1990

PADS'89: SCS Multiconference on Distributed Simulation

Venue • Tampa, Florida, USA, 28–31 March 1989
General Chair • Brian Unger
Program Chair • Richard Fujimoto
Proceedings • published by the SCS as Simulation Series, Vol. 21, No. 2, March 1989

PADS'88: SCS Multiconference on Distributed Simulation

Venue • San Diego, California, USA, 3–5 February 1988
General Chair • Brian Unger
Program Chair • David Jefferson
Proceedings • published by the SCS as Simulation Series, Vol. 19, No. 3, July 1988

PADS'85: SCS Conference on Distributed Simulation

Venue • San Diego, California, USA, 24–26 January 1985
General Co-Chairs • Bernard Zeigler and Sallie Sheppard
Program Co-Chairs • Paul Reynolds and Horst Wedde
Proceedings • published by the SCS as Simulation Series, Vol. 15, No. 2, January 1985

Session 1
Challenges for future research

Advanced Distributed Simulation: What we learned, where to go next
Keynote speaker: W. H. (Dell) Lunceford, Jr.

Advanced Distributed Simulation: What we learned, where to go next

W. H. (Dell) Lunceford, Jr.[*]

US Army Model and Simulation Office
Arlington, VA, U.S.A.

Abstract

It has been a little less than ten years since modeling and simulation (M&S) hit the knee on the curve. During these past few years a great deal of marketing of the potential of M&S has occurred, which resulted in a significant influx of funding for research and development (R&D) projects, especially in the area of distributed simulation.

One of the significant experiments in this area — the DARPA Synthetic Theater of War program — officially ended this year, bringing to an end one of the more robust experiments in distributed simulation. We are now in a time where most of the M&S funding is targeted at production programs, with much fewer dollars going into R&D or experimentation.

Although it is good that major programs are capitalizing on previous R&D efforts, it would not be true to say that the necessary R&D has been completed to realize the vision of distributed simulation. It would be true to say that we now have a much better understanding of the issues. What is needed now is a period of reflection on the vision, where we are, what was done right, what hasn't worked well, and where we should be headed for the next five to ten years.

Overview of talk

Mr. Lunceford will give his perspective on what we have learned in the field of distributed M&S over the past few years, and provide some insights of where this technology area — and the PADS community — should focus its efforts over the next few years.

About the speaker

W. H. (Dell) Lunceford, Jr., is Director of the US Army Model and Simulation Office (AMSO), which is responsible for shaping and guiding the US Army's use of simulation technology. He has over twenty-five years of modeling and simulation experience, including program management, systems engineering and R&D for some of the US Department of Defense's largest simulation-based programs. His recent position as Program Manager for DARPA's Advanced Simulation Technology Thrust program included the opportunity/responsibility to fund PADS research. In addition to his position at AMSO, Mr. Lunceford is also Vice Chair/Secretary of the Simulation Interoperability Standards Organization, and editor of its on-line Simulation Technology Magazine.

---

[*] The speaker can be reached at Wendell.Lunceford@hqda.army.mil.

Session 2
Parallel simulation for continuous and real-time applications

Parallel Mixed-Technology Simulation
P. Frey, R. Radhakrishnan, H. W. Carter, and P. A. Wilsey

Applying Parallel Discrete Event Simulation to Network Emulation
R. Simmonds, R. Bradford, and B. Unger

Repeatability in Real-Time Distributed Simulation Executions
T. McLean and R. Fujimoto

Parallel Mixed-Technology Simulation*

Peter Frey
Cadence Design Systems,
2655 Seely Avenue,
San Jose, CA 95134
pfrey@cadence.com

Radharamanan Radhakrishnan,
Harold W. Carter, and Philip A. Wilsey
Dept. of ECECS, University of Cincinnati,
Cincinnati, OH 45221–0030
{ramanan,hcarter,paw}@ececs.uc.edu

Abstract

Circuit simulation has proven to be one of the most important computer aided design (CAD) methods for the analysis and validation of integrated circuit designs. A popular approach to describing circuits for simulation purposes is to use a hardware description language such as VHDL. Similar efforts have also been carried out in the analog domain that has led to tools such as SPICE. However, with the growing trend of hardware designs that contain both analog and digital components, design environments that seamlessly integrate analog and digital circuitry are needed. Simulation of such circuits is however, exacerbated by the higher resource (CPU and memory) demands that arise when analog and digital models are integrated in a mixed-mode (analog and digital) simulation. One solution to this problem is to use PDES algorithms on a distributed platform. However, a synchronization interface between the analog and digital simulation environment is required to achieve integrated mixed-mode simulation. In this paper, we present the issues involved in the construction of synchronization protocols which support mixed-mode simulation in a distributed simulation environment. The proposed synchronization protocols provide an interface between an optimistic (Time Warp based) discrete-event simulation kernel and any continuous time simulation kernel. Empirical and formal analyses were conducted to ensure correctness and completeness of the protocols and the results of these analyses are also presented.

1 Introduction

Advances in computer aided design (CAD) technology have nurtured and facilitated the use of analog components

---

*Support for this work was provided in part by the Defense Advanced Research Projects Agency under contracts J-FBI-93-116 and DABT63–96–C–0055.

together with digital components in today's high end integrated circuit designs. Design and analysis tools such as discrete-event simulators are now required to analyze large circuit designs that contain both analog and digital components. This has resulted in the development of the *mixed-mode simulation* domain. Mixed-mode simulation is the combination of *mixed-level* and *mixed-signal* simulation. The mixed-level paradigm enables the hardware designer to model a design at different levels of abstraction. The ability to combine different signal domains (*e.g.*, analog and digital) in a single model is called mixed-signal simulation. Thus, as mixed-mode simulation enables the designer to model and simulate at different levels of abstraction in different domains, it introduces unique complications for the modeler and the simulator developer. It is clear that interaction via some type of interface functions will have to be supported for correct simulation to take place. This implies that the simulation is split into distinct simulation time intervals in which no interaction between the two simulation models takes place. Hence, there are distinct points in simulation time where the interaction (or communication) does take place. To model this interaction, the simulation models are defined as interacting processes. Discrete-event processes define the behavior of the discrete-event model whereas differential equation processes define the behavior of the analog/continuous (usually modeled using differential equations) model. The interface functions are responsible for handling the communication between these processes, but the different notions of time will need to be addressed by the simulator. Resolving the different notions of time is critical for correct simulation. Figure 1 illustrates the temporal behavior of a discrete-event process and a differential equation process. Execution of a discrete-event process is instantaneous as time is not advanced *during* execution. A differential equation process's execution may advance the simulation time during execution. This is why a differential equation process is also known as a *self-advancing* process.

A mixed-mode simulator must coordinate between these

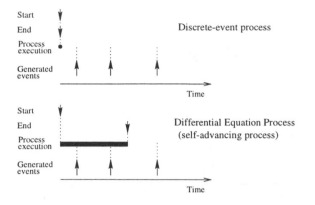

Figure 1. Mixed-Mode Processes

different simulation processes. There are two basic approaches to this problem: (a) define and provide an interface to a simulation backbone such that the interface takes care of providing individual processes with the necessary simulation and timing information [3]; and (b) partition every differential equation process into a set of discrete-event processes [1]. While the first case has to deal with the design and support of a complex interface, the latter case has high communication costs due to the large number of processes. Despite the limitations of the basic approaches, a parallel execution environment is ideal for mixed-mode simulation as a mixed-mode design is by default, naturally partitioned along the boundaries of its digital and analog regions. We present a solution that tries to establish a tradeoff between the complex interface or high communication costs by using a new parallel synchronization scheme between the mixed-mode simulation processes. This new scheme adopts a process based approach towards synchronization and is called *process synchronization*. The remainder of this paper is organized as follows. Section 2 reviews mixed-mode simulation and motivates the need for efficient synchronization protocols. Section 3 describes the process synchronization approach and presents two synchronization protocols that have been successfully used to synchronize a Time Warp based parallel kernel with a continuous time differential equation simulation kernel. Section 4 presents the prototype simulation environment in which the process synchronization protocols have been implemented and studied. In addition, Section 4 also presents the series of experiments that have been carried to formally and empirically validate the correctness of the process synchronization protocols. Finally, Section 5 presents some concluding remarks.

2 Background and Related Work

Mixed-mode simulation is the combination of two mathematical models. Zeigler [15] classified these two mathematical models as the class of discrete event models and the class of differential equation models. Differential equation models exhibit continuous changes in time as well as continuous changes in state; thus, the time derivatives (i.e., rates of change) are governed by the differential equations. Cellier [4] states that differential equation models, in general, are simulated as a discrete-time model on a digital computer to avoid infinitely many state changes. Values between the discrete-time stamps are then interpolated. The time increments of the differential equations is usually smaller than the time increments of the discrete event models.This is attributed to the fact that as a continuous signal's value changes rapidly, smaller time increments are needed to correctly sample the signal's value. Zeigler also concluded that no more than a finite number of events can occur in a finite time interval. Discrete event models, on the other hand, exhibit discrete changes in time and state. State changes only occur at time points (events) and are always discontinuous.

The traditional mixed-mode simulation implementations were restrictive in nature as they mainly dealt with individual differential equation solvers (communication through a backplane) or a large set of discrete-event processes. Instead of dividing the self-advancing process into individual discrete-event processes, the *process synchronization* approach deals with the self-advancing processes as discrete-event processes. Process synchronization protocols are required to bridge the differences between the self-advancing process and a discrete representation of the same process. This has several advantages. There is a large set of algorithms available for differential equation model simulation. Each of these algorithms have different properties and performance factors. Depending on the model descriptions, the algorithm that gives the best performance may vary. With the process synchronization approach, the differential equation model simulation algorithm can be dynamically selected during the simulation or statically determined before the simulation. Memory requirements for state saving are lower for the single self-advancing process when compared to the memory requirements of the discrete-event representation of a self-advancing process (since a self-advancing process is usually split into several discrete-event processes). This is because the self-advancing process advances in its own time domain, such that state saving is only required at synchronization points. As synchronization is limited to specific simulation intervals, the number of states saved will be much lower than the number of states saved in the traditional optimistic discrete-event simulation (even if an infrequent state saving strategy is employed in the optimistic simulator). Communication is reduced to interface function communication in the case of the self-advancing processes. As self-advancing processes have high internal communication demands, this communication is kept local (and not sent across the network of a distributed platform).

Tahawy *et al* [13] was the first to investigate synchronization of processes for mixed-mode simulation. However, the process synchronization scheme introduced by Tahawy only considered sequential event-driven simulation kernels with a single self advancing process. Given that parallel simulation methods are required to simulate today's large scale simulation models, the usability of Tahawy's scheme is, at best, limited.

3 Parallel Process Synchronization

Correct parallel simulation is dependent on the behavior of the discrete-event processes, the self-advancing processes, and the interface between the different time domains. During our investigations of this problem, we have developed two different synchronization protocols. These two protocols are presented in this section. A graphical representation (*synchronization diagrams*) of the protocols is provided for aiding the discussion.

A single synchronization diagram represents a snapshot of the interface between a single self-advancing process and the parallel discrete-event simulator. The state of a self-advancing process is marked by a state indicator. All state indicators shown in the diagram, belong to the monitored self-advancing process. The same applies to the events shown in the diagram (*i.e.*, the diagram does not show all the events in the system). There are two kinds of state indicators. The black triangles represent the saved states (i.e states that were saved in the previous execution cycle). These states are accessible and rollbacks to these states can be initiated. The white triangles represent states that are going to be saved at the completion of the current execution cycle. Note that each saved state is associated with a discrete-event. This implies that a self-advancing process saves state only if there is an interaction with the discrete-event simulator. Between these points of interaction, the self-advancing process may have any number of changes to its state which will not be recorded. In the following subsections, synchronization diagrams are used to introduce the synchronization protocols. Two process based synchronization protocols are introduced. The protocols are named after their fundamental property of synchronization: (a) *First Event Synchronization* (FES) and (b) *Second Event Synchronization* (SES).

3.1 First Event Synchronization protocol

In the First Event Synchronization (FES) protocol, the differential equation process is handled as a discrete event process that is triggered by an event arriving at the start of the simulation interval. However, the process synchronization protocol has to handle some exceptions, due to the

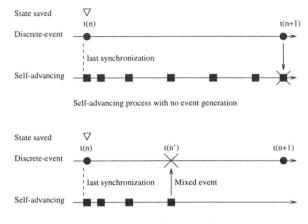

Self-advancing process with no event generation

Self-advancing process with generation of an event

Figure 2. First Event Synchronization (FES)

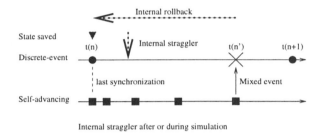

Internal straggler after or during simulation

Figure 3. First Event Synchronization error

process's self-advancing nature. Figure 2 gives a graphical representation of the FES protocol. The self-advancing process is activated by the first event (t_n). The previous state stored contains the system state up to the event time (t_n). The self-advancing process attempts to simulate to the time of the next scheduled event (t_{n+1}) of the process. If no event is generated, the self-advancing process calculates all intermediate values, stops computation at t_{n+1}, and stores its state. The state stored will be associated with the activation event (t_n) but it will contain the self-advancing process state up to time t_{n+1}. After the state is saved, a new synchronization point is reached. In case a threshold cross (event generation) occurs during computation of the internal values of the self-advancing process, the FES protocol requires the storage of the state and an artificial event at time $t_{n'}$ needs to be generated to force another synchronization point. Synchronization is accomplished since the artificial event will cause activation and the stored state will have the self-advancing process's values stored up to time $t_{n'}$. This protocol appears straightforward, but several assumptions must be satisfied to guarantee correct execution. The most obvious assumption is that the protocol assumes the time stamp t_{n+1} of the next event is available. This can not always be guaranteed. Therefore, if no further event is scheduled, a simulation interval end time must be selected. In reality, this may not be an issue as the self advancing process is compute-intensive and is often the slowest process in the simulated system. Due to this, the next event (which is used as the simulation end time) is usually available. However, a more serious issue arises from the use of the optimistic discrete event simulator. Although the optimistic protocol does not enforce the execution of events in causal order, it will ensure the causal order of events before the current event (t_n). This, however, is not enough in a mixed-mode simulation because the computation in the self-advancing process has its own notion of time.

Figure 3 shows this error case. Due to the event at time t_n, the self-advancing process is triggered to calculate the system behavior till $t_{n'}$ (the same error would occur if the self advancing process did not cross the threshold). Now any event which arrives between the current trigger event at t_n and the final time $t_{n'}$ (or t_{n+1}) produces a self-advancing process error. Events in this interval (internal straggler) are not considered to be a causality error by the discrete system because the event receive time is greater then the time of the trigger event. On the other hand, the self-advancing process has already advanced to the end time $t_{n'}$ (or t_{n+1}). Therefore a rollback is required to restore correct initial conditions, remove unnecessarily created events, and resume execution from t_n up to the new received event time. The FES protocol is responsible for all tasks from the recognition of the internal straggler to the initiation of a rollback. This implies that there is a relationship between the time interval for the self-advancing process and the internal rollbacks. Therefore, the selection of the time step (which is either pre-selected or decided at run-time) is a critical performance factor in the basic FES protocol.

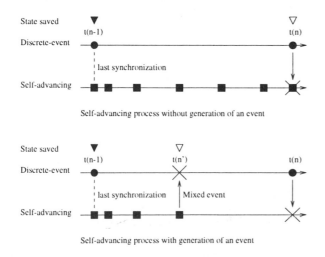

Self-advancing process without generation of an event

Self-advancing process with generation of an event

Figure 4. Second Event Synchronization (SES)

Optimistic discrete-event simulators require a saved state (or a regenerated state if an infrequent state saving strategy is employed) at any time point to which the simulation may rollback. This requires that every process called during initialization return a valid state. However, if the self-advancing process proceeds as described above, this can not be ensured. Therefore, the FES protocol must ensure that this property can be supported by the self-advancing process. One solution is to prohibit time advancement during initialization and enforce re-execution by scheduling an event with no delay. This results in a safe synchronization state from which the protocol can continue.

3.2 Second Event Synchronization protocol

In the Second Event Synchronization (SES) protocol, synchronization is attempted on the receive time of the event(s) determining the end of the self-advancing simulation interval. With synchronization at the end of the interval, the protocol does not need to pick a simulation end time. The general approach is illustrated by the synchronization diagram in Figure 4. The previously executed event at time t_{n-1} marks the previous synchronization point to which the self-advancing process has simulated. The self-advancing process is activated by the event at time t_n (since a simulation interval end time is now available) and continues to simulate from t_{n-1} to t_n. If no threshold is crossed, the simulation reaches the time t_n and stops. A new synchronization point is automatically generated after the state is stored. The synchronization is complete because the self advancing simulation time as well as the discrete time is now t_n and all causality errors will have been handled by the discrete-event system. If an event is generated during the self-advancing simulation interval, the self-advancing process must be interrupted. In addition to sending the generated event at time $t_{n'}$, the state associated with the time $t_{n'}$ must be stored and the discrete-event simulator notified that the self-advancing process did not complete the calculations up to time t_n. One possible solution is to insert a dummy event at time $t_{n'}$ and make the system believe that the self advancing process was activated by this event. The change of the triggering event involves reactivating the event at time t_n. The state will then automatically be stored with the correct time stamp because of the change in the triggering event. A synchronization point is now reached as the time of the self-advancing process is the same as the discrete-event time.

Although there is no need for additional rollback detection, there exists some additional processing overhead. The state has to be saved if an event occurs during the self-advancing process execution. If not, the system can run into deadlock as shown in Figure 5. In this case, assume that an event occurred at $t_{n'}$. However, no state was saved and the

10

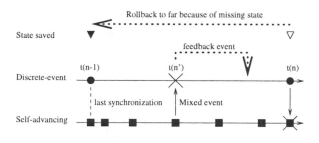

Figure 5. Second Event Synchronization error

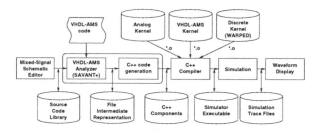

Figure 6. Architecture of SEAMS

self-advancing process continued up to t_n. If the discrete event at time $t_{n'}$ is responsible for an event in the interval $[t_{n'}, t_n]$ for the self-advancing process, a system rollback will be determined. Through the initiated rollback, the system is now reset to the last synchronization point. This how-ever, causes the removal of both the event at time $t_{n'}$ and the feedback event that initiated the rollback. The system will reset itself to the same state as before (namely the state at time t_{n-1}). Because no change in the system occurred, the simulation would again create the event at $t_{n'}$ that will re-sult in an infinite loop.

To ensure a second event at any time, the SES proto-col needs to ensure that at least one element is scheduled at the end of the simulation time. However, this could result in a larger than necessary simulation interval. This is not ideal as the simulation interval is an important performance issue. Increasing the simulation interval results in a pro-portional increase in the probability of a rollback. Due to this phenomenon, the SES protocol allows the user to select a pre-specified *maximum simulation interval* or the *analog simulation interval* (ASI). This ASI value is again a ran-dom value and the optimum is dependent on the simulation model. Compared to the FES protocol, the ASI is an addi-tional option for the SES protocol and not a requirement.

The process synchronization approaches presented here are not specific to any differential equation simulator. In-stead, the protocols can synchronize any self-advancing process as long as the following assumptions hold: (a) The process progresses monotonically in time after activation; (b) At any change of output or at a specified simulation end time, the process interrupts execution; and (c) Processes can resume execution from a previously established simu-lation point once its internal state is regenerated. If these preconditions hold, the process synchronization approach restricts the interface to input and output communication (including input and output of simulation time) and occa-sional state changes. Many differential equation simulators satisfy these conditions or can be easily adapted to use these protocols. The interface approach used for process synchro-nization enables the simulator to incorporate several self-advancing processes during a single simulation. Given the

domain of circuit simulation, this implies that parallel sim-ulation of individual sub-circuits is supported and the actual circuit simulator may be chosen separately for each individ-ual differential equation model.

4 Experimental Framework

With the growing trend of hardware designs that contain significant analog and digital sections, comprehensive de-sign environments that seamlessly integrate analog and dig-ital circuitry are necessary. Toward this end, the VHDL [9] language (for which there are several design tools) was ex-tended to support (in addition to digital) analog and mixed-signal simulation. These extensions to VHDL have re-sulted in a new language called VHDL-AMS [8]. In ad-dition to the electrical-domain, VHDL-AMS also supports mixed-domain modeling. There are several ongoing en-deavors in the academic and industrial worlds to develop design environments to create and simulate models written in VHDL-AMS. Simulation Environment for VHDL-AMS (SEAMS) [6], is one such mixed-signal simulator that is the product of our research.

SEAMS [6] consists of several modules that are inte-grated into a single simulation system. Figure 6 shows the architecture of SEAMS. The input to the system is VHDL-AMS text of the model that is to be simulated. The model is parsed and analyzed (the syntax and the semantics of the system are verified). The parser/analyzer converts the VHDL-AMS code to an intermediate format from which C++ code is automatically generated. The generated C++ program is then compiled and linked with the different ker-nels in the system, namely the TyVIS VHDL Kernel [14], the Analog Simulation Kernel, and the WARPED optimistic discrete-event simulation kernel [11].

4.1 Formal and Empirical Analysis

The complexity and the nondeterministic execution be-havior of the Time Warp protocol make it a difficult algo-rithm to implement and extend. Years of development have shown that even a simple implementation of the basic Time

Warp protocol is often error prone due to difficulties in understanding the protocol. The discussion of the FES and the SES protocols in the earlier sections serve only as an introduction. The descriptions only introduced the protocols and elaborated on their general design. However, the informal description is ambiguous, difficult to comprehend and often does not convey a complete picture of the issues involved. Formal methods provide the means to overcome these shortcomings and provide a framework for conducting proofs of correctness. Towards this end, we have developed an extensible formal framework for the specification and the verification of the optimistic discrete-event simulation paradigm (Time Warp) and the synchronization protocols. For the sake of brevity (and since this is not the focus of this paper), we do not detail the specification and verification process in this paper. Details regarding the specification are available in the literature [5, 7] and the formal specification itself is available on-line at www.ececs.uc.edu/~pfrey/pvs.

While the PDES domain has matured enough to be able to sufficiently characterize and compare the performance of parallel discrete-event simulators, the same cannot be said of mixed-mode simulators. The set of parameters concerning parallel mixed-mode simulation is large. Memory requirements, communication latencies, execution time, event granularity, and process granularity are just a few of the metrics that exist in PDES [2]. These metrics must be expanded to address the attributes of differential-equation simulation to obtain an accurate index of parallel mixed-mode simulation performance. Some metrics native to differential-equation simulation include the accuracy of the solution, the sample interval of the signals, the analog simulation interval, the effect of partitioning on performance, the generality of the simulation method and several other parameters that are completely alien to discrete-event simulators. Given the myriad ways that we could analyze the performance of the synchronization protocols, we selected three indices that were the most interesting: (a) execution time, (b) the effect of partitioning on the mixed-mode simulation performance, and (c) the effect of the analog simulation interval. As test circuits, we chose three circuits from a set of six circuits that Saleh [12] had specifically designed to stress test the mixed-mode simulation interface. The three circuits are: a two-bit adder with an RLC circuit as the delay line, a clock generator consisting of a RC circuit connected to two NOT gates and a combination of two clock generators working in parallel.

The timings presented in Figure 7 are the average of three different runs. Since these experiments were carried out on a dedicated machine (a 4 processor SPARC Center 1000) and the runs are large heavy-weight processes, three different runs were enough to get a good estimate. In addition, in case of multiprocessor execution, three different

process distributions (or partitions) were simulated. Figure 7 also presents a comparison of the different synchronization protocols. The effect of increased computation power and communication cost on the synchronization protocols can be investigated by varying the number of processors. Keeping the number of processors constant but changing the process partitions, illustrates the effect of locality of related processes on the protocol performance. The preliminary performance evaluation illustrates some interesting facts about the individual protocols. The performance values in almost all cases favor the SES protocol when it is a multiprocessor simulation. In most cases, the SES protocol performs as good as or better than the FES protocol. A reason why SES is more efficient than FES is that SES is a less optimistic approach (with the synchronization performed on the second event). Unlike FES, where a significant amount of unnecessary computation may occur (and be rolled back), SES limits the number of such occurrences and reduces the wasted simulation time. Reducing the amount of wasted computation is a primary goal in mixed-mode simulation using an optimistic simulation approach. Another interesting observation is the effect of partitioning on the performance of the simulator, especially in the two clock generator example. If both self-advancing processes are assigned to the same partition (same processor), the high process granularity affects the simulator's performance adversely.

As explained earlier, for a given simulation run, the analog simulation intervals (ASIs) are the time periods for which an analog (continuous) process is allowed to simulate. Of course, it must be realized that if the ASI is set to be equal to the total simulation time, the analog process will attempt to simulate from the start time of simulation to the end time of simulation. This would be fine if the simulation were for a purely analog model, where there are no possibilities for rollbacks in case of erroneous computation. In this scenario, the simulation proceeds from the start time to the finish time. However, in the case of a mixed signal model, the behavior of the simulator is not quite as simple as in the case of the analog model. In a mixed signal circuit, it is possible that the analog (continuous) process might produce signals which are then sent out to other processes in the simulation domain as discrete events. The analog process must halt computation at this particular time point and save the current state. The analog process will resume its simulation from this point sometime in the future. If the opposite case occurs, *i.e.*, the analog process receives some event from some other process in the simulation whose time-stamp is lower than the current local time of the analog/continuous process, it will need to halt computation immediately, roll back to the previously saved state and resume simulation from this point. Note that if the ASI is set to be a large time value, there is a higher probability of the analog process

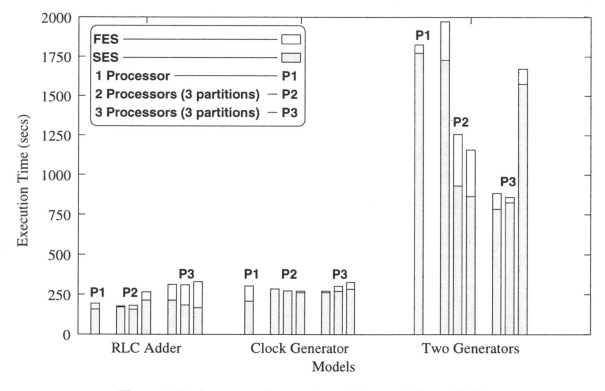

Figure 7. Performance Comparison between FES and SES

being interrupted in the middle of its simulation interval because either events are being generated within it, or events are being sent to it from outside processes. This results in the suspension of the analog process and possible rollbacks if the time-stamp of arriving events is lower than the current simulation time. So how does the ASI affect a mixed-mode simulation's execution?

The results illustrated in Figure 8 show the execution time for the two clock generators model executing on up to four processors (randomly distributed). Each simulation run was performed over the same simulation time of $10s$ ($1e + 16$ femto-seconds (fs)), whereas the ASI was varied from $10\mu s$ to $10s$. A minimum in execution time can be clearly identified in all cases. Note that reducing the ASI below this optimal value leads to an increase in simulation time. This identifies the ASI as a model dependent parameter and raises the question of finding an optimum value for a given model dynamically during the simulation [10]. We have identified some factors that contribute to the determination of an optimum ASI:

(a) *State size:* With a frequent state saving strategy, a state of the simulation object is saved after each execution cycle. A small ASI increases the number of state saving operations, whereas a larger may reduce the state saving costs. As the cost of state saving is not negligible, especially for the relatively large states of a continuous solver, this

factor has to be considered when the ASI is selected.

(b) *Rollback frequency:* Only if a rollback occurs, should the ASI be set different from the simulation end time. Similarly, if rollbacks are infrequent, the ASI should be set as large as possible as this requires less state saving and less solution points calculated in the analog islands.

(c) *Analog solution points:* Any analog solver has several variables determining the number of solution points calculated in a given simulation interval. Most variables are tolerance-related, which enforces additional solution points in circuits with small time constants. In addition, the user can restrict the maximum possible advancement to increase accuracy. All of these factors increase the granularity of the analog process behavior and make re-execution more expensive. As a result, more solution points (higher execution granularity) favor smaller ASIs.

(d) *Event generation:* Since the generation of events by the analog solver disrupts the analog simulation interval, a highly active circuit might be able to perform better with a large ASI.

5   Conclusions

Two approaches for synchronizing any generic continuous time differential equation simulation kernel with an optimistic (Time Warp) discrete-event simulation paradigm

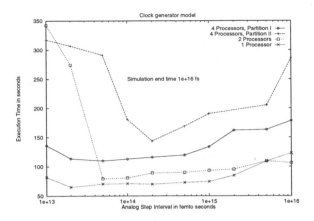

Figure 8. Execution time vs. ASI

were presented. Both protocols follow a process-based synchronization approach which requires independent self-advancing processes to synchronize only at the beginning or end of an interval. When compared with a purely event-driven mixed-mode simulation approach, the process synchronization approach exhibits several advantages: (a) there is a significant reduction in memory usage as states are saved only at the beginning/end of the simulation interval and not for every intermediate value; (b) the problem is naturally partitioned, making it more amenable for parallel execution (the modeler can improve the simulation performance by subdividing circuits into separate islands); and (c) there is freedom to select from a large set of algorithms for differential equation model simulation.

The exact requirements of the FES and SES protocol were identified with the help of the formal specification. The formal specification and verification clarified inconsistencies in the design and description of the algorithms. The specification provided an insight into the exact semantics of the protocols and provides a framework for future optimizations. Although the performance characteristics support the claims of the process-based synchronization protocols, the experiments only profile a subset of the known performance parameters. The discrete and continuous simulation domain each provide a large set of performance parameters. In mixed-mode simulation, these parameters are merged together and new parameters due to synchronization are introduced. It is therefore, critical to define a set of suitable performance parameters to report and compare performances of several mixed-mode simulators.

References

[1] ACUNA, E. L., DERVENIS, J. P., PAGONES, A. J., YANG, F. L., AND SALEH, R. A. Simulation techniques for mixed analog/digital circuits. *IEEE Journal of Solid-State Circuits 25*, 2 (Apr. 1990), 353–363.

[2] BALAKRISHNAN, V., FREY, P., ABU-GHAZALEH, N., AND WILSEY, P. A. A framework for performance analysis of parallel discrete event simulators. In *Proceedings of the 1997 Winter Simulation Conference* (Dec. 1997).

[3] CAD FRAMEWORK INITIATIVE, INC, A. Simulation backplane programming interface specification, 1993. (available on the ftp at ftp.cfi.org).

[4] CELLIER, F. E. *Continuous System Modeling*. Springer-Verlag, 1991.

[5] FREY, P. *Protocols for Optimistic Synchronization of Mixed-Mode Simulation*. PhD thesis, University of Cincinnati, Aug. 1998.

[6] FREY, P., NELLAYAPPAN, K., SHANMUGASUNDARAM, V., MAYILADUTHURAI, R. S., CHANDRASHEKAR, C. L., AND CARTER, H. W. SEAMS: Simulation Environment for VHDL-AMS. In *1998 Winter Simulation Conference (WSC'98)* (December 1998).

[7] FREY, P., RADHAKRISHNAN, R., WILSEY, P. A., ALEXANDER, P., AND CARTER, H. W. An extensible formal framework for the specification and verification of an optimistic simulation protocol. In *Proceedings of the 32nd Hawaii International Conference on System Sciences (HICSS'99)* (jan 1999), Sony Electronic Publishing Services.

[8] IEEE COMPUTER SOCIETY. *IEEE Draft Standard VHDL-AMS Language Reference Manual*, 1997.

[9] LIPSETT, R., MARSCHNER, E., AND SHAHDAD, M. VHDL — the language. *IEEE Design & Test 3*, 2 (Apr. 1986), 28–41.

[10] MANAVALAN, J. K. Performance evaluation and speed improvement of the seams vhdl-ams simulator using dynamic adjustment of the analog simulation interval. Master's thesis, University of Cincinnati, November 1998.

[11] RADHAKRISHNAN, R., MARTIN, D. E., CHETLUR, M., RAO, D. M., AND WILSEY, P. A. An Object-Oriented Time Warp Simulation Kernel. In *Proceedings of the International Symposium on Computing in Object-Oriented Parallel Environments (ISCOPE'98)*, D. Caromel, R. R. Oldehoeft, and M. Tholburn, Eds., vol. LNCS 1505. Springer-Verlag, Dec. 1998, pp. 13–23.

[12] SALEH, R., JOU, S.-J., AND NEWTON, A. R. *Mixed-mode simulation and analog multilevel simulation*. Kluwer Academic Publishers, 1994.

[13] TAHAWY, H. E., RODRIGUEZ, D., GARCIA-SABIRO, S., AND MAYOL, J.-J. Vhd$_e$ldo: A new mixed mode simulation. *EURO DAC 1993* (Sept. 1993).

[14] WILSEY, P. A., MARTIN, D. E., AND SUBRAMANI, K. SAVANT/TyVIS/WARPED: Components for the analysis and simulation of VHDL. In *VHDL Users' Group Spring 1998 Conference* (Mar. 1998), pp. 195–201.

[15] ZEIGLER, B. P. *Theory of Modelling and Simulation*. John Wiley & Sons, Inc., New York, 1976.

Applying
Parallel Discrete Event Simulation
to Network Emulation

Rob Simmonds, Russell Bradford[†] and Brian Unger
simmonds@cpsc.ucalgary.ca, rjb@maths.bath.ac.uk
unger@cpsc.ucalgary.ca
University of Calgary, Canada.
[†]University of Bath, UK.

Abstract

The simulation of wide area computer networks is one area where the benefits of parallel simulation have been clearly demonstrated. Here we present a description of a system that uses a parallel discrete event simulator to act as a high speed network emulator. With this, real Internet Protocol (IP) traffic generated by application programs running on user workstations can interact with modelled traffic in the emulator, thus providing a controlled test environment for distributed applications.

The network emulator uses the TasKit conservative parallel discrete event simulation (PDES) kernel. TasKit has been shown to be able to achieve improved parallel performance over existing conservative and optimistic PDES kernels, as well as improved sequential performance over an existing central-event-list based kernel. This paper explains the modifications that have been made to TasKit to enable real-time operation along with the emulator interface that allows the IP network simulation running in the TasKit kernel to interact with real IP clients. Initial emulator performance data is included.

Keywords: *Parallel Discrete Event Simulation (PDES), Computer Network Emulation, Conservative Protocol, Critical Channel Traversing, Real-Time Simulation, Internet Protocol (IP).*

1. Introduction

This paper describes the *Internet Protocol Traffic and Network Emulator* (IP-TNE), a computer network emulator that uses a fast parallel discrete event simulation (PDES) kernel. IP-TNE models interactions between real IP packets generated by external sources and IP packets generated

within a network simulation. IP-TNE uses the TasKit [10] PDES kernel that has been modified in order to operate as a real-time system. We describe both the IP handling mechanisms and the modifications that have been made to TasKit.

IP-TNE enables the testing of real distributed systems under the controlled conditions provided by the network simulation. This is useful for testing how the traffic being modelled in the simulator affects the IP streams passing through the emulator and how the traffic being generated by the real IP clients affects the simulated traffic streams.

IP-TNE uses a new IP level simulator called the *Internet Protocol Traffic and Network* (IP-TN) simulator currently being developed at the University of Calgary. IP-TN uses the TasKit kernel and is designed to complement the existing ATM-TN [9] simulator. IP-TN models at the IP packet level whereas ATM-TN models at the ATM cell level.

IP-TNE is not the first system to provide network emulation. Both *NS* [4] and *NIST Net* [1] provide network emulation functionality. NIST Net works by adding fixed delays to the time taken to pass an IP packet from its source to its destination, while NS, like IP-TNE, models interactions between packets routed through the emulator and simulated packet events in the emulator. However, the performance of NS is poor due to its interpreter based architecture. While there are projects underway to parallelise NS, to the best of our knowledge these projects are aimed primarily at improving scalability rather than increasing the performance of simulations of the type of networks we feel will be of interest to users of an emulator. Both NS and NIST Net use a simple IP routing strategy, while IP-TNE has multiple routing modes making it more flexible than either of these existing systems.

The remainder of this paper is laid out as follows. Section 2 gives an example of how IP-TNE could be used. Section 3 gives a brief description of the TasKit PDES kernel. Then section 4 explains how real IP packets are read into the emulator and how packets from the modelled network are sent to the IP clients. This section explains the two different IP routing strategies supported by IP-TNE. Section 5 explains the architecture of IP-TNE and section 6 gives some initial performance data. The paper is summarised in section 7.

2. Motivation

This section provides motivation for the creation of IP-TNE by providing a concrete example of how the system could be used. This is for testing the protocols for an Internet gaming system. The current trend in computer game design is to allow consoles connected to the Internet to interact, allowing multi-user games to be played over wide area networks. The aim is to create protocols that give all users taking part an equal opportunity to perform well.

Testing of multi-user games usually involves subjective analysis from game players. To test an Internet-ready game, such a subjective test should really be carried out using computers connected to the Internet in different locations, using different interconnect technologies (e.g., audio, ADSL, or cable modems). Tests would need to be performed at different times of the day since the amount of background traffic on the Internet links connecting the player's consoles will vary throughout the day. Testing a system in this way is fraught with difficulties. Problems detected during a test could be hard to pinpoint since the network conditions at the time the problem was detected could not be reproduced. Also, subjective testing with users in distant locations is difficult to moderate.

Now consider testing such a system using IP-TNE. All the testers could be located at the same site with the configuration of the virtual network in the emulator determining how and where each user's console appears to be connected to the Internet. The testers could switch consoles or the simulated network could be reconfigured to give different tester's consoles different connection characteristics. This should allow more thorough testing to be performed. Also, all of the background network traffic will be generated in a deterministic way within the simulated network. This will allow traffic patterns that appear to cause problems to be replayed allowing repetitive testing to be performed.

The gaming example is only one instance of where IP-TNE could be employed. Other examples would be to test the effects of network load on connections to a transaction processing system or on a wide area distributed file system.

Modelling network conditions for IP streams passing between real IP clients is not the only way in which IP-TNE could be used. It could also be used to generate traffic directed at an external server. An example of this would be the testing of a transaction processing system such as an on-line bidding system. The bid requests could be generated within the simulated network and routed to the real host running the bid server. This would allow the responsiveness of the real bid server to be analysed using the statistics gathering capability provided by the IP simulator.

3. The TasKit Kernel

TasKit is a simulation kernel that implements the *Critical Channel Traversing* (CCT) algorithm [10]. CCT is an extension of the *Chandy-Misra-Bryant* (CMB) [3][2] algorithm that incorporates scheduling decisions into the conservative causality maintenance calculations. It uses a dynamic load balancing scheme that has been shown to work well when used with computer network simulations with irregular workloads [7].

TasKit uses the *logical process modelling view* [3] of discrete event simulation. With this, the system being modelled is represented by *logical processes* (LPs) which communicate using timestamped event messages. TasKit also employs a *channel based event messaging view*. With this only LPs that have a channel connecting them to each other can communicate with each other, so any pair of LPs that may ever exchange event messages must have channels constructed between them.

TasKit uses a partitioning scheme where LPs are grouped into collections referred to as *tasks*. A task is formed using simple topological information based on the graph whose edges represent channels and vertices represent LPs in the model. This is different from most systems where execution load information has to be used when determining the best way to partition a model. The topological partitioning scheme used by TasKit, along with the scheduling scheme used to take advantage of this partitioning makes TasKit less sensitive to changes in the values of input parameters than other systems we have explored [8].

TasKit works by scheduling tasks, which in turn schedule the LPs within them. The LPs execute any events that are currently safe to execute determined by the constraints provided by the *channel times* (the timestamp of the next event that could arrive on each channel) of the LP's input channels. A task can be scheduled in one of two ways depending on whether it is a *source task*, which is a task with no external input channels (no channels leading from LPs in another task to LPs in this task), or a *non-source task*, that is a task with at least one external input channel. A source task schedules itself at the end of each execution session and sets its local clock to the timestamp of the next event that will be executed in the task, while a non-source task sets a *critical channel* at the end of its execution session. The task's critical channel is the external input channel with the lowest clock value; its clock value must advance in order for any more events to be executed within this task. A non-source task is scheduled by a neighbouring task when an LP in that neighbouring task updates the channel clock of the critical channel. This means that a task is not scheduled for execution until it is known that it is likely that its local clock will be able to advance during the ensuing execution session.

Tasks can be scheduled from a single task queue for all processors. When a task is scheduled for execution it is inserted into the task queue which is ordered by the task clock values. Since the next processor to become available will take the task at the head of the task queue, TasKit is always working to increase the lowest LP clock in the system.

The original implementation of TasKit provided two task types, the *pipe-task* type and the *cluster-task* type. The pipe-task type enables pipeline parallelism and improves memory access locality since essentially the same set of event buffers can be reused by each LP in the pipeline as, for example, one or more simulated IP packets passes along the pipeline. Many LP pipelines can be found in a computer network model. The cluster-task type allows LPs that appear in zero weight sum cycles in the communication graph to be grouped and scheduled using lowest timestamp first (LTF) scheduling within the task.

4. IP Packet Handling

This section describes how real IP packets are read from the network, passed to the simulated network and resent to their destination IP client. Also described are the two primary routing modes that make IP-TNE more flexible than the other network emulators that are available. Finally the way in which virtual hosts in the simulator appear to real IP clients is explained.

4.1 Reading and Writing IP Packets

In order to read packets into the simulator a socket needs to be opened for each interface connecting IP-TNE's host computer to a network. This may be a packet socket or a packet filter socket [6] according to the operating system and requires superuser access privileges on Unix systems. Initially we used the portable *pcap* library to provide packet reading functionality, but we replaced this with a simple packet reader that performs just the tasks required by IP-TNE.

The reader has to be able to read and respond to address resolution protocol (ARP) requests for the IP address of a gateway to a virtual network. This allows hosts to resolve the (ficticious) IP address and send packets to the virtual router. Note that if the real IP address of the host running IP-TNE were used, the operating system would attempt to route these packets itself using its own routing mechanism.

Writing packets back to the network requires the use of a raw socket [6]. This allows packet headers to be written directly by IP-TNE rather than being added by the operating system. Before a packet is written out, a checksum has to be computed and inserted into the header. There is no need to compute checksums within the simulator since simulated data corruption can simply be indicated by a flag, but checksums are needed on the real network. For packets that have been routed between real clients, only the IP checksum needs to be recomputed. This is required since the time-to-live of the packet as it leaves the emulator will be less than when it arrived. For packets that are generated within the emulator additional checksums may have to be computed and inserted into the header. For example, a TCP packet generated within the emulator requires a TCP checksum to be added to the TCP header.

4.2 Emulator Routing

In order for IP packets from real clients to be routed through IP-TNE, routes have to be set appropriately on the client hosts. IP-TNE provides two primary modes of routing to allow the user to choose the most appropriate for their test environment. We describe these two modes of operation as the *virtual host* method and the *virtual router* method.

4.2.1 Virtual Host Method

Suppose host **A** with IP address 192.168.1.2 wishes to communicate with **B** (192.168.1.3) via the emulator **E** (192.168.1.99). Instead of using the address 192.168.1.3 some virtual addresses are allocated on an unused network, 10.0.1 say, with each real IP address corresponding to one virtual address. Then, to contact **B**, **A** sends packets addressed to the virtual host 10.0.1.3.

The emulator listens to all packets on the host interface for packets addressed to 10.0.1 and reads them for its own use. On entering the emulator the source address 192.168.1.2 in the IP header of the packet is mapped to the virtual 10.0.1.2. The packet can then be manipulated as required by the emulator before being put back on the interface destined for **B**. On output the virtual destination address 10.0.1.3 is mapped to the real 192.168.1.3, and thus is forwarded to **B**. The packet's return address is still the virtual 10.0.1.2.

Notice that this requires the emulator to respond to ARP requests for the address of a (virtual) gateway to 10.0.1, 192.168.1.254, say, and **A** and **B**'s routing tables must be set to route to 10.0.1 via this virtual gateway. Without this, the default routes on **A** and **B** would send these packets to the real network gateway, and thus on to the wider Internet. The address 192.168.1.254 must be otherwise unused on this network to prevent other hosts mistakenly trying to route these packets.

Also note that **A** can still connect to **B** directly (without going via the emulator) by using **B**'s real address. Therefore the simulation can be run regardless of other traffic between the machines (e.g., other users).

The major problem with this technique is that it fails for application protocols where IP addresses are carried as data and then used by the recipient to connect back to the originator. Examples of such protocols include FTP, Quake and IRC. This could be resolved by using protocol specific mapping routines in the emulator that can rewrite data segments. Modules exist for rewriting certain examples (e.g., the above and others) in the IP-chains firewall package [5], though these are designed to run within the Linux kernel and are difficult to port for use in IP-TNE.

Instead of rewriting packet data, the virtual router method described next can be used to ensure all packets are correctly routed through IP-TNE.

4.2.2   Virtual Router Method

With this method, the hosts' own IP addresses are used. As **A** and **B** are on the same network, they would normally send packets directly to each other. We prevent this by simply setting **A**'s route to **B** to be via **E**. Similarly for **B** to **A**. Now packets go via the emulator as required. Note that the address of **E** needs to be a virtual address for which the emulator responds to ARP requests. As before, if the real address of the host running the emulator were used, the host operating system would route the packets directly to the destination IP-client most likely resulting in duplicate packets then being delivered from the emulator.

Now the problem is that a route has to be set up on each machine for each real destination within the simulation. If we are lucky with the way IP addresses are allocated to us, careful use of netmasks could make this easy. However, now *all* packets between **A** and **B** will travel via the emulator, which may not be what other users of these computers want.

4.2.3   Internal Hosts

Simulated hosts within the emulator appear "real" to real hosts outside. An internal host can respond to pings, and show up on traceroutes through the emulator. This is achieved by implementing small parts of the Internet Protocol: for example traceroute requires the manipulation of the time-to-live fields in a packet header, and the generation of suitable Internet Control Message Protocol (ICMP) messages. Similarly, internal hosts can provide trivial services like daytime or echo, or be programmed gracefully to reject attempted Transmission Control Protocol (TCP) and User Datagram Protocol (UDP) connections.

Again, the emulator must respond to ARP requests on behalf of the internal hosts in order that the real hosts on the local network can route their packets to the emulator. The

internal hosts can be either on the same network as the real hosts, or on other virtual networks.

5. Emulator Architecture

This section explains the architecture of IP-TNE and includes a description of the modifications made to the TasKit kernel to enable real-time operation. Figure 1 shows the main components of IP-TNE. This shows that separate I/O threads are used and that a new task type, the RT-task type, has been added to TasKit to enable real-time operation. The exact configuration of the TasKit simulator component depends on whether it is executing on a single processor, or on multiple processors of a shared memory parallel computer. When executing sequentially, the TasKit simulator runs on a single thread. When executing in parallel, a thread is allocated for each processor and if possible each thread is bound to an individual processor.

5.1. I/O Threads

IP-TNE uses separate threads for reading data from and for writing data to the network. A reader thread could be used for each network interface on the host computer, though a single thread could handle multiple interfaces by monitoring all the interfaces simultaneously. A single writer thread handles the writing of data out of the simulator at the required wall clock time.

5.1.1   Reader Thread

The packet reader must be ready to read a packet from the network whenever a packet arrives. In IP-TNE a separate thread is used to achieve this. The packet reading mechanism was explained in section 4.1. Once a packet is read, the header is packed into a packet header structure and is placed in the input queue (see figure 1) ready to be read by the simulator. The packet data is packed into a separate buffer and a reference to this placed in the packet header structure. There is no need to modify the data section from within the simulator, so there is no need to copy the data to the simulation event structure.

5.1.2   Writer Thread

The writer code is run on a separate thread since this has been found to be a good method of ensuring that messages are sent out from the emulator at the wall clock time calculated. The method used to write the packets out was described in section 4.1. When a packet structure is read from the output queue by the writer thread, if this packet structure refers to an IP packet being routed through the emulator

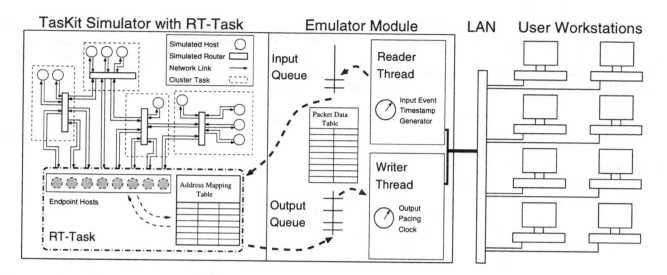

Figure 1. IP-TNE configuration showing a single RT-task in the Taskit simulator along with the reader and writer threads. Within TasKit, channels connect the emulated endpoints in the RT-task and LPs representing switches and routers in the simulated network.

with its data unchanged, the IP packet data is recovered using the reference held in the packet header structure. At this point a new checksum is calculated for the packet as described in section 4.1. If the packet was generated within the emulator some extra checksums may need to be calculated at this point.

Once scheduled, the execution session for the writer thread continues while there are packets to be written out with timestamps less than $wct + \Delta_{send}$, where wtc is the current wall clock time and Δ_{send} is a small constant to account for the amount of time taken to write out the packet. When there are no packets left for which this condition is true, the thread suspends. If there were any packet structures queued to be sent when the execution session ends, a timeout is set to wake the thread in time to send the next packet. Whether or not a timeout is set, the thread is woken whenever a new packet is placed in the output queue that has a timestamp less than that of the packet currently at the top of the output queue, or if the queue had been empty before the new packet was added.

When messages are passed to the writer thread a test is made to determine if the message has arrived soon enough to attain its real-time deadline. Statistics are then kept to indicate the number of packets failing to attain the deadline, the maximum amount by which a deadline has been missed and the mean amount by which deadlines are missed. These statistics can either be output when the emulator terminates, or periodically while it is running.

5.2. Simulator Interface

As described in the previous section, the real-time input and output from the emulator is handled by separate I/O threads that put packets into the input queue and take packets out of the output queue. This section explains how packets are taken from the input queue and inserted into the IP-TN simulation model, and how packets that need to be dispatched to IP clients are placed into the output queue.

5.2.1 RT-Task Type

A new task type has been added to TasKit to enable real-time interaction. This is the *real-time task*, or *RT-task*. In the current implementation of IP-TNE, a single RT-task is used; there could be advantages in using more than one RT-task and this is discussed in section 5.2.3. All interactions between the emulator I/O queues and the simulator are handled by the RT-task.

The RT-task implementation is similar to that of the cluster-task type described in section 3, though the method for updating the task clock has been changed to work correctly in a real-time environment. The RT-task follows the rules for CCT execution that were described in [10] apart from stage 3 of the algorithm where the task clock is updated to the current wall clock time instead of being set to the safe-time; the safe-time is the value of the lowest clock of an empty input channel observed in the proceeding execution session. This ensures that the channels leading from the RT-task are not updated beyond the next possible timestamp of a packet event taken from the emulator input queue. The execution session of the RT-task is outlined below.

First, the external input channels are examined and the identity of the empty channel with the lowest clock value is recorded. This lowest clock value is also recorded as the safe-time. If no channels are empty at this stage this fact is indicated by the channel identity remaining undefined and the safe-time remaining at ∞.

The second stage of the algorithm involves executing events contained in the RT-task's event queue. Each time an event that arrived on an external input channel is executed, an attempt is made to recover another event from the same input channel. If such an event exists, this event is inserted into the task's event queue. Otherwise, if the channel's clock is less than the current safe-time, the identity of the channel is recorded. Also in this case, the safe-time is set to the channel's clock value. The execution session continues until there are no events in the task's event queue with timestamps less than the safe-time.

Next the task clock, $Clock_{RT}$, is set to the current wall clock time. Then for each external output channel (i, j), the channel clock is set to $Clock_{RT} + \delta_{i,j}$, where $\delta_{i,j}$ is the delay value attributed to channel (i, j) and represents the smallest timestamp increment for any message passed along this channel.

Finally a check is made on the input channel with the lowest clock value that was found to be empty during the safe-time calculation. If the channel clock (saved as the safe-time) has not advanced since the channel identity was recorded, this channel is set to critical so that the RT-task will be scheduled using the CCT rules. If the clock value has increased, then the RT-task reschedules itself (i.e., places itself back into the task queue ready for execution). This completes the current execution session.

5.2.2 Emulator Endpoints

For each real host that is registered to interact with IP-TNE, an *endpoint host* is instantiated in the RT-task. An endpoint host is simply a host LP as used in IP-TNE, but with an emulator endpoint object replacing the traffic model object that it would normally contain. The emulator endpoints are all registered with the RT-task allowing packets to be inserted directly into an endpoint by the RT-task.

A packet read from the emulator input queue has to be mapped to the emulator endpoint representing the IP client that sent the packet. A table is maintained for this purpose (see figure 1), with all of the real addresses of IP hosts registered to interact with IP-TNE mapped to the virtual host endpoints. Also contained in this table are the corresponding *reduced addresses* used in the simulator so that the source and destination address in each packet can be converted to reduced addresses used within the IP-TN simulator. Reduced addresses are simply a convenient form of internal addressing used to speed up packet routing in the

simulator. Once this is done, the packet is passed to the host endpoint which does an internal routing lookup and sends the packet to the modelled network on the appropriate virtual interface.

When a simulated packet arrives at a virtual endpoint, the table is used to map the reduced source and destination addresses to real addresses. Then the packet is placed into the output queue ready to be read by the emulator writer thread.

5.2.3 Multiple RT-Tasks

Currently IP-TNE uses a single RT-task to interact between the emulator I/O queues and the network simulation. It may be possible to increase the amount of parallelism available to the emulator by using multiple RT-tasks. In order to achieve this, multiple input queues could be used, with the reader thread using a mapping table and placing packet structures into the input queue of the RT-task holding the packet's source emulated endpoint. Care would be needed not to place too much additional load on the reader thread however, since this could lead to it failing to read packets from the network. For small multi-processor machines the use of the single RT-task seems appropriate, though experimentation with other ways of implementing the emulator endpoints will continue.

6. Preliminary Testing and Performance

This section explains how IP-TNE has been tested and provides initial performance results. IP-TNE has been tested by running multiple IP streams through the emulator and checking that packets arrive correctly at the real IP clients. The end-to-end time to pass packets between the IP clients was checked to make sure that these were consistent with the configuration of the network model in the emulator.

Apart from the testing described above, some initial benchmarks have been performed. These benchmarks have used a simplified version of IP-TN since the full version of IP-TN will only operate in conjunction with a channel based PDES kernel such as TasKit and we wished to compare the performance of IP-TNE using TasKit to IP-TNE using *CelKit*, a central-event-list sequential discrete event simulation kernel. These benchmarks are important since they show the advantage of using a PDES kernel even when running on a single processor computer.

The benchmarking version of IP-TN uses simple routers which are adequate for the experiments performed and can be used with or without a channel based simulation kernel. CelKit has been modified to work with IP-TNE by adding a regulator into the event execution loop. This prevents event ev from being executed until $ts(ev) \leq wct + \Delta_L$, where $ts(ev)$ is the timestamp of event ev, wct is the current wall

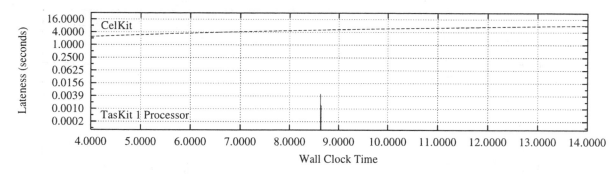

Figure 2. Graph showing a 10 second sample of the lateness of packets (using a log_2 scale) for a model with two emulator endpoints, two routers and two hosts acting as aggregate traffic sources. Plots for CelKit and TasKit running on a single processor are shown. During the sample period 0.1% of messages arrived late in TasKit (all arriving in one short interval), while all messages arrived late in CelKit.

clock time and Δ_L is the minimum time increment that will be given to any IP packet that could arrive from a real IP client. Δ_L is equivalent to the minimum delay value ($\delta_{i,j}$) of channels leading from an RT-task to the simulated network in the channel based simulator.

The network models used for the benchmarks each have a simulated host acting as an aggregate traffic generator along with one simulated router for each emulated endpoint. The simulated hosts communicate with each other, passing messages via the routers where this traffic interacts with traffic being routed between emulator endpoints. To avoid the effects of network contention in the real network, all the IP packets are generated by a simple simulator running on the benchmarking host; a server with greater interconnect bandwidth would be required to run these benchmarks otherwise. The benchmarks were performed on an SGI R8000 Power Challenge.

Figure 2 shows the lateness of packets arriving at the output queue when a simple network model is used in the emulator. This model has two emulated endpoints and two simulated hosts acting as constant rate aggregate traffic generators. Two routers are also present. As can be seen, the CelKit version was not able to keep up with real-time, so the lateness of packets increases linearly with wall clock time. TasKit running on a single processor was able to keep up, with just one small batch of packets arriving late during the sample period. A four processor parallel run of TasKit showed similar behaviour to the single processor run.

Figure 3 shows the lateness of packets for a model using sixteen emulated endpoints, routers and simulated hosts. This model used a lower rate for the generation of packets at the simulated hosts, so the total number of events generated in this simulation was a little less than twice the number generated in the first benchmark. The larger number of LPs in this model increases the total LP scheduling cost. Not

surprisingly given that this is a larger model, CelKit again fails to run fast enough to keep up with wall clock time and delays increase linearly. In this case the single processor TasKit also fails to operate fast enough, though the rate at which the delay is increasing is lower. The jagged plot is thought to be due to the RT-task not being scheduled often enough; this is currently being investigated. The four processor TasKit does run fast enough, but still 16% of packets miss their deadlines by small amounts. In general this should not be a problem for the types of systems that will use IP-TNE, but we believe that this situation can be improved as the implementation is fine tuned.

7. Summary

This paper has described a network emulator called IP-TNE. IP-TNE allows programs that operate in a distributed environment to interact with a wide area network simulation running in the emulator. These programs could be user applications such as video conferencing or games applications, or could be system level programs such as distributed databases or file-systems.

IP-TNE uses the parallel discrete simulation kernel TasKit to provide fast network simulation and thus enable IP-TNE to attain real-time deadlines. Other network emulation systems are available, but IP-TNE's PDES approach should offer a considerable performance advantage. Also, IP-TNE provides a flexible external routing model allowing IP-TNE to be used on both dedicated test networks and on shared networks.

We have presented preliminary performance results for the system. These show that IP-TNE is capable of outperforming an emulator using a central-event-list simulation kernel when running on a single processor, as well as when

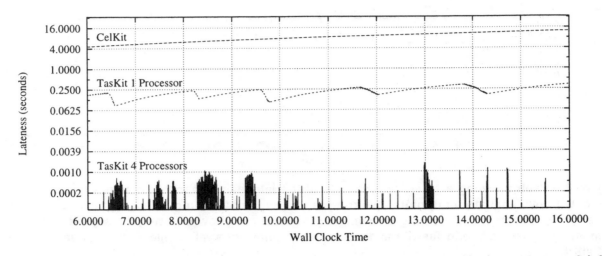

Figure 3. Graph showing a 10 second sample of the lateness of packets (using a log_2 scale) for a model with sixteen emulator endpoint / router / aggregate traffic source sets. Plots for CelKit, TasKit running on a single processor, and for TasKit running on four processors are shown. 16% of packets arrived late in the four processor TasKit experiment, while all packets arrived late in the other experiments.

running on multiple processors of a shared memory parallel computer. While IP-TNE is not yet capable of attaining hard real-time deadlines, i.e., it cannot guarantee to always meet all deadlines, soft real-time deadlines are all that are usually required from such a system.

We would like to thank the following people for providing code that has been used in IP-TNE. Zhong-e Xiao, the author of TasKit, Cameron Kiddle who has been responsible for providing the routers and initial modelling framework for IP-TN and Julie Doerksen who has provided the host models and simulated traffic models. We would also like to thank our industrial sponsors including Nortel Networks, Telus Advanced Communications and Electronic Arts for supporting us in this work. We also thank the Natural Sciences and Engineering Research Council of Canada and the Alberta Science and Research Authority for providing grants that help support the TeleSim group at the University of Calgary. This work was done while Russell Bradford was on sabbatical at the University of Calgary.

References

[1] N. Advanced Network Technologies Division. NIST Net home page, 1999. http://www.antd.nist.gov/itg/nistnet/.

[2] R. Bryant. Simulation of packet communication architecture computer systems. Technical Report MIT/LCS/TR-188, MIT, November 1977.

[3] K. M. Chandy and J. Misra. Asynchronous distributed simulation via a sequence of parallel computations. *Communications of the ACM*, 24(11):198–206, 1981.

[4] B. N. research group. NS home page, 1999. http://www-mash.cs.berkeley.edu/ns/ns.html.

[5] R. Russell. The Linux IP firewall chains page, 1999. http://www.rustcorp.com/linux/ipchains/.

[6] W. R. Stevens. *Unix Network Programming, Networking APIs: Sockets and XTI, Volume 1.* Prentice-Hall, 1998.

[7] B. Unger, Z. Xiao, and J. Cleary. High performance task-based parallel simulation of ATM networks. In preparation., 2000.

[8] B. Unger, Z. Xiao, J. Cleary, J. Tsai, and C. Williamson. Parallel shared-memory simulator performance for atm networks. Submitted to TOMACS, 2000.

[9] B. W. Unger, F. Gomes, X. Zhonge, P. Gburzynski, T. Ono-Tesfaye, S. Ramaswamy, C. Williamson, and A. Covington. A high fidelity ATM traffic and network simulator. In *Proceedings of the 1995 Winter Simulation Conference*, pages 996–1003. The Society for Computer Simulation, 1995.

[10] Z. Xiao, B. Unger, R. Simmonds, and J. Cleary. Scheduling critical channels in conservative parallel discrete event simulation. In *Proceedings of the 13th Workshop on Parallel and Distributed Simulation*, May 1999.

Repeatability in Real-Time Distributed Simulation Executions

Thom McLean
College of Computing
Georgia Institute of Technology
Atlanta, GA, 30332
thom@cc.gatech.edu

Richard Fujimoto
College of Computing
Georgia Institute of Technology
Atlanta, GA, 30332
fujimoto@cc.gatech.edu

Abstract

Real-time distributed simulations, such as on-line gaming or military training simulations are normally considered to be non-deterministic. Analysis of these simulations is therefore difficult, depending solely on logging and runtime observations. This paper explores an approach for removing one major source of non-determinism in these simulations, thereby allowing repeatable executions. Specifically, we use a synchronization protocol to ensure repeatable delivery of messages. Through limited instrumentation of the simulation code, we maintain a virtual time clock, by which message delivery is governed. The additional overhead imposed by the scheme is shown to be reasonable, although additional reductions in this overhead are anticipated. The results are demonstrated in the context of a simple combat model, whose only source of non-determinism is communications latency. The simulation is shown to be made repeatable, and the perturbation on the execution compared to the non-repeatable execution small. The paper is one step in bridging the gap between the traditional PDES perspective and real-time simulation world.

1. Introduction

Distributed interactive simulations have been pressed into service for a variety of new uses. Beginning with the US Army's SimNET, sets of previously stand-alone simulators have been used in larger scale simulation systems [20]. Typically, these simulators have synchronization models that are designed to meet real-time human-in-the-loop response requirements. The lack of a general mechanism for synchronization for real-time simulators led to the development of protocols that do not rely on timestamps to order the delivery of messages. Recently, similar techniques have been used in on-line gaming environments, where communication latency may be large, and a strict timestamp order protocol is infeasible.

The inability to repeat an execution makes it difficult to debug these distributed simulation systems. The conditions that lead to the occurrence of an anomaly, for instance, are not guaranteed to recur on subsequent executions. This hinders discovery of the cause of the anomaly or bug. To compensate, developers typically rely on logging individual messages. However, logging techniques may consume large resources, and are not guaranteed to yield the desired data. In STOW-97, a large-scale simulation [19], it was estimated that terabyte-order storage requirements were foreseeable for medium and large-scale simulations. Message logs are of limited use, since no explicit causal or temporal relationships are enforced at runtime, and comprehensive logs can, at best, show one possible ordering of messages. Further, the merging of temporally indeterminate event logs is not straightforward [17].

In training simulations, a particularly useful capability is the ability to replay an execution back to the training audience. Replay of the simulation may allow one to understand cause and effect relationships after the training session has finished. Replay may also permit a specific activity to be repeated, until the desired training objective has been met. This capability to replay an execution, inherent in many stand-alone simulators, is frequently sacrificed when operating in an integrated distributed mode. Neither SimNET nor Distributed Interactive Simulation (DIS) protocols, for example, can easily support a deterministic ordering of events, since no regulation of delivery order is specified in the protocol. Training goals may be more easily reached using repeatable simulation executions. Through a combination of replay and live interaction, alternative courses of action may be investigated. Repeatability would enable investigation of alternatives based on a repeatable decision point.

The problems highlighted above may be more easily resolved if a mechanism existed for producing repeatable simulation executions. This problem has been studied before, in the context of distributed system debugging, and in direct execution simulation. Here, we extend the previous research to provide general techniques for producing repeatable execution in real-time distributed simulation. By embedding ordered delivery of time-stamped messages, we transform non-time-managed, distributed simulations into familiar time-managed logical processes, without impact on the original systems' synchronization mechanics.

Repeatability provides a mechanism for post hoc investigation of causal phenomena and provides an alternative to message logging.

2. Background

Repeatability is a property of a simulation where multiple executions with the same input produce the exact same results. Here, we focus on distributed simulation, and message passing simulations in particular. Inputs to a simulation may include user interactions, wall clock time values, etc. Therefore, we apply an observability criterion to this property, basing our determination of a repeated execution upon the messages a simulation sends and receives. This yields a practical definition for repeatable simulation execution. A simulation execution is repeatable when, for a given initial condition, the simulation will send and receive the exact same messages, in the same order, for every execution. (Note that we have not used the term *timestamp* in this definition.)

2.1 Models of RT Execution

Our definition of real-time execution simply implies that the execution of the simulation is synchronized with a single external reference of time. Commonly, the simulation community uses local wall-clock time (WCT) as the reference, ignoring any variance between local clocks. Such variance can be accounted for, if required.

We note that, in order to ensure that real-time simulations remain synchronized with the real world clock, they must execute in one of two manners. A simulation may execute at an explicit time step, in which case it will suspend execution until the expiration of the time step interval. Alternatively, a simulation may request the wall clock time at the end of a time step and, based upon the return value, vary the time step interval accordingly. These methods are explained below.

Time stepped execution is the predominant model for

"DIS" style applications. The simulation is executed as a series of discrete intervals, of length Δt. Table 1 shows pseudocode for a typical time stepped execution. In each interval, the application must 1)retrieve incoming messages, 2)compute the new internal state, and 3)send appropriate messages to other logical processes. At the end of this processing cycle, internal time is incremented by Δt, and the application suspends execution until that time is reached. Timestamps, if present, are not used to order delivery of the messages. All messages are delivered in receive order (RO), and are assumed to be relevant for NOW (the current wall-clock time).

This method of execution has the benefit of providing regular, periodic state updates. Such a method is appropriate for a visualization routine, where each cycle yields a new frame in the animation.

There are a few drawbacks to this approach, however. In order to ensure that a queue of incoming events does not grow, the application must normally flush the incoming event (message) queue in each cycle. Since the intervals are fixed at Δt length, all processing must be completed in Δt time. However, variance in the number of incoming messages and other factors in the computation may increase the time spent in each processing cycle. Therefore, Δt must be at least as large as the longest total time that can be spent processing. The difference between Δt and the actual time spent during a cycle is called the *slack time*. This is shown in Figure 1.

```
while (not done) {
  flush incoming message queue ( "tick()" )
  process messages
  for each object {
    integrate (over •t)
    post results (send messages)
  }
  now = now + •t
  wait until WallClockTime = (now * scalefactor)
}
```

Table 1 - Time Stepped Execution

The existence of positive slack time in each cycle ensures that the simulation time is able to stay correctly synchronized with wall clock time. If the cycle take longer than Δt, then simulation time will lag wall-clock time.

The *no-wait* model is designed to post updates as quickly as possible. It may be appropriate when response time of the system to any input is the most important factor in the design. It permits synchronization to wall-clock time without the requirement for slack time. We can find examples of this type of system in human-in-the-loop simulators. For this model, the processing cycle may include the same basic functions as in time stepped. The difference is how simulation time is advanced. In the no-wait model, the current value of WCT is sampled to determine the new simulation time. Messages are again

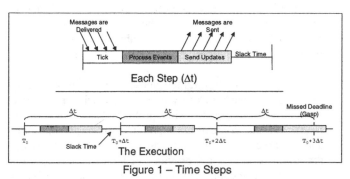

Figure 1 – Time Steps

processed in receive order, and are assumed to be relevant for NOW. Notice that in this model there is no need for slack time, because variance in processing time is accounted for each time the wall-clock time is sampled. In order to make a no-wait simulation repeatable, a mechanism must be derived to provide a repeatable value for WCT. Although this is an interesting problem; that function is not the main focus of this study, and will be reserved for later research.

Outside the distributed simulation community, distributed real-time computing commonly involves scheduling remote and local events with real-time execution constraints. In this model, all processing is scheduled to be done at (or completed by) a specified deadline. A logical process (LP) can schedule processing for itself, or for another LP. Messages are simply one class of remotely scheduled processing. Most distributed simulation systems do not employ such a methodology, it is mentioned here for completeness.

2.2 Sources of Non-determinism

In distributed simulation systems, there are several factors that make it difficult to ensure repeatable executions. The simulations have non-deterministic input from a variety of sources. The human operator, for instance, cannot be made to be repeatable. Because unreliable transport mechanisms can be used, messages may be lost or ordered differently from one execution to the next.

To attack the problem of creating repeatable executions, we examine the sources of non-determinism. Bacon and Copen classify the sources of non-determinism as arising from 3 sources: input-data; systems calls; and interrupts [5]. Since we're dealing with distributed simulation, we, for convenience, separate the input data into 2 sub-categories: a) that which is a result of messages passed between simulation Logical Processes (LPs), and b) all other input data. This yields four sources of non-determinism for real-time distributed simulation:

(1a)   Message Delivery (order, timing, loss)
(1b)   External Inputs (operators, or other system inputs)
(2)   Operating System Calls (which are not guaranteed to be reproducible)
(3)   Interrupts (which may cause non-determinism at the system level)

The focus of this paper is (1a), ensuring repeatable message delivery.

3. Related Work

Much of the previous research, relevant to creating repeatable real-time distributed simulations, comes from two research communities. First, significant research has been conducted into the **optimization and debugging of complex parallel codes** [1,4,5,6,10,18]. Some the

debugging researchers focused on creating a deterministic execution environment. Others focused on creating minimal logging devices, with separate record and playback functionality.

A second body of research deals with **direct execution simulation of parallel processors** [7,8,11]. Some of the same challenges to repeatability are encountered in parallel computer engineering. While more focused on measuring the expected performance of a processor or code, the research is nonetheless relevant insofar as it provides a synchronization scheme that is transparent to the executing processes. In doing so, it creates an environment for deterministic communications.

At least two general approaches for producing repeatable executions have been developed. *Log-based approaches* record needed simulation events as they occur, such that a replay will provide any needed information, in a repeatable fashion. A *message ordering approach* assumes that the LPs are repeatable except to the degree that relative message timing yield non-determinism [1].

Most practical implementations combine aspects of both approaches. While a comprehensive log-based approach can shield every LP from non-determinism, it typically requires too much overhead. Conversely, a strict synchronization based approach is not sufficient if there are any other sources of non-determinism. Moreover, fast, conservative synchronization without lookahead guarantees is hard. [3, 6]

3.1 Log Based Approaches

Several log-based approaches have been proposed to achieve repeatability. Instant Replay [4] uses partial order message logging for each LP. LeBlanc and Mellor-Crummey note that in many cases, processes are deterministic, if the inputs are known. Using the partial log, Instant Replay ensures that at any point of the execution the appropriate inputs, and return values are presented to each LP. The technique is refined by noting that the *content of messages* need not be logged if the messages are reproduced in the same order. The logging is accomplished by source code instrumentation.

Shen and Gregory assume that a source-to-source transformation is necessary [1]. Generally, in source-to-source conversion techniques, difficulty exists in identifying sources of non-determinism, and replacing the offending code with a deterministic variant. However, RecPlay [18], a system used for cyclical debugging of parallel codes, employs an alternative technique called "just in time instrumentation." This is a technique for code conversion in which the non-deterministic code blocks are cloned at execution time, and modified during execution.

Bruegge notes some desirable features in his Basis for a Distributed Event Environment (BEE) execution environment in [6]. Among his set is the ability to work with several programming languages, and insensitivity to network hardware underpinnings. Bacon and Copen note that software-based replay often suffers from various probe effects, time and space overhead, and the requirement to perform artificial code modifications to support replay. [5] They also generally note that software based replay may require recording impossibly large data sets. Although this may be valid for a general software debugging environment, it is not necessarily appropriate for other intents. .

When one assumes or ensures that the individual LPs are deterministic, we are left with a less strict message ordering requirement. As noted in [5], we must only ensure that the per-process, partial order is repeated in order to guarantee repeatability. This implies that, in our situation, the order of local events can be completely arbitrary, and still be made repeatable.

3.2 Direct Execution Approaches

In the research and design of parallel computers, simulations have been developed that emulate execution of a target machine by directly executing much of the instruction set. This class of simulation, know as a direct execution simulation, must also provide for functionality that is available in the target machine, which is not available on the simulation host. Two good examples of this type of simulation are the Wisconsin Wind Tunnel (WWT) [8] and the Large Application Parallel Simulation Environment (LAPSE) [7]. Both WWT and LAPSE exploit knowledge of the target machines' architecture in the design of the simulation

Brewer and Weihl identify source-code compatibility as a critical feature of PROTEUS, a direct execution simulator [11]. We can translate this requirement into our domain by proposing that any repeatable execution solution should be achievable within any expected execution environment for the application. Practically, this means that an appropriate implementation *will not be architecture dependent*. Brewer and Weihl propose that non-intrusiveness and machine independence are desirable traits for debugging. In our research this tends to support a *common virtual machine* implementation in which any simulation code may run, independent of the actual hardware.

3.3 Insufficiency of Existing Approaches

Instant Replay and LAPSE require that the code be transformed extensively. This is not a desirable attribute of our system. The process of transforming existing codes into "repeatable codes" is not generally suitable for real-time simulations. Our solution must function predominately at a layer beyond any existing communications interface. The simulation run-time

infrastructure (RTI) is a convenient abstraction layer into which to embed repeatability functions [13]. Since its functionality is hidden from the simulation, any transformation of code within the RTI is likewise hidden.

In both the WWT and LAPSE systems, the assignment of timestamps for the messages is based upon the architecture of the modeled system. There is no flexibility in the assignment of timestamps. For our domain, the logical processes are advancing at a real time pace. Timestamps are completely irrelevant to the application execution. Because we are not constrained by a target architecture performance, we may choose to arbitrarily assign timestamps based on other criteria.

Performance of the simulation code is not a motivating factor in our domain. In a direct execution simulation, the measurement of the expected performance on the target machine is more important than actual execution time. In our problem domain, we do not care about measurement of the execution time, only that the execution is able to support the individual LPs in their respective real-time execution.

4. Approach

Our approach to achieving repeatability can simply be thought of as placing the entire system within a distributed virtual machine, which replaces existing communications and synchronization functions with their repeatable counterparts. Per our definition of repeatable execution, we are primarily concerned with repeatable delivery of messages. We note, therefore, that known, conservative time management techniques can be used to guarantee repeatable message delivery, given two conditions: 1) a message is given the same, unique timestamp during every execution, and 2) each logical process advances (is granted) to the same series of times for every execution. Using this knowledge we can modify our description of the problem to take advantage of existing time management techniques. Our approach to repeatability has three parts.

1. **Map the entire computation to a virtual time scale.** Every event in the execution will correspond to a specific time on a virtual clock. Any operation or computation will have some non-zero duration in virtual time, by which we advance virtual time.

2. **Use time management algorithms to order the delivery of messages.** Once a repeatable timestamp has been assigned to a message, we can use existing methods to provide a repeatable order. The time management will also ensure that the local virtual time (LVT) values of all logical process local virtual clocks stay synchronized.

3. **Replace any non-deterministic calls with deterministic mechanisms.** This caveat removes other sources of non-determinism. This aspect is not

the focus of this paper, and has been explored extensively in previous research as mentioned in Section 3.1.

Finally, our approach assumes reliable communications. While message losses could be recorded and replayed, reliable communications is a necessary for the conservative time management, and simplifies repeatable message delivery.

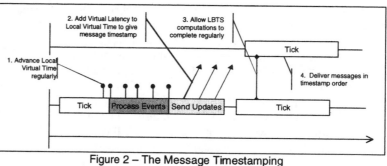

Figure 2 – The Message Timestamping

5. Implementation

Given the above approach, there are three central problems to be addressed: 1) Advancing Local Virtual Time, 2) Assignment of Timestamps, 3) Delivery of the messages.

5.1 Advancing Local Virtual Time

During a repeatable execution, a clock is kept for each logical process to represent its progress during the computation. The value of this clock is *local virtual time (LVT)*. To advance the virtual time we assign a specific duration to each major block of code, T_{BLOCK} and increment LVT by T_{BLOCK} whenever that block is executed. An analogous approach is used in WWT, except that actual machine code execution time was used to advance the clock [8]. The division of the application code into "major blocks" is arbitrary, however, the decision can have a significant impact on performance of the infrastructure. LVT must be advanced between each message send (or another method must be employed to serialize the messages). LVT must be advanced between consecutive tick calls, which poll the RTI for incoming messages (or no messages will be received/reflected).

We use a two step approach to determining the divisions between code blocks and the assignment of T_{BLOCK} values. As a first step, instrumentation code is inserted into the simulation application at the beginning and end of each candidate code block. The application is then run in a non-repeatable execution (its original configuration) to determine the amount of wall-clock time spent executing that block. The results of this profiling are used to adjust the divisions between code blocks until an acceptable characterization is produced. The goal of this profiling is to 1) find blocks of code which, when executed, are very predictable in the amount of wall-clock time used, and 2) keep the total number of blocks as small as possible. The second step of the process occurs after we are satisfied with the divisions between code blocks. The profiling information is used to pick a T_{BLOCK} value for each block[1]. We remove the instrumentation code

used for the profiling and substitute code that advances LVT by the chosen value for T_{BLOCK}.

5.2 Timestamp Assignment

All messages that a logical process sends are mapped to a specific LVT. This value is specified by a timestamp, TS, for the message. In choosing a timestamp for each message, we could intuitively assign the sending logical processes' LVT. However, just as each operation or computation performed by an LP has some non-zero duration in virtual time, so does any network communication. We thus define *virtual latency* to be the interval, on the virtual time scale, between the transmission of a message by some LPi and its earliest delivery at some other LPj. Conceptually, virtual latency corresponds to lookahead for the simulation. The timestamp for each message n from LPi to LPj can be simply assigned the sum of the virtual latency and current local virtual time of the sender.

$$TS_n = VL_{ij} + LVT_i$$

This assignment of a timestamp is hidden from the logical processes, which continue to operate as if the messages are sent and received in receive order. This assignment is illustrated in Figure 2.

5.3 Message Delivery

Once a unique timestamp is assigned to a message, it can be used to order the delivery. This is necessary but not sufficient to ensure repeatable delivery. To be repeatable, the messages must be delivered in the same order, and at the same point in the execution. For a receive order LP, each call to tick() (see Table 1)

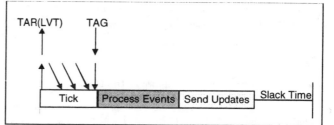

Figure 3 - Delivering Messages

---

[1] In our implementation we simply chose the average value for the time spent in the respective block. There may be merit to choosing another value, such as the maximum time spent in each block, but this issue is reserved for future research.

would simply flush the incoming message queue. We replace this behavior with a call to advance the (global) virtual time. Because we have already mapped the computation to a virtual time scale, this is simply a request to advance to the current LVT. As the ordered messages are received, they are stripped of their timestamp and passed to the LP until time has been advanced to LVT, at which point tick() returns. (Figure 3) We have already shown how the value of LVT can be repeated during each execution, and how the messages can be assigned the same timestamp. Therefore, the surrogate behavior for tick() will have the effect of delivering the same set of messages, in the same order, and will ensure that each LP's virtual time remains synchronized with LVT[2].

5.4 Repeatability Infrastructure

The implementation of this approach to repeatability is based on the DoD HLA RTI interface specification [21], and can be used to gain repeatability with receive-order[3] federations. Architecturally, the software is placed between the federate and the RTI. Functionally, the software acts as a *repeatability ambassador*. (Figure 4) The repeatability functions are independent of any communications or network hardware. Below, we assume the reader is familiar with the HLA's Interface Specification.

The system of software for repeatable executions is referred to as the Repeatable RTI (RRTI). The current implementation is based on the Georgia Tech Federation Developers Kit (FDK). The FDK includes example RTIs[4]. One of the example RTIs was subclassed and extended to include repeatability functions. An application programmer uses the RRTI exactly as if it were the original RTI. Use of the RRTI does not require extensive code modifications to existing RT federates. Basic calls to the HLA RTI such as join(), publish(), sendInteraction(), UpdateObjectAttributes() and tick()

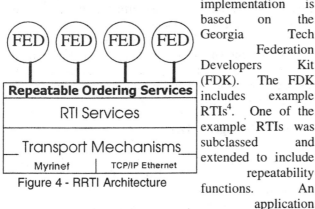

Figure 4 - RRTI Architecture

---

behave identically in the RRTI compared to the original RTI.

5.5 Software Modules

The RRTI is composed of two logical sets of functions. The first are the extended implementations of HLA RTI calls. The second set of functions represent new functions required for instrumentation of the application and advancing LVT. The list below explains the extensions.

joinFederationExecution() This HLA call is extended to include initialization of LVT and default values for lookahead and virtual latency.

tick() This HLA call is overridden, as previously explained. The RRTI version of tick first performs a timeAdvanceRequest (an HLA call to advance simulation time) for the current value of LVT. Then the RepeatableRTIambassador::tick calls the RTIambassador::tick until a timeAdvanceGrant is received. As messages (reflects and receives) arrive at the RRTI ambassador, the timestamps are stripped and the messages are passed on to the federate ambassador.

updateAttributeValues/sendInteraction() Both of these methods are extended to timestamp outgoing messages based upon the current LVT.

advanceRunTimeClock() This is a new method that allows LVT to be incremented.

setRunTimeClock() This method permits setting LVT explicitly.

setVirtualLatency() This call sets the value that is added to LVT to compute the timestamp of an outgoing message.

The software also includes a set of macros to simplify the instrumentation of existing software. The macros are placed at the beginning and end of each block of code to be instrumented. During the profiling of the simulation, the macros function as timers. When the simulation is run in a repeatable execution, the macros instead call advanceRunTimeClock() with chosen values.

6. Experiments

To test the repeatable execution capability of the RRTI, a simulation was developed which models a simple combat interaction. The simulation, called *Phalanx*, is set in a battlefield of two opposing forces (red and blue), akin to a musket battle. Each force is initialized with a number of soldiers, which can be distributed among any number of LPs. The soldiers follow a three-state behavior to Aim, Reload and, if shot, enter a terminal state of Dead..

This simulation was developed to be easy to distribute. The behavior of the combat is very regular and should not be affected by degree of parallelism or distribution. Additionally, the expected outcome is predictable by a well-known mathematical model [16]. The results are easy to interpret.

6.1 Experimental Executions

The execution environment was a set of 8 Sun UltraSparc 1 cpu computers, running Solaris 5.5. The tests were executed for both Myrinet and TCP. Prior to

---

[2] This assumes that virtual latency has been set to correspond to the minimum network latency.
[3] Receive order federations are composed of DIS-like federates, which are neither time regulating, nor time constrained.
[4] The RTIs included in the FDK are research vehicles that do not completely conform to HLA RTI API specifications. In some cases, the included RTIs extend the functionality specified for HLA.

execution, the simulation application was profiled to determine execution times for various blocks of code. Using the profile information, the simulation was recompiled for repeatable execution.

Each configuration was executed with several sets of parameters on 2, 4 and 8 CPUs. Executions were made in repeatable and non-repeatable mode, for Δt varying from 100 to 1 millisecond. For the repeatable executions, the virtual latency was set to 100, 50 25, 10, 5, 2.5, and 1 millisecond.

7. Results

The system was able to produce repeatable executions in all configurations. The ability to produce this repeatable execution is the first and foremost result of this project. The results of repeatable and non-repeatable executions were used to estimate the overhead required to support repeatable execution. Given our model of real-time simulation, two basic measures of impact were intuitive: message delay and tick() delay.

7.1 Expectations with this Approach

For the non-repeatable runs, the processes run asynchronously. If the various LPs send messages at random times during the execution, we would expect an even distribution of messages across Δt. The minimum latency would, of course, be bound by the limits of physical communications. Since all messages are flushed, the maximum observed latency would be the maximum communications delay, plus Δt. This would result in an average message delay, or latency-to-delivery of approximately

$$1/2(\Delta t) + physical\ latency. \qquad (EQ-1)$$

This is not the best case, however. Ideally, each LP could send its messages just prior to when the receiver polls the incoming delivery routines (in this case "tick()"). This would result in messages more frequently being delivered with latencies close to the physical limit. Practically, however, this rarely occurs.

For the repeatable runs, we artificially enforce an additional lower bound to the communications latency by specifying virtual latency. Since we know that a message cannot be delivered before We might expect that a lower bound on latency-to-delivery for virtual latency > physical latency would be

$$1/2(\Delta t) + virtual\_latency. \qquad (EQ-2)$$

However, we also must synchronize virtual time, which equates to a lower-bound timestamp (LBTS) computation, prior to delivery of the messages. Therefore, we expect that our total latency-to-delivery would be approximately

$$1/2(\Delta t) + virtual\_latency + time\_to\_compute\_LBT, \qquad (EQ-3)$$

provided that our messages are sent evenly over the execution.

Observe, however, that because we perform a synchronization step during every cycle, if the message sends occur at the same point in each cycle of the execution, then we tend not to have an even distribution of messages sends, but rather, many message sends at the same time, each cycle. In our timing model, the message sends occur prior to the slack time (spin-wait). The messages will not be delivered until the receiver has completed spinning. For large Δt, we may expect that spin time approaches Δt. As Δt decreases, so must spin time, until no slack exists, and the LP begins to gasp (shown later in this section). At this point, the message delay should be at a minimum value, bound by either the virtual latency, or by physical latency. Additionally, at small values of Δt, the RTI will be delivering very few messages per tick(), so the RTI overhead will be dominated by the LBTS computation. Substituting from above, this yields an expected repeatable message delay of

$$MAX(\Delta t, (1/2(\Delta t) + virtual\_latency + RTI\_overhead)). \qquad (EQ-4)$$

7.2 Message Delay Results

As explained above, message delay is the amount of wall-clock time that elapses between the time a message is sent and when it is delivered to the LP. Figure 5 shows that a message may not be delivered immediately, depending on the receiving LP. Since the message may sit in a queue, waiting to be delivered, this is not a measurement of network latency, but rather a more practical *latency-to-delivery*.

Figure 6 compares the repeatable and receive order message delay results for Myrinet and TCP. Results are

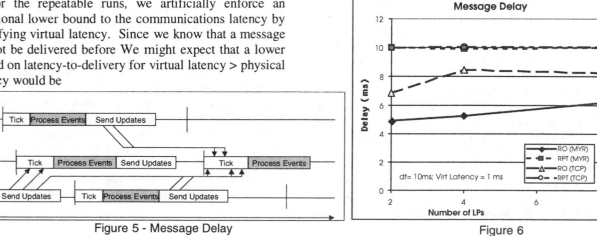

Figure 5 - Message Delay

Figure 6

shown for executions of 2,4, and 8 CPUs. The virtual latency for the runs was set to 1 ms, and Δt was 10 ms. We see that the delay for both repeatable runs is approximately Δt, as was expected from EQ-4. For the receive order runs, delay for Myrinet shows slightly better than expected results, while TCP is slightly worse, indicating that virtual latency is approaching the physical communication limit (EQ-1).

Figures 7 and 8 show the effect of decreasing Δt for various values of virtual latency. From these charts we can also see the effect that virtual latency has on the message delay. As we reduce Δt for the receive-order runs (RO) we see a corresponding reduction in message delay. For the repeatable runs, when Δt is large compared to virtual latency, the reductions in Δt also have a corresponding effect on message delay. However, as Δt decreases, message delay is bound from below by the value of virtual latency.

For Myrinet runs (figure 8), we see that the message delay quickly approaches this lower-bound, for all values of virtual latency, 10ms to 1 ms. However, for the TCP runs (figure 7), we observe that for values of virtual latency less that 5 ms, the message delay reaches a minimum at Δt of 2.5 ms and thereafter increases. This phenomenon is due to limits of physical communication speeds and the time required to perform the LBTS computation, and indicates that no further reduction in latency may be produced by changes in Δt or virtual latency.

7.3 Tick Time

In the time-stepped execution, the simulation application assumes that all processing and OS overhead for each cycle will not take longer than Δt. This defines the bounds of imposable load due to repeatable message delivery. If after imposing the load, the simulation can execute at the desired rate, the solution is appropriate. Else, the "wait" period must be increased, which implies that the time step interval will need to be increased.

The overhead load for this implementation consists of three factors: 1) the time spent updating local virtual time, 2)the additional time spent assigning timestamps during message sending, and 3)the time required for LBTS computation and TSO message delivery (dominant)

The first two loads are incurred through the processing cycle at the end of each instrumented block and any time a message is sent, respectively. These loads will be apparent if one were to measure the total processing load during each cycle. In practice, however, the load from 1) and 2) load is small relative to 3).

The third factor is accounted for in the RRTI tick() method (Figure 9, 10). Figure 9 shows the delay in milliseconds when calling tick() for a typical execution configuration. The delay accounts for the delivery of

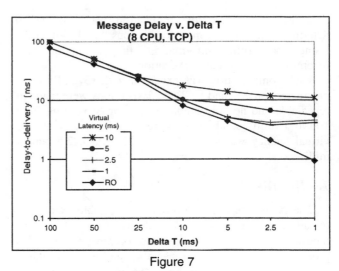

Figure 7

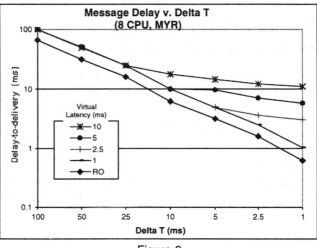

Figure 8

messages, and in the repeatable run, the time required to advance virtual time.

Figure 9 shows how RTI overhead is effected by the Δt. As Δt is increased, the overhead increases due to the number of messages that must be delivered during each tick. At small values of Δt, there are fewer messages per tick, however, the RTI must wait for transient messages and the completion of the LBTS before returning. This is also evident by the increase in the number of missed deadlines (next section).

When we examine RTI overhead as a percentage of Δt, (Figure 10) we can see that for this simulation, the repeatability overhead for Δt less than 5ms will produce missed deadlines every cycle. This means that the execution will slow down to accommodate the time management, and will not be able to run in real-time. However, for Myrinet, a Δt of 2.5 ms was found to be acceptable, causing relatively few missed deadlines.

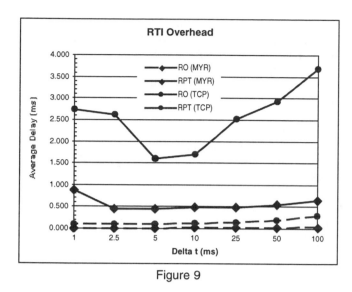

Figure 9

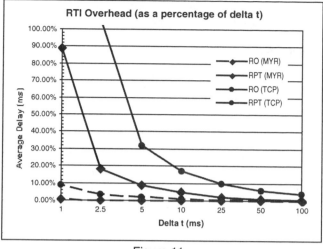

Figure 11

7.4 Gasps

Gasps are a measure of the ability of the simulation to meet its real-time processing requirements. Gasps are comparable to missed processing deadlines. However, gasps do not indicate a failure, or error, but rather a lack of slack time during a cycle. An LP may recover from this condition in the subsequent cycle(s). If the LP is continually unable to complete its processing in the allotted Δt, the gasp condition persists, and the execution will run slower than real-time. The chart below shows the behavior of this particular simulation. It is an indication of how similar data can be used to determine if a system is functioning properly (in real-time) during a repeatable execution.

The unshaded blocks show configurations of virtual latency and Δt where the repeatable simulation ran with very few gasps. It was thus able to keep up with real-time without exception. The yellow (lightly shaded) blocks show configurations where the simulation missed

deadlines, but was able to recover. The simulation could be operated in this configuration, but would not be guaranteed to run at real-time continuously. The heavily shaded blocks indicate that the repeatable infrastructure placed a significant burden on the simulation and it was not able to run at real-time.

One can see that there are many configurations of the simulation that would produce real-time execution. This leads us to conclude that the infrastructure places a reasonable load on the simulation, and could be used to produce repeatable, real-time executions.

8. Future Work

Some refinements may be made to the process of virtual time management. Specifically, the determination of a good value for virtual latency, and the process of instrumentation may yield additional performance gains. Although it is beyond the scope of this study, mechanisms need to be explored which will allow a more generalized remedy for non-deterministic behavior. Approaches such as event logging may be explored in the context of data collection also as in [17].

9. Conclusions

The paper has shown the viability of the notion of a repeatable execution system for real-time distributed simulations. The concepts explored here have been implemented and tested on a real-time, receive order simulation. Using a repeatable infrastructure patterned after the DoD HLA RTI, we have shown how a simulation can be made to executed in a repeatable fashion. We have measured the impact of the repeatability mechanism on the simulation performance, and find it to be reasonable in most cases. Based on data from experiments presented herein, it appears likely that this mechanism could be applicable to a large number of existing real-time (DIS-like) simulation systems. This would provide and

Gasps per execution			Delta t (sec)						
Network	Exec	Virtual Latency (sec)	0.1	0.05	0.03	0.01	0.01	0.0025	0.001
Myrinet	RO	NA	0	0	0	0	5	15	49
	RPT	0.1000	160	91	78	136	189	418	1053
		0.0500	0	160	101	138	138	1027	642
		0.0250	0	0	206	42	143	158	419
		0.0100	0	0	60	284	106	117	1431
		0.0050	0	0	0	0	455	267	2157
		0.0025	0	0	0	0	7	1130	5350
		0.0010	0	0	0	0	40	175	117208
TCP	RO	NA	0	0	0	1	4	18	110
	RPT	0.1000	308	172	139	143	185	691	2856
		0.0500	0	346	230	185	168	370	3625
		0.0250	16	0	582	16	253	256	7418
		0.0100	0	0	0	841	308	6837	15336
		0.0050	0	0	0	1011	1669	1992	132263
		0.0025	0	0	0	6	103	9457	157581
		0.0010	0	0	0	0	68	45914	158744

☐ Few gasps during the execution
☐ Modest/acceptable numbers of gasps due to message que overhead
▨ Large numbers of gasps due to RTI time management overhead

Figure 10

important link between real-time, receive order simulation and time managed simulation systems.

References

[1]   K. Shen and S. Gregory, "Instant Replay Debugging of Concurrent Logic Programs," New Generation Computing, 14(1), pp. 79-107, January 1996..

[2]   R. M. Fujimoto, "Parallel Discrete Event Simulation," Communications of the ACM, vol. 33, pp. October 1990, 1990.

[3]   D. M. Nicol, "Performance Bounds on Parallel Self-Initiating Discrete-Event Simulations," ACM Transactions on Modeling and Computer Simulations, vol. 1, 1991.

[4]   T. J. LeBlanc and J. M. Mellor-Crummey, "Debugging Parallel Programs with Instant Replay," IEEE Transactions on Computers, vol. C-36, pp. 471-481, 1987.

[5]   D. F. Bacon and S. C. Goldstein, "Hardware-Assisted Replay of Multiprocessor Programs," Proceedings of the ACM/ONR Workshop on Parallel and Distributed Debugging, published in ACM SIGPLAN Notices, 26(12), pp. 194-206, December 1991.

[6]   B. Bruegge, "A Portable Platform for Distributed Event Environments," Proceedings of the ACM/ONR Workshop on Parallel and Distributed Debugging, published in ACM SIGPLAN Notices, 26(12), pp. 184-193, December 1991.

[7]   P. Dickens, P. Heidelberger, and D. M. Nicol, "Parallel Direct Execution Simulation of Message-Passing Parallel Programs," IEEE Transactions on Parallel and Distributed Systems, vol. 7, pp. October 1996, 1996.

[8]   S. K. Reinhardt, M. D. Hill, J. R. Laurus, A. R. Lebeck, J. C. Lewis, and D. A. Wood, "The Wisconsin Wind Tunnel: Virtual Prototyping of Parallel Computers," ACM Sigmetric, 1993.

[9]   D. M. Nicol, "The cost of conservative synchronization in parallel discrete-event simulations," Journal of the ACM, vol. 40, pp. 304-333, 1993.

[10]   R. H. B. Netzer and B. P. Miller, "Optimal tracing and replay for debugging message-passing parallel programs," presented at Supercomputing '92, 1992.

[11]   E. A. Brewer and W. E. Weihl, "Developing Parallel Applications Using High-Performance Simulation," Proceedings of the Workshop on Parallel and Distributed Debugging, ACM SIGPLAN Notices, Vol. 28_12, pp. 158-168, ACM Press, May 1993.

[12]   D. M. Nicol, "Noncomittal Barrier Synchronization," Parallel Computing, vol. 21, 1995.

[13]   R. M. Fujimoto, "Zero Lookahead and Repeatability in the High Level Architecture," .

[14]   K. M. Chandy and J. Misra, "A Nontrivial Example of Concurrent Processing: Distributed Simulation," Proceedings of COMPSAC, pp. 822-826, 1978.

[15]   R. L. Bagrodia, K. M. Chandy, and J. Misra, "A Message-Based Approach to Discrete-Event Simulation," IEEE Transactions of Software Engineering, vol. SE-13, pp. June 1987, 1987.

[16]   F. W. Lanchester, Aircraft in Warfare, the Dawn of the Fourth Arm. Tiptree, Constable and Co. Ltd, 1916.

[17]   T. McLean, L. Mark, M. Loper, and D. Rosenbaum, "Relating the High Level Architecture to Temporal Database Concepts," Proceedings of the 1998 Winter Simulation Conference, Washington DC, Dec 12, 1998

[18]   M. Ronsse, K. De Bosschere, "RecPlay: A Fully Integrated Practical Record/Replay System," ACM Transactions on Computer Systems, vol. 19, pp. 133-152. May 1999.

[19]   S. Bachinsky, G. Tarbox, E. T. Powell, "Data Collection in an HLA Environment," Proceedings of the 1997 Spring Simulation Interoperability Workshop, Orlando FL, March 1997.

[20]   C. Kanarick, "A Technical Overview and Histroy of the SIMNET Project" Proceedings of the SCS Multiconference on Advances in Parallel and Distributed Simulation, pp. 104-111, 1991.

[21]   Defense Modeling and Simulation Office, "HLA Interface Specification" Available on-line at hla.dmso.mil, Version 1.3 DRAFT 1, 02 April 1998

Session 3
Optimistic system performance

**Analytic Performance Model for Speculative,
Synchronous, Discrete-Event Simulation**
B. L. Noble and R. D. Chamberlain

Slow Memory: The Rising Cost of Optimism
R. A. Meyer, J. M. Martin, and R. L. Bagrodia

ROSS: A High-Performance, Low Memory, Modular Time Warp System
C. D. Carothers, D. Bauer, and S. Pearce

Analytic Performance Model for Speculative, Synchronous, Discrete-Event Simulation

Bradley L. Noble
Dept. of Electrical and Computer Engineering
Southern Illinois University Edwardsville
Edwardsville, IL
bnoble@siue.edu

Roger D. Chamberlain
Computer and Communications Research Center
Department of Electrical Engineering
Washington University, St. Louis, MO
roger@ccrc.wustl.edu

Abstract

Performance models exist that reliably describe the execution time and efficiency of parallel discrete-event simulations executed in a synchronous iterative fashion. These performance models incorporate the effects of processor heterogeneity, other processor load due to shared computational resources, application workload imbalance, and the use of speculative computation. This includes modeling the effects of predictive optimism, a technique for improving the accuracy of speculative assumptions. We extend these models to incorporate correlated workloads across the set of processors and validate the models with two different applications.

1. Introduction

Speculative computation has received a great deal of attention in the parallel computing community as a technique for balancing computational load and masking latencies in interprocessor communications [8]. It has even found its way into processor design at the instruction level, with proposals for *value prediction*, speculating the results of individual instructions or basic code blocks [11]. In discrete-event simulation, parallel algorithms that perform computation in a speculative manner are generally referred to as *optimistic* algorithms.

While both synchronous and asynchronous optimistic algorithms exist, our interest is in synchronous algorithms. This is due to a desire to avoid the inconsistent (and sometimes inexplicable) performance associated with many asynchronous protocols. Lin and Lazowska [13] coined the term "S phenomenon" to describe the observation that speedup curves for an optimistic asynchronous algorithm often have several local minima and maxima. This observation was made over a large set of different simulation appli-

cations [4, 10, 12, 22]. In addition, synchronous algorithms have an inherent simplicity and ease of implementation that is not present in asynchronous techniques.

As with many other algorithms, there is a tradeoff between simplicity and performance; the simplicity of the synchronous algorithm comes with a potential cost in performance. If frequent synchronizations are required, the algorithm becomes more fine grained. Since the critical path lies with the slowest processor at each iteration, idle time can accumulate at the other processors and the total execution time is lower bounded by the execution time of the slowest processor in each iteration. In an attempt to alleviate these performance concerns for synchronous discrete-event simulation, techniques used in asynchronous simulation algorithms (e.g., speculative computation) have been applied to the synchronous algorithm, while retaining the iterative nature of the algorithm.

In [18], we described a performance model for synchronous iterative algorithms that incorporates the effects of speculative computation. Included in this model is the degree to which speculative computations are correct (i.e., what is the impact of predictive optimism). This model assumed that the computational workload is relatively independent across the processors. However, there are many simulation applications (e.g., VLSI logic simulation) for which the workload is highly correlated. Here, we present extensions to this model that enable accurate performance prediction for correlated workloads. This new model is validated using two applications, queueing network simulation and VLSI logic simulation.

2. Speculative Computation and Predictive Optimism

The model developed here is not restricted to discrete-event simulation applications, but can be applied to any synchronous iterative algorithm. Synchronous iterative algorithms include many of the compute intensive numerical methods used in science and engineering applications [1]. Figure 1 illustrates a typical set of iterations of a synchronous iterative algorithm executing on four processors (labeled 1 through 4). An iteration can be seen as consisting of 3 phases:

1. Computation – performing the computational tasks associated with the application.

2. Idle – time between first and last processor to complete work in an iteration.

3. Synchronization – time to complete the barrier synchronization operation.

Computation starts on all processors immediately following the barrier synchronization. During this phase, each processor executes all the tasks assigned to it that iteration. For discrete-event simulation, this consists of processing simulation events. Interprocessor data communication may be concurrent with computation. At the end of the computation phase, each processor enters a barrier and waits for its completion. The *idle* phase is a result of variation in computation times between processors due to imbalances in workload as the algorithm progresses, multitasking other unrelated processes (background load), or processor heterogeneity. *Synchronization* time is determined by the communication performance of the parallel platform in completing the barrier synchronization. After the barrier synchronization completes, the processors proceed to the next iteration, repeating the cycle until the algorithm completes. In the performance model for synchronous iterative algorithms described in [20], the quantity of computation to be performed on each processor during each iteration is modeled by a random variable with a known stationary distribution. The mean completion time for an iteration executing on P processors can then be modeled as the expectation of the maximum of P instances of the random variable.

Speculative computation utilizes the idle phase of the above algorithm by allowing processing to proceed into future iterations. While waiting for the barrier synchronization to complete, computation progresses speculatively, with the hope that a message arrival from a remote processor does not subsequently invalidate the computation. Once the barrier synchronization is complete, the speculated computation is tested for correctness and either committed or discarded.

To support processing during the execution of the barrier synchronization, a fuzzy barrier implementation is used [9]. Processors signal their willingness to complete the barrier and, rather than blocking, proceed to compute speculatively. A "barrier complete" signal indicates the end of the current iteration. The execution time line, illustrated in Figure 2, shows the speculative computation occurring during the idle

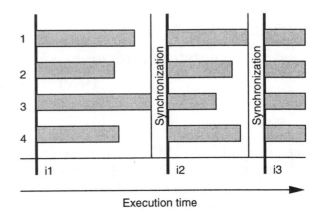

Figure 1. Synchronous iterative algorithm execution. The horizontal bars represent computation during each iteration.

times and while waiting for the barrier to complete. Note that the time required to complete iteration 2 is less than in the previous figure, since some of the computation has been completed during the otherwise idle time of iteration 1.

Mehl [14] proposed essentially this technique in the context of a conservative asynchronous algorithm, but did not report on its performance. We previously reported a set of empirical performance results in [17, 19]. Dickens et al. [3] present a performance model for a similar algorithm that predicts performance gains over a purely conservative synchronous algorithm. Steinman's Breathing Time Buckets algorithm [21] has been implemented in the SPEEDES environment and exhibits good performance on a pair of simulation models (queueing networks and proximity detection). In [18], the model of [20] is extended to incorporate the effects of speculation. A recurrence relation is developed that relates the original workload distribution, the distribution of time available for speculation, and the resulting workload distribution.

Predictive optimism is a technique for improving the accuracy of the guesses used to guide speculative computation. In traditional optimistic discrete-event simulation algorithms, the standard optimistic assumption is that if a message has not arrived on an input channel, none will arrive, and processing can continue assuming the channel is unchanged.

In predictive optimism, information theoretic techniques are used to improve the accuracy of this assumption. A predictor is placed an each input channel, and the predictor retains historical information about the messages on the channel. If a message has not arrived on a channel, the predictor can be interrogated to determine if (and when) a message is likely to arrive. If the answer is no, processing proceeds as before. If the answer is yes, speculative computation is

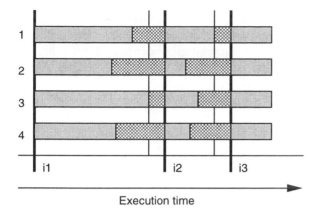

Figure 2. Speculative computation execution time line. The crosshatched areas represent speculative computing, potentially decreasing the computation needed during the subsequent iteration.

Table 1. Parameters for performance model.

Param.	Definition
R_P	application run time with P processors
P	number of processors
I	number of iterations
t_s	serial computation time per iteration
t_p	parallel computation time per iteration
t_{ov}	parallelism overhead time per iteration
$w_{i,j}$	parallel work during iteration i on processor j, no speculation
W	vector-valued random process representing work each iter., no speculation
W_j	component of W representing work on processor j
$v_{i,j}$	parallel work during iteration i on processor j, with speculation
V	vector-valued random process representing work each iter., with speculation
V_j	component of V representing work on processor j
$s_{i,j}$	work available to speculate during iteration i on processor j
S	vector-valued random process representing available speculation each iter.
S_j	component of S representing speculation on processor j
r	speculation success ratio: fraction of speculative computation that is correct

suspended, since the results are likely to be discarded, and the bookkeeping overhead of managing the speculation can be diminished.

We have previously investigated predictive optimism in the context of VLSI systems simulation [16]. In that study, the "no message arrival" assumption was compared to a first order finite state predictor and an incremental parsing predictor based on Lempel-Ziv data compression techniques [5]. Both predictors significantly decreased (or eliminated) cases where the standard assumption performed poorly (i.e., was wrong most of the time). In [6], Ferscha describes a similar mechanism, called probabilistic direct optimism control, and reports peformance for four different predictors of message interarrival time: arithmetic mean, exponential smoothing, approximated median, and an autoregressive moving average process predictor. The analytic model presented here includes mechanisms for evaluating the performance implications of variations in prediction accuracy, in order to investigate the usefulness of predictive optimism techniques.

3. Model Development

The set of variables used in the performance model is summarized in Table 1. A more complete definition of each variable is given in the text near the first use of the variable.

The execution time of a synchronous iterative algorithm requiring I iterations and running on a set of P processors can be modeled by a function consisting of three distinct terms. In any particular iteration i, there is a portion of work which is serial in nature. The first term represents the time required to complete the portion which cannot be

parallelized, which we denote as $t_{s,i}$. Each processor j has some assigned work to be performed during the parallel portion of each iteration. The time for each processor to complete this work is denoted by $t_{p,i,j}$. However, the parallel portion of each iteration is not complete until the last processor completes its assigned work. This gives the second term as $\max_{1 \leq j \leq P}(t_{p,i,j})$. Finally, the time required for the overheads associated with the parallel algorithm itself during iteration i are denoted by $t_{ov,i}$.

Combining these terms gives a model for the execution time as

$$R_P = \sum_{i=1}^{I} \left[t_{s,i} + \max_{1 \leq j \leq P} t_{p,i,j} + t_{ov,i} \right] \quad (1)$$

Although this equation effectively models the execution time, it requires specific knowledge of each individual iteration. By treating each of the terms as an i.i.d.[1] random process and taking the expected value, the references to a

---
[1] Independent and identically distributed.

specific iteration are eliminated. A new expression for runtime is given by

$$
\begin{aligned}
R_P &= \sum_{i=1}^{I} \left(E\left[t_{s,i}\right] + E\left[\max_{1 \le j \le P} t_{p,i,j}\right] + E\left[t_{ov,i}\right] \right) \\
&= I\left(t_s + E\left[\max_{1 \le j \le P} t_{p,j}\right] + t_{ov} \right)
\end{aligned} \tag{2}
$$

Previous work has shown this model to be effective for estimating run time for several different types of synchronous iterative algorithms [20]. By examining the effects of speculation on the terms in this model, we incorporate both speculative computation and the impact that successful speculation has on the run time.

3.1. Speculative Workload Characterization

For the discrete-event simulation applications we are interested in, both the serial term $t_{s,i}$ and the parallel overhead term $t_{ov,i}$ do not vary significantly between iterations. As such, these terms can be treated as constants. We focus on characterizing $E\left[\max_{1 \le j \le P} t_{p,i,j}\right]$ for the both the initial workload without speculative computation and for the resulting workload with speculative computation.

Let us define $w_{i,j}$ as the work to be completed on processor j during iteration i without speculative computation. Assuming the units of work are relatively constant in time (e.g., event evaluations with similar computational complexity), $t_{p,i,j}$ will be proportional to $w_{i,j}$. When speculative computation is performed, it will take work away from future iterations whenever a processor completes before the barrier synchronization. We will define this new workload as $v_{i,j}$, the work to be completed on processor j during iteration i with speculation. In this case, $t_{p,i,j}$ is proportional to $v_{i,j}$ which, by definition, must be less than or equal to $w_{i,j}$.

The development of $v_{i,j}$ from $w_{i,j}$ can be made by examining a specific iteration, i, of a synchronous algorithm that incorporates speculative computation. Examining Figure 2, we determine that the work to be completed during iteration i is $\max_{1 \le j \le P} v_{i,j}$. Therefore, the amount of work that can be speculated on processor j during iteration i is given by

$$
s_{i,j} = \max_{1 \le j \le P} (v_{i,j}) - v_{i,j}, \tag{3}
$$

provided we limit speculation to one iteration into the future. This yields a recursive formulation that relates $v_{i+1,j}$ to $v_{i,j}$:

$$
v_{i+1,j} = w_{i+1,j} - r s_{i,j} \tag{4}
$$

with initial condition

$$
v_{0,j} = w_{0,j}. \tag{5}
$$

The scalar r that is introduced in equation (4) represents the speculation success ratio, or the fraction of the speculated work that was successfully committed. Substituting (3) into (4) gives:

$$
v_{i+1,j} = w_{i+1,j} - r\left(\max_{1 \le j \le P}(v_{i,j}) - v_{i,j} \right) \tag{6}
$$

Although the case outlined above is limited to one iteration into the future, a similiar expression can be developed relating $v_{i+2,j}$ to $v_{i+1,j}$ and $v_{i,j}$ for speculation two iterations into the future. Similiarly, this can be extended to $i+n$ iterations into the future.

These expressions can be used to empirically evaluate $v_{i,j}$ for a specific instance where $w_{i,j}$ is known, however, it does not generalize beyond the circumstances where one has knowledge of workload during individual iterations. To accomplish this, we develop a stochastic workload model.

3.2. Stochastic Workload Model

We model the workload without speculation as an i.i.d., vector-valued random process W, with component W_j representing the work to be completed on processor j. Although described in other terms, this is consistent with the model of [18]. In [18], however, the components of W were assumed to be independent. Here, we model the vector W as correlated, with a given joint density function $f_W(x_1, ..., x_P)$. Essentially, this implies that we are modeling the workload at each iteration on each processor, $w_{i,j}$, as independent in the i dimension (iterations), and correlated in the j dimension (processors).

We model the workload with speculation as an i.i.d., vector-valued random process V. As above, the component V_j represents the work to be completed on processor j. Again, the components of V are assumed to be correlated, and an important piece of the model is evaluating the unknown joint density function $f_V(x_1, ..., x_P)$.

Provided a stationary distribution for V exists, we can define the vector-valued random process S as the amount of work that can be speculated each iteration, where:

$$
S = E\left[\max_{1 \le j \le P}(V_j)\right] \mathbf{1} - V \tag{7}
$$

and

$$
V = W - rS. \tag{8}
$$

Substitution of (7) into (8) yields:

$$
V = W + rV - rE\left[\max_{1 \le j \le P}(V_j)\right] \mathbf{1} \tag{9}
$$

Although (9) gives the fixed point conditions that V must meet, it does not directly support the calculation of its distribution. However, by adding a superscript k to equation

(9), we define an iterative approach which may be used in an attempt to solve for the distribution of V.

$$V^{k+1} = W + rV^k - rE\left[\max_{1 \le j \le P}(V_j^k)\right]\mathbf{1} \quad (10)$$

For the initial iteration, $V^0 = W$. Convergence is reached when the distributions of V^{k+1} and V^k are equal.

Clearly, there is no guarantee that (10) will converge to a stationary distribution for V. In some applications, the speculation process itself may be highly unstable, even oscillatory. If convergence is achieved, the result is a viable steady state distribution of the parallel workload.

4. Model Validation

The validation of the performance model is in three stages. We first discuss how to evaluate the model (i.e., compute the distribution of the random process V). We next investigate the correctness of the distribution of V. We then investigate the accuracy of the middle term in equation (2), which is represented by $E[\max_{1 \le j \le P} W_j]$ for executions that do not exploit speculation and by $E[\max_{1 \le j \le P} V_j]$ for executions that do employ speculative computation. To perform the validation, we will use empirical data from two discrete-event simulation applications.

The first application is a closed queueing network simulation of the style used in [7] and [15] to investigate the performance of asynchronous algorithms. The topology is a regular network with FCFS queueing discipline, the service requirements are exponentially distributed with a specified minimum service time, and the routing probabilities are uniformly distributed to each of the neighboring queueing stations. The second application is a VLSI logic simulation of several of the ISCAS-89 sequential benchmark circuits [2]. For each circuit, a gate-level simulation is executed using a unit delay timing model driven with random input vectors.

Our validation methodology starts with a set of trace data that directly represents $w_{i,j}, 1 \le i \le I, 1 \le j \le P$. Workload data from both the queueing network simulation and the logic simulation applications were recorded for a variety of queueing networks and logic circuits respectively. Example trace data from both applications (queuing network simulation q8000pm3 and VLSI logic simulation s9234) on four processors ($P = 4$) is shown in Figures 3 and 4. The units of work shown are simulation event counts.

Figures 5 and 6 show a normalized histogram of $w_{i,j}$ for the example trace data in Figure 3 and Figure 4 respectively. These histograms will be used to approximate the joint distribution of workload without speculation, $f_W(x_1, ..., x_P)$. It is useful to note that for the queueing network simulation, the histogram workload for each processor is very similiar

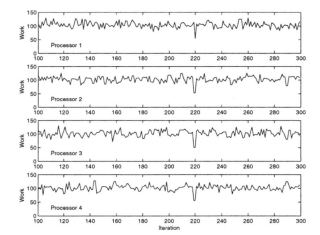

Figure 3. Example trace data for queueing network simulation application (QNS).

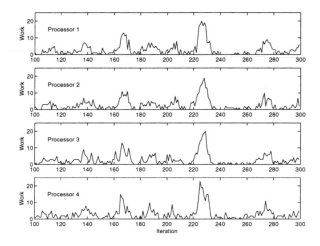

Figure 4. Example trace data for VLSI logic simulation application (VLS).

in shape. This implies a relatively uniform workload distribution across the processors. This view is also supported by a statistical analysis of the queueing networks. For example, the correlation coefficients (across j) of $w_{i,j}$ range from 0.20 to 0.24 for queueing network q8000pm3.

In the logic simulation case, although each histogram has the same basic shape, there are distinct differences in each distribution. The logic simulator workload, shown in Figures 4 and 6, exhibits a large degree of correlation across the processors. Again, this view is supported by a statistical analysis of the logic circuits and is to be expected since the logic circuits being simulated are governed by a clock. Iterations immediately following the clock signal have a high degree of activity which trails off in iterations later in the clock period. The correlation coefficients of $w_{i,j}$ range from 0.70 to 0.76 for circuit s9234.

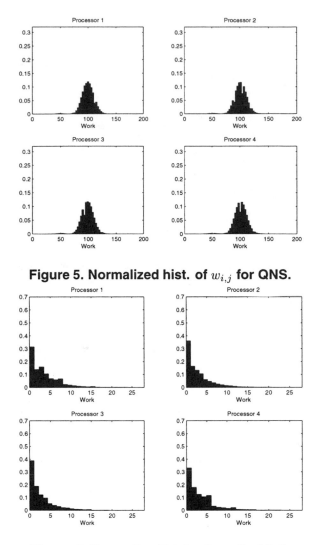

Figure 5. Normalized hist. of $w_{i,j}$ for QNS.

Figure 6. Normalized hist. of $w_{i,j}$ for VLS.

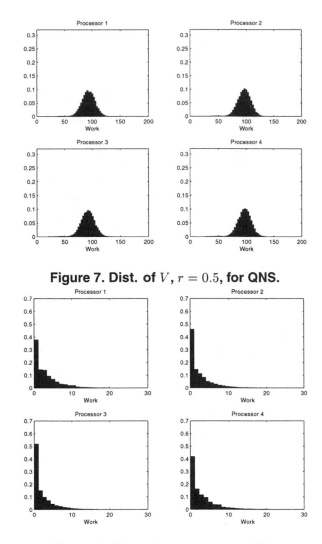

Figure 7. Dist. of V, $r = 0.5$, for QNS.

Figure 8. Dist. of V, $r = 0.5$, for VLS.

4.1. Model Evaluation

To evaluate the model, we use the empirical histogram data to represent the distribution of the random process W. However, to preserve the joint workload dependencies, this histogram must be P-dimensional. Equation (10) is then numerically evaluated using samples drawn from this approximation to the distribution of V^k to obtain a new P-dimensional histogram approximation of the distribution of V^{k+1}. This is repeated until the distributions of V^{k+1} and V^k have converged.

For the sample queueing network and logic circuit workloads of Figures 5 and 6 the resulting distribution of V is shown in Figures 7 through 10 for two different values of the speculation success ratio, r. Once $f_V(x_1, ..., x_P)$ is known, we can calculate $E[\max_{1 \leq j \leq P} V_j]$. These values are tabulated in Table 2.

4.2. Model Analysis

To quantify the accuracy of the model, we compare the distribution of the random process V to empirical results. The empirical data for the two applications, $w_{i,j}$, is evaluated using equation (6) to determine $v_{i,j}$. This evaluation constitutes a trace-driven simulation of the speculative execution algorithm. Histograms of the resulting workloads are shown in Figures 11 through 14 for the same two values of the success ratio, r. A good match between the histograms of Figures 7 to 10 with those in Figures 11 to 14 implies that the analytic model is effective in matching the empirical results in its estimate of $f_V(x_1, ..., x_P)$.

For the final stage of evaluating the model, we are interested in comparing $E[\max_{1 \leq j \leq P}(W_j)]$ and $E[\max_{1 \leq j \leq P}(V_j)]$ to the mean (across iterations) of $\max_{1 \leq j \leq P}(w_{i,j})$ and the mean (across iterations) of $\max_{1 \leq j \leq P}(v_{i,j})$. This comparison lets us quantify the ac-

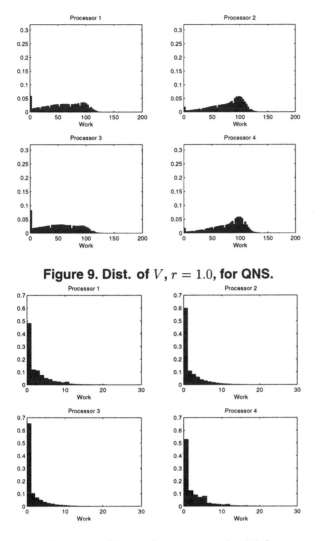

Figure 9. Dist. of V, $r = 1.0$, for QNS.

Figure 10. Dist. of V, $r = 1.0$, for VLS.

Table 2. Model results for $P = 4$.

	$E[\max_{1 \leq j \leq P} V_j]$ for q8000pm3	$E[\max_{1 \leq j \leq P} V_j]$ for s9234
$r = 0.5$	106.17	4.39
$r = 1.0$	102.02	4.08

reasonable approach.

The last two columns in the tables correspond to parallel workload when speculation is present. The column labeled $E[\max_{1 \leq j \leq P} V_j]$ corresponds to the modeled results, and the column labeled mean of $\max_{1 \leq j \leq P} v_{i,j}$ corresponds to the empirical results. This data is also plotted in Figures 15 and 16. In the queueing network simulation, the model of the workload with speculation, V, closely matches the empirically calculated speculative workload, $v_{i,j}$, for all queueing networks and for different values of the speculation success ratio, r. These results are what we expected for the queueing network application, since the previous model (of [18]) worked well under these circumstances.

The limitations of the previous model were apparent for the VLSI logic simulation application. The independence assumption (across processors) caused the earlier model to consistently overstate the execution time. Here, however, we have an excellent match between modeled and empirical results. Explicitly modeling the correlation in workload across the processors has enabled us to reliably predict the performance of an application that is not well characterized when an independence assumption is made.

5. Summary and Conclusions

This paper has presented and validated a performance model for synchronous iterative algorithms that include speculative computation. The model was applied to two discrete-event simulation applications: queueing network simulation and VLSI logic simulation. Unlike earlier models, the model presented here effectively handles circumstances where the parallel workload across the processors is highly correlated, such as is the case for VLSI logic simulation.

We believe the usefulness of this model will come in two forms. First, any good analytic model can be used to better understand the performance issues associated with a parallel application execution. This can point to improvements in efficiency via changes in the algorithm, execution platform modifications, or various other forms of performance tuning.

Second, since the analytic model only requires empirical data that can be collected from a serial execution of the simulation, it can be used to predict the performance of a new application prior to parallel implementation. This can

curacy of the model at characterizing the workload both with and without speculation. Tables 3 and 4 provide such a comparison for a variety of queueing networks and logic circuits with different numbers of processors, P, and values of r. Figures 15 and 16 plot these results for the case where speculation is present.

The first two data columns in the tables correspond to parallel workload when no speculation is present. The first column (labeled $E[\max_{1 \leq j \leq P} W_j]$) corresponds to the modeled results, and the second column (labeled mean of $\max_{1 \leq j \leq P} w_{i,j}$) corresponds to the empirical results. To calculate the empirical results, the max operator was applied at each iteration, and the mean was taken across iterations. As seen in both tables, the model of the workload, W, strongly matches the empirical workload, $w_{i,j}$, for both the queueing network and logic simuation for a variety of topologies and circuits. This points to the fact that modeling the original workload via an i.i.d. random process is a

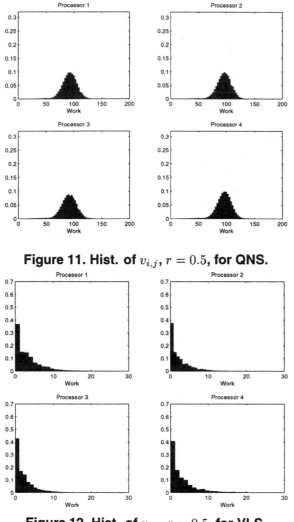

Figure 11. Hist. of $v_{i,j}$**,** $r = 0.5$**, for QNS.**

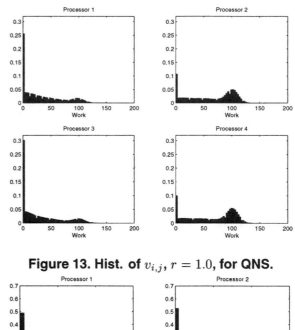

Figure 13. Hist. of $v_{i,j}$**,** $r = 1.0$**, for QNS.**

Figure 12. Hist. of $v_{i,j}$**,** $r = 0.5$**, for VLS.**

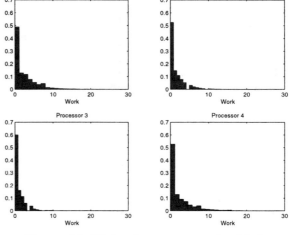

Figure 14. Hist. of $v_{i,j}$**,** $r = 1.0$**, for VLS.**

help a simulation practitioner to evaluate whether or not it is worth the effort to implement a synchronous parallel version of the application.

References

[1] D. P. Bertsekas and J. N. Tsitsiklis. *Parallel and Distributed Computation: Numerical Methods.* Prentice Hall, NJ, 1989.

[2] F. Brglez, D. Bryan, and K. Kozminski. Combinational Profiles of Sequential Benchmark Circuits. In *Proc of the Int'l Symp. on Circuits and Systems*, pages 1929–1934, May 1989.

[3] P. M. Dickens, D. M. Nicol, P. F. Reynolds, Jr., and J. M. Duva. The Impact of Adding Aggressiveness to a Non-Aggressive Windowing Protocol. In *Proc. of the 1993 Winter Simulation Conf.*, pages 731–739, December 1993.

[4] M. Ebling, M. Di Loreto, M. Presley, F. Wieland, and D. Jefferson. An Ant Foraging Model Implemented on the Time Warp Operating System. In *Proc. of the SCS Multiconference on Distributed Simulation*, pages 21–28, March 1989.

[5] M. Feder, N. Merhav, and M. Gutman. Universal Prediction of Individual Sequences. *IEEE Trans. on Information Theory*, 38(4):1258–1270, July 1991.

[6] A. Ferscha. Probabilistic Adaptive Direct Optimism Control in Time Warp. In *Proc. of 9th Workshop on Parallel and Distributed Simulation*, pages 120–129, June 1995.

[7] R. M. Fujimoto. Performance Measurements of Distributed Simulation Strategies. *Trans. of Society for Computer Simulation*, 6:89–132, 1989.

[8] V. Govindan and M. Franklin. Speculative Computation: Overcoming Communication Delays. In *Proc. of*

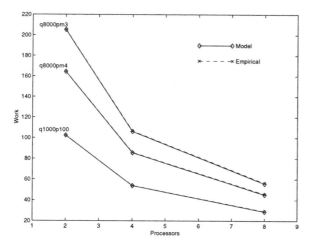

Figure 15. Speculative model validation for queueing network simulation.

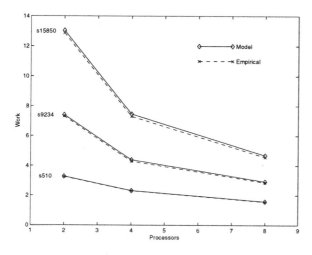

Figure 16. Speculative model validation for VLSI logic simulation.

the 1994 Int'l Conf. on Parallel Processing, volume III, pages 12–16, August 1994.

[9] R. Gupta. The Fuzzy Barrier: A Mechanism for the High Speed Synchronization of Processors. In *Proc. of the Int'l Conf. on Architectural Support for Programming Languages and Operating Systems*, pages 54–63, April 1989.

[10] P. Hontalas, B. Beckman, M. Di Loreto, L. Blume, P. Reiher, K. Sturdevant, L. Van Warren, J. Wedel, F. Wieland, and D. Jefferson. Performance of the Colliding Pucks Simulation on the Time Warp Operating System (Part 1: Asynchronous Behavior and Sectoring). In *Proc. of the SCS Multiconference on Distributed Simulation*, pages 3–7, March 1989.

[11] J. Huang and D. Lilja. Exploiting Basic Block Value Locality with Block Reuse. In *Proc. of 5th Int'l Symp. on High Performance Computer Architecture*, pages 106–114, January 1999.

[12] D. Jefferson et al. Distributed Simulation and the Time Warp Operating System. In *Proc. of the 11th ACM Symp. on Operating Systems Principles*, 1987.

[13] Y.-B. Lin and E. D. Lazowska. Processor Scheduling for Time Warp Parallel Simulation. In *Proc. of the SCS Multiconference on Advances in Parallel and Distributed Simulation*, pages 11–14, January 1991.

[14] H. Mehl. Speedup of Conservative Distributed Discrete Event Simulation Methods by Speculative Computing. In *Proc. of the SCS Multiconference on Advances in Parallel and Distributed Simulation*, pages 163–166, January 1991.

[15] D. M. Nicol. High Performance Parallelized Discrete-Event Simulation of Stochastic Queueing Networks. In *Proc. of the 1988 Winter Simulation Conf.*, 1988.

[16] B. L. Noble and R. D. Chamberlain. Predicting the Future: Resource Requirements and Predictive Optimism. In *Proc. of 9th Workshop on Parallel and Distributed Simulation*, pages 157–164, June 1995.

[17] B. L. Noble and R. D. Chamberlain. Performance of Speculative Computation in Synchronous Parallel Discrete-Event Simulation on Multiuser Execution Platforms. In *Proc. of the 8th IASTED Int'l Conf. on Parallel and Distributed Computing and Systems*, pages 489–494, October 1996.

[18] B. L. Noble and R. D. Chamberlain. Performance Model for Speculative Simulation Using Predictive Optimism. In *Proc. of 32nd Hawaii Int'l Conf. on System Sciences*, January 1999.

[19] B. L. Noble, G. D. Peterson and R. D. Chamberlain. Performance of Synchronous Parallel Discrete-Event Simulation. In *Proc. of 28th Hawaii Int'l Conf. on System Sciences*, Vol. II, pages 185–186, January 1995.

[20] G. D. Peterson and R. D. Chamberlain. Parallel Application Performance in a Shared Resource Environment. *Distributed Systems Engineering*, 3:9-19, 1996.

[21] J. S. Steinman. SPEEDES: A Multiple-Synchronization Environment for Parallel Discrete-Event Simulation. *Int'l Journal in Computer Simulation*, 2:251–286, 1992.

[22] F. Wieland, L. Hawley, A. Feinberg, M. Di Loreto, L. Blume, P. Reiher, B. Beckman, P. Hontalas, S. Bellenot, and D. Jefferson. Distributed Combat Simulation and Time Warp: The Model and Its Performance. In *Proc. of the SCS Multiconference on Distributed Simulation*, pages 14–20, March 1989.

Table 3. Model validation for QNS.

Queueing network	P	r	$E[\max_{1 \leq j \leq P} W_j]$	mean of $\max_{1 \leq j \leq P} w_{i,j}$	$E[\max_{1 \leq j \leq P} V_j]$	mean of $\max_{1 \leq j \leq P} v_{i,j}$
q8000pm3	2	0.5	208.42	208.38	205.19	205.35
		1.0	208.36	208.38	201.96	201.96
	4	0.5	110.45	110.43	106.17	106.56
		1.0	110.42	110.43	102.02	102.16
	8	0.5	60.06	60.05	55.70	56.29
		1.0	60.06	60.05	51.46	51.96
q8000pm4	2	0.5	167.27	167.28	164.43	164.58
		1.0	167.28	167.28	161.65	161.57
	4	0.5	89.38	89.36	85.55	85.90
		1.0	89.37	89.36	81.79	81.91
	8	0.5	49.04	49.04	45.15	45.68
		1.0	49.05	49.04	41.40	41.85
q1000p100	2	0.5	104.76	104.77	102.46	102.49
		1.0	104.78	104.77	100.16	99.76
	4	0.5	56.80	56.80	53.78	53.91
		1.0	56.80	56.80	50.74	50.59
	8	0.5	31.87	31.87	28.86	29.20
		1.0	31.86	31.87	25.98	26.25

Table 4. Model validation for VLS.

Logic circuit	P	r	$E[\max_{1 \leq j \leq P} W_j]$	mean of $\max_{1 \leq j \leq P} w_{i,j}$	$E[\max_{1 \leq j \leq P} V_j]$	mean of $\max_{1 \leq j \leq P} v_{i,j}$
s38584	2	0.5	92.41	92.30	91.32	90.79
		1.0	91.91	92.30	90.17	89.75
	4	0.5	49.30	49.51	47.84	47.48
		1.0	49.58	49.51	47.32	45.95
	8	0.5	27.49	27.50	26.08	25.17
		1.0	27.44	27.50	25.33	23.82
s15850	2	0.5	13.57	13.59	13.04	12.87
		1.0	13.57	13.59	12.73	12.41
	4	0.5	8.22	8.22	7.46	7.30
		1.0	8.20	8.22	7.05	6.58
	8	0.5	5.46	5.47	4.69	4.57
		1.0	5.46	5.47	4.33	4.05
s9234	2	0.5	7.92	7.92	7.41	7.32
		1.0	7.95	7.92	7.13	6.87
	4	0.5	4.98	4.98	4.39	4.29
		1.0	4.99	4.98	4.08	3.84
	8	0.5	3.58	3.59	2.93	2.87
		1.0	3.59	3.59	2.62	2.47
s510	2	0.5	3.53	3.53	3.28	3.26
		1.0	3.53	3.53	3.15	3.09
	4	0.5	2.70	2.70	2.32	2.31
		1.0	2.69	2.70	2.14	2.09
	8	0.5	2.01	2.01	1.59	1.57
		1.0	2.01	2.01	1.40	1.31

Slow Memory: the Rising Cost of Optimism

Richard A. Meyer, Jay M. Martin, and Rajive L. Bagrodia
Computer Science Department
University of California at Los Angeles

Abstract

Rapid progress in the design of fast CPU chips has outstripped progress in memory and cache performance. Optimistic algorithms would seem to be more vulnerable to poor memory performance because they require extra memory for state saving and anti-messages. We examine the performance of both optimistic and conservative protocols in controlled experiments to evaluate the effects of memory speed and cache size, using a variety of applications.

1 Introduction

During the last 20 years, the field of parallel discrete event simulation (PDES) algorithms has achieved a state of technological maturity. Recent publications show marginal improvements, usually in restricted domains, but no quantum leaps forward. During those same 20 years, advances in hardware design have made efficient parallel execution harder to achieve. Processor speed doubles every 18 months, but memory speed and interconnection latency between processors improve more slowly. For example, as of PADS '98, Intel was shipping Pentium II processors at 350 MHz, and Celeron processors at 266 MHz. At the time of PADS '99, Intel was shipping 550 MHz Pentium III and 466 MHz Celeron processors, using essentially the same 100MHz system bus and memory.

PDES algorithms are typically divided into two orthogonal categories: optimistic [11] and conservative [2, 4]. Conservative techniques are so called because events can only be executed when they are known to be safe. By comparison, optimistic algorithms execute events aggressively, but must roll back to a previous saved state if a causality error occurs. A third set of adaptive or hybrid algorithms [12] combine the two primary techniques.

In this paper, we examine the premise that architectural changes will have a measurably larger impact on optimistic algorithms by running a series of controlled experiments, using primarily "real" benchmarks. Considerable work has been done in measuring the performance of optimistic methods with respect to total memory usage [7], cache performance [14], and the cost of state saving versus reverse computation [3]. No one, to our knowledge, has directly compared the two PDES protocol families in terms of cache or memory performance. In the following section, we will describe the simulation library used in this study, and then describe two applications used as benchmarks. Section 3 presents the results of a series of experiments using these applications. In Section 4, we draw conclusions and suggest future research directions.

2 Applications and Environment

To compare, as fairly as possible, optimistic and conservative algorithms, we use a PDES library called COMPOSE that supports both families of protocol while sharing a significant amount of code between them. The experiments are done using two "real" applications -- a parallel database system and a theatre air missile defense (TAMD) model – and one synthetic model: PHOLD [8]. Each model will be described in moderate detail after a brief introduction to the simulation environment.

2.1 COMPOSE

COMPOSE (Conservative Optimistic and Mixed Parallel Object-oriented Simulation Environment) [13] is a C++ PDES library that provides a null-message conservative algorithm and a time warp derived optimistic algorithm. COMPOSE also supports mixed mode simulations, with some optimistic and some conservative elements [12]. Models with well-behaved subsystems, for example source or sink objects that don't require state saving, can sometimes benefit from mixed mode execution. The programming model used in COMPOSE is that of messages being exchanged between objects.

COMPOSE's conservative null message algorithm is similar to that of PARSEC [1], with additional

* This work was funded in part by the Defense Advanced Research Projects Agency (DARPA) under the DOMAINS (Design of Mobile Adaptive Networks Using Simulation and Agent Technology) project, contract DAAB07-97-C-D321, a part of the Global Mobile Information Systems (GloMo) program.

optimization for shared memory architectures. Per-pair channel variables are directly modified [5], without locking, instead of sending explicit null messages.

The Time Warp implementation is very like that of GTW [9] with some exceptions. COMPOSE has an entity queue (heap) and message queues (splay tree) for each entity. Incremental state saving is provided by having the programmer implement a class interface that has rollback and deadwood collection procedures. COMPOSE does not have fixed sized memory buffers, but allows messages and state memory to be of any size. When saving an entity's state, the runtime copies each entity state block into a circular memory queue. COMPOSE implements a simple Moving Time Window [9] scheme for optimistic throttling and a simple non-blocking GVT algorithm based on keeping track of the smallest time-stamped message observed within globally defined phases.

2.2 Parallel Database Model

This model simulates a parallel database running on a cluster of symmetric multiprocessors (SMP). In this architecture, each processor can access a unique set of memory and disk elements. Access to remote disks or memory is via messages that use the interconnection network, as shown in Figure 1. This architecture is able to directly exploit advances in processor, memory and disk technologies, is scalable, and hence is widely used by commercial parallel databases.

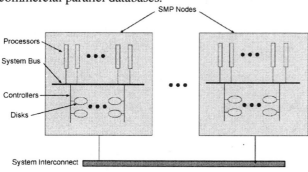

Figure 1 Parallel Database Schematic

Intra-query parallelism is the most widely exploited form of parallelism in databases and its performance can have a substantial impact on overall database performance. This parallelism is obtained by decomposing a complex query into multiple steps, which may be executed in parallel on multiple partitions on the multiple disks in the database.

The database model described here was used to evaluate the performance of a parallel database that exploits intra-query parallelism to improve complex query response times. The goal of the study was to evaluate the impact of changes in architectural features including disk access times, communication times, as well as data partitioning strategies on query response times.

Jobs (queries) are executed on the simulated parallel

database system using a set of pre-generated execution plans. Each job is represented by a "job thread" and is assigned to a particular node of the simulated parallel system. For each parallel step, the job thread in the model creates "worker threads" on all nodes. For example, a complete scan of the database could be accomplished by spawning one worker thread for every CPU in the system and having these worker threads scan independent parts of database. After all worker threads have reported their results, the job thread can start a new parallel step or it can simulate reporting the scan's results and terminate.

The executing worker threads and job threads reserve time on various resources (CPUs, disks, interconnect). If a resource is busy, the thread must wait in a FIFO queue until it is available. Once a thread has obtained a resource, it can hold it for a period of simulation time and then release it. For example, to simulate a scan, a worker thread performs a large number of reads. Each disk read uses a disk, a disk controller, the system bus, and a CPU. In addition, more accesses to the CPU are necessary to process what was read.

To improve performance, the resources are implemented as shared non-simulation objects, which must be accessed in increasing time order. (Implementing them as separate simulation objects was terribly inefficient.) To guarantee sequential access to these shared variables, it was necessary to use some form of aggregation of the entities that share resources. All job threads, worker threads and resources within a single node were aggregated into a combined *node entity* that does its own sequential scheduling. While less intuitive for the programmer, an aggregated implementation typically provides much better (sequential) efficiency and better scalability [16].

The aggregation makes parallelization difficult, complicating lookahead calculation and making the state very large, as well as constraining the available parallelism, since the real system can consist of as few as four nodes. The lookahead of the node entity is the minimum delay before any internal thread will send a message to (an internal thread in) another entity. Lookahead is calculated by computing a conservative estimate of the delay until a thread will send its next message. The aggregation also limits the effectiveness of lazy cancellation, because most straggler events will make use of a shared resource (e.g. the CPU resource), delaying the timestamp of any previously generated message. For most scenarios, incremental state saving must be employed because of the large state.

Two test cases were used: a low communication *scan* operation where each worker thread processes a large chunk of local data before communicating with others, and a more typical high communication *hash join* operation with frequent data redistribution.

2.3 TAMD Model

A comprehensive missile defense simulation environment is under development at the Joint National Test Facility (JNTF) as part of the Wargame 2000 project. The project is developing both national missile defense (NMD) and theatre air missile defense (TAMD) models. The fully functional model will take years to develop, so as a risk reduction measure, simplified models were developed to evaluate each of the functional models for potential speedup [15]. These evaluation models were designed to duplicate the functional models in number of objects, communication pattern, and computation grain.

The TAMD evaluation model includes three types of enemy missiles: long range, short range, and air-to-air, with three corresponding types of interceptors (two instances per missile). There are command and control centers, fire units, and a collection of sensors. The evaluation model executes timed spin loops to emulate the computation of the functional model. The spin delays are calculated by running the code from the functional model on the target architecture. Message counts are estimated using a probabilistic model, and each object self-schedules these events. The resulting simulation is calibrated with the functional model in terms of both message counts and computation granularity. The size of the state is smaller than the functional model, just enough to track several runtime statistics and store protocol-specific information, such as lookahead.

Though simpler than the functional model, the evaluation model is far from trivial. It can contain thousands of objects (the scenario used herein has approximately 1200), and alternates between phases of intense activity – missile launch, interceptor launch, interception, impact (for those not intercepted) – and phases of inactivity. Both the communication topology and the lookahead characteristics change drastically between phases.

For these experiments, the spin loops were disabled. With spin loops active, the computation grain is large enough to allow virtually any simulation protocol to produce good speedup (12 on 16 processors with conservative, 15 on 18 processors with optimistic). Without spin, no speedup is expected, so the differences in overhead of the various protocols are clearly evident.

2.4 PHOLD

For the experiments, simple PHOLD test cases were constructed with 64 PHOLD simulation entities connected in a torus mesh to their immediate neighbors (including diagonals). Two jobs per entity are initially inserted into the simulation. The hold time for the entities is from an exponential distribution with a mean of 10 clock ticks with a bias of +1 tick. The lookahead is one tick and on average is less than 10% of the actual delay, so the null message algorithm should struggle on this test case. There are three versions of this PHOLD model – PHOLD, PHOLD-Hit, and PHOLD-Miss. The first has the random seed as the only state variable. For added state, PHOLD-Hit has ten dynamically allocated blocks of 512 bytes, and PHOLD-Miss has 20 such blocks. The latter two cases add granularity, and exercise the cache, by reading and writing 8 bytes of each data block (each on a different cache line) per event. The sizes and number of the blocks were chosen to emphasize cache effects on the Dell PowerEdge. PHOLD-Hit fits pretty well in the Dell's cache, while PHOLD-Miss doesn't. For optimistic execution with periodic state saving, an empirically determined state saving interval of 20 events was used for the tests with artificial state.

3 Results

Three sets of experiments were conducted to measure how memory speed and cache size affect performance. Scenarios were chosen for each application to ensure that the program fits entirely in main memory on every machine, eliminating any need for virtual memory paging. Each experiment will be described in turn.

The first experiment runs each of the applications on a four CPU Dell PowerEdge 6100 with alternately two-way and four-way interleaved memory. The four-way interleaved memory is calculated to have 37% more bandwidth than the two-way. The results demonstrate that the optimistic protocol is especially sensitive to memory performance.

The second experiment measures the cost of state saving (without rollback) on several architectures – a 233MHz Pentium Pro system, a Sun Enterprise 6500, an SGI Origin 2000, and an 884MHz AMD Athlon system. The purpose of the experiment is to measure the overhead of state saving in the optimistic algorithm. The Athlon, with the slowest memory relative to CPU speed, has the highest state saving cost.

The third experiment makes use of performance modeling tools provided by SGI to compare the performance of several programs on three SGI Origin 2000 multiprocessors: one with a 1MB L2 cache, and the others with a 4MB L2 cache. Because of state saving and rollback, optimistic methods have poor cache performance relative to conservative. The experiment will show that the optimistic protocol is more sensitive than conservative to cache size as well as memory speed.

Table 1: Reference Speedups (4-way interleave)

	Sequential	Opt/Periodic	Opt/Incremental	Conservative	Mixed Mode
Database High Comm	1	0.7	1.6	3	-
Database Low Comm	1	2.2	1.6	3	-
TAMD	1	0.94	-	2.2	2
PHOLD	1	1.76	-	0.73	-
PHOLD-Hit	1	1.72	-	1.02	-
PHOLD-Miss	1	1.11	-	1.27	-

Table 2: Percentage Speedup for four-way over two-way interleaved memory

	Sequential	Opt/Periodic	Opt/Incremental	Conservative	Mixed Mode
Database High Comm	0%	17.6%	11.2%	2.2%	-
Database Low Comm	0%	11%	10%	2.7%	-
TAMD	0%	8.8%	-	7.2%	6.8%
PHOLD	0%	4.3%	-	1%	-
PHOLD-Hit	0%	11%	-	1%	-
PHOLD-Miss	0%	19%	-	1%	-

3.1 Slow Memory on a Dell Quad Pentium Pro.

Experiments were conducted to test the effect of memory speed on a Dell PowerEdge 6100 with four 200 MHz Pentium Pro processors, each with a 512K cache. The Dell has a single bank of 512MB 60μs fast page mode (FPM) memory shared by the four processors. To measure the effect of memory speed, the models were run with the central memory bank in both two-way and four-way interleaving modes. In the Dell architecture, "interleaving" means wider memory banks, with 2-way interleaving being 16 bytes wide and 4-way interleaving 32 bytes wide (one cache line) [10]. Assuming fairly scattered memory references, four-way interleaving allows the central memory bank to output one 32 byte cache line every 8 bus cycles, while two-way interleaving needs an extra 3 cycles (FPM) to get the second half, for a total of 11 bus cycles. With four-way interleaving the central bank has about 1.375 times more memory bandwidth than two-way. For the memory latency experienced by the processor, 3 cycles must be added to traverse the system bus and memory system giving a ratio of 14/11, i.e., four-way interleaved latency is 1.27 times quicker. Both latency and bandwidth are significant. If the system has many memory transactions pending, then the memory bandwidth ratio will be the key performance barometer, while for sparse memory activity the latency ratio will be the effective difference. For demanding optimistic test cases with large states, the memory bandwidth ratio is the driver.

Table 1 shows the speedups achieved for the application set with four-way interleaving using all four CPUs. Table 2 shows the relative performance difference between two-way and four-way memory configurations. Unfortunately, due to the overlap of memory access with computation and with other memory access, one can't give hard percentages for the time the program (in either fast or slow memory mode) spends waiting for memory. But the ratio of application performance increase to the increase in memory speed gives a nice metric to evaluate the memory dependence of an application.

The results show that sequential execution time has little dependence on small changes in memory speed (0% change in all cases). Conservative execution also shows little difference in performance with the exception of the (large) TAMD model. For optimistic execution with periodic state saving, the database model with high communication (with its large aggregated node states) and the PHOLD-Miss model are definitely thrashing the memory system, as shown by the respective 17.6% and 19% performance change. Given the 37.5% increase in memory bandwidth, this gives a performance difference ratio of (17.6/37.5) = .47 and (19/37.5) = .51. In other words, a one percent change in memory bandwidth gives about a 1/2 percent change in application performance. The poor parallel speedup numbers for these test cases show that these models are struggling on the Dell even for the faster memory mode. PHOLD-Hit cuts the performance degradation of PHOLD-Miss significantly, from 19% to 11%, apparently crossing a threshold on the size of application that can run efficiently on this machine.

The low communication database test case using periodic state saving doesn't thrash memory like the high communication test case, due to an extremely large (unrealistic for most systems) state saving interval. Incremental state saving continually saves small chunks of data at each event, showing about the same performance for both the high and low communication test cases, an 11.2/37.5 = .3 dependence ratio on memory speed. It also allows the more typical high communication test case to achieve a speedup of 1.6 (unlike the dismal performance of periodic state saving).

These tests show that sufficient memory bandwidth is an important requirement for a parallel machine running an optimistic simulator.

Table 3: *Slowdown* due to State Saving on a 233MHz Pentium Pro

	Incremental	Periodic
Normal x222 memory Avg 14 cycles per line.	2.6	2.5
Slowed x444 memory Avg 20 cycles per line.	2.95	3.2
AMD Athlon 884 MHz	4.2	3.1

Table 4: Slowdowns on Parallel Systems

	Incremental	Periodic
Sun Enterprise 6500 336 MHz – 4 MB Cache	2.05	2.2
SGI Origin 2000 180 MHz – 1 MB Cache	2.6	2.2
Dell PowerEdge 6100 200 MHz – 512K Cache	1.85	1.8

3.2 Sequential Execution with Optimistic State Saving Overhead

To measure the cost of state saving, an 8-node database model executing a light communication scenario was shrunk to ¼ its size to approximate the state saving load for one CPU in a 4 CPU parallel simulation run. Since the test case is running sequentially, no rollbacks will occur. During the run, states were saved after every 100 events and were garbage collected during the GVT calculation (frequency 100/sec). This experiment represents a lower bound on the overhead of optimistic execution of our simulator. The first test system is a Pentium Pro 233 which is tested in both normal mode and an artificial state where the memory timing is artificially slowed (1.43 times slower) via BIOS memory settings. The results are given in Table 3.

The difference in performance for incremental and periodic state saving modes for this model, for the Pentium Pro processor, was 13% and 28% respectively, giving performance change to memory change ratios of 0.3 for the incremental and 0.53 for the memory thrashing periodic test case. The next entry shows the performance of the new AMD Athlon processor. For the more efficient incremental state saving, it shows even worse performance than the artificially slowed Pentium Pro system. The improvement in memory speed of the Athlon system (SDRAM at 104 MHz) over the Pentium Pro system (EDO RAM at 66 MHz) is not as significant as the increase in CPU performance (233MHz to 884MHz plus other advances). Also, the 512K L2 cache of the Athlon runs at 2/5 of the core speed while the Pentium Pro runs at full speed, so the cache speed isn't keeping up either.

Table 4 shows the performance of these test cases for the parallel machines used in this paper, all of which gave better results than the state of the art Athlon.

3.3 The Effect of Cache Size

Like memory speed, cache size has not improved in proportion with processor speed. If the relative performance of memory is degrading, the cache performance of programs becomes more critical. As the programs themselves grow larger, they must be tuned such that they don't outgrow the cache. The goal of this experiment is to measure the effect of cache size on algorithm performance. To do this, we use three Origin 2000 machines.[1] The first has ten 180MHz processors, each with a 32KB L1 instruction cache, a 32KB L1 data cache, and a 1MB combined L2 cache. The second Origin has 56 195MHz processors, both 32KB L1 caches and a 4MB L2 cache. The third Origin, with 128 250MHz processors and 4MB L2 cache, was used for one experiment because of usage limits on the slower systems. The L1 cache returns data in two or three cycles. A cache miss on either L1 cache invokes a load from the L2 cache at a cost of 8-10 clock cycles [6]. An L2 cache miss requires a load from memory, which varies in cost because of the Origin's NUMA architecture. Assuming the requested page is on the same node, the cost of an L2 cache miss is 75 cycles (for a 195MHz CPU system). For memory located on another node, the cost could be as much as 250 cycles. (As shown in [3], a TLB miss increases the cost substantially more. But TLB misses were almost completely eliminated in these experiments by increasing the page size (from 16K to 1MB), so we can ignore them for this paper.) By default, both caches use an LRU replacement policy.

SGI provides tools – perfex and SpeedShop – for measuring specific hardware performance counters, including misses on both the L1 and L2 caches, and providing analysis of the memory performance of programs. Although the L2 cache is shared between instructions and data, the hardware can distinguish between the two types of requests.

The difference in CPU speed of the three Origins will of course affect the absolute execution time, and makes it difficult to precisely measure the effect of cache size. According to the results derived in the previous experiments, an increase in processor speed should increase the relative penalty for a cache miss. If cache size were unaffected, we would expect the speedup due to the faster processor to be less than the percentage increase in processor speed. The relative speedup (over a sequential execution on the same machine) would also degrade because of the relative increase in IPC cost.

---

[1] The Origin has a hierarchical memory system, and SGI provides tools to place programs on specific processors so that these experiments can be accurately compared on the three machines.

3.3.1 Database Model Results. The high communication hash-join test of the parallel database model was run on the 180MHz and 195MHz Origins. The sequential performance improved by 9.9%, slightly more than the 8.3% increase in processor speed, the rest due to the larger cache. Figure 2 shows the speedups achieved by each protocol, relative to the corresponding sequential execution time, on the two Origins. The speedup (relative to sequential) of optimistic improves slightly, benefiting from the larger cache, while that of conservative gets worse, though still better than optimistic. The conservative performance degrades on the faster machine because of its larger inter-processor latencies (relative to processor speed).

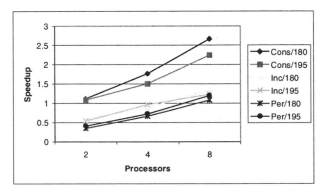

Figure 2: Database Model Performance

A significant performance factor is the L1 cache hit rate. These experiments can have little influence on the L1 cache hit rate, so it will not be considered further, but the data in Table 5 shows a dramatic difference in cache performance of the various protocols. If this difference extends to all levels of the memory hierarchy, it will be very difficult for optimistic techniques to compete, as misses become more expensive in the future.

Table 6 shows the L2 cache hit rates on the Origins for two, four, and eight processors. It is worth noting that a single node conservative run has a cache hit rate of 99.5%. Virtually all of its cache misses during parallel execution can therefore be attributed to communication. In fact, a SpeedShop analysis of the program shows that more than 2/3 of the L2 cache misses in the eight CPU test are caused by null messages, and these are unavoidable. A write to a shared channel variable will caused the remote cache to be invalidated, and force a cache miss on the next access. The cache hit rate for conservative is only slightly affected by the larger caches on the faster machine. The cache hit rates for optimistic improve more consistently. The percentages in Table 6 are somewhat deceptive, as conservative still has fewer cache misses than optimistic, despite its poor hit rate.

Table 5: L1 Cache misses, in millions

	Processors			
	1	2	4	8
Sequential	190			
Conservative		252	203	202
Incremental		539	492	437
Periodic		1495	1234	1267

Table 6: L2 Cache Hit Rates

Protocol	2	4	8
Cons/180	88.71%	75.55%	58.24%
Inc/180	89.55%	84.24%	80.17%
Periodic/180	91.57%	90.37%	90.67%
Cons/195	88.85%	73.84%	65.49%
Inc/195	92.84%	87.85%	82.50%
Periodic/195	97.88%	94.25%	92.04%

Table 7: L2 Data/Instruction cache misses

Protocol	Data cache misses	Inst. cache misses
Conservative/180	38M	26K
Optimistic-periodic/180	145M	4M
Optimistic-inc/180	80M	2M
Conservative/195	37M	5K
Optimistic-periodic/195	59M	400K
Optimistic-inc/195	42M	32K

Table 8: Time Spent Waiting for Memory

	2	4	8
Conservative/180	42.68%	35.99%	32.14%
Incremental/180	59.72%	54.51%	46.22%
Periodic/180	68.43%	58.22%	47.11%
Conservative/195	41.56%	35.44%	31.40%
Incremental/195	57.55%	46.41%	38.71%
Periodic/195	68.20%	51.77%	44.01%

An interesting result is the remarkable difference in L2 *instruction* cache misses. Table 7 lists the number of L2 cache misses, both data and instruction, for the slow and fast Origins for two CPUs. The bulk of the difference in cache performance is in the data cache, but the ratio of data cache misses for optimistic and conservative is about 3.5 to 1. The ratio of instruction cache misses is 40 to 1. A possible explanation is that the optimistic algorithm has a larger working set of instructions. For example, during rollback, a new set of instructions would be required, possibly pushing the forward progress instructions out of the L1 cache. Because of rollback, cache lines for both the saved states and the newly restored states would have been more recently accessed than the instructions, so the instructions could get pushed out of the L2 cache as well. When forward progress resumes, those instructions must be re-fetched. A SpeedShop run on that test case shows the two methods causing the most cache misses are memcpy (save state), and the scheduler (go forward again).

Perfex can be used to estimate the percentage of time a program spends waiting for memory. Table 8 shows these numbers for the database model. The optimistic models see a noticeably larger decrease in this metric, particularly for larger numbers of processors.

The results in this section have shown that optimistic execution of the database model benefits more from an increase in cache size, or conversely, is damaged more by a decrease in cache size than is conservative.

3.3.2 PHOLD Results. The three PHOLD test cases produced such a remarkable affinity in their relative performance that only the results for PHOLD-Hit will be shown. Figure 3 shows the relative speedup on the two machines for conservative, and optimistic with periodic state saving. As with the database model, the increased cache size benefits optimistic, while the increased processor speed hurts conservative. This for an application that, unlike the database model, generally performs better with optimistic. Table 9 shows the L2 cache hit rates on the two machines. The optimistic protocol gets consistently better cache performance on the faster machine, while conservative usually does only slightly better.

Table 9: PHOLD-Hit L2 Cache hit rates

	1	2	4	8
Sequential/180	99.5%			
Conservative/180		88.02%	69.93%	71.67%
Optimistic/180		86.25%	87.08%	85.73%
Sequential/195	99.92%			
Conscrvativc/195		88.62%	75.07%	70.48%
Optimistic/195		94.18%	91.02%	91.05%

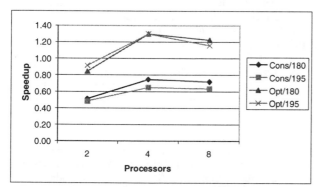

Figure 3: Speedup of PHOLD-Hit

3.3.3 TAMD Results. The previous models have a very small memory signature; the TAMD model does not. Even in sequential, it requires 87MB memory. Both the conservative and optimistic executions require more, and

even multiprocessor jobs do not fit neatly into the L2 cache. The functional version of the TAMD model would be even more resource intensive.

Table 10: TAMD L2 Cache hit rates

	1	2	4	8
Sequential/180	97.16%			
Conservative/180		71.13%	79.84%	85.03%
Optimistic/180		75.28%	75.10%	76.32%
Mixed/180		82.33%	76.39%	76.69%
Sequential/250	99.74%			
Conservative/250		92.35%	91.24%	93.04%
Optimistic/250		90.15%	84.14%	83.60%
Mixed/250		89.71%	80.62%	79.91%

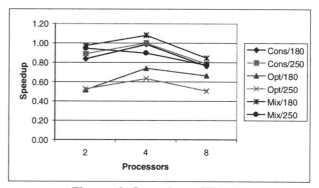

Figure 4: Speedup of TAMD

Because of usage limits on the 195MHz system, these tests were run on the 180MHz and 250MHz Origin systems. In addition to the Time Warp optimistic and null message conservative protocols, the TAMD model was implemented with a mixed model, in which most of the LPs were conservative while the most communicative LPs were optimistic. The mixed model outperformed both conservative and optimistic. Table 10 shows the L2 cache performance. Unlike in the earlier cases, where the largest beneficiary of the larger cache was the optimistic protocol, here the conservative benefits most, improving from a hit rate of 71% on two processors to 92%. This is because the model was initially too big to get good cache performance with the 1MB caches. By increasing to 4MB caches, the conservative now "fits" and its performance improves. The optimistic and mixed models still don't fit, so their performance, as shown in Figure 4, improved relatively little. (Recall that speedup is not expected in these models because of very small computation grain.)

4 Conclusion

This paper studied the impact of three architectural features on performance of PDES models: memory speed, relative memory and processor speeds, and cache sizes. Our hypothesis is that improvements in processor performance relative to memory performance would have a detrimental effect on optimistic protocol performance, because state saving causes relatively poor cache performance, and a correspondingly greater reliance on memory performance. The experiments presented in this paper demonstrate that the performance of the COMPOSE optimistic protocol is more sensitive to the speed and capacity of memory than its conservative protocol. The absolute numbers are rather modest, for example a 19% improvement in one test, but this was caused by a mere 37% increase in memory bandwidth, a dramatic .5 correlation. Another experiment showed a clear advantage in cache performance of incremental state saving over periodic. Comparisons between the very new AMD Athlon and approximately two year old CPUs from Sun and SGI show nearly a doubling in the cost of state saving. As applications continue to grow, the performance of optimistic techniques will rely more and more heavily on intensive memory optimization, for example aggressive throttling and timely GVT calculation.

This paper is a preliminary attempt to measure the performance effects of architectural features on PDES models. A premise of this paper was that improvements in processor speed have outstripped improvements in memory speed over the last several years. Architectural advances are still sometimes of the revolutionary sort, and are hard to predict. The long awaited recent introduction of Rambus memory may reverse the trend of slower memory for a while, and we expect that eventually memory and CPU will be combined on a single chip. But revolutions in processor speed – quantum and/or chemical computers – are also in the offing, and these may swing the trend back the other way.

There are clearly many opportunities for further research. The SGI performance analysis tools, and similar ones from Intel, can be used for performance tuning of PDES protocols. Architectures can be compared for their suitability for PDES. For example, we have found the cc-NUMA Origin 2000 to be a poor architecture for parallel simulation because of generally poor memory latency between processors (five times slower than the PowerEdge with comparable CPU speed). This has a particularly negative effect on the conservative protocol, which relies heavily on frequent null messages (i.e. cache misses) to keep the simulation moving.

Acknowledgements

We would like to thank Pat Talbot of the JNTF for help in defining the TAMD model. We are also grateful to John Greene and Tom Julien for discussions on the database model. The 195MHz and 250MHz Origin 2000 machines are administered by the NCSA at UIUC. The Sun Enterprise 6500 is administered by the Advanced Computing Research group at the UCLA Medical School.

References

[1] R. Bagrodia, R. Meyer, M. Takai, Y. Chen, X. Zeng, J. Martin, and H. Song, "Parsec: a parallel simulation environment for complex systems," *Computer*, vol. 31, pp. 77-85, 1998.

[2] R. E. Bryant, "Simulation of Packet Communications Architecture Computer Systems," Massachusetts Institute of Technology MIT-LCS-TR-188, 1977 1977.

[3] C. D. Carothers, K. S. Perumalla, and R. M. Fujimoto, "The effect of state-saving in optimistic simulation on a cache-coherent non-uniform memory access architecture," presented at WSC'99. 1999 Winter Simulation Conference Proceedings., Phoenix, AZ USA, 1999.

[4] K. Chandy and J. Misra, "Asynchronous Distributed Simulation via a Sequence of Parallel Computations," *Communications of the ACM*, vol. 24, pp. 198-206, 1981.

[5] Y. A. Chen and R. Bagrodia, "Shared memory implementation of a parallel switch-level circuit simulator," presented at Twelfth Workshop on Parallel and Distributed Simulation PADS '98, Banff, Alberta, Canada, 1998.

[6] D. Cortesi, "Origin2000 and Onyx2 Performance Tuning and Optimization Guide," Silicon Graphics, Inc. 1998.

[7] S. R. Das and R. M. Fujimoto, "Adaptive memory management and optimism control in Time Warp," *ACM Transactions on Modeling and Computer Simulation*, vol. 7, pp. 239-71, 1997.

[8] R. Fujimoto, "Performance of time warp under synthetic workloads," presented at Distributed Simulation, SCS Multiconference, San Diego, CA, USA, 1990.

[9] R. Fujimoto, *Parallel and Distributed Simulation Systems*, 1st ed. New York: John Wiley & Sons, 2000.

[10] Intel, "450KX/GX PCIset Datasheet 29052301," Intel Corp. 1996.

[11] D. Jefferson, "Virtual time," *ACM Transactions on Programming Languages on Systems*, vol. 7, pp. 404-425, 1985.

[12] V. Jha and R. Bagrodia, "A unified framework for conservative and optimistic distributed simulation," presented at 8th Workshop on Parallel and Distributed Simulation, Edinburgh, UK, 1994.

[13] J. M. Martin and R. L. Bagrodia, "Compose: an object-oriented environment for parallel discrete-event simulations," presented at Proceedings of 1995 Winter Simulation Conference, Arlington, VA, USA, 1995.

[14] K. S. Panesar and R. M. Fujimoto, "Adaptive flow control in Time Warp," presented at 11th Workshop on Parallel and Distributed Simulation, Lockenhaus, Austria, 1997.

[15] P. Talbot, "Performance Benchmarking of a Parallel Discrete Event Simulation for a Command and Control Application," presented at 14th Workshop on Parallel and Distributed Simulation, Bologna, Italy, 2000.

[16] X. Zeng, R. Bagrodia, and M. Gerla, "GloMoSim: a library for parallel simulation of large-scale wireless networks," presented at Proceedings of the 12th Workshop on Parallel and Distributed Simulation, Banff, Alberta, Canada, 1998.

ROSS: A High-Performance, Low Memory, Modular Time Warp System

Christopher D. Carothers, David Bauer and Shawn Pearce
Department of Computer Science
Rensselaer Polytechnic Institute
110 8th Street
Troy, New York 12180-3590
{chrisc,bauerd,pearcs}@cs.rpi.edu

Abstract

In this paper, we introduce a new Time Warp system called *ROSS: Rensselaer's Optimistic Simulation System*. ROSS is an extremely modular kernel that is capable of achieving event rates as high as 1,250,000 events per second when simulating a wireless telephone network model (PCS) on a quad processor PC server. In a head-to-head comparison, we observe that ROSS out performs the Georgia Tech Time Warp (GTW) system on the same computing platform by up to 180%. ROSS only requires a small *constant* amount of memory buffers greater than the amount needed by the sequential simulation for a constant number of processors. The driving force behind these high-performance and low memory utilization results is the coupling of an efficient pointer-based implementation framework, Fujimoto's fast GVT algorithm for shared memory multiprocessors, *reverse computation* and the introduction of *Kernel Processes (KPs)*. KPs lower fossil collection overheads by aggregating processed event lists. This aspect allows fossil collection to be done with greater frequency, thus lowering the overall memory necessary to sustain stable, efficient parallel execution.

1 Introduction

For Time Warp protocols there is no consensus in the PDES community on how best to implement them. One can divide Time Warp implementation frameworks into two categories: *monolithic* and *modular* based on what functionality is directly contained within the event scheduler. It is believed that the *monolithic* approach to building Time Warp kernels is the preferred implementation methodology if the absolute highest performance is required. The preeminent monolithic Time Warp kernel is *Georgia Tech Time Warp (GTW)* [10, 14]. One only needs to look at GTW's 1000 line "C" code `Scheduler` function to see that all functionality is directly embedded into the scheduling loop. This loop includes global virtual time (GVT) calculations, rollback, event cancellation, and fossil collection. No subroutines are used to perform these operations. The central theme of this implementation is *performance at any cost*.

This implementation approach, however, introduces a number of problems for developers. First, this approach complicates the adding of new features since doing so may entail code insertions at many points throughout the scheduler loop. Second, the all-inclusive scheduler loop lengthens the "debugging" process since one has to consider the entire scheduler as being a potential source of system errors.

At the other end of the spectrum, there are *modular* implementations which break down the functionality of the scheduler into small pieces using an object-oriented design approach. SPEEDES is the most widely used Time Warp system implemented in this framework [25, 26, 27]. Implemented in C++, SPEEDES exports a *plug-and-play* interface which allows developers to easily experiment with new time management, data distribution and priority queue algorithms.

All of this functionality and flexibility comes at a performance price. In a recent study conducted on the efficiency of Java, C++ and C, it was determined that "C programs are substantially faster than the C++ programs" (page 111) [22]. Moreover, a simulation of the National Airspace System (NAS), as described in [28], was originally implemented using SPEEDES, but a second implementation was realized using GTW. Today, only the GTW implementation is in operation. The reason for this shift is largely attributed to GTW's performance advantage on shared-memory multiprocessors. Thus, it would appear that if you want maximum performance, you cannot use the modular approach in your implementation.

Another source of concern with Time Warp systems is memory utilization. The basic unit of memory can be generalized to a single object called a *buffer* [9]. A buffer contains all the necessary event and state data for a particular LP at a particular instance in virtual time. Because the optimistic mechanism mandates support of the "undo" operation, these buffers cannot be immediately reclaimed. There have been several techniques developed to reduce the number of buffers as well as to reduce the size of buffers required to execute a Time Warp simulation. These techniques include infrequent state-saving [2], incremental state-saving [15, 27], and most recently reverse computation [6].

Rollback-based protocols have demonstrated that Time Warp systems can execute in no more memory than the corresponding sequential simulation, such as Artificial Rollback [19] and Cancelback [17], however performance suffers. Adaptive techniques [9], which adjust the amount of memory dynamically, have been shown to improve performance under "rollback thrashing" conditions and reduce memory consumption to within a constant factor of sequential. However, for small event granularity models (i.e., models that require only a few microseconds to process an event), these adaptive techniques are viewed as being too heavy weight.

In light of these findings, Time Warp programs typically allocate much more memory than is required by the sequential simulation. In a recent performance study in retrofitting a large sequential Ada simulator for parallel execution, SPEEDES consumed 58 MB of memory where the corresponding sequential only consumed 8 MB. It is not known if this extra 50 MB is a fixed constant or a growth factor [24].

In this paper, we introduce a new Time Warp system called *ROSS: Rensselaer's Optimistic Simulation System*. ROSS is a modular, C-based Time Warp system that is capable of extreme performance. On a quad processor PC server ROSS is capable of processing over 1,250,000 events per second for a wireless communications model. Additionally, for this particular low event granularity application, ROSS only requires a small *constant* amount of memory buffers greater than the amount needed by the sequential simulation for a constant number of processors. The key innovation driving these high-performance and low memory utilization results is the integration of the following technologies:

- pointer-based, modular implementation framework,
- Fujimoto's GVT algorithm [12],
- reverse computation, and
- the use of *Kernel Processes(KPs)*.

KPs lower fossil collection overheads by aggregating processed event lists. This aspect allows fossil collection to be done with greater frequency, thus lowering the overall memory necessary to sustain stable, efficient parallel execution.

As a demonstration of ROSS' high-performance and low memory utilization, we put ROSS to the test in a head-to-head comparison against one of the fastest Time Warp systems to date, GTW.

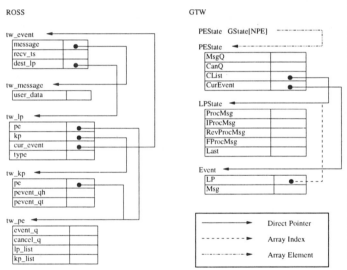

Figure 1: Data Structure Comparison: ROSS vs. GTW.

2   Data Structure and System Parameter Comparison

2.1   Algorithm and Implementation Framework

GTW is designed to exploit the availability of shared-memory in a multiprocessor systems. With that view in mind, a global structure called GState is the backbone of the system as shown in Figure 1. This array represents all the data used by a particular instantiation of a Scheduler thread, which is executed on a distinct processor.

Inside each GState element is a statically defined array of LP pointers, locks for synchronizing the transfer of events between processors, pointers to manage the "free-list" of buffers,

and timers for performance monitoring. To obtain the pointer for LP i, the follow access is required:

$$LP\_Ptr \;\; = \;\; GState[TWLP[i].Map].CList[LPNum[i]];$$

where, i is the LP number, $TWLP[i].Map$ is the processor on which the LP resides and $LPNum[]$ array specifies to which slot within a processor's CList array the LP's pointer was located (see Figure 1.

Now, using these data structures, GTW implements an optimistic time management algorithm that throttles execution based on the availability of memory. On each processor, a separate pool of memory is created for each remote processor. When the application requests a free memory buffer, the owning processor will use the LP destination information provided in the TWGetMsg routine to determine which processor's pool to allocate from. If that pool is empty, the *abort* buffer is returned and no event is scheduled. When the current event has completed processing, the Scheduler will rollback (i.e., abort) that event and attempt to reclaim memory by computing GVT. This arrangement is called *partitioned buffer pools* [13]. The key properties of this approach is that over-optimism is avoided since a processor's forward execution is throttled by the amount of buffers in its free-list. Also, this approach precludes false sharing of memory pages since a memory buffer is only shared between a pair of processors.

To implement GVT, GTW uses an extremely fast asynchronous GVT algorithm that fully exploits shared memory [12]. To mitigate fossil collection overheads, an "on-the-fly" approach was devised [12]. Here, events, after being processed, are immediately threaded into the tail of the appropriate free-list along with being placed into the list of processed events for the LP. To allocate an event, the TWGetMsg function must test the *head* of the appropriate free-list and make sure that the time stamp of the event is less than GVT. If not, the abort buffer is returned and the event that is currently being processed will be aborted. As we will show in Section 3, "on-the-fly" fossil collection plays a crucial roll in determining GTW's performance.

ROSS' data structures, on the other hand, are organized in a bottom-up hierarchy, as shown on the left panel of Figure 1. Here, the core data structure is the tw_event. Inside every tw_event is a pointer to its source and destination LP structure, tw_lp. Observe, that a pointer and not an index is used. Thus, during the processing of an event, to access its source LP and destination LP data only the following accesses are required:

$$my\_source\_lp \;\; = \;\; event- > src\_lp;$$
$$my\_destination\_lp \;\; = \;\; event- > dest\_lp;$$

Additionally, inside every tw_lp is a pointer to the owning processor structure, tw_pe. So, to access processor specific data from an event the following operation is performed:

$$my\_owning\_processor \;\; = \;\; event- > dest\_lp- > pe;$$

This bottom-up approach reduces access overheads and may improve locality and processor cache performance. Note that prior to adding Kernel Processes (KPs), the tw_kp structure's elements were contained within the tw_lp. The role of KPs will be discussed in Section 3.4.

Like GTW, the ROSS' tw_scheduler function is responsible for event processing (including reverse computation support), virtual time coordination and memory management. However, that functionality is decomposed along data structure line. This decomposition allows the tw_scheduler function to be compacted into only 200 lines of code. Like the scheduler function, our GVT computation is a modular implementation of Fujimoto's GVT algorithm [12].

ROSS also uses a memory-based approach to throttle execution and safeguard against over-optimism. Each processor allocates a *single* free-list of memory buffers. When a processor's free-list is empty, the currently processed event is aborted and a GVT calculation is immediately initiated. Unlike GTW, ROSS fossil collects buffers from each LP's processed event-list after each GVT computation and places those buffers back in the owning processor's free-list. We demonstrate in Section 3 that this approach results in significant fossil collection overheads, however these overheads are then mitigated through the insertion of Kernel Processes into ROSS' core implementation framework.

2.2 Performance Tuning Parameters

GTW supports two classes of parameters: one set to control how memory is allocated and partitioned. The other set determines how frequently GVT is computed. The total amount of memory to be allocated per processor is specified in a configuration file. How that memory is partitioned for a processor is determined by the TWMemMap[i][j] array and is specified by the application model during initialization. TWMemMap[i][j] specifies a *ratioed* amount of memory that processor j's free-list on processor i will be allocated. To clarify, suppose we have two processors and processor 0's TWMemMap array has the values 50 and 25 in slots 0 and 1 respectively. This means that of the total memory allocated, 50 buffers out of every 75 will be assigned to processor 0's free-list on processor 0 and only 25 buffers out of every 75 buffers allocated will be assigned to processor 1's free-list on processor 0.

To control the frequency with which GVT is calculated, GTW uses *batch* and $GVT_{interval}$ parameters. The *batch* parameter is the number of events GTW will process before returning to the top of the main event scheduling loop and checking for the arrival of remote events and anti-messages. The $GVT_{interval}$ parameters specifies the number of iterations through the main event scheduling loop prior to initiating a GVT computation. Thus, on average, $batch * GVT_{interval}$ is the number of events that will be processed between successive GVT computations.

ROSS, like GTW, shares a *batch* and $GVT_{internal}$ parameter. Thus, on average, $batch * GVT_{interval}$ events will processed between GVT epochs. However, because ROSS uses the fast GVT algorithm with a conventional approach to fossil collection, we experimentally determined that ROSS can execute a simulation model efficiently in:

$$C \times NumPE \times batch \times GVT_{interval}$$

more memory buffers than is required by a sequential simulation. Here, $NumPE$ is the number of processors used and C is a constant value. Thus, the additional amount of memory required for efficient parallel execution only grows as the number of processors is increased. The amount per processor is a small constant number.

The intuition behind this experimental phenomenon is based on the previous observation that memory can be divided into two categories: *sequential* and *optimistic* [9]. Sequential memory is the base amount of memory required to sustain sequential execution. Every parallel simulator must allocate this memory. Optimistic memory is the extra memory used to sustain optimistic execution. Now, assuming each processor consumes $batch \times GVT_{interval}$ memory buffers between successive GVT calculations, on average that is the same amount of memory buffers that can be fossil collected at the end of each

GVT epoch. The multiplier factor, C, allows each processor to have some reserve memory to schedule new events into the future and continue event processing during the asynchronous GVT computation. The net effect is that the amount of *optimistic* memory allocated correlates to how efficient GVT and fossil collection can be accomplished. The faster these two computations execute, the more frequently they can be run, thus reducing the amount of optimistic memory required for efficient execution. Experimentally, a value of $C = 2$ yields the best performance for the PCS model used here since each event when processed only schedules at most one new event into the future. Values as low as 1 have been observed to yield performance that is only 4% below the best.

3 Performance Study

3.1 Benchmark Application

The benchmark application used in this performance study is a personal communications services (PCS) network model as described in [7]. For both, GTW and ROSS, the state size for this application is 80 bytes with a message size of 40 bytes and the minimum lookahead for this model is *zero* due to the exponential distribution being used to compute call inter-arrivals, call completion and mobility. The event granularity for PCS is very small (i.e., less than 4 microseconds per event). PCS is viewed as being a representative example of how a "real-world" simulation model would exercise the rollback dynamics of a optimistic simulator system.

3.2 Computing Testbed and Experiment Setup

Our computing testbed consists of a single quad processor Dell personal computer. Each processor is a 500 MHz Pentium III with 512 KB of level-2 cache. The total amount of available RAM is 1 GB. Four processors are used in every experiment.

The memory subsystem for the PC server is implemented using the Intel NX450 PCI chipset [16]. This chipset has the potential to deliver up to 800 MB of data per second. However, early experimentation determined the maximum obtainable bandwidth is limited to 300 MB per second. This performance degradation is attributed to the memory configuration itself. The 1 GB of RAM consists of 4, 256 MB DIMMs. With 4 DIMMs, only one bank of memory is available. Thus, "address-bit-permuting" (ABP), and bank interleaving techniques are not available. The net result is that a single 500 MHz Pentium III processor can saturate the memory bus. This aspect will play an important roll in our performance results.

For all experiments, each PCS cell was configured with 16 initial subscribers or *portables*, making the total event population for the simulation, 16 times the number of LPs in the system. The number of cells in the system was varied from 256 (16x16 case) to 65536 (256x256 case) by a factor of 4.

$GVT_{interval}$ and *batch* parameters were set at 16 each. Thus, up to 256 events will be processed between GVT epochs for both systems. These settings where determined to yield the highest level of performance for both systems on this particular computing testbed. For ROSS, the C memory parameter was set to 2. In the best case, GTW was given approximately 1.5 times the amount of memory buffers required by the sequential simulations for large LP configurations and 2 to 3 times for small LP configuration. This amount of memory was determined experimentally to result in the shortest execution time (i.e., best performance) for GTW. Larger amounts of memory resulted in longer execution times. This performance degradation is attributed to the memory subsystem being a bottleneck.

Smaller amounts of memory resulted longer execution times due to an increase in the number of aborted events.

GTW and ROSS use precisely the same priority queue algorithm (Calendar Queue) [4], random number generator and associated seeds for each LP. The benchmark application's implementation is identical across the two Time Warp systems. Moreover, for all performance runs, *both systems deterministically commit precisely the same number of events*. Consequently, the only performance advantage that one system has over the other can only be attributed to algorithmic and implementation differences in the management of virtual time and memory buffers.

3.3 Initial Performance Data

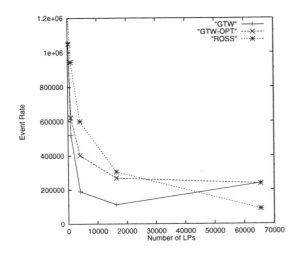

Figure 2: Performance Comparison: GTW vs. ROSS. The "GTW" line indicates GTW's performance without optimized memory pool partitioning. "GTW-OPT" indicates GTW's performance with optimized memory pool partitioning.

The data for our initial performance comparison between GTW and ROSS is presented in Figure 2. Here, the event rate as a function of the number of LPs is shown for ROSS, GTW and GTW-OPT. "GTW" represents the Georgia Tech Time Warp system without proper settings of the TWMemMap array (i.e., $TWMemMap[i][j] = 1 \forall i, j$). "GTW-OPT" uses the experimentally determined optimal settings for TWMemMap.

For GTW-OPT, this setting was determined to be 50 when i and j are equal and 5 for all other cases. This allocation strategy is very much inline with what one would expect for this *self-initiated* simulation model [21]. This ratio for memory allocation was used for all cases.

We observe that in the comparison, GTW-OPT out performs GTW in all cases. In the 64x64 case, we see a 50% performance gap between GTW-OPT (400,000 events per second) and GTW (200,000 events per second). These results underscore the need to find the proper parameter settings for any Time Warp system. In the case of GTW, the local processor's free-list (i.e., TWMemMap[i][i] was not given enough memory to schedule events for itself and a number of aborted events resulted. This lack of memory caused a severe performance degradation.

Now, when GTW-OPT is compared to ROSS. We observe that ROSS out performs GTW-OPT in every case except one:

the 64K LP case. For ROSS, the biggest win occurs in the 4K LP case. Here, a 50% performance gap is observed (600,000 events per second for ROSS and 400,000 for GTW-OPT). However, in the 16K LP case, the gap closes and in the 64K LP cases GTW-OPT is outperforming ROSS by almost a factor of 4. Two major factors are attributed to this performance behavior.

For both GTW-OPT and ROSS, the under powered memory subsystem is a critical source of performance degradation as the number of LPs increase. The reason for this is because as we increase the number of LPs, the total number of pending events increase by a factor of 16. This increase in memory utilization forms a bottleneck as the memory subsystem is unable to keep pace with processor demand. The 4K LP case appears to be a break point in memory usage. ROSS, as shown in Table 1 uses significantly less memory than GTW. Consequently, ROSS is able to fit more of the free-list of events in level-2 cache.

In terms of overall memory consumption, GTW-OPT is configured with 1.5 to 3 times the memory buffers needed for sequential execution depending on the size of the LP configuration. As previously indicated, that amount of memory was experimentally determined to be optimal for GTW. ROSS, on the other hand, only allocates an extra 2048 event buffers (512 buffers per processor) over what is required by the sequential simulation, regardless of the number of LPs. In fact, we have run ROSS with as little as 1024 extra buffers ($C = 1.0$, 256 buffers per processor) in the 256 LP case. In this configuration, ROSS generates an event rate of over 1,200,000. These performance results are attributed to the coupling of Fujimoto's GVT algorithm for shared memory multiprocessors with memory efficient data structures, reverse computation and a conventional fossil collection algorithm, as discussed in Section 2.

However, this conventional approach to fossil collection falls short when the number of LPs becomes large, as demonstrated by 64K LP case. Here, GTW-OPT is 4 times faster than ROSS. The culprit for this sharp decline in performance is attributed to the overwhelming overhead associated with searching through 64,000 processed event-lists for potential free-event buffers every 256 times though the main scheduler loop. It is at this point where the low-overhead of GTW's "on-the-fly" approach to fossil collection is of benefit.

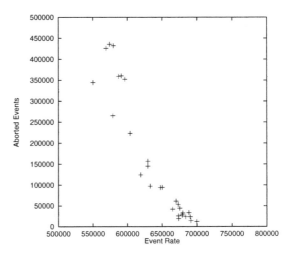

Figure 3: The impact of *aborted* events on GTW event rate for the 1024 (32x32 cells) LP case.

Table 1: Event Buffer Usage: GTW-OPT vs. ROSS. The buffer size for both GTW and ROSS is 132 bytes.

	Memory Usage in Buffers	Amount Relative to Sequential
GTW-OPT 16x16 case	11776	287%
ROSS 16x16 case	6144	150% (seq + 2048)
GTW-OPT 32x32 case	31360	190%
ROSS 32x32 case	18432	113% (seq + 2048)
GTW-OPT 64x64 case	93824	143%
ROSS 64x64 case	67584	103% (seq + 2048)
GTW-OPT 128x128 case	375040	143%
ROSS 128x128 case	264192	100.8% (seq + 2048)
GTW-OPT 256x256 case	1500032	143%
ROSS 256x256 case	1050624	100.2% (seq + 2048)

To summarize, ROSS executes efficiently so long as the number of LPs per processor is kept to a minimum. This aspect is due to the ever increasing fossil collection overheads as the number of LPs grow. To mitigate this problem, "on-the-fly" fossil collection was considered as a potential approach. However, it was discovered to have a problem that results in a increase in the amount of memory required to efficiently execute parallel simulations.

The problem is that a processors ability to allocate memory using the "on-the-fly" approach is correlated to its rollback behavior. Consider the following example: suppose we have LP A and LP B that have been mapped to processor i. Assume both LPs have processed events at $TS = 5, 10$ and 15. With GTW, processor i's free-list of event buffers for itself (i.e., GState[i].PFree[i]) would be as follows (with the head of the list being on the left):

$$5.0_A, 5.0_B, 10.0_A, 10.0_B, 15.0_A, 15.0_B$$

Note how the free-list is ordered with respect to virtual time. Suppose now LP B is rolled back and re-executes those events. The free-list will now appear as follows:

$$5.0_A, 10.0_A, 15.0_A, 5.0_B, 10.0_B, 15.0_B$$

Observe that because LP B has rolled back and re-executed forward, the free-list is now unordered with respect to virtual time. Recall that after processing an event it is re-threaded into the tail of the free-list. This unordered free-list causes GTW to behave as if there are no free buffers available, which results in events being falsely aborted. This phenomenon is caused by the event at the head of the free-list not being less than GVT, yet deeper in the free-list are events with a timestamp less than GVT.

On-the-fly fossil collection under tight memory constraints can lead to large variations in GTW performance, as shown Figure 3. Here, the event rate as it correlates to the number of aborted events for the 1024 LP case is shown. We observe the event rate may vary by as much as 27%. This behavior is attributed to the rollback behavior increasing the "on-the-fly" fossil collection overheads as the free-list becomes increasingly out-of-order, which leads to instability in the system. To avoid this large variance in performance, GTW must be provided much more memory than is required for sequential execution. This allows the free-list to be sufficiently long such that the impact of it being out-of-order does not result in aborted events and allows stable, predictable performance.

A solution is to search deeper into the free-list. However, this is similar to aborting events in that it introduces a load imbalance among processors who are rolling back more than others (i.e., the more out-of-order a list becomes, the longer

the search for free-buffers). In short, *the fossil collection overheads should not be directly tied to rollback behavior*. This observation lead us to the creation of what we call *Kernel Processes (KPs)*.

3.4 Kernel Processes

A Kernel Process is a shared data structure among a collection of LPs that manages the processed event-list for those LPs as a single, continuous list. The net effect of this approach is that the tw_scheduler function executes forward on an LP by LP basis, but rollbacks and more importantly fossil collects on a KP by KP basis. Because KPs are much fewer in number than LPs, fossil collection overheads are dramatically reduced.

The consequence of this design modification is that all rollback and fossil collection functionality shifted from LPs to KPs. To effect this change, a new data structure was created, called tw_kp (see Figure 1). This data structure contains the following items: *(i) identification field, (ii) pointer to the owning processor structure, tw_pe, (iii) head and tail pointers to the shared processed event-list and (iv) KP specific rollback and event processing statistics.*

When an event is processed, it is threaded into the processed event-list for a shared KP. Because the LPs for any one KP are all mapped to the same processor, mutual exclusion to a KP's data can be guaranteed without locks or semaphores. In addition to decreasing fossil collection overheads, this approach reduces memory utilization by sharing the above data items across a group of LPs. For a large configuration of LPs (i.e., millions), this reduction in memory can quite significant. For the experiments done in this study, a typical KP will service between 16 to 256 LPs, depending on the number of LPs in the system. Mapping of LPs to KPs is accomplished by creating sub-partitions within a collection of LPs that would be mapped to a particular processor.

Our primary concern with this approach is the issue that "false rollbacks" would degrade performance. A "false rollback" occurs when an LP or group of LPs is "falsely" rolled back because another LP that shares the same KP is being rolled back. As we will show for this PCS model, this phenomenon was not observed. In fact, a wide range of KP to LP mappings for this application were found to result in the best performance for a particular LP configuration.

3.5 Revised Performance Data

Like the previous set of experiments, ROSS utilizes the same settings. In particular, for all results presented here, ROSS again only uses 2048 buffers above what would be required by the sequential simulator.

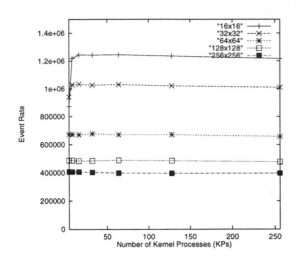

Figure 4: Impact of the number of kernel processes on ROSS' event rate.

In Figure 4, we show the impact of the number of kernel processes allocated for the entire system on event rate. This series of experiments varies the total number of KPs from 4 to 256 by a factor of 2. In the 4 KP case, there is one "super KP" per processor, as our testbed platform is a quad processor machine. We observe that only the 256 (16x16) and the 1024 (32x32) LP cases are negatively impacted for a small number of KPs. All other cases exhibit very little variation in event rate as the number of KPs is varied. These flat results are not what we expected.

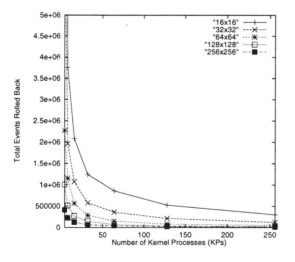

Figure 5: Impact of the number of kernel processes on events rolled back.

If we look at the aggregate number of rolled back events , as shown in Figure 5, for the different LP configurations, we observe a dramatic decline in the number of rolled back events as the number of KPs is increased from 4 to 64. So,

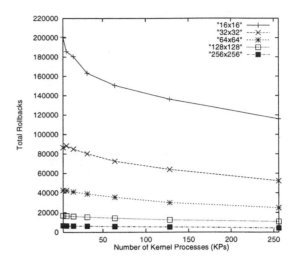

Figure 6: Impact of the number of kernel processes on total rollbacks.

then why is performance flat? The answer lies in the fact that we are trading rollback overheads for fossil collection overheads. Clearly as we increase the number of KPs, we increase fossil collection overheads since each processor has more lists to sort through. Likewise, we are also reducing the number of "false rollbacks". This trade-off appears to be fairly equal for KP values between 16 and 256 across all LP configurations. Thus, we do not observe that finding the *absolute best* KP setting being critical to achieving maximum performance as was finding the best TWMemMap setting for GTW. We believe this aspect will allow end users to more quickly realize top system performance under ROSS.

Looking deeper into the rollback behavior of KPs, we find that most of the rollbacks are primary, as shown in Figures 6 and 7. Moreover, we find that as we add KPs, the average rollback distance appears to shrink. We attribute this behavior to a reduction in the number of "false" rolled back events as we increase the number KPs.

As side note, we observe that as the number of LPs increase from 256 (16x16 case) to 64K (256x256 case) LPs, the event-rate degrades by a factor of 3 (1.25 million to 400,000), as shown in Figure 4. We attribute is performance degradation to the sharp increase in memory requirements to execute the large LP configurations. As shown in Table 1, the 64K LP case consume over 1 million event buffers, where the 256 LPs only requires 6,000 event buffers. This increase in memory requirements results in higher cache miss rates, placing a higher demand on the under-powered memory subsystem, and ultimately degrades simulator performance.

The performance of ROSS-OPT (best KP configuration) is now compared to that of GTW-OPT and ROSS without KPs in Figure 8. We observe that ROSS-OPT outperforms GTW-OPT and original ROSS across all LP configurations. In the 64K (256x256) LP case, ROSS-OPT using 256 KPs has improved its performance by a factor of 5 compare to original ROSS without KPs and is now 1.66 times faster than GTW-OPT. In the 16K (128x128) LP case ROSS-OPT using 64 KPs is 1.8 times faster than GTW-OPT. These significant performance improvements are attributed to the reduction in fossil collection overheads. Moreover, KPs maintain ROSS' ability to efficiently execute using only a small constant number of memory buffers per processor greater than the amount required

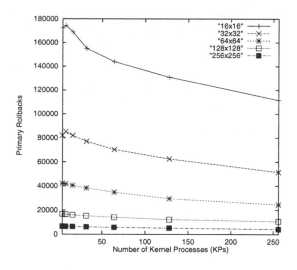

Figure 7: Impact of the number of kernel processes on primary rollbacks.

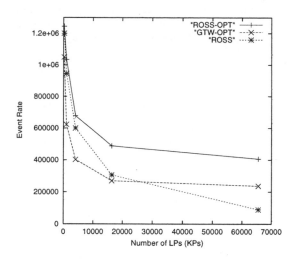

Figure 8: Final Performance Comparison: ROSS-OPT with KPs (best among those tested), "GTW-OPT" indicates GTW's performance with optimized memory pool partitioning, and "ROSS" indicates ROSS' original performance without KPs.

by a sequential simulator.

4 Related Work

The idea of Kernel Processes is very much akin to the use of clustering as reported in [1, 5, 11], and [23]. Our approach, however, is different in that it is attempting to reduce fossil collection overheads. Moreover, KPs , unlike the typical use of clusters, are not scheduled in the forward computation and remain passive until rollback or fossil collection computations are required.

Additionally, while low memory utilization is experimentally demonstrated, we do not consider KPs to be an adaptive approach to memory management, as described by [8] and [9]. That work focused on the efficient operation of Time Warp under "rollback thrashing" conditions. The PCS application used in this performance study is much more well behaved, despite its low event granularity.

In addition to "on-the-fly" fossil collection, Optimistic Fossil Collection (OFC) has been recently proposed [29]. Here, LP states histories are fossil collected early without waiting for GVT. Because we are using reverse computation, complete LP state histories do not exist. Thus, this technique will not immediately aide in ROSS' approach to fossil collection.

5 Final Remarks and Future Work

In closing, there are a number of caveats to this performance study. First, while the `TWMemMap` setting for GTW-OPT is experimentally the best, there is some reason to believe it may not be the absolute best. Our experience with GTW seems to indicate that the absolute best setting is configuration specific. Meaning that for every processor, LP, *batch* and $GVT_{interval}$ setting combination, there is a best setting for `TWMemMap`. Finding such a setting is a difficult, time consuming task due to interdependencies with other parameters. Consequently, the performance results of GTW presented here should not be taken as an absolute.

Additionally, the final performance advantage that ROSS has over GTW needs to be better quantified before final conclusions can be made. While it is true that ROSS with KPs outperforms GTW, we are unclear as to how much of that performance advantage is due to the under-powered memory subsystem. As previously indicated, GTW requires much more memory than ROSS. This puts GTW at a serious performance disadvantage on this computing platform. If we correct the memory bus problem by adding more memory, would ROSS' performance advantage disappear? These questions need to be answered before any definitive statements can be made.

ROSS demonstrates that a modular Time Warp kernel can yield high-performance as well efficient memory utilization. However, it does so using a well-behaved simulation model as the benchmark application. It it unclear how ROSS will perform under more adverse "rollback thrashing" conditions. This aspect needs to examined.

Acknowledgements

This work was supported by NSF Grant #9876932 and an Intel Equipment Grant made to the Scientific Computation Research Center (SCOREC).

References

[1] H. Avril, and C. Tropper. "Clustered Time Warp and Logic Simulation". In *Proceedings of the 9th Workshop on Parallel and Distributed Simulation (PADS'95)*, pages 112–119, June 1995.

[2] S. Bellenot. "State Skipping Performance with the Time Warp Operating System". *In Proceedings of the 6th Workshop on Parallel and Distributed Simulation (PADS '92)*, pages 53–64. January 1992.

[3] S. Bellenot. "Performance of a Riskfree Time Warp Operating System". *In Proceedings of the 7th Workshop on Parallel and Distributed Simulation (PADS '93)*, pages 155–158. May 1993.

[4] R. Brown. "Calendar Queues: A Fast *O(1)* Priority Queue Implementation for the Simulation Event Set Problem". *Communications of the ACM (CACM)*, volume 31, number 10, pages 1220–1227, October 1988.

[5] C. D. Carothers and R. M. Fujimoto. "Background Execution of Time Warp Programs". In *Proceedings of the 10th Workshop on Parallel and Distributed Simulation (PADS'96)*, pages 12–19, May 1996.

[6] C. D. Carothers, K. S. Permalla, and R. M. Fujimoto. "Efficient Optimistic Parallel Simulations using Reverse Computation", In *Proceedings of the 13th Workshop on Parallel and Distributed Simulation (PADS'99)*, pages 126–135, May 1999.

[7] C. D. Carothers, R. M. Fujimoto, and Y-B. Lin. "A Case Study in Simulating PCS Networks Using Time Warp." In *Proceedings of the 9th Workshop on Parallel and Distributed Simulation (PADS'95)*, pages 87–94, June 1995.

[8] S. Das and R. M. Fujimoto. "A Performance Study of the Cancelback Protocol for Time Warp". *In Proceedings of the 7th Workshop on Parallel and Distributed Simulation (PADS '93)*, pages 135–142. May 1993.

[9] S. Das, and R. M. Fujimoto. "An Adaptive Memory Management Protocol for Time Warp Parallel Simulator". *In Proceedings of the ACM Sigmetrics Conferences on Measurement and Modeling of Computer Systems (SIGMETRICS '94)*, pages 201–210, May 1994.

[10] S. Das, R. M. Fujimoto, K. Panesar, D. Allison and M. Hybinette. "GTW: A Time Warp System for Shared Memory Multiprocessors." *In Proceedings of the 1994 Winter Simulation Conference*, pages 1332–1339, December 1994.

[11] E. Deelman and B. K. Szymanski. "Breadth-First Rollback in Spatially Explicit Simulations", *In Proceedings of the 11th Workshop on Parallel and Distributed Simulation (PADS'97)*, pages 124–131, June 1997.

[12] R. M. Fujimoto and M. Hybinette. "Computing Global Virtual Time in Shared Memory Multiprocessors", *ACM Transactions on Modeling and Computer Simulation*, volume 7, number 4, pages 425–446, October 1997.

[13] R. M. Fujimoto and K. S. Panesar. "Buffer Management in Shared-Memory Time Warp Systems". *In Proceedings of the 9th Workshop on Parallel and Distributed Simulation (PADS'95)*, pages 149–156, June 1995.

[14] R. M. Fujimoto. "Time Warp on a shared memory multiprocessor." In *Proceedings of the 1989 International Conference on Parallel Processing*, volume 3, pages 242–249, August 1989.

[15] F. Gomes. "Optimizing Incremental State-Saving and Restoration." Ph.D. thesis, Dept. of Computer Science, University of Calgary, 1996.

[16] Personal correspondence with Intel engineers regarding the Intel NX450 PCI chipset. See www.intel.com for specifications on on this chipset.

[17] D. R. Jefferson. "Virtual Time II: The Cancelback Protocol for Storage Management in Distributed Simulation". *In Proceedings of the 9th ACM Symposium on Principles of Distributed Computing*, pages 75–90, August 1990.

[18] P. L'Ecuyer and T. H. Andres. "A Random Number Generator Based on the Combination of Four LCGs." *Mathematics and Computers in Simulation*, volume 44, pages 99–107, 1997.

[19] Y-B. Lin and B. R. Preiss. "Optimal Memory Management for Time Warp Parallel Simulation", *ACM Transactions on Modeling and Computer Simulation*, volume 1, number 4, pages 283–307, October 1991.

[20] Y-B. Lin, B. R. Press, W. M. Loucks, and E. D. Lazowska. "Selecting the Checkpoint Interval in Time Warp Simulation". *In Proceedings of the 7th Workshop on Parallel and Distributed Simulation (PADS '92)*, pages 3–10. May 1993.

[21] D. Nicol. "Performance Bounds on Parallel Self-Initiating Discrete-Event Simulations". *ACM Transactions on Modeling and Computer Simulation (TOMACS)*, volume 1, number 1, pages 24–50, January 1991.

[22] L. Perchelt. "Comparing Java vs. C/C++ Efficiency Differences to Interpersonal Differences". *Communications of the ACM (CACM)*, volume 42, number 10, pages 109–111, October, 1999.

[23] G. D. Sharma *et al.* "Time Warp Simulation on Clumps". In *Proceedings of the 13th Workshop on Parallel and Distributed Simulation (PADS '99)*, 1999, pages 174–181.

[24] R. Smith, R. Andress and G. M. Parsons. "Experience in Retrofitting a Large Sequential Ada Simulator to Two Versions of Time Warp". In *Proceedings of the 13th Workshop on Parallel and Distributed Simulation (PADS'99)*, pages 74–81, May 1999.

[25] J. S. Steinman. "SPEEDES: Synchronous Parallel Environment for Emulation and Discrete-event Simulation". *In Advances in Parallel and Distributed Simulation*, volume 23, pages 95–103, SCS Simulation Series, January 1991.

[26] J. S. Steinman. "Breathing Time Warp". *In Proceedings of the 7th Workshop on Parallel and Distributed Simulation (PADS '93)*, pages 109–118, May 1993.

[27] J. S. Steinman. "Incremental state-saving in SPEEDES using C++." *In Proceedings of the 1993 Winter Simulation Conference*, December 1993, pages 687–696.

[28] F. Wieland, E. Blair and T. Zukas. "Parallel Discrete-Event Simulation (PDES): A Case Study in Design, Development and Performance Using SPEEDES". *In Proceedings of the 9th Workshop on Parallel and Distributed Simulation (PADS '95)*, pages 103–110, June 1995.

[29] C. H. Young, R. Radhakrishnan, and P. A. Wilsey. "Optimism: Not Just for Event Execution Anymore", *In Proceedings of the 13th Workshop on Parallel and Distributed Simulation (PADS '99)*, pages 136–143, May 1999.

Session 4
Interoperability issues

An Approach for Federating Parallel Simulators
S. L. Ferenci, K. S. Perumalla, and R. M. Fujimoto

Safe Timestamps and Large-Scale Modeling
D. Nicol, J. Liu, and J. Cowie

An Approach for Federating Parallel Simulators

Steve L. Ferenci
Kalyan S. Perumalla
Richard M. Fujimoto
College Of Computing
Georgia Institute of Technology
Atlanta, GA 30332-0280
{ferenci,kalyan,fujimoto}@cc.gatech.edu

Keywords: federating, parallel simulators, proxy entity

ABSTRACT

This paper investigates issues concerning federations of sequential and/or parallel simulators. An approach is proposed for creating federated simulations by defining a global conceptual model of the entire simulation, and then mapping individual entities of the conceptual model to implementations within individual federates. Proxy entities are defined as a means for linking entities that are mapped to different federates.

Using this approach, an implementation of a federation of optimistic simulators is examined. Issues concerning the adaptation of optimistic simulators to a federated system are discussed. The performance of the federated system utilizing runtime infrastructure (RTI) software executing on a shared memory multiprocessor (SMP) is compared with a native (non-federated) SMP-based optimistic parallel simulator. It is demonstrated that a well designed federated simulation system can yield performance comparable to a native, parallel simulation engine, but important implementation issues must be properly addressed.

1. Introduction

There are two principal paradigms for constructing parallel and distributed simulations today. The first, widely utilized by the parallel discrete event simulation (PDES) research community, is to define a parallel simulation engine, associated languages, libraries, and tools to create new high performance simulators. Numerous examples of this approach exist today, e.g., TeD/GTW [1], SPEEDES [2], and Task-Kit [3] to mention a few. Simulation models are specific to the environment for which they were developed, making it difficult, in general, to port models to new environments.

A second paradigm that has emerged in the distributed simulation community is to federate disparate simulators, utilizing runtime infrastructure (RTI) software to interconnect them. This approach is utilized

in efforts such as Distributed Interactive Simulation (DIS) [4], Aggregate Level Simulation Protocol (ALSP) [5] and the High Level Architecture (HLA) [10]. This approach places few restrictions concerning the realization of individual simulators. This results in coarse-grained federations, where entire simulations are viewed as black boxes, and designated as federates. The runtime infrastructures used to interconnect the simulations are typically designed for coarse granularity concurrency.

Here, we explore an alternate approach. Unlike the traditional PDES paradigm, explicit support for model interoperability and reuse is defined. Unlike traditional federated approaches such as the HLA, we impose certain restrictions concerning the structure of the simulators that are included in the federation in order to enable entity level interactions between federates. Thus, this approach does not attempt to address the general problem of interoperability and reuse of *arbitrary* legacy simulators. Rather, this paper attempts to explore the question of how simulators might be defined in the future in order to support both model reuse and highly efficient concurrent execution.

A second, related problem addressed in this paper concerns the difficulty of constructing federations of optimistic simulators, and the efficiency of their execution. While interfaces such as the HLA support federations of optimistic simulators, few, if any, federations to date have included multiple optimistic federates. We compare the efficiency of a federation of optimistic simulations with a native (non-federated) implementation executing the same simulation model.

We next describe our approach to realizing federated simulations. The prototype federated simulation is then described that uses an RTI to interconnect optimistic simulations. Implementation issues associated with federating optimistic simulations are discussed, and performance measurements presented.

2. Approach to Federating Simulations

At the highest level, our approach to realizing federated simulations is based on:

- defining a *global conceptual model (GCM)* for the entire (federated) simulation model based on an entity/message-passing paradigm,
- standard entity types and data exchange definitions to achieve semantic interoperability among entities realized in different federates, and
- defining a *mapping* of the GCM to realization of individual model components.

The GCM is central to this approach. Use of conceptual models is not new. Such models are used at least informally as part of the federation development process in the HLA. Our approach differs from that currently used in the HLA in that we formalize this notion so that it can be used to automatically generate and configure federated simulations.

Here, we do not address the second issue concerning standard entity types and data definitions. These must be realized by defining consensus within the modeling and simulation community for each specific domain. Work of this nature is in progress within the Defense community, for example.

2.1. Global Conceptual Model

The GCM is based on an entity/message-passing paradigm. This means the entire federated simulation is viewed as a collection of entities that interact by exchanging time stamped messages.

Each entity in the GCM is viewed as a black box. The GCM makes no assumptions concerning the internal realization of an entity, e.g., whether it is based on an event-oriented or a process-oriented world-view. Further, the GCM makes no assumption concerning the actual mechanism for passing information in or out of an entity. This could be done through procedure calls or method invocations, for example. In general, different federates may use entirely different mechanisms to implement and pass information among entities.

We assume each entity defined in the GCM has a corresponding implementation in at least one of the simulators (federates) making up the federation. Thus, we assume each simulator is internally composed of interacting entities. We do not view this as an overly constraining assumption because the entity concept is widely used in modern discrete event simulation. For example, object-oriented and object-based simulation systems typically utilize this approach. Parallel discrete event simulations almost universally are based on logical processes that interact by exchanging messages, so they naturally fall into the entity/message-passing paradigm.

Here, we preclude the use of modifiable, shared state variables between entities. In principle, mechanisms to allow shared state could be easily allowed by the GCM. However, shared state introduces well-known difficulties concerning synchronization. Specifically, references to shared-state inevitably result in zero lookahead interactions, which can have severe performance consequences. Extension of the GCM to allow shared state is an area of future research.

It is clear that not all simulators will be able to conform to the restrictions outlined above. In some cases, it may be necessary to encapsulate the entire simulation as a single entity of the GCM. In other situations, it may not be possible to compose legacy simulations without major redevelopment efforts.

Figure 1. Mapping GCM to Federates. Pr_A is a

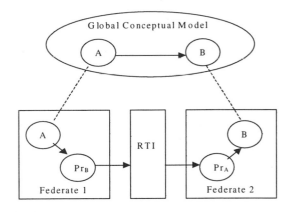

proxy of A, and Pr_B is a proxy of B.

2.2. Mapping the GCM to Federates

Each entity in the GCM must have a realization in one of the simulators making up the federation. For this purpose, a table is defined that maps each GCM entity to its corresponding realization in a federate. This mapping is depicted in Figure 1, where entity A is mapped to federate 1, and entity B is mapped to federate 2.

Interactions between entities that reside within the same federate are handled using the mechanisms defined internally within that federate. Interactions between entities residing in different federates are handled using a mechanism called *proxy entities*. A proxy entity is a local representation of an entity that resides within another federate.

An entity initiates an interaction with a remote entity by interacting with the local proxy entity, using whatever interaction mechanisms are defined within the simulator. For example, in Figure 1, suppose entity A wishes to interact with entity B. This will be accomplished by entity A in federate 1 initiating an interaction with Pr_B, the proxy entity for B residing in federate 1. In general, the entity initiating the interaction need not be aware that it is interacting with a proxy rather than the actual entity.

The proxy entity Pr_B is responsible for converting the local interaction to one or more messages that are sent through the RTI to the destination federate, or in this case, Federate 2. These messages are delivered to a second proxy entity (Pr_A) in Federate 2 that represents the entity initiating the interaction. Proxy entity Pr_A must translate the incoming message(s) to interactions with the destination entity B. Pr_A interacts with B using the local interaction mechanisms defined within Federate 2. Again, entity B need not be aware that it is interacting with a local or remote entity.

The principal task performed by the proxy entities is to convert local interactions using the mechanisms defined within the local simulator to interactions that are transmitted through the RTI, and vice versa. A common interface is defined for the RTI, e.g., the Interface Specification defined for the High Level Architecture.

To simplify the previous discussion, we assumed a separate proxy entity was used to represent each remote entity that interacts with a local entity. In some cases it may be more efficient to realize a collection of proxy entities within a single entity, and time multiplex the usage of that realization.

In general, proxy entities may be created or destroyed dynamically during the execution. For example, consider a simulator modeling the operation of a sensor, e.g., radar. As other vehicles, represented in other federates, move within range of the sensor, new proxy entities must be created within the radar simulator to represent them. Further, such proxy entities can be discarded once the simulated vehicles move out of range.

Of particular interest here is the case where each federate is a parallel discrete event simulation. Such simulations are normally defined as collections of logical processes that interact by exchanging messages. Thus, each logical process represents a single entity in the GCM. The mapping of logical processes to federates can be defined as a mapping function:

$$LPtoFed(LPi) = Fedj$$

LPtoFed identifies the federate on which each LP is instantiated.

An example better illustrates the role the GCM plays. Suppose two disparate simulators are to be integrated with one another. The first is an air battle simulation comprised of aircraft entities, the second is a ground battle simulation comprised of tank entities. In the GCM each aircraft entity and each tank entity will be represented as an entity. Each entity in the GCM is permitted to interact with any other entity in the GCM. At this point information about the communication topology between entities can be used to more efficiently federate the simulators. If an entity communicates only with local entities then there is no need to create a proxy entity to represent this entity in the other federates. Next the entities in the GCM are mapped to the federates and proxy entities are created to facilitate communication between the federates.

We will now consider the techniques for implementing the proxy-based federating approach. We illustrate the techniques using an LP-based prototype system, followed by some performance characteristics of the system.

3. Prototype Overview

An initial prototype was developed to enable exploration of this approach to realizing federated simulations, and to identify and evaluate performance issues. As a first step, a realization of a *homogeneous* federation was developed. Specifically, each federate is an instance of the TeD / GTW (Telecommunication Description Language implemented over the Georgia Tech Time Warp parallel simulator) [1, 6]. RTI software from the Federated Distributed Simulation Kit (FDK) was used to interconnect the simulators. In the rest of this section, we describe the relevant aspects of the GTW implementation and the RTI interface, which have a bearing on the effort necessary to realize a federated implementation.

3.1. GTW Overview

Georgia Tech Time Warp (GTW) is an optimistic simulator based on Time Warp [7]. GTW has three main data structures: a message queue (MsgQ) holds incoming messages, a cancellation queue (CanQ) that holds messages that have been canceled (anti-messages), and an event queue (EvQ) that holds processed and unprocessed events. Each processor has each of these structures present and executes a loop that does the following three steps:

(1) All incoming messages are removed from the MsgQ data structure, and the messages are filed one at a time into the EvQ data structure. If a message has a timestamp smaller that the last event processed by the LP, the LP is rolled back. Messages sent by rolled back events are enqueued into the CanQ of the processor holding the event.
(2) All incoming canceled messages are removed from the CanQ data structure, and are processed one at a time. Rollbacks may also occur here, and are handled in essentially the same manner as rollbacks caused by normal messages.
(3) A single unprocessed event is selected from the EvQ, and processed by calling the LP's event handler procedure.

The principal atomic unit of memory in GTW is a buffer. Each buffer contains the storage for a single event, a copy of the automatically checkpointed state, pointers to scheduled messages (direct cancellation) and incremental state-save buffers, and miscellaneous status flags, and other information. Each buffer utilizes a fixed amount of storage. Each processor maintains a list of buffers that are not in use. A buffer may be reused for future events once it has been determined that the time stamp of the event is less than global virtual time (GVT) [7]. GTW uses an efficient GVT algorithm described in [8]. In addition to the GVT algorithm, GTW also employs on-the-fly fossil collection that enables efficient storage reclamation for simulations containing large numbers of simulator objects [8].

3.2. FDK and BRTI Overview

FDK is a modular and reusable set of libraries designed to facilitate the development of Run Time Infrastructures (RTIs) for developing or integrating parallel and distributed simulation systems [9]. Using the libraries provided by the FDK, an RTI was built that implements a subset of the High Level Architecture (HLA) services. This RTI is called the BRTI, and the following is a brief description of the BRTI services that are pertinent to this paper.

- **Publish Object Class/Subscribe Object Class Attribute** - These two services establish a communication pathway between two federates. A federate first publishes an object with Publish Object Class. Other federates can subscribe to the published objects using Subscribe Object Class Attribute.
- **Update Attribute Values/Reflect Attribute Values** - Update Attribute Values sends a message to all federates that have subscribed to an object notifying them of the change in the object's state. On the receiving side, Reflect Attribute Values is the means by which the RTI notifies the federate that an object has been updated.
- **Retract/Request Retraction** - Given an Event Retraction Handle, Retract can be used to cancel a previously sent message. The retraction mechanism is used to implement Time Warp's anti-message mechanism between federates.
- **Flush Queue Request** - This is used by the federate to notify the RTI that the federate wishes all messages currently residing within the RTI to be delivered to the federate as soon as possible. Additionally, Flush Queue Request will also attempt to advance time to the specified time.
- **Time Advance Grant** - This is used by the RTI to notify the federate that its logical time has been advanced to the specified time.
- **Tick** - This is used by the federate to provide the RTI with execution time to perform communication services, time management services, and deliver messages to the federate.

The BRTI includes an underlying efficient asynchronous algorithm for periodically computing lower bound on the timestamp (LBTS) of future incoming events at any federate.

4. Federated GTW

Using the proxy-based approach, we have implemented a system for federating multiple instances of GTW simulations. Each instance of GTW acts as a federate, which communicates using the BRTI with the other GTW federates The implementation process mainly involved three items:
1. Defining a common abstraction of the application objects, called the federation object model, for use by all GTW federates
2. Defining a proxy framework that is used across all GTW applications
3. A set of modifications to GTW for adapting its initialization, message sends, message cancellations and GVT computation modules, to accommodate the proxy-based model.

We describe each of these items next.

4.1. Federation Object Model

A federation object model is necessary so that all the federates agree on a certain abstraction of the entities in the GCM. The object model for the GTW federation is defined as follows. Each logical process (LP) has input ports and output ports. Each output port of an LP is mapped at initialization time to an input port of another LP. Whenever an LP sends a message on one of its output ports, the LP that owns the corresponding mapped input port receives the message. The LP actually sends a message by "assigning" the event data as the value of the port object variable. This model based on ports allows the application to expose its communication topology, which is necessary to prevent broadcast semantics for inter-federate communication; at the same time, it does not exclude applications that do need all-to-all communication.

During initialization, the communication links between federates are established with the help of BRTI services **Publish Object Class** and **Subscribe Object Class Attribute**, using port names as unique object classes. Each federate publishes a list of output ports corresponding to the LPs that are owned by this federate. A federate will subscribe to an output port if it owns an LP whose input port is mapped to that output port. Port mapping can be specified in a file that is read in at run time. If no file is specified then all-to-all communication is assumed by default.

At runtime, event exchanges are realized using the ports as follows. Since each port is an RTI object, its value can be updated by the federate that can publish new values to the object. Events (event data) are assigned as *values* for the port objects. This is done using the **Update Attribute Values** service of the BRTI. On the other side of the output port, updates to the output port are received via the **Reflect Attribute Values** callback service of the BRTI.

Based on the port descriptions of the LPs, the object class creation, publication and subscription services are automatically invoked by GTW, in order to initialize the communication services.

4.2. Proxy Framework

By default, a replication-based proxy framework is supported. In this framework, every federate instantiates every LP that is present in the simulation's GCM. At any federate, only those LPs that are mapped to that federate are executed as regular LPs. The rest of the LPs are executed as proxies. Exactly one federate *owns* any given non-proxy LP. When any proxy LP receives an event, it forwards exactly one copy of that event to the federate that owns that LP. In

addition to the forwarding semantics, every GTW proxy LP implements an initialization function, which is the same as its corresponding non-proxy LP initialization function. This is used in constructing global read-only data structures during the initialization stage at each GTW federate, as described next.

4.3. Initialization and Read-only State

The GTW federations are initialized as usual, similar to the non-federated GTW simulation, with one important distinction as follows. When LPs are created and initialized in GTW, they are permitted not only to schedule their initial events, but also to cooperate in creating and initializing global data structures intended for read-only use during the actual simulation. It is clear that, if the initialization procedures of *all* the LPs are invoked in *all* the federates, then identical copies of the global state are correctly created automatically in *all* the federates. This approach is what the proxy framework as described previously supports.

This approach has the advantage that no source-code changes are required for the applications. Since we are interested in minimizing the changes to the application, we implemented this approach. The initialization must be carefully controlled, however, in order to preserve the semantics of proxy LPs. This is done at each federate by ignoring any message-sends performed by a proxy LP during its initialization, permitting the proxy LP to cooperate in the global data creation, but disallowing it to be scheduled during simulation at this federate. Turning off message-sends was quite easy to implement in GTW -- for any message-send by a proxy LP, a dummy "abort" message buffer is supplied by GTW to the LP, which is later discarded, instead of being scheduled, by the kernel.

4.4. Sending and Receiving Messages and Message Cancellations

The original native GTW includes a mechanism for sending messages and cancellations among LPs. This mechanism needed to be augmented such that events and cancellations destined to a proxy LP at a federate get automatically forwarded to the federate where the destination LP is actually simulated. For events exchanged between regular (non-proxy) LPs, the usual fast communication path of GTW is preserved. At each GTW federate, the processor whose ID is zero acts as the gateway to route events to and from other GTW federates.

With a view to minimizing the source-code changes, while not compromising on efficiency, we preserved the method by which any GTW LP sends an event to another LP, irrespective of whether the destination LP is a proxy or not. This essentially appends the event to the MsgQ of the owner processor of the event's destination LP. The distinction between local and proxy LPs is, however, made at the time the event is actually extracted from the MsgQ by the destination processor. If the event is for a local LP then the event handler is called as usual. Otherwise (if the LP is a proxy), then this message is forwarded to the federate that owns the LP by invoking **Update Attribute Values** on the object of the corresponding port.

On the receiver side, the BRTI accepts the message and stores it internally until the federate notifies the BRTI to deliver the messages. In the main scheduling loop of GTW, **Flush Queue Request** is invoked to notify BRTI to delivery any messages received so far. (The messages are actually delivered when the next time Tick is called). Messages are delivered to the GTW federate by the BRTI via **Reflect Attribute Values** callback. Once the message has been delivered it is appended to the MsgQ of the processor that owns the destination LP.

Message cancellations (retractions) are treated in a manner analogous to normal events. If the cancellation is meant for a local LP, then the existing GTW mechanism for processing cancellations is performed. If the retraction was in fact destined to a proxy LP, then the BRTI services will have to be used to cancel the message. Every time a normal message is sent using **Update Attribute Values,** an event retraction handle is returned. This handle is stored in the event buffer so that the handle can be used if it has to be canceled. When a proxy LP receives a cancellation it invokes the BRTI **Retract** service with the event retraction handle. When a federate receives a retraction, it makes a call back specified by the GTW federate. The GTW federate performs a handle-to-pointer hash to identify the retracted event, and places it on the CanQ of the processor who owns the destination LP. Cancellations then proceed as usual in GTW.

4.5. Synchronization
Both GTW and BRTI have their own concept of a global time. In GTW it is GVT (Global Virtual Time) and in BRTI it is LBTS (Lowest Bound on Time Stamps). Coordinating the algorithms is crucial to obtaining correct and efficient performance. In the main scheduling loop of GTW, Flush Queue Request is called to notify the BRTI to deliver all messages it has received. A target time is passed as argument to the BRTI, which indicates when the next event is scheduled to the best of GTW's knowledge at that time. When this federate participates in an LBTS computation it will use this to determine its contribution to the computation. When the LBTS computation completes, BRTI issues a Time Advance Grant which notifies the GTW federate that time has been advanced. This time is what is used as the global GVT. In the federated GTW, LBTS is equivalent to GVT of the non-federated GTW.

5. Insights, Lessons, and Challenges
The process of federating GTW was straight forward. The GTW kernel was augmented to use RTI services where necessary, e.g., sending messages to remote LPs or performing necessary time management services. Only the GTW kernel was modified, thus avoiding making significant modifications to the applications. In the case of phold and PNNI no changes were required in these applications. During the course of the implementation it became apparent that care must be taken to ensure good performance as well as correctness. Two major challenges included coordinating the GVT computation and LBTS computation, and buffer management.

5.1. GVT and LBTS
The GVT algorithm [8] incorporated into GTW is specially optimized for a shared-memory implementation, which relies on the actual order of operations on the MsgQ, CanQ and EvQ for handling transient messages efficiently. When such an algorithm is integrated with an RTI, which presents incoming events at unpredictable moments, race conditions can arise with respect to accounting for transient messages in both the local GVT and LBTS computation, potentially leading to incorrect GVT values being computed.

Ensuring that the LBTS computation and the incoming message delivery do not overlap with the local GVT computation easily solves this problem. In our implementation, an LBTS computation gets initiated when a Flush Queue Request is made. By calling Flush Queue Request only when no GVT computation is active locally, we can prevent the race condition. This ensures that all messages that have to be considered in the local GVT computation have already been delivered by BRTI, and the most accurate local GVT value is used in the LBTS computation. Thus, we were able to preserve the efficient asynchronous GVT algorithm of GTW without compromising its correct integration with the time management services of the BRTI.

5.2. Buffer Management

The second major challenge actually became relatively simple to solve using the proxy-entities. When sending or receiving messages using the BRTI we either had to decide what to do with a buffer once used, in the case of sending, or where to obtain a buffer when receiving a message. Message sends occur when an event is removed from the MsgQ and its destination is a non-local LP. At this point, the BRTI is used to send the message, but what can be done with the buffer after the send? The solution is quite simple: mark the buffer as 'processed', as if an event handler was called for this event, and place it on the LP's processed list. This way, the on-the-fly fossil collection can recover the buffer and place it on the free buffer list. The proxy LPs essentially served as convenient buffer repositories for remote messages, to facilitate in generating anti-messages if necessary. This made it relatively easy to integrate the proxy behavior with on-the-fly fossil collection, GVT computation and cancellations, thus minimizing the amount of code changes required.

When receiving messages, BRTI first asks GTW where it can place messages arriving off the wire. This ensures that there will not be a need for an extra memory copy from a BRTI buffer to a GTW buffer. GTW will give BRTI a buffer from processor 0's free buffer list to store the message. At this point the message will be stored in BRTI's internal message queue and delivered when GTW requests that the message be delivered. When the messages are delivered, processor 0 will forward the message to the destination LP's owner processor as if processor 0 scheduled it. As far at the destination processor is concerned processor 0 sent the message. Using the proxy-entities makes buffer management much simpler since the existing buffer manager can be relied on.

5.3. Deadlocks and Flow Control

Deadlock is another disconcerting possibility that arises when the simulators are federated together. Even though the native simulators are designed to be deadlock free in isolation, the deadlock problem arises all over again when they are federated together. In fact, we have observed this problem empirically early on in our implementation. Even though GTW is deadlock free in isolation, a naïve implementation of a GTW federation can deadlock due to a circular hold-and-wait condition on memory buffers used for sending events between federates.

The flow control problem also shares this feature with respect to federating, and deserves careful attention in a federation.

6. Performance Study

We used two separate GTW applications in our performance study. The first is the PHOLD application, which is a synthetic benchmark commonly used for parallel simulators. The second is a practical application, called the PNNI (Private Network to Network Interface) model suite, written in the TeD language, and compiled as a GTW application. The two applications exhibit contrasting characteristics compared to each other. PHOLD is a relatively fine-grained application, with small state and event sizes. PNNI, on the other hand, is a relatively coarse-grained application, with very large state and event sizes.

With both applications, we compared two scenarios:
1. A non-federated multi-processor parallel simulation, using a single instance of the original GTW kernel. The LPs of the application are statically mapped to different processors.
2. A federated simulation in which multiple instances of single-processor GTW kernels communicate using the BRTI. The LPs are partitioned across the federates, but proxies are instantiated for non-local LPs in every federate.

The LP-to-federate mapping used in the federated simulation is the same as the LP-to-processor mapping of the corresponding native GTW simulation.

The test configuration for PHOLD included 40 LPs with a message population of 40. The test configuration for PNNI included a 200-node real-life network with a user node attached to each network node, giving a total of 400 LPs. All the simulations were run on an SGI Origin multiprocessor (R10K processors) and 4GB RAM. All communication is through shared memory.

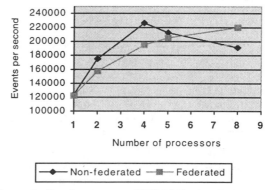

Figure 2. Performance of PHOLD simulation.

The performance of PHOLD is shown in the Figure 2. The rollback statistics of the federated and non-federated simulations were comparable on smaller number of processors. But when larger number of processors was used, the federated simulation incurred fewer rollbacks, accounting for its higher performance than the non-federated simulation.

The performance of PNNI is depicted in the Figure 3. In all cases, the rollback behavior of federated and non-federated simulations was comparable.

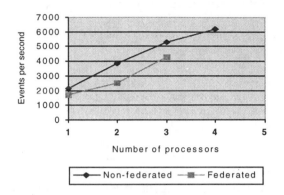

Figure 3. Performance of PNNI.

In both types of applications, we observe that the performance of the federated simulation is comparable to that of the optimized monolithic parallel simulator. This indicates that for an application, not only the reuse capabilities but also performance needs can be met using a standards-based federated implementation.

7. Conclusions and Future Work

In this paper we presented an approach to federating parallel simulations. We introduced the Global Conceptual Model (GCM) as a key concept to federating parallel simulations, and presented the implementation techniques for a prototype federation of GTW optimistic parallel simulators. The implementation of a proxy-based GTW federation involved a relatively small amount (15%) of source-code changes to the GTW kernel, along with the use of the RTI library. Our implementation ensured that GTW applications written to run on non-federated GTW would run on the GTW federation with almost no source-code changes. By keeping overheads low, such as by minimizing memory copy operations via careful buffer management, and by adopting asynchronous GVT/LBTS algorithms, we demonstrated that the federation of parallel simulators could perform nearly as well as native parallel simulators. We intend to extrapolate further from this observation: if any parallel simulator shall be developed from scratch in the future, it is actually feasible to develop it as a federation of sequential simulators (rather than as yet another monolithic parallel simulator) without the fear of a significant performance penalty! The system presented here is one of the first works to evaluate the performance of a standards-based federation of optimistic parallel simulators.

Although there has been much work on GVT algorithms, the problem of hierarchical composition of different GVT/LBTS algorithms appears to be an interesting research area to be explored further. Specifically, this is a problem that becomes more relevant in a federation of heterogeneous *parallel* simulators, rather than of sequential simulators.

8. Acknowledgements
This work was supported under contract #DASG-60-99-C-0052 from the U.S. Army Space and Missile Defense Command

9. References
1. Bhatt, S., *et al.*, *Parallel Simulation Techniques for Large-Scale Networks.* IEEE Communications, 1998. **36**(8): p. 42-47.
2. Steinman, J.S., *SPEEDES: A Multiple-Synchronization Environment for Parallel Discrete Event Simulation.* International Journal on Computer Simulation, 1992: p. 251-286.
3. Unger, B., *et al.*, *Scheduling Critical Channels in Conservative Parallel Discrete Event Simulation*, in *Proceedings of the Workshop on Parallel and Distributed Simulation.* 1999.
4. IEEE Std 1278.1-1995, *IEEE Standard for Distributed Interactive Simulation -- Application Protocols.* 1995, New York, NY: Institute of Electrical and Electronics Engineers, Inc.
5. Wilson, A.L. and R.M. Weatherly, *The Aggregate Level Simulation Protocol: An Evolving System*, in *Proceedings of the 1994 Winter Simulation Conference.* 1994. p. 781-787.
6. Das, S., *et al.*, *GTW: A Time Warp System for Shared Memory Multiprocessors*, in *Proceedings of the 1994 Winter Simulation Conference.* 1994. p. 1332-1339.
7. Jefferson, D., *Virtual Time.* ACM Transactions on Programming Languages and Systems, 1985. **7**(3): p. 404-425.
8. Fujimoto, R.M. and M. Hybinette, *Computing Global Virtual Time in Shared Memory Multiprocessors.* ACM Transactions on Modeling and Computer Simulation, 1997. **7**(4): p. 425-446.
9. Fujimoto, R.M. and P. Hoare, *HLA RTI Performance in High Speed LAN Environments*, in *Proceedings of the Fall Simulation Interoperability Workshop.* 1998: Orlando, FL.
10. Defense Modeling and Simulation Office, http://hla.dmso.mil.

Safe Timestamps and Large-Scale Modeling *

David Nicol   Jason Liu   James Cowie
Dartmouth College   Cooperating Systems

Abstract

This paper visits issues that recur in consideration of simulation time-stamps, in the context of building very large simulation models from components developed by different groups, at different times. A key problem here is "safety", loosely defined to mean that unintended model behavior does not occur due to unpredictable behavior of timestamp generation and comparisons. We revisit the problems of timestamp format and simultaneity, and then turn to the new problem of timestamp inter-operability. We describe how a C++ simulation kernel can support the concurrent evaluation of submodels that internally use heterogeneous timestamps, and evaluate the execution time costs of doing so. We find that use of a safe timestamp format that explicitly allows different time-scales costs less than 10% over a stock 64-bit integer format, whereas support for completely heterogeneous timestamps can cost as much as 50% in execution speed.

1 Introduction

Ordering the execution of events is the central activity in any discrete-event simulation. Intuitively (but informally) one thinks of events as being ordered with respect to some scalar-valued timeline; an event's timestamp positions the event in this ordering. Complications quickly cloud this simple intuition, e.g., events sharing the same timestamp value may or may not be further ordered using a tie-breaking rule; numerical overflow when scheduling new events may inadvertently cause inversion of intended event execution. Tie-breaking rules, when used, tend to be system specific. Threat of anomalies due to round-off leads many simulation systems to use integer-valued timestamps; greater flexibility and ease of use leads others to use floating-point representation, but this (as we will see) is inherently unsafe.

Against this backdrop of heterogeneity in timestamp treatment there is a growing thrust for generality in model development. The High Level Architecture (HLA) [7]

targets the coordination of separately developed federate simulators. The RunTime Infrastructure (RTI) of the HLA is a specification for middleware that binds inter-operating federate simulations. In principle, an RTI implementation deals with any timestamp definition the federates are designed to use. This is accomplished by having the RTI call federate provided functions whenever RTI needs to compare event timestamps. HLA and the RTI state simply that the timestamp type is abstract. One can see that two federates developed using two different timestamp implementations will not inter-operate unless both are aware, a priori, of each other's timestamp formats and time-scales. To inter-operate without such coordination is inherently unsafe. A simulation submodel that assumes millisecond units does not without intervention inter-operate with a submodel that assumes seconds. This is serious business: the Mars Climate Observer in October 1999 was lost because one of its subsystem used English units while all others used metric. We have experienced similar (but less disastrous) errors when incorporating model code written assuming one time-scale into a model that assumes another.

These problems also arise in a system designed for model reuse. Imagine a model of a complex system, clocked periodically at one millisecond. Interactions between its subsystems are assumed to take zero time with respect to this time-scale. Further imagine that a detailed model is separately developed by another group for some subsystem S, but using a micro-second time-scale and different timestamp format. A system supporting model reuse would allow us to replace the coarse-grained model of S with the fine-grained model, and have the whole thing hang together logically (there are of course other interface issues, timestamps are only part of the problem). Intermingling of different time-scales stresses dynamic range of timestamps that can be represented exactly, in ways that are not experienced by the coarser models individually. Independently developed submodels need a common timestamp basis if they are to inter-operate, and should have access to a run-time mechanism for detecting numerical problems, if any, caused by inter-operation.

A simulation *language* like VHDL [1] can address inter-operability by standardizing timestamp representa-

---

*This research is supported in part by DARPA Contract N66001-96-C-8530, NSF Grant ANI-98 08964, and NSF Grant EIA-98-02068

tion, standardizing tie-breaking rules, and requiring any reference to time to include units (e.g. nanoseconds). On the other hand, a large segment of the simulation community uses library-based simulators where a model is expressed in a general purpose programming language, using an Application Programmer's Interface (API) to a simulation kernel library. Virtually every extant PADS simulator is of this type. Generality brings flexibility, but failure of specification also creates problems for simulator inter-operability and model re-use. A quick survey of commonly used simulators reveals only the sort of heterogeneity mentioned earlier. CSIM [16] and C++SIM[12] employ floating-point timestamps, provide no user control over tie-breaking, and leave time-scale to be understood by the modeler. GTW[6] can be compiled to use any scalar type as timestamp; Parsec[3] and UserSimulation Kernel 2.0 [4] use integer timestamps. We have seen no evidence in these systems' documentation that they provide kernel support for tie-breakers, heterogeneous time-scales, or detection of timestamp overflow.

Use of language-native scalars as timestamps is not safe in the general case. Numerical overflows or rounding may silently occur, affecting timestamp accuracy, thereby affecting ordering, thereby affecting the simulation's results. The problem is exacerbated when simulations run long enough that the scale of simulation time is significantly different from the scale of a very small timestamp increment. This occurs if most of the simulation's activity occurs at a coarse time-scale (say, days), but infrequently engages in activity at a fast time-scale (say, picoseconds).

The contribution of this paper is development of a coherent strategy for dealing with timestamps, simultaneous events, tie-breaking strategies, and timestamp safety that is suitable for use in library based C++ and Java based simulators. Our definition of safety is apophatic—defined in terms of what it prevents—this being the more intuitive (and most easily expressed) definition. While the strategy supports flexibility in timestamp design and tie-breaking strategies, at the same time it proposes concrete instances of timestamp classes and tie-breaking rules that, if used, yield tremendous flexibility of expression while ensuring that the simulation does not silently fail due to numerical problems, and does not live-lock due to unintentioned consequences of tie-breaking rules. Although we are not directly addressing RTI, we believe that RTI federates could use the classes we discuss to achieve inter-operability between federates developed using heterogeneous timestamps.

One of our objectives is to assess the execution time costs as a function of functionality offered. We are involved in a large project, SSF (Scalable Simulation Framework) [5], that defines a public domain simulation kernel API that supports modeling in the large. Critical components of large-scale model building are standard-

ization where necessary, support for model re-use, and assurance that the underlying ordering mechanisms do not silently fail as a result of bringing separately developed models together.

SSF is a parallel simulator, and while the main thrust of this paper is tangential to usual PADS themes, the problems we address directly impact the practice of parallel and distributed simulation. Parallel simulators are used to accelerate very long runs, and very long runs push the limits of timestamp accuracy and representation. Parallel simulators use lookahead whose computation and use is easily befouled by rounding error. Distributed simulations integrate models developed by different groups, using different timestamp time-scales and representations. This paper addresses those problems.

2 Simulation Time is a Scalar

Simulation time is, intuitively, a one-dimensional quantity[1]. One could think of a "timestamp" class as a generalization of simulation time, and augment it with tie-breaking fields, such as those proposed in [14]. After defining appropriate arithmetic and comparison operators for the timestamp class, the code can abandon all distinctions between simulation time and timestamp, and manipulate instances of a timestamp class just as though it would if the timestamp were integer or floating point, e.g. in the event-list implementation. If an RTI-controlled federated simulation were to include tie-breaking priorities, the fields carrying those priorities need to be part of a timestamp class[2]. However, this approach runs into conceptual trouble in parts of an API where when the kernel returns a simulation time that is not clearly linked to a single event. Most APIs allow a user to query the kernel for the current system time—the value returned by the kernel must be a timestamp, not a simulation time. What values ought the tie-breaking fields have? This example is just one of many (lookahead is another) that cropped up as we considered the ramifications of supporting a truly general abstract time-stamp within the framework of SSF. In the end we concluded that in SSF we need to clearly separate the focused notion of *simulation time* (a scalar) from the broader notion of *abstract timestamp*, which might include auxiliary information for tie-breaking.

If we are to have an object-oriented kernel that supports both user-defined events through inheritance, and user-defined timestamps, the considerations above lead us to an organization where the kernel API defines an abstract base class for timestamps, and another for events, with the

---

[1]One exception is the newly proposed "approximate time"[8] that defines upper and lower bounds on a scalar notion of simulation time. We will not directly address such timestamps.

[2]assuming that an RTI implementation *truly* supports abstract timestamps. At last report RTIKit supports only double precision timestamps.

event class containing a timestamp (or a pointer to one). We will say more about this in Section 6. Technically this a minor matter of arrangement. Conceptually it makes a big difference to the kernel API.

3 Issues of Type

Implementation of simulation time as a floating point number is common, but dangerous to the unwary. The central issue is round-off error. A common technique in simulations of "clocked" systems is to coordinate sub-model states at pre-compute instants of simulation time, e.g. at millisecond resolution. The user actively pursues construction of events to occur at the same simulation time. Floating point time cannot assure this simultaneity because negative powers of ten cannot be represented *exactly* in IEEE 754 standard format; there is always rounding error associated with powers-of-ten fractions of whatever time-scale a simulation uses. Furthermore the rounding is not uniform in the direction it takes. $99.999 + 0.001$ evaluates to be less than a coded valued of 100, whereas $99.998 + 0.001 + 0.001$ evaluates to be greater than it. Users of floating point timestamps know to test for equality within some user defined tolerance, but are still at the mercy of the hidden rounding mechanism for their models' correctness.

Integer clocks bring their own problems. The modeler is responsible for managing the scale of those integers, and for doing explicit scaling whenever a floating-point number is used to define an event's time. However, floating-point timestamps are extremely convenient when simulation time is driven by samples from continuous probability distributions. One could argue that timestamps ought to be stored in fixed-point representation, as a compromise that avoids the problem areas of integer and floating-point types. C++ classes exist to support fixed-point arithmetic; rules for rescaling and arithmetic are encapsulated in overloaded operators. A small but dedicated group would argue that all arithmetic ought to have infinite precision; C++ classes are available to support this philosophy as well.

While we will propose a concrete timestamp class, the diversity of timestamps in use motivates us to look at the performance impacts of permitting a user to define a timestamp class, and rebuild the SSF kernel to use that class. In section §7 we will also examine kernel issues related to *safely* supporting multiple time-scales, and multiple timestamp classes simultaneously.

4 Simultaneity Revisited

The topic of simultaneous events (events occuring at the instant of simulation time) crops up continually in simula-

tion. It is worth visiting this topic, if only briefly, because of the importance it has to simulationists, and the threat that mishandling of simultaneous events has on timestamp safety.

The key issues to consider are what the simulation kernel should do with regards to simultaneous events, what (if anything) the simulation modeler should be allowed to do to break ties among simultaneous events, and if so, how. Our position is that the kernel must take at least minimal action to protect itself against livelock. This can happen under the following sequence:

1. at time t simultaneous events A and B exist, both of which must be executed to make forward progress,

2. A executes first and schedules C at time t, with higher priority than B,

3. C executes and schedules A at time t, with higher priority than B, and control loops back to step 1.

This is not an artificial problem, it is easy to construct this example in logic network simulations. A solution is to order simultaneous events with respect to causality (in a Lamport clock sense [11]). Doing this so as to restrict the scheduling of as few events as possible is a computationally expensive proposition. Instead we may order simultaneous events with respect to "causality waves", which is a stricter ordering but which is easily implemented. If event A has causality wave number n, we assign wave $n + 1$ to B if B is scheduled by A to occur at the same simulation time as A, otherwise B is assigned wave number 0. If two simultaneous events have different wave indices, priority is given to the smaller index. The notion of "wave" comes from two simultaneous events have different wave indices, priority is given to the smaller index. the notion of a set of simultaneous events in wave 0 scheduling (in zero-time) a second wave of events with index 1, and so on. Causality wave ordering can be done implicitly, by the simple device of ensuring that when an event at time t is scheduled, it is not processed before *all* pre-existing events with timestamp t are processed first. This condition is a requirement in the SSF API, and has long been a part of the CSIM[16] system. Obviously one can also build explicit representation of causality wave counters in events; a complicated version of this, tailored to problems in Time Warp simulations, is proposed in [14].

A second issue is whether a simulation modeler should be given control over simultaneous events. We believe this freedom is necessary. In some contexts it is desirable that a group of concurrent events be presented all at once to model code, e.g., a model of a 64-bit adder with clocked inputs. At the point the inputs are released to the adder there may be as many as 128 different input events. Logical clarity of the model and efficiency in execution argue for those input events to be presented all at once for evaluation. Likewise, treatment of vanishing states in timed Petri net simulations involves simultaneous events, presented to the modeler, for which processing is fairly complex. The SSF API supports this operation, and supports application-specific construction of a layer to separate complex processing of simultaneous events from orthogonal model code. As applied to the class TimeStamp, the user would provide a tie-breaker that always flagged equality, and then allow SSF to deliver a *vector* of simultaneous events to model code.

In other contexts a modeler may wish for the kernel to enforce a tie-breaking rule. For example, Wieland[17] points out that most simulation languages encode tie-breaking rules (sometimes arbitrary ones) and that the choice of tie-breaking rule can skew the simulation results. In his view, if there are N events with the same timestamp, then the characteristic behavior ought to be obtained by averaging the results of considering all N orderings of event execution. Wieland's view is statistically equivalent to the assumption that any of these N events are as likely to be picked first as any other. We observe that *this* sampling that can be achieved by the simple device of assigning to every event (upon its generation) a random tie-breaking priority, sampled from the uniform distribution. The kernel can easily do this, as can a user in the sort of class-based framework we describe. Statistically this is equivalent to uniformly sampling from among simultaneous events whenever such sets develop.

Throughout the PADS literature one finds vector-valued information associated with timestamps[2, 10, 13]. The class-based strategy we propose supports inclusion of such information. Users establish their own secondary ordering rules through the interface to the event abstract base class. Obviously such application is not the main point of this paper, but it's worthwhile noting the possibilities.

5 Timestamp Inter-operability

Simulators differ in their timestamp formats, time-scales, and tie-breaking schemes. Differences may be more than just a matter of the native scalar type used to represent the time. The IEEE 1278.1 timestamp standard for DIS specifies a timestamp to be a 32-bit entity. The least significant bit (LSB) describes how to interpret the other 31 bits. If the LSB is 1 then the time is "absolute"—the number of seconds since January 1, 1970; if the LSB is 0 the time is "relative", and the upper 31 bits represent time up to one hour. The unit per tick of a relative clock is $3600/(2^{31}-1)$ seconds. A legacy DIS model that uses this format has a challenge inter-operating with models that don't. Modeling in the large will mean different groups will develop (or reuse) components using differently defined notions of time and ordering. We now consider how to provide inter-operability between such component models.

5.1 Common Timestamp Format

The most obvious problem for inter-operability is event comparison. Events may differ in their timestamp representation, in their time-scale, and in their tie-breaking schemes. Clearly a common basis of comparison is required. We define here the *Common Timestamp Format* (CTF) to provide that basis. Any user-defined timestamp class must be derived from an abstract base class which specifies a method for returning an "equivalent" CTF instance, on demand. One compares two events of the same subclass using their subclass-specific comparison mechanism, one compares differently subclassed events by obtaining CTF representations from each, and comparing those.

CTF accommodates representation from timestamps based on either integer and floating-point clocks, and it supports different time scales. Our implementation of CTF supports automatic detection of numerical problems when performing timestamp arithmetic. The CTF format is a big integer counter with an associated power-of-ten scale tag; (t, e) represents $t \times 10^e$ simulation seconds. More formally, CTF defines an auxiliary class tick_t to be an unsigned integer counter of at least 64 bits and includes the interface

```
class CTF {
 public:
  tick_t get_ticks();
  int    get_tick_size();
  CTF (tick_t t, int e);
  CTF (double t, int u, int e);
  ...
  double get_double(int u);
  ...
};
```

One CTF constructor accepts the CTF description in terms of ticks and tick size; the other constructor accepts a double, with one argument u specifying units (in 10^u seconds) and the other e specifying required accuracy (to 10^e). This constructor essentially turns a floating-point number into a fixed point number, with a user-specified level of accuracy. Accessor methods produce the count, and tick size. One can extract a double from a CTF, specifying the desired units; the accuracy is that specified by the tick size method.

If d is an IEEE 754 double precision number, our CTF implementation guarantees that

$$d - \text{CTF}(d, u, e).\texttt{get\_double}(u) \leq 10^e,$$

which is to say that accuracy of doubles is retained to the degree specified at construction, and that rounding is accomplished by truncation. There is no free lunch. A timestamp value that cannot or should not be represented as a 64-bit tick count scaled by a power of 10 will lose information when being cast to CTF, but the degree of loss is controlled by the modeler, and the modeler knows exactly how a value will be rounded. This is the inescapable price paid for inter-operability.

Our CTF implementation provides overloaded '+' and '-' operators for addition and subtraction between CTF instances, and overloaded operators for virtually all arithmetic between a CTF and an integer scalar (the scalar is interpreted to to have the same scale as the CTF instance).

To compare, add, or subtract two CTF instances (t_1, e_1) and (t_2, e_3), one of t_1 and t_2 is first multiplied by $10^{|e_1 - e_2|}$. It is possible for the results of that multiplication to be a tick count larger than can be represented by tick_t. Indeed, the larger the difference in exponents, the smaller that tick count must be if overflow is to be avoided. Mixing time-scales reduces the range of simulation times that can be represented in the coarser time-scale, because it must be transformed to the finer time-scale. For example, if tick_t is 64 bits, then tick counts may rise as high as 1.8×10^{19}, at the smallest time-scale specified by the model. If that scale is pico-seconds (10^{-12}), the range is 1.8×10^7 seconds—equivalently, several months. While it is unrealistic to expect a simulation to work through a single day at a pico-second scale, it is not unthinkable for a model working at the minute level (say, a vehicle moving in a road network) to infrequently use a submodel modeling laser photonics at the pico-second scale. One doesn't design a simulation this way from scratch, but one may end up assembling a simulation this way from diverse component libraries. If this were to happen in an extremely long running simulation, overflow could occur. There is also danger of overflow when sampling from heavy tailed distributions, as is frequently done in models of communication traffic. An obscenely large number might be generated, incur overflow when involved in arithmetic, and (if undetected) be transformed into a reasonable looking number.

The modeler needs to be able to analyze the consequences of mixing time-scales. To support this analysis, the SSF implementation of CTF guarantees that it will never create a CTF instance with exponent either larger or smaller than the maximum or minimum exponent explicitly used by a modeler, or explicitly given as a result of retrieving the CTF representation of a modeler provided timestamp class.

Our CTF implementation is able to detect overflow from any arithmetic operation, using standard techniques[9]. However, runtime overflow checking is often not necessary: a static analysis can demonstrate freedom from overflow if the maximum simulation time, largest and smallest timestamp scale, and maximum

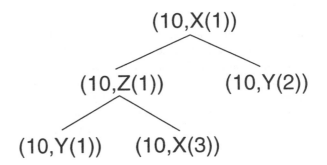

Figure 1: Heap organization of mixed subclasses

operands used in any arithmetic operation are all known. Runtime overflow protection *is* needed though as simulation technology moves into a realm where models are assembled semi-automatically from libraries distributed across the Internet. We'll later quantify the cost of providing such checks.

5.2 Maintaining Simultaneity Ordering

The CTF interface allows one to mix events from different subclasses together in one event-list; there is no mechanism for breaking ties between events with the same CTF timestamp values (except for causality counters that are implemented in the Event base class). Even though two events of the same subclass will be compared using a subclass-specific function, events from different classes will be compared using CTF. Without extra care, even if commonly subclassed events A and B are ordered $A < B$ (as they might if their simulation times are equal but a tie-breaker is defined or if conversion to CTF loses ordering information), if their timestamps both have the same CTF value it is possible for B to be executed before A.

Figure 1 illustrates the threat. The event-list is implemented as a heap; shown are 5 events, all of which have the same CTF value at time 10, from subclasses X, Y, and Z. The priority within , and a class is shown, so the event at timestamp $(10, Y(1))$ should be executed before the event with timestamp $(10, Y(2))$. The configuration of events shown occurs if the insertions are done in the order $(10, X(1))$, $(10, Z(1))$, $(10, Y(2))$, $(10, Y(1))$, $(10, X(3))$. After event $(10, X(1))$ is executed, the new "minimum" timestamp is identified by moving the last event in the heap—$(10, X(3))$—to the top and pushing it towards the leaves. In this process it is possible for the positions of $(10, X(3))$ and $(10, Y(2))$ to be interchanged, making $(10, Y(2))$ the next event to execute, *before* $(10, Y(1))$! This is an inversion over the Y class internal ordering, and must be avoided.

One can resolve this problem by engineering the base and derived event classes to establish integer codes that distinguish between derived classes, and use these codes

75

as type identifiers. Events from the same subclass are grouped into a common event-list; an additional min-priority structure is maintained over the CTF representations of the minimum elements in each subclass event-list. This arrangement ensures that events within a subclass are executed in the order specified by that subclass. The overall next event (or set of simultaneous next events) is found by fetching the minimum event(s) from the CTF min-priority structure.

6 Classes

The framework we describe consists of a few abstract base classes, and CTF. Class TSO (TimeStamp Object) is the abstract base class for a user-defined timestamp. Its critical methods are `clone` (to make a copy), `cmp` (to compare two TSO objects), and `ctf` (to return the corresponding CTF representation). It also contains virtual methods for arithmetic on TSO objects. All of these methods must be provided by any subclassed TSO object. Subclass TSODefault implements the CTF timestamp.

Class `ltime` is an abstract base class for logical time. For concrete implementations it contains an instance of a subclassed TSO as its sole data member. For virtual implementations it contains a pointer to a virtual TSO class. `ltime` also contains a function for comparing two timestamps, `int ltime::cmp(ltime &t1, ltime &t2)`, and a full set of overloaded operators and constructors to support the underlying TSO object. In SSF the modeler sees only instances of `ltime` objects.

Class `Event` is the abstract base class for a simulation event. Its critical methods are `clone()` for making a copy of itself, `cmpCaus(Event &e1, Event &e2)` for comparing the causality counters of two events (not needed in SSF, but provided for completeness should other implementations use this class), `cmpPri(Event &e1, Event &e2)` for comparing other tie-breaking priorities, `setCaus(int c)` for setting the event's causality counter, and `setTime(ltime now, ltime delay)` for marking an `Event` with both the current simulation time, and a scheduling increment. Each event has a `ltime` data member, `ts`.

Assuming the various compare functions take the usual Unix meaning[3] the kernel would order events using a comparison function such as

```
int Event::cmp(Event &e1, Event &e2)
{
  int lcomp = ltime::cmp( e1.ts, e2.ts );
  if( !lcomp ) return 0;
```

---

[3] < 0 implies the first argument is less than the second, $== 0$ implies equality, and > 0 implies the first argument is greater than the second.

```
  lcomp = Event::cmpCaus(e1,e2);
  if( !lcomp ) return 0;
  return Event::cmpPri(e1,e2);
}
```

A framework like this can be used in different ways. One way is to have kernel designers define a general timestamp class (like CTF) and build a kernel that uses only concrete instances of that class. All models that link to that kernel use that class. This approach is effective with a timestamp class that provides for explicit declaration and management of time-scale. A more general way allows users to define their own concrete timestamp classes. An API for timestamp class definition would allow a *user* that had access to the kernel source to rebuild the kernel to work with the new timestamp class. All models run on that kernel would use that class. In the most aggressive scenario the kernel is engineered to work with virtual timestamp classes, making it possible to introduce a new timestamp class by relinking to the kernel—not recompiling the kernel. This option also requires an API for timestamp class definition, but allows one this level of generality without access to the kernel source code (a consideration if the kernel is commercially sold or is merely strongly protected by its authors.)

Different grades of flexibility consume different degrees of computing power that otherwise would be available for advancing model state. The next section looks at how costs escalate with generality in the SSF parallel simulator.

7 Implementation Costs

Moving from a native scalar to virtual class timestamps will cost performance. We next take up an assessment of these cost, by looking at six scenarios, in a C++ implementation of SSF . In the first `ltime` is a symbolic name for a native scalar, `long long`. This is the baseline case reflecting common practice in many simulators. To assess the cost of using class-based representation, the second scenario uses the same native scalar representation, but as a concrete member of a full developed timestamp class with a full compliment of overloaded operators, and a fixed (static) time-scale. The memory used and operators applied are exactly the same as the first case, just within the machinery of a class definition. The third scenario is of a concrete TSO class (the CTF class) with the additional memory cost, with all the overhead of scaling when comparing timestamps or performing arithmetic operations on them, but *without* overflow testing. The fourth is the same as the third, with overflow detection logic engaged at all times. These scenarios represent the case where an implementation provides some model reuse, provided that all submodels use one timestamp class with flexible scale. These experiments use two different timescales. The last two scenarios mix two fundamentally different timestamp classes in a kernel that supports a virtual TSO base class. Every reference to a timestamp involves a reference through an object's virtual table. This is the most general, but obviously the most expensive case. We look at a version that performs overflow checking, VirtTSO(check), and one that does not, VirtTSO(free).

For each scenario we rebuilt the SSF kernel on a 550MHz Pentium III based processor, using the g++ 2.9.1 compiler from the Cygnus GnuPro Toolkit for Linux, with level 3 optimizations enabled. We report only serial runs, since we are trying to isolate the effects of different timestamp representations. However, because of the structure of SSF, virtually all of the timestamp arithmetic and comparisons that would be done in a parallel run are also being done in these serial runs.

We examine the execution speed of a packet-switched communications network, with stochastically generated workload. The network is large—there are approximately 1/2 million traffic sources and routers—to stress the contribution of event-list operations. The computational grain of the simulation is small. Networking applications simulating protocol stacks typically have greater granularity, and so the costs we observe here contribute less to overall running time.

Table 1 describes performance. SSF is process-oriented; we describe raw performance in terms of the number of context switches it performs each second. Typical activity corresponding to a context switch is receipt of a packet, check for buffer problems, and transmission of a packet.

There is absolutely no difference in performance between using a native `long long`, or using a class-wrapper around it, complete with overloaded operators. The compiler was able to do all the in-lining and memory optimizations that were possible. Remembering that over 1/2 million objects are present (as are well over one million threads), the raw performance of over 1/3 million context switches per second is noteworthy. Moving to implementations that use CTF as the TSO object in `ltime`, we compare an implementation that does not check overflow, CTF(free), and another that does, CTF(check). The CTF(free) experiments show that the cost of supporting multiple time-scales is a reduction of less than 10% over native scalar; the version that includes overflow checking reduces this further by about 1%. The kernel that supports completely general user-defined timestamps without overflow checking runs at 49% the rate of the native scalar implementation; including overflow checking it runs at 48%.

The results are interesting in showing that the cost of carrying scale factors along in timestamps is quite acceptable, and that doing overflow testing is comparatively inexpensive. CTF timestamps require one word more of

Timestamp	CommNet
long long	353K/s
class	353K/s
CTF(free)	324K/s
CTF(check)	318K/s
VirtTSO(free)	174K/s
VirtTSO(check)	171K/s

Table 1: Context switching rate (in thousands per second) of different timestamp schemes on network model

memory than does native scalar, but against the backdrop of all other memory demands by SSF this addition is hardly noticeable. Added memory cost *is* more noticeable in the virtual TSO versions, we observed that the memory useage high-water mark is 18% higher. While all these costs are not negligible, nor are they overwhelming in the face of the functionality those implementations provide. One may well be willing to pay a factor of two in computational speed and 20% in memory overhead to be able to inter-operate very different SSF models. One should certainly be will to pay 10% in performance to let the system manage time-scale.

8 Conclusion

Event ordering is the soul of discrete-event simulation. Despite the ubiquity of DES, disputed complications quickly arise over issues of timestamp representation, arithmetic on timestamps, and simultaneous events. New problems of timestamp inter-operability emerge as we consider the process of building large models from libraries of smaller models.

We are concerned that timestamp manipulation be safe, in the sense of avoiding event inversions due to numerical rounding or overflow, in avoiding live-lock due to user-defined tie-breaking functions, and in avoiding logical confusion due to mixing submodels that assume different time-scales. We believe solutions to these problems exist in (i) using a general, integer-based timestamp class that requires a user to specify time-scale and accuracy, (ii) making causality ordering a mandatory highest priority tie-breaker among concurrent events, (iii) making run-time overflow detection on timestamp arithmetic available for simulations that need it. While meeting these concerns, we aim also to make simulation kernels flexible enough to allow user-defined timestamps. An important application of such is the inter-operability of the timestamps of separately developed models, within the SSF context.

The problems we consider are generic to discrete-event simulation, yet have particular importance to parallel and distributed simulation. Overflow problems arise in very long runs—and length of run is a strong motivating reason for using parallelism. Numerical problems with timestamps have in the past caused problems with conservative synchronization methods, in computing lookahead (too far) or establishing appointments (when timestamps computed on different processors must agree exactly). Distributed simulation will tie together separately developed submodels; indeed, the CTF class we describe could in principle be used by RTI federates and circumvent the problem of agreeing upon a time-scale. In the bargain the federates will benefit from a timestamp class that is safe to use.

References

[1] Peter J. Ashenden. *The Designer's Guide to VHDL*. Morgan Kaufmann, San Francisco, CA, 1996.

[2] A. Back and S. Turner. Timestamp generation for optimistic parallel computing. In *Proceedings of the 28th Annual Simulation Symposium*, pages 144–153, Phoenix, AZ, April 1995.

[3] R. Bagrodia, R. Meyer, M. Takai, Y. Chen, X. Zeng, J. Martin, B. Park, and H. Song. Parsec : A parallel simulation environment for complex systems. *IEEE Computer*, 3(10):77–85, October 1998.

[4] Columbia University. *UserSimulation Kernel 2.0*, 1996. See http://comet.ctr.columbia.edu/software/TeleSoft.

[5] J. Cowie, D. Nicol, and A. Ogielski. Modeling the Global Internet. *Computing in Science and Engineering*, 1(1):42-50, Jan.-Feb. 1999.

[6] S. Das, R. Fujimoto, K. Panesar, D. Allison, and M. Hybinette. GTW: A Time Warp system for shared memory multiprocessors. In *1994 Winter Simulation Conference Proceedings*, pages 1332–1339, December 1994.

[7] Defense Modeling and Simulation Office. *High Level Architecture Interface Specification, V1.3*, April 1998. (http://www.dmso.mil).

[8] Richard Fujimoto. Exploiting temporal uncertainty in parallel and distributed simulation. In *Proceedings of the 1999 Workshop on Parallel and Distributed Simulation*, pages 46–53, Atlanta, Ga, May 1999.

[9] J.L. Hennessy and D.A. Patterson. *Computer Organization and Design, The Hardware/Software Interface*. Morgan Kaufmann Publishers, Inc., Palo Alto, CA, 1994.

[10] Murray Pearson, John Cleary, J.A. David McWha. Timestamp representations for virtual sequences. In *Proceedings of the 1997 Workshop on Parallel and Distributed Simulation*, pages 98–105, Lockenhaus, Austria, June 1997.

[11] L. Lamport. Time, clocks, and the ordering of events in distributed systems. *Communications of the ACM*, 21(7):558–565, July 1978.

[12] M.C. Little and D.L. McCue. Construction and use of a simulation package in c++. *C User's Journal*, 3(12), 1994. Also available as Technical Report 437, Dept. of Computing Science, University of Newcastle on Tyne, 1993.

[13] D. Nicol and X. Liu. The dark side of risk : What your mother never told you about time warp. In *Proceedings of the 1996 Workshop on Parallel and Distributed Simulation*, pages 188–195, Lockenhaus, Austria, 1996. IEEE Press.

[14] Robert Rönngreen and Michael Liljenstam. On event ordering in parallel discrete event simulation. In *Proceedings of the 1999 Workshop on Parallel and Distributed Simulation*, pages 38–45, Atlanta, Ga, May 1999.

[15] David Prochnow, Ernest Page, Bryan Youmans. Development of a Federation Management Tool: Implications for HLA. In *Proceedings of the Spring 1998 Simulation Interoperability Workshop*, Orlando, Florida, March 1998.

[16] H. Schwetman. CSIM: A C-based, process oriented simulation language. In *Proceedings of the 1986 Winter Simulation Conference*, pages 387–396, 1986.

[17] Frederick Wieland. The threshold of event simultaneity. In *Proceedings of the 1997 Workshop on Parallel and Distributed Simulation*, pages 56–59, Lockenhaus, Austria, June 1997.

Session 5
Making parallel simulation a success

Strategies for Success in Parallel Simulation Applications
Keynote speaker: Frederick Wieland

Strategies for Success in Parallel Simulation Applications

Frederick Wieland[*]

The MITRE Corporation
Center for Advanced Aviation Systems Development
McLean, VA, U.S.A.

Abstract

While the PADS community has traditionally focused on—and done a great job with—the technical aspects of developing simulations that run fast and can be connected to other simulations, it has paid little or no attention to the overall strategies required to produce a marketable, useful, and successful parallel simulation. This lack of market focus has led to many fears of the demise of the PADS community, complaints of its lack of general acceptance by the broader simulation community, and predictions that it will become merely another venue for simulation interconnection.

These fears, complaints, and predictions are unnecessary. There are several examples of successful parallel simulations—in domains as far apart as aviation modeling and wargames. What can we learn from their successes? How can we translate their general acceptance into other parallel simulation domains? Are there market opportunities that we are missing? In short, what is the parallel simulation community lacking, and what does it need to do in order to be more successful?

The purpose of this talk is to begin a discussion on the answers to these questions (as opposed to definitively answering them). We will draw on numerous examples of successful applications, and make some concrete suggestions for furthering the community.

Overview of talk

In recent years, there have been many cries from parallel simulation researchers as to the lack of utility of their products in the marketplace. Some have suggested that the only viable market is the simulation interconnection market as embodied by the US Department of Defense's High Level Architecture. Others have actively pointed to the paucity of simulation applications in PADS proceedings as a metric that the community has lost its focus. Still others claim that the market for fast-time parallel simulations has been overtaken by other technologies.

We will argue in this talk that the discussion of the demise of the parallel simulation community is ill timed and needless. However, for the community to thrive and grow it must begin to address marketing and customer concerns in addition to its traditional technical focus. The lack of market focus, and the almost complete absence of any papers or talks addressing the real needs of simulation end-users, is itself a problem with the community that needs to be addressed.

So what are the needs of the simulation community? How can a simulation that has been retrofitted with PADS-type technology be successfully marketed to sponsors or business customers? How can the community reach out to new venues of simulation development? We will discuss all these questions—and beyond—in this talk. We are not claiming to have the definitive answer to these problems, only a starting point for fruitful discussion.

About the speaker

Frederick Wieland has been involved in parallel and distributed simulation for over 15 years, first as a member of the Time Warp Operating System (TWOS) team and lately as a developer of Web-based parallel simulations for the aviation industry. Fred has published over forty papers in conferences and journals in the areas of parallel simulation, aviation modeling, physics-based simulation, and biology. Fred's latest simulation, DPAT, has been used in over forty studies of the National Airspace System by MITRE, the FAA, airlines, and a university.

[*] The author can be reached at fwieland@mitre.org, or +1 (703) 883-5385.

Session 6
Applications

**Efficient Distributed Simulation of a Communication
Switch with Bursty Sources and Losses**
A. S. McGough and I. Mitrani

Optimizing Cell-size in Grid-Based DDM
R. Ayani, F. Moradi, and G. Tan

Distributed, Parallel Simulation of Multiple, Deliberative Agents
A. M. Uhrmacher and K. Gugler

Efficient Distributed Simulation of a Communication Switch with Bursty Sources and Losses

A.S.M^{C}Gough and I. Mitrani
Computing Science Department, University of Newcastle,
Newcastle upon Tyne, NE1 7RU
a.s.mcgough@ncl.ac.uk   isi.mitrani@ncl.ac.uk

Abstract

Algorithms for simulating an ATM switch on a distributed memory multiprocessor are described. These include parallel generation of bursty arrival streams, along with the marking and deleting of lost cells due to buffer overflows. These algorithms increase the amount of computation carried out independently by each processor, and reduce the communication between the processors. When the number of cells lost is relatively small, the run time of the simulation is approximately $O(N/P)$, where N is the total number of cells simulated and P is the number of processors. The cells are processed in intervals of fixed length; that length affects the structure and the performance of the algorithms.

1. Introduction

Consider an ATM switch with transmission capacity C cells / second (i.e. a service time of $c = 1/C$). The switch contains a finite buffer of size Q cells, which is filled from arrivals generated by merging M independent bursty sources of the "on"/"off" type, see figure 1 below. Suppose that the performance measure of interest is the cell loss probability, i.e. the long–term fraction of cells that are lost due to buffer overflow. If the "on", "off" and cell inter-arrival intervals for the different sources are different and generally distributed, that quantity cannot normally be determined by analysis. On the other hand, estimating the loss probability by simulation tends to be a very time-consuming task because the overflow events are usually rare and so a large number of cell arrivals and departures have to be generated in order to obtain an accurate result.

In order to reduce these large simulation times, considerable effort has gone into exploring parallel computation techniques. In particular, the parallel simulation of Multiplexers, as used in ATM networks, has attracted much at-

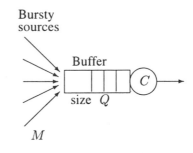

Figure 1. ATM Switch with multiple sources

tention over recent years. Space-parallel simulation techniques, where different nodes of the network are allocated to different processors, have been proposed in [6, 7, 8]. These techniques do not help in speeding up a long simulation of a single ATM node. Nikolaidis [9] and Fujimoto [10] presented a method of simulating an ATM multiplexer at the level of bursts. Since individual cells are not simulated, this approach can only provide approximate results or ones that require particular assumptions. Wang and Abrams [11] presented another approximate method for the parallel simulation of the G/G/1/n queue. That method becomes exact when the service times are constant but it requires the computation of all departure times as well as all arrivals. A similar approach to ours is adopted by Andradóttir and Ott [13]. They apply time-parallel and relaxation techniques to the simulation of queuing networks. However, they do not handle bursty arrivals and do not report the achieved speedup in either shared-memory or distributed environment. Chen [3] presents an alternative approach to the parallel simulation of finite buffers, based on longest-path algorithms to compute departure times. That approach does not apply easily to our model.

A parallel simulation algorithm for the present model was described in [5]. It used the parallel prefix approach

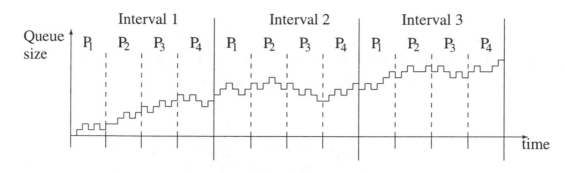

Figure 2. The division of the sample path into intervals

of [1, 12], together with parallel merge and relaxation techniques for deciding which cells are lost. That algorithm achieved almost linear speedup on a shared-memory multiprocessor. However, if it is run without modification on a distributed memory multiprocessor, such as a cluster of workstations connected by a fast Ethernet, the benefits of parallelism are overcome by the communication overheads. While generating the merged arrival stream, large amounts of data have to be passed around among the processors. In that environment we have found that increasing the number of processors (up to eight) does not reduce significantly the simulation execution time.

That is why it is necessary to develop different and more efficient parallel simulation algorithms, which is the subject of this paper. The emphasis of the new approach is to use a method for generating arrivals which allows the majority of cells to be generated and handled on the correct processor. This allows the merging of streams and the marking of lost cells to be done locally, thus significantly reducing the communication costs.

1.1. Outline of the distributed algorithm

The total simulation period is broken up into intervals of B seconds. Within each interval the work is divided approximately equally between the P processors. Figure 2 illustrates a sample path where a simulation over the interval 0 to $3B$ is split among four processors.

If the chosen value for B is great enough then the average amount of work performed by each processor will be approximately the same. This coupled with low communication costs between processors allows the simulation to reach almost linear speed–up.

The actions taken by the processors in parallel are:

- **1. Generate all arrivals for the next B seconds.** Processor k first computes the "on"and "off"periods for arrival source i that fall within its own sub-interval of the time line. It can then compute the list of arrivals from that source which occur during this sub-interval.

These two steps are performed using the modified version of the parallel prefix algorithm described in section 2 below. Some arrivals may be generated on the incorrect processor due to the random nature of the arrival sources. These arrivals need to be communicated to the correct processor. Provided that the number of such cells is small, in comparison with the total number of arrivals generated, this should have little effect on the performance of the simulation. Repeating these steps for all sources and merging the resulting cells produces the total arrival stream that processor k needs to handle.

- **2. Mark and remove lost cells.** The algorithm used for this task is an adaptation of an algorithm introduced in [5]. It can be used with an arbitrary sized collection of arrivals, and works by generating a step function of the queue size over a given time interval. Each processor generates a portion of the sample path corresponding to its own sub-interval, assuming some initial conditions for the state of the queue. That step is iterated using new initial conditions obtained from the previous processor and passing new initial conditions to the next one. This process, known as 'relaxation', continues until two consecutive iterations produce identical sample paths. If the cell loss fraction is small then the number of iterations should be small.

The technique of using relaxation to refine the current state of knowledge of individual processors was discussed, in general context, by Chandy and Sherman [4]. Relaxation does not always help, but it can be implemented efficiently in our case.

To obtain a point estimate and a confidence interval for the cell loss probability, it is enough to compute the number of cells, L, that are lost during the simulation period. It should be pointed out, however, that with simple modifications the above algorithms can generate other performance measures for the ATM switch, such as average buffer occupancy or average cell response time.

It is also worth pointing out that these algorithms can be modified to accommodate more general models, including cells of different priority types, reservation of buffer space for higher priority cells, and sources with dependent "on"and "off"periods (provided that the "on"periods are large compared to the inter-arrival times).

Finally, it should be mentioned that although we have considered a continuous time model (arrival instants are real and transmissions can start at arbitrary points) for this work, the method can easily be adapted to a discrete–time model.

The following sections provide a more detailed description of the stages described above.

2. Generation of arrival instances

It is assumed that the bursty nature of each source can be simulated by an alternating sequence of "on" periods during which cells arrive, and "off" periods without arrivals. All sources start with an "on" period. The n th "on" , "off" and inter-arrival periods for source i are denoted by $\xi_{i,n}$, $\eta_{i,n}$ and $\alpha_{i,n}$, respectively. These are sequences of i.i.d. random variables with general distributions.

The generation of a sequence of arrivals during an interval of length B for source i is carried out in two steps. First, the "off" periods are ignored and an 'unadjusted' arrival sequence is calculated as if the source was "on" all the time (see the lower part of figure 3, where the "off" periods have been condensed to 0).

The 'unadjusted' arrival time of cell n from source i, $a_{i,n}$, satisfies the following recurrence relation:

$$a_{i,n+1} = a_{i,n} + \alpha_{i,n+1} \; ; \; n = 1, 2, \dots , \qquad (1)$$

where $\alpha_{i,n+1}$ is the inter-arrival interval between cells n and $n + 1$. These recurrences can be solved in parallel by applying the parallel prefix algorithm (see [1]). A total of N_i arrival instants can be calculated on P processors in time on the order of $O(N_i/P)$ when N_i, the number of arrivals that are generated from source i over the interval of length B, is much larger than P.

The second step consists of adjusting $a_{i,n}$ by inserting the missing "off" periods in the appropriate positions (see upper part of figure 2, where the inserted "off"periods are denoted by O). To ascertain how many "off" periods occurred before a particular 'unadjusted' arrival time, the index of the "on" period during which $a_{i,n}$ occurs must be determined. Given the lengths of the consecutive "on" periods for source i, $\xi_{i,j}$, we need to find, for each $a_{i,n}$, an index l such that

$$\sum_{j=1}^{l-1} \xi_{i,j} < a_{i,n} \le \sum_{j=1}^{l} \xi_{i,j} , \qquad (2)$$

where an empty sum is 0 by definition.

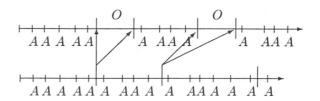

Figure 3. Unadjusted and adjusted arrival instants

Having solved the inequalities (2) for l, the actual arrival instant of cell n from source i, $A_{i,n}$, is obtained from

$$A_{i,n} = a_{i,n} + \sum_{j=1}^{l-1} \eta_{i,j} . \qquad (3)$$

The adjustment procedure described above assumes that the realizations of $\xi_{i,j}$ and $\eta_{i,j}$ have been pre-computed. Since the total number of "on" and "off" periods that are generated during the simulation is typically much smaller than the total number of cells, we treat that pre-computation as an overhead. Of course, the sequences of partial sums for $\xi_{i,j}$ and $\eta_{i,j}$ can also be obtained by means of the parallel prefix algorithm, and infact are in this case.

Solving (2) and (3) is essentially equivalent to merging the two sequences of arrival and "off" instants. Since there are many more arrival instances than "on"/ "off"periods, that operation together with the calculation of the actual arrival times, can be carried out on P processors in time approximately equal to $O(N_i/P)$.

2.1. Generation of "off"and "on"periods

The first step of the new algorithm for generating the arrival instances is to compute the prefix sums of "on"and "off"periods involved in (2) and (3). Each of the P processors computes all "on"and "off"instants that occur within a sub-interval of length B/P. For processor k that sub-interval is $[(k-1)B/P, kB/P]$, $k = 1, 2, ..., P$. All processors follow the four stages of the algorithm outlined below. For simplicity the algorithm only describes the computation of the first interval of the simulation. All other intervals are processed in a similar manner.

1. Processor k assumes that the beginning of its sub-interval, $(k - 1)B/P$, is the start of an "on"period for every source. It then computes sets of partial sums $\Xi'_{i,j}$ and $\Theta'_{i,j}$ according to the following equations.

$$\Xi'_{i,j} = \xi_{i,1} + \xi_{i,2} + ... + \xi_{i,j} \quad j = 1, 2, 3, ... \; ; \quad (4)$$

$$\Theta'_{i,j} = \eta_{i,1} + \eta_{i,2} + \dots + \eta_{i,j} \quad j = 1,2,3,\dots \ . \quad (5)$$

where i indexes the source and j indexes the "on"/ "off" pair. Partial sums are computed until

$$(k-1)B/P + \Xi'_{i,j} + \Theta'_{i,j} > kB/P \quad i = 1,2,\dots,M. \quad (6)$$

Denote the values of $\Xi'_{i,j}$ and $\Theta'_{i,j}$ which satisfy (6) by $\Xi_i^{(k)}$ and $\Theta_i^{(k)}$ respectively.

2. Processor k sends $\Xi_i^{(k)}$ and $\Theta_i^{(k)}$ for each i to processors $k+1, k+2, \dots, P$. It also receives similar values from all the processors $1,2,\dots,k-1$. Processor k computes

$$\Xi_i = \Xi_i^{(1)} + \Xi_i^{(2)} + \dots + \Xi_i^{(k-1)} \quad i = 1,2,\dots,M \ ; \quad (7)$$

$$\Theta_i = \Theta_i^{(1)} + \Theta_i^{(2)} + \dots + \Theta_i^{(k-1)} \quad i = 1,2,\dots,M \ . \quad (8)$$

3. The true "on" and "off" starting points are computed as

$$\Xi_{i,j} = \Xi'_{i,j} + \Xi_i \quad j = 1,2,3,\dots \ ; \quad (9)$$

$$\Theta_{i,j} = \Theta'_{i,j} + \Theta_i \quad j = 1,2,3,\dots \ . \quad (10)$$

4. Find the last pair $(\Xi_{i,j}, \Theta_{i,j})$ which satisfies

$$\Xi_{i,j} + \Theta_{i,j} < kB/P. \quad (11)$$

Copy that, and all subsequent pairs $(\Xi_{i,j}, \Theta_{i,j})$, to processor $k+1$. Receive similar pairs from processor $k-1$. This is necessary for computing the burst of arrivals that may straddle the boundary between the kth and the $k+1$st sub-intervals. Processor k then renumbers its (increasing) sequences $\Xi_{i,j}$ and $\Theta_{i,j}$ such that $\Xi_{i,1} + \Theta_{i,1} < (k-1)B/P$. Thus the first "on"-"off" cycle for processor k in fact starts before the beginning of its sub-interval.

2.2. Distributed generation of arrival instances

In this section we present the algorithm for generating the arrival instances from all sources. To do that for source i, start by eliminating all corresponding "off" periods and consider the "on" periods joined end to end. On this 'compressed' time line the start of the k'th sub-interval, for source i, moves from $(k-1)B/P$ to

$$s_i^{(k)} = \begin{cases} \Xi_{i,1} & \text{if } (k-1)B/P \text{ is in} \\ & \text{an "off" period} \\ (k-1)B/P - \Theta_{i,1} & \text{otherwise.} \end{cases}$$

The arrival generation algorithm proceeds as follows.

1. Processor k starts by assuming that there is an arrival instance for source i at time $s_i^{(k)}$. It computes the partial sums

$$a'_{i,n+1} = a'_{i,n} + \alpha_{i,n+1} \quad ; \quad n = 1,2,\dots \ , \quad (12)$$

until

$$s_i^{(k)} + a'_{i,n} > s_i^{(k+1)} \ . \quad (13)$$

Denote the first value $a'_{i,n}$ which satisfies (13) by $a_i^{(k)}$.

2. Processor k sends $a_i^{(k)}$ for each i to processors $k+1, k+2, \dots, P$. It also receives similar values from all the processors $1,2,\dots,k-1$. Processor k computes

$$a_i = a_i^{(1)} + a_i^{(2)} + \dots + a_i^{(k-1)} \quad i = 1,2,\dots,M \ . \quad (14)$$

3. The arrival instances for source i on the 'compressed' time line are computed as

$$a_{i,n} = a'_{i,n} + a_i \quad n = 1,2,3,\dots \ . \quad (15)$$

4. Any arrival instances which satisfy

$$s_i^{k+r} < a_{i,n} < s_i^{(k+r+1)}. \quad (16)$$

are sent to processor $k+r$, where they will finish their processing.

5. The true arrival time $A_{i,n}$ can now be computed by first finding the index l of the relevant "on" period. That index satisfies

$$\Xi_{i,l-1} < a_{i,n} < \Xi_{i,l} \ . \quad (17)$$

Adjust $a_{i,n}$ by adding to it the sum of all previous "off" periods:

$$A_{i,n} = a_{i,n} + \Theta_{i,l-1} \ . \quad (18)$$

In practice, when the sub-interval length B/P is large compared to the inter-arrival times, step 4 only requires arrivals to be passes to processor $k+1$.

The arrivals from all M sources are then merged to produce the full list of arrivals within the kth sub-interval.

3. Mark and remove lost cells

Denote, for convenience, the merged arrival instants in the current sub-interval by A_n, $n = 1,2,\dots$ (in practice, the numbering carries on sequentially from one sub-interval to the next). It is now necessary to determine, in parallel, which cells are accepted into the buffer and which are lost as a result of finding it full. An algorithm to achieve this result is presented below.

3.1. Acceptance Algorithm

Processor k now computes the queue size at the arrival instants in its sub-interval, assuming some initial conditions. The latter are then refined in subsequent iterations. For the purpose of determining the lost cells, it is only necessary to calculate some of the departure instants.

For cell n within a sub-interval, let q_n be the queue size 'just before' A_n; this is the queue size 'seen' by the incoming cell. Also, let d_n be the time of the last departure before A_n if $q_n > 0$; otherwise $d_n = A_n$. For the first cell, assume initially that $q_1 = 0$ and $d_1 = A_1$. This definition of d_n is illustrated in figure 4. The actual departure times D_n are marked on for clarity.

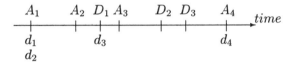

Figure 4. The values of d_n

Clearly, cell n is accepted if $q_n < Q$ and is lost otherwise. Denote by σ_n the indicator of that event:

$$\sigma_n = \begin{cases} 1 & \text{if } q_n < Q \\ 0 & \text{if } q_n = Q. \end{cases}$$

Let δ_n be the number of cell transmissions that can be completed in the interval (d_n, A_{n+1}):

$$\delta_n = \left\lfloor \frac{A_{n+1} - d_n}{c} \right\rfloor ,$$

where $\lfloor x \rfloor$ is the largest integer not exceeding x.

Now, the values of q_n and d_n are computed by means of the following recurrence relations:

$$q_{n+1} = \max(q_n + \sigma_n - \delta_n, 0) , \qquad (19)$$

$$d_{n+1} = \begin{cases} d_n + \delta_n c & \text{if } q_{n+1} > 0 \\ A_{n+1} & \text{if } q_{n+1} = 0. \end{cases} \qquad (20)$$

These equations rely on the fact that cell service times are constant. If that is not the case, they would be modified in a straightforward manner, but would still remain recurrences.

Processor k solves (19) and (20) for its sub-interval, using known or assumed initial values of q_1 and d_1 (in the case of processor 1, these are known from the previous interval; the other processors start by assuming that their first cell arrives into an empty buffer). The computed values of q_n and d_n for the last cell in the sub-interval are then passed

to processor $k+1$ and serve as the latter's new initial values. This procedure is iterated until the new initial conditions of all processors are the same as the old ones. In the worst case P iterations are required, but when the number of losses is small, fewer iterations suffice.

There are several strategies that can be employed to reduce the amount of computation performed by each processor during an iteration. They are based on the following ideas:

1. Let I_k be the total idle time during sub-interval k, as computed by processor k in one of the iterations:

$$I_k = \sum_n I(q_n = 0)[A_n - d_{n-1} - c(q_{n-1} + \sigma_{n-1})] , \quad (21)$$

where the summation is over all arrival instants in the sub-interval, and $I(x) = 1$ if the event x occurs, 0 otherwise. Suppose that $I_k > cQ$, i.e. a full buffer can be cleared during an interval of length I_k. Then the index of the last accepted cell in the sub-interval, and the queue size seen by that last cell, are independent of the initial conditions. Hence, the new initial conditions for processor $k + 1$ are correct and it can perform its final iteration, regardless of the future state of processor k.

2. More generally, if for a given iteration the increase of the initial queue size (passed from processor $k - 1$) does not exceed the old value of I_k/c, then the new initial conditions for processor $k + 1$ will be the same as the old ones.

3. If j consecutive cells, $\{n + 1, n + 2, \ldots, n + j\}$, have the property that none of them are lost and none of them, except perhaps the first, finds an empty buffer, then that collection can be treated as a single 'packet' for the purpose of calculating the evolution of the queuing process. Instead of computing j pairs of recurrences (19) and (20), a single pair is evaluated:

$$q_{n+j} = q_n + j - \delta_{n,j} , \qquad (22)$$

$$d_{n+j} = d_n + \delta_{n,j}c , \qquad (23)$$

where

$$\delta_{n,j} = \left\lfloor \frac{A_{n+j} - d_n}{c} \right\rfloor .$$

The effectiveness of this technique has not been evaluated empirically. However, it appears to have the potential for reducing the amount of computation significantly.

Figure 5 illustrates the application of **1 & 2** above, where the interval is 20 seconds long and the buffer size Q is 3, with the work distributed over four processors. During the first iteration each processor computes the queue size trajectory for all of the cells in its sub-interval. Note that the algorithm only computes the queue size immediately before and after a cell arrival, the departures have been added to the

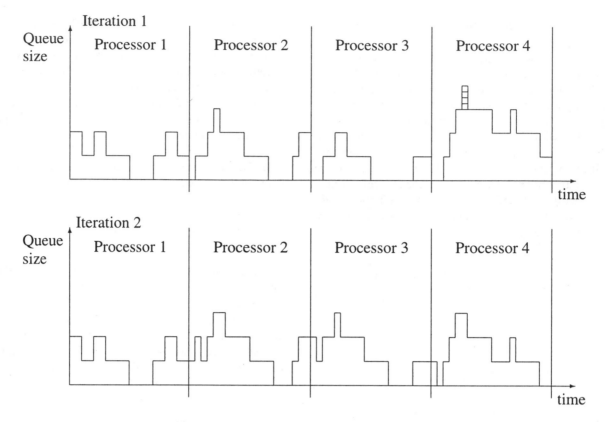

Figure 5. Example graph of queue sizes

diagram for clarity. In the case of processor 4 its fourth arrival will exceed the queue size, marked in the diagram as a shaded block. However in a future iteration this cell may be accepted, thus it is marked as lost here but is still kept in the list of arrivals.

Processor 2 contains enough idle time to absorb one cell in the queue from the previous processor. Processor 3 contains enough idle time to absorb any valid queue size from the previous processor. All cells that arrive to processor 3 after cQ idle time can be computed as final and the end state of its sub-interval is finalized.

In iteration 2 the end state (queue size after the last arrival and time of the last departure) from each processor is passed onto the next processor as the start state. Processor 2 receives a queue of size 1 from processor 1 and needs only to compute those cells that arrive before the first point where the queue size reaches zero, likewise for processor 3. Processor 4 receives a queue size of one and marks cell 4 as lost. It is removed from the arrival list and does not appear in the diagram for the final iteration. The end conditions are now passed from processor k to processor $k + 1$, as these new start conditions are identical for all processors the iterations terminate.

4. Experimental Results

The results were generated from running the test program on a cluster of eight PentiumII 233Mhz workstations, connected by fast Ethernet. The simulation was written using the LAM [14], implementation of MPI [15], running under Linux. Experimental results were also produced from the same cluster with the addition of a shared memory quad processor system running at 450MHz. This allows the number of processors to be increased to twelve.

Varying numbers of processors were used to produce results for two ATM systems, the first having eight bursty sources and the second having 24 sources. The offered load was chosen to ensure that the fraction of lost cells was just under 10^{-4}. Each simulation run represents 10^7 seconds of simulated time. During that time, approximately 1.2×10^7 cell arrivals occured in all cases. For simplicity, the cell inter-arrival times, the "on"and "off"periods were assumed to be exponentially distributed, with the cell transmission time assumed to be constant.

Since the object of this study is to examine the efficiency of the parallel simulation algorithms and the speedups that can be achieved, the only metric plotted is the ratio T_0/T_n, where T_0 is the execution time of the best *sequential* sim-

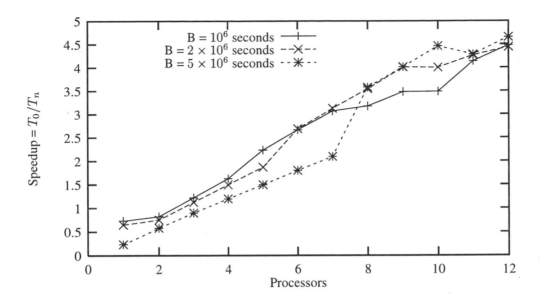

Figure 6. Results from a cluster with 8 input sources

ulation run on a single processor and T_n is the execution time of the parallel simulation run on n processors. This ratio is commonly known as the 'speedup' achieved by the algorithm. Note that T_1, the execution time of the parallel simulation run on 1 processor, is normally larger than T_0. If T_0/T_n is proportional to n, the parallel algorithm is said to achieve 'linear speedup'. Statistics about the lost cells were collected, but neither the point estimates nor the confidence intervals are displayed in the following graphs.

Figures 6 and 7 illustrate the speedup achieved as a function of the number of processors. Each figure shows the results for running the simulation with different interval sizes B. Figure 6 illustrates the situation with eight input sources, showing almost linear speedup for all interval lengths. Altering the interval length appears to have little effect on the overall speedup of the simulation. For very large intervals there is a difference, although slight. There is an apparent jump in performance between seven and eight processors, when the batch size is 5×10^6. This seems to be a consequence of the removal of page swapping as the amount of data handled by each processor decreases as the processor count increases.

Processors nine to twelve are included by using the use of the quad processor workstation. These processors are faster than the others and therefore compute their sections of the simulation path quicker. However, since there is no attempt at load balancing, the trend of the speedup remains as before.

Figure 7 shows similar results for the case of 24 bursty input sources. Here again we observe an almost linear speedup. The larger jump between seven and eight processors for $B = 5 \times 10^6$ is present here too, and probably has the same explanation.

5. Conclusion

We have demonstrated that a large sample path for a nontrivial communication system can be simulated in parallel on a distributed cluster of processors. Moreover, the parallelization is efficient, in the sense that a linear speedup is achieved. The major obstacle that has been overcome by the algorithms presented here is the large amount of data communicated between the processors. Normally the communication overheads swamp the benefits of parallelism. We have been able to eliminate most of the overheads by delegating more intelligence to the individual processors. Each processor is now able to decide accurately which arrivals to generate, so that they can be handled locally.

Dependencies between sub-intervals, due to lost cells, require some repetition of work performed by processors. However these iterations can be carried out efficiently without destroying the benefits of parallel simulation.

The relaxation techniques described here are not restricted to this model. The idea that each processor can work on an interval of the sample path, subsequently refining its knowledge in light of information received from other processors, can be applied to many different systems. However, the details of that allocation can have an important effect on performance. Unless all intervals converge quickly to their final states, the advantage of parallel processing can be lost.

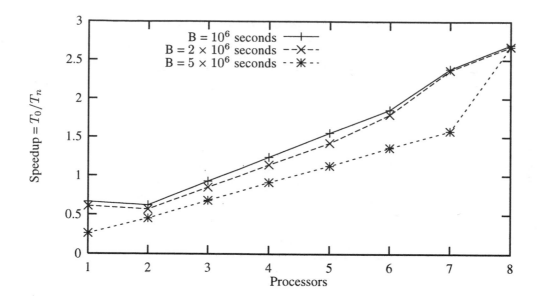

Figure 7. Results from a cluster with 24 input sources

References

[1] A.G. Greenberg, B.D. Lubachevsky, and I. Mitrani. Algorithms for Unboundedly Parallel Simulations, ACM TOCS, 91(9):201-221, August 1991.

[2] C.P. Kruskal, I. Rudolph and M. Snir. The Power of Parallel Prefix, IEEE Trans. Comp., 85(34):965-968, October 1985.

[3] L. Chen. Parallel Simulation by multi-instruction, longest-path algorithms, Queueing Systems, 97(27 no 1-2):37-54, 1997.

[4] K.M. Chandy, R. Sherman. Space-Time and Simulation, Proceedings of the SCS Multiconference on Distributed Simulation, Tampa, Florida, Society for Computer Simulation, 89:53-57, July 1989.

[5] A.S. McGough, I. Mitrani. Parallel Simulation of ATM Switches using Relaxation, IFIP ATM'98, 98(54), July 1998.

[6] Z. Xiao, B. Unger, R. Simmonds, J. Cleary. Scheduled Critical Channels in Conservative Parallel Discrete Event Simulation, PADS '99, 99:20-28, May 1999.

[7] C. Williamson, B. Unger, Z. Xiao. Parallel Simulation of ATM Networks: Case Study and Lessons Learned, CCBR '98, 98:78-88, June 1998.

[8] C.D. Caróthers, K.S. Perumalla. Efficient Optimistic Parallel Simulations using Reverse Computation, PADS '99, 99:126-135, May 1999.

[9] I. Nikolaidis, R. Fujimoto, C.A. Cooper. Time-Parallel Simulation of Cascaded Statistical Multiplexers, ACM Sigmetrics, 94:231-239, May 1994.

[10] R.M. Fujimoto, I. Nikolaidis, C.A. Cooper. Parallel Simulation of Statistical Multiplexers, Discrete Event Dynamic Systems-Theory and Applications, 95(5):115-140, April 1995.

[11] J.J. Wang, M. Abrams. Approximate Time-Parallel Simulation of Queuing systems with losses, 1992 Winter Simulation Conference, 92:700-708, December 1992.

[12] F. Baccelli, M. Canales. Parallel Simulation of Stochastic Petri Nets Using Recurrence Equations, ACM Transactions on Modeling and Computer Simulation, 93(Vol. 3, No. 1):20-41, January 1993.

[13] S. Andradóttir, T.J. Ott, Time-Segmentation Parallel Simulation of Networks of Queues with Loss or Communication Blocking, ACM Transactions on Modeling and Computer Simulation, 95(Vol. 5, No. 4):269-305, October 1995.

[14] LAM / MPI Parallel Computing, http://www.mpi.nd.edu/lam/, 09/1999.

[15] Message Passing Interface Forum, http://www.mpi-forum.org/, 09/1999.

Optimizing Cell-size in Grid-Based DDM

Rassul Ayani[*], Farshad Moradi and Gary Tan
School of Computing
National University of Singapore
Singapore 119260
Corresponding Email: rassul@comp.nus.edu.sg
Fax: (+65) 779 4580

Abstract

In a large-scale distributed simulation with thousands of dynamic objects, efficient communication of data among these objects is an important issue. The broadcasting mechanism specified by the Distributed Interactive Simulation (DIS) standards is not suitable for large scale distributed simulations.

In the High Level Architecture (HLA) paradigm, the Runtime Infrastructure (RTI) provides a set of services, such as data distribution management (DDM) among federates. The goal of the DDM module in RTI is to make the data communication more efficient by sending the data only to those federates that need the data, as opposed to the broadcasting mechanism employed by DIS.

Several DDM schemes have appeared in the literature. In this paper, we discuss grid-based DDM and develop a DDM model that uses grids for matching the publishing/subscription regions, and for data filtering. We show that appropriate choice of the grid-cell size is crucial in obtaining good performance. We develop an analytical model and derive a formula for identifying the optimal cell size in grid-based DDM.

Keywords: distributed simulation, HLA, data communication, group communication, and data filtering

1. Introduction

In High Level Architecture (HLA) paradigm, the Runtime Infrastructure (RTI) is similar to a distributed operating system for the simulation federates. The RTI provides a set of services, including data distribution management (DDM) among federates. In DDM, each federate may inform the RTI about its intention to *publish* some data or it may *subscribe* to receive a subset of the published data.

For instance, consider a war gaming scenario where hundreds of objects (e.g., tanks or airplanes) are moving within a battlefield. An object (e.g., a tank) may publish its current position, or it may subscribe to receive the relevant position update data published by other objects (e.g., those objects that are within its radar range).

The DDM can be formulated as a producer/consumer problem, where the goods supplied by the producers (the publishers) are changing and similarly the consumers (the subscribers) demands are also changing with time. The task of DDM consists of two parts:

(i) to match the dynamic supplies to the dynamic demand, and

(ii) to distribute the goods to the consumers.

Thus, the main concern is *how to match the dynamic supplies with the dynamic demands, and how to distribute the products to the consumers efficiently.*

In this problem formulation, one may employ the following two-step approach:

a) Matching phase: determine the **potential** consumers of each producer for the next T time units. Since the groups are dynamic, it would be very difficult to select the consumers accurately. Hence, the approach would be to determine the **potential** consumers for each producer.

b) Refinement phase: refine the selected set by eliminating the less likely consumers.

Several researchers have applied the grid-based technique to the "Matching phase" of the two-step approach described above. Cohen and Kemkes [2, 3]

---

[*] On leave from the Royal Institute of Technology (KTH), Sweden

discuss the impact of the update/subscription rate on performance of DDM. Hook and Calvin [11] and Rak and Hook [8] study the performance of grid-based DDM and show the impact of grid cell size on communication costs. Rizik et al [7] use a predator-prey model to identify the impact of cell size on performance of DDM.

In this paper, we employ a grid-based DDM to match the supplied data to the demands, but we also use the grid cells to refine the set of customers (Refinement phase of the above approach), i.e., we use the grids for both matching and filtering. We partition the routing space into a grid of cells (see Figure 2) and map supplies and demands to the grid cells. We assign two lists to each cell, namely:

(i) a list of those federates that publish within the cell (list of publishers), and

(ii) a list of federates that are interested to receive the data published within the cell (list of subscribers). Since the objects are moving and their publishing/subscribing region will be changing, the lists associated with each cell will be changed accordingly.

In grid-based DDM, an important issue is the size of the grid cells. We develop a model to study the impact of cell size on performance. *Our main contribution is the development of the grid-based filtering model and derivation of a formula that can be used to identify the optimal grid-cell size (see section 3).*

The rest of the paper is organized as follows. In section 2, we review some of the data filtering mechanisms discussed by HLA community. In section 3 we develop a model to identify the optimal cell size of a grid-based filtering algorithm. In section 4 we discuss some of our results and finally in section 5 we summarize our findings.

2. Data filtering mechanisms

Several filtering mechanisms have appeared in the literature and some of them have been implemented in RTI. Below, we will briefly describe these mechanisms and discuss their expected performance.

2.1. Class-based DDM

In this approach, a group of objects (e.g., all tanks) is defined as a class. A federate may subscribe to an object class' attribute values (or to an interaction class) and it will receive all updates of the specified attribute values for *all* objects of that class. This type of data distribution eliminates the delivery of attributes of the class (e.g., position of tanks) to those who have not subscribed to it. However, a federate cannot subscribe to a subset of a *class*. For instance, an object cannot subscribe to all *red* tanks only, if all tanks are defined as a class. The class-based filtering approach may be acceptable for a small federation with few objects in each class. However, for

simulations with a large number of objects in each class some additional filtering mechanism is needed.

2.2. Region-based DDM

A fundamental construct used by DDM is the routing space (RS). A routing space is a multidimensional coordinate system through which a federate may express its interest in receiving data (subscription region) or declares its intention to send data (publishing region). When a publishing region P and a subscription region S have a non-empty intersection, the RTI matches these two and establishes communications connectivity between the publishing and subscribing federates. Figure 1 shows one subscription region (S_1) and two publishing regions P_1 and P_2. In this example S_1 and P_1 overlap and thus the attribute updates from the object associated with P_1 will be routed to the federate that created S_1. However, S_1 and P_2 do not overlap and thus P_2's attributes will not be routed to S_1.

In figure 1, S_1 (more precisely the federate associated with S_1) *should* receive updates of (the object associated with) P_1 as long it stays in the shaded area. However, in region based filtering S_1 receives *all* updates within P_1. Thus, S_1 receives some ***irrelevant data*** (those within P_1, but outside of the shaded area) as well.

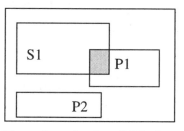

Figure 1: region based filtering

The region-based filtering described above suffers from two drawbacks:

1. Each subscriber S_i may receive a large number of irrelevant messages, as explained above

2. If a publisher i changes its publishing region P_i, the RTI must find P_I's intersection with each and every subscriber. If the number of subscribers, m, is high the cost will be unacceptable. The grid-based filtering discussed in the next subsection provides a better alternative.

2.3. Grid-based filtering

In the grid-based DDM, the routing space is divided into a grid of cells. The publishing and subscription regions are mapped into the grid-cells. A subscription region S is assigned to a publishing region P, if they share at least one cell (matching phase). For instance, in figure 2, S1 and P1 share cell C22 and thus S1 is seen as P1's consumer.

The grid-based filtering mechanism used in this paper is different from the traditional grid-based DDM. In our DDM model, each routing space is partitioned into a grid of cells. The application user specifies the subscription and publication areas as regions, but the DDM maps these regions into cells. This means that the user uses regions as in DMSO RTI, whereas our DDM works with cells as explained below. We associate two lists with each cell.

a) A list identifying those federates whose publishing region overlaps with the cell (list of cell's publishers), and

b) A second list identifying those federates that have shown interest to receive data published within the cell (list of cell's subscribers).

Based on these two lists, we identify the subscribers and publishers of each cell. As opposed to the region-based, where a whole region is assigned to a publisher, here we assign a portion of a publisher's region to a subscriber. For instance, in figure 2, P_1 and S_1 overlap in one cell only (cell C22) meaning that S_1 is interested to receive the data published in cell C_{22} only. As opposed to the region based filtering and the traditional grid-based filtering, the data published in cell C_{21} by P_1 will not be sent to S1. This is the refinement phase of the approach. Hence, our grid-based filtering reduces the amount of unnecessary communications by refining the subscribers' area of interest.

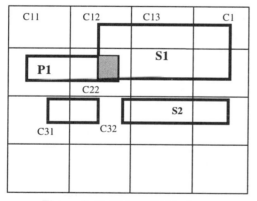

Figure 2: Grid-based filtering

We claim that our grid-based filtering is better than region-based and the traditional grid-based filtering in many situations, though it does not produce a 100% filtering of data. For instance, in Figure 2, P2 publishes in cell C32 and (according to our scheme) S2 has subscribed for C32. Thus, the data published by P2 in C32 is sent to S2. However, these data is outside of S2's subscription region and will not be used. This *irrelevant data* lies within the boundary cells of the subscription region only and depends on the grid cell size. The unnecessary (irrelevant) data communicated in our grid-based filtering model is generally less than the irrelevant data

communicated in the region-based (and traditional grid-based) DDM. In our model, the larger the cell size the greater is the amount of unnecessary data that is communicated. On the other hand, the smaller the grid cell size the larger is the amount of work required to update the cell's subscribers and publishers lists. Hence, there should be an optimal size for the grid cells.

In the next section we will develop a mathematical model to determine the optimal cell size for our grid-based filtering scheme.

3. Performance of the grid-based filtering mechanism

Consider a simulation model with m subscribers and n publishers. Assume that the two-dimensional routing space (RS) has been partitioned into a grid with quadratic cells and length g (i.e., the cell area, s, is g^2). Similarly, assume that each subscriber j has a quadratic subscription region S_j with length $L_{j,s}$ ($S_j = L_{j,s}^2$) and each publisher i has a publishing region P_i with length $L_{i,p}$ ($P_i = L_{i,p}^2$). Consider the time-stepped simulation algorithm given in Figure 3. In this algorithm, the regions are updated every *k* time-steps, but the published data (e.g., position of the objects in the simulation model) are updated in each time-step. Each region is defined in such a way to ensure that the object (publisher or subscriber) remains in its region until the next region update. For instance, if an object can move at most 50m (in any possible direction) in each time-step, its region for the next k time steps can be defined as a square of length 100*k.

Initialization:
- partition the routing space into cells with length g
- create two empty lists for each cell, publishers (P-list) and subscribers (S-list)
end_initialization
  for t= t_o, t_o + kdt, t_o + 2kdt, ..., do
    begin
    - calculate new publishing region for each publisher;
      map it to the grid and update the cells P-list
    - calculate new subscription region for each subscriber;
      map it to the grid and update cells S-list
    - for each publisher, those cells with at least one subscriber, i.e., **non-empty** cells, are identified
    - for t_1=t, t+dt, t+2t, ..., t +(k-1)dt
      begin
        -each publisher sends its update to the subscribers of its current position, if the corresponding cell is non-empty
        -each subscriber eliminates the irrelevant data it receives
      end
  end

Figure 3: a distributed simulation algorithm using grid-based filtering

3.1. Updating the publishing regions

Consider n publishers moving in a two-dimensional routing space. Consider the time-stepped simulation algorithm depicted in Figure 3, where a new publishing region is calculated after every **k** time steps. Consider a publisher P_i with coordinate (x_i, y_i) and define a quadratic publishing region $R_{i,p}$ with length $L_{i,p}$ such that P_i remains in $R_{i,p}$ during the next k time-steps. Thus, $R_{i,p}$ determines the boundaries for P_I's movement in the next k time-steps. Further, assume that $R_{i,p}$ is based on the maximum speed of the publisher and thus remains constant in size during the simulation. For instance, if the maximum speed of P_i is V_i then it may move at most $k* V_i$ in each direction, and thus $L_{i,p} = 2*k* V_i$. If P_i with coordinate (x_i, y_i) is placed at the center of its region and in each k time-steps its x and y coordinates are changed by (dx_i, dy_i), then

$$dx_i \leq \frac{L_{i,p}}{2} \quad and \quad dy_i \leq \frac{L_{i,p}}{2}.$$

The changes in P_I's region (the non-shaded area in figure 4 denoted by $R_{i,u}$) must be updated due to movement of P_i. The area of $R_{i,u}$ can be calculated according to equation (1)

$$R_{i,u} = 2L_{i,p}^2 - 2(L_{i,p} - dx_i)(L_{i,p} - dy_i) = 2L_{i,p}(dx_i + dy_i) - 2dx_i dy_i$$
(1)

Consequently, the corresponding number of cells, $P_{i,u}$ that must be updated would be:

$$P_{i,u} = \frac{R_{i,u}}{g^2}$$
(2)

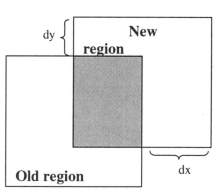

Figure 4: updating a region

3.2. Updating the subscription region

Similarly, assume that a subscriber S_j moves (dx_j, dy_j) units away from its previous position after k time-steps.

The changes in its region, $R_{j,u}$, and the corresponding number of cells $S_{j,u}$ that must be updated would be:

$$R_{j,u} = 2L_{j,s}^2 - 2(L_{j,s} - dx_j)(L_{j,s} - dy_j)$$
(3)

$$S_{j,u} = \frac{R_{j,u}}{g^2}$$
(4)

3.3. Number of irrelevant messages

A subscriber j may receive irrelevant messages at its boundary cells, as discussed in
Section 2.3 and shown in the Figure 2. If we assume that the publishers are uniformly
distributed in the boundary cells, then the number of irrelevant messages received by
a subscriber at the boundary cells would be proportional to the uncovered boundary area (shaded in fig. 5).
Let us denote the uncovered boundary (shaded) area in figure 5 by A_s and the density of the publishers in the subscription region by D. The number of irrelevant messages in each iteration of the Simulation Algorithm (Figure 3) received by a subscriber j, denoted by I_j, will be:

$$I_j = D.A_s$$
(5)

But, how can A_s be calculated?
Consider a grid with cell size g. How can we map a subscription region S that is equal with a cell area (i.e., $S = g^2$) to this grid? S may be mapped to one, two, or four cells as shown in Figure 6. Consequently, the uncovered boundary area, denoted by A_s would be 0, g^2 or $3g^2$ respectively, as shown in Figure 6. Intuitively, one could claim that the uncovered area on each side of S is uniformly distributed. Hence, we hypothesized that that A_s can be approximated by

$$A_s = (L_{i,s} + g)^2 - L_{i,s}^2 = g^2 + 2gL_{i,s}$$
(6)

To test this hypothesis, we developed a Monte Carlo simulation and ran it for a given g and different values of S, $S = L_{j,s} * L_{j,s}$
Where $L_{j,s}$ is the length of the subscription region of subscriber j, and g is the length of a grid cell.

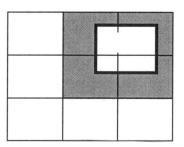

Figure 5: Irrelevant messages

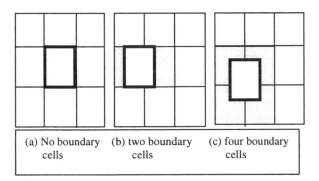

| (a) No boundary cells | (b) two boundary cells | (c) four boundary cells |

Figure 6: mapping a region to the grid cells

For each given cell and region size we generated 10000 objects and place them randomly in the two-dimensional routing space and calculated the value of A_s for each object. The result of this simulation for various values of g is presented in Table 1. As this table illustrates, for each given pair of g and L there are always three different estimated (experimented) values for A_s, but one of them occurs with much higher frequency. In Figure 7, we illustrate the discrepancy between the value of A_s obtained by this simulation (denoted as expt) and the calculated value (denoted by calc) using equation (6) for various sizes of g.

Based on these results, one may substitute A_s by its approximated measure given in (6) and obtain:

$$I_j = D.((L_{j,s} + g)^2 - L_{j,s}^2) = D.(g^2 + 2.L_{j,s}.g)$$
(7)

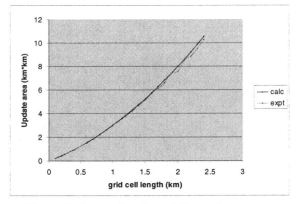

Figure 7: Approximation of the update area

3.4. Cost of grid-based filtering

The cost associated with the grid-based filtering algorithm described in Figure 3 consists of the following parts:
(i) Mapping of the regions to the grid-cells and update of the two lists (P-list and S-list) associated with each cell

(ii) Communication of the irrelevant messages in the boundary cells, and
(iii) Detection and elimination of the irrelevant messages by subscriber.

Obviously, choosing smaller cell size will increase the cost of updating the two lists, but it will decrease the number of irrelevant messages at the boundary cells. On the other hand, a larger cell size would decrease the list update costs but increase the number of irrelevant messages. Hence, there should be an optimal cell size.

In each super-step of the simulation (an iteration of the upper loop in Figure 3 is denoted as a super step) the new subscription/publishing regions are calculated, and the corresponding P-lists and S-lists are updated. However, in each time-step the publisher sends its published data (e.g., the position of the moving object) directly to its subscribers. In each super-step of the simulation (Figure 3) the overhead of the grid-based filtering consists of mapping the P and S regions onto grid cells, updating the cell lists (P-lists and S-lists), and the cost associated with the irrelevant messages.

Assuming that c_1 is the amortized cost of updating one item of the lists (it includes amortized cost of mapping regions onto cells and updating the cell lists) and c_2 is the cost of one irrelevant message (including communication, detection and elimination), the cost of one step of the simulation can be expressed as a function of grid-cell size by equation (8):

$$C(g) = c_1 \sum_{i=1}^{m} P_{i,u} + c_1 \sum_{j=1}^{n} S_{j,u} + k.c_2.\sum_{j=1}^{n} I_j$$
(8)

3.5. Minimization of the grid-based filtering cost

Using equation (2), (4) and (7) and (8), we obtain:

$$C(g) = c_1 \sum_{i=1}^{m} \frac{R_{i,u}}{g^2} + c_1 \sum_{j=1}^{n} \frac{R_{j,u}}{g^2} + k.c_2.D.\sum_{j=1}^{n} (g^2 + 2.L_{j,s}.g)$$
(9)

where $R_{j,u}$ and $R_{i,u}$ are independent of g.

The value of g that minimizes the cost can be obtained by setting $C'(g) = 0$

$$C'(g) = -\frac{2c_1.(\sum_{i=1}^{m} R_{i,u} + \sum_{j=1}^{n} R_{j,u})}{g^3} + 2kc_2.D.\sum_{j=1}^{n} (g + L_{j,s}) = 0$$
(10)

If we assume that g>0, we may multiply equation (9) by g^3 and obtain equation (11).

$$kc_2 D \sum_{j=1}^{n} (g^4 + L_{j,s}g^3) - c_1(\sum_{i=1}^{m} R_{i,u} + \sum_{j=1}^{n} R_{j,u}) = 0$$
(11)

Or

$$\sum_{j=1}^{n}(g^4+L_{j,s}g^3)-\frac{c_1}{k.c_2 D}(\sum_{i=1}^{m}R_{i,u}+\sum_{j=1}^{n}R_{j,u})=0 \quad (12)$$

We can find the optimal value of g (for given values of m, n, L_s, L_p, dx_s, dy_s, dx_p, dy_p, D, c_1 and c_2) by solving equation (12). Approximation techniques such as Newton-Raphson method can be used to solve this equation.

4. An example

Consider a war gaming scenario where n tanks are attacking a target T and m aircraft are defending T. In this scenario the aircraft are equipped with radar to detect the tanks (the range of the radar corresponds to the subscription region of the aircraft). However, the tanks have no radar and thus cannot detect the aircraft. Thus, tanks have no subscription region and only publish their position while aircraft subscribe to the data published by the tanks and do not publish anything. For simplicity, assume that all tanks have the same speed, and similarly all aircraft have the same air speed. In our simulation, we make the following assumptions:

-The publishing and subscription regions are updated every 60 seconds (i.e., k=60), but the position of the tanks are updated every second (i.e., dt=1).
- The tanks move with an average speed of 60km/h and a maximum of 90km/h (i.e., Lp=2*90*60/3600=3km).
- The aircraft fly with an average speed of 900km/h and max 1200km/h (i.e., Ls=2*1200*60/3600=40km).
- Number of aircraft=10; number of tanks=50; density of tanks near the target is 1 tank/10km^2 , i.e., D=0.1.
- We assume that c1=1ms and c2=5ms (we will discuss the impact of these two parameters on performance in the next section).

Figure 8 illustrates the overhead of grid-based filtering. In this Figure, P/S denotes the cost of updating the cell lists (P-lists and S-lists), I_m denotes the cost of communicating, detecting and eliminating the irrelevant messages; and C denotes the total overhead of the grid-based filtering (C is sum of P/S and I_m). These values are calculated for various sizes of g using equations (2), (4), (6), and (8). As this figure clearly shows, the choice of cell size substantially affects the grid-based filtering overhead. For instance, for g=0.2 the cost is 312312ms to execute one time-step of the simulation loop and if we choose g=5 the cost would be 127992ms.

Further, we have used equation (12) to find the optimal value of g. For this homogeneous system, equation (12) is simplified as

$$(g^4+L_s g^3)-\frac{c_1}{n.k.c_2 D}(m.R_p+n.R_s)=0 \quad (13)$$

where Rp and Rs denote the publishing and subscription regions respectively. Replacing the parameters by their

corresponding values will transfer equation (13) to equation (14)

$$g^4+40g^3-41=0 \quad (14)$$

Solving equation (14), e.g., by Newton-Raphson's method, gives $g_{optimal}=1$. And thus the minimum cost is obtained for this grid-cell size which is $C(g_{optimal}=1)=36600ms$.

5. Discussion

We have developed a simple model to investigate the communication costs in grid-based time-stepped distributed simulations. Our model can be used:
- To estimate the costs of grid-based data filtering
- To find the optimal cell size of the grid
In our analysis, several issues deserve further discussion:
(1) We assumed quadratic regions, but the analysis can be easily extended to models with "circular" regions.
(2) The parameters we used in our analysis can be classified into three categories:

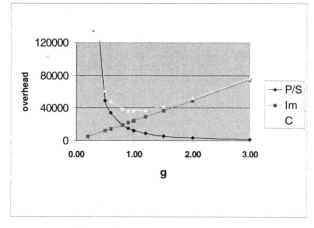

Figure 8: Impact of cell size on overhead

(i) System dependent, i.e., parameters of the system being simulated such as speed of the moving objects and radar ranges.
(ii) Model dependent, i.e., parameters that depend on the characteristics of the simulation model such as size of the regions and frequency of updating the regions (parameter k).
(iii) Platform dependent, i.e., parameters, that depend on the simulation platform (including both hardware and software being used) such as c1 and c2.
The value of the parameters in category (i) and (ii) are rather easy to capture. However, the platform dependent parameters are much more difficult to estimate.
In our notation c_1 and c_2 denote the cost of updating one element of the cell lists and the cost of communicating

one irrelevant message respectively. Obviously, these parameters depend on the software and hardware being used. For instance, if the interconnection network of a distributed system is upgraded (to a faster one) the value of c2 will decrease. For this reason, we calculated the optimal cell size for different values of c_1 and c_2 using equation (8). In Figure 9 we show the impact of processing to communication ratio (i.e., c_1/c_2) on the optimal value of g. As this Figure illustrates, the higher the ratio of processing to communication cost the greater the value of g-optimal will be.

(3) We presented a time-stepped simulation model in Figure 3, where all objects of the simulation (all publishers and subscribers) modify their regions after k time-steps. Certainly the choice of k will be essential to the performance of the simulation. Increasing k decreases the region update frequency, but increases the number of irrelevant messages. On the other hand, decreasing k will increase the region update cost but decrease the cost of irrelevant messages. Further research is needed to identify the optimal size of k for a given application

(4) Figure 3 represents a simple time-stepped simulation, but in many practical situations the objects move with different speeds and the update frequencies of the regions are different (for instance a fast moving airplane may update its regions more frequently than a slow object such as a tank). In such a case one may prefer an event-driven simulation. . In Figure 10 we illustrate a sketch of an event-driven simulation, where each object modifies its position after moving a certain distance D, and calls a routine to update its region whenever it approaches the end of its current publication (or subscription) region. Thus, different objects may modify their position and their regions at different points in time. Fortunately, our analysis is easily extendable to event-driven simulations. For instance, consider an event-driven simulation model with two objects, a fast and a slow one. Assume that the slow object modifies its regions after T time units, while the fast object modifies its regions K times within T. We can use this frequency weight and develop a formula similar to equation (12) for calculating g-optimal for the event-driven simulations.

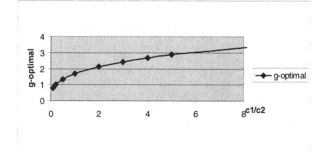

Figure 9: Optimal size of g for various c1/c2 ratio

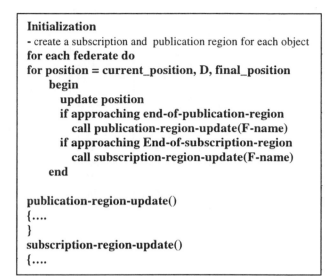

```
Initialization
- create a subscription and  publication region for each object
for each federate do
for position = current_position, D, final_position
    begin
        update position
        if approaching end-of-publication-region
            call publication-region-update(F-name)
        if approaching End-of-subscription-region
            call subscription-region-update(F-name)
    end

publication-region-update()
{....
}
subscription-region-update()
{....
```

Figure 10: a sketch of an event-driven DDM

6. Conclusions

Efficient data distribution is an important issue in large-scale distributed simulations with several thousands of entities. The broadcasting mechanism employed in Distributed Interactive Simulation (DIS) standards generates unnecessary network traffic and is not suitable for large scale and dynamic simulations. An efficient data distribution mechanism should filter the data and forward to a client only those data that are needed.

In this paper we discussed grid-based data filtering and its impact on performance of distributed simulation. We have developed a grid-based DDM model, where a grid is used to match the subscribers to the publishers, but also for the purpose of data filtering. We have also developed an analytical model to study the impact of cell size on performance of grid-based filtering. We derived a formula for finding the optimal cell size in a grid-based filtering in a time-stepped simulation. Our main contribution can be summarized as:

We have developed a grid-based filtering scheme that is different from those which have appeared in the literature.

We have shown that the grid cell size has a substantial impact on the network traffic and hence affects the performance of distributed simulations.

We have derived a formula for the calculation of the optimal grid cell size for a time-stepped distributed simulation scenario. The optimal cell size minimizes the cost of network traffic and updating the group lists associated with each cell.

We discussed how our model could be extended to event-driven simulations.

Grid cell size	Calculated value	Avg. Expmtl value	Alt. 1	Frequency of Alt. 1 (%)	Alt. 2	Frequency of Alt. 2 (%)	Alt. 3	Frequency of Alt. 3 (%)
10	2100	1887	2100	82	1000	17	0	1
20	4400	4161	4400	90	2000	10	0	0
30	6900	6609	4400	50	8000	42	12500	9
40	9600	9287	9200	49	4400	28	15600	23
50	12500	12213	12500	96	5000	4	0	0
60	15600	15200	11600	46	22400	42	4400	12
70	18900	18573	19400	49	9600	34	34100	17
80	22400	21832	15600	59	28400	35	47600	5
90	26100	25615	22400	81	38600	18	62900	1
100	30000	29571	30000	98	10000	2	0	0
150	52500	51430	12500	12	35000	46	80000	42
200	80000	75484	70000	49	30000	29	150000	21
250	112500	105006	52500	42	115000	46	240000	13
300	150000	144971	170000	43	80000	47	350000	10
350	192500	185130	112500	54	235000	39	480000	7
400	240000	222784	150000	63	310000	33	630000	4

Table 1: Result of the Monte Carlo simulation (with 10000 objects) for different values of g (grid cell size) with constant region size L=100. The three experimented A_s values are indicated with their frequencies in the table, as well as the weighted average experimental value and the calculated A_s derived from equation 6.

7. References

1. Berrached, A., Beheshti, M., and Sirisaengtaksin, O. (1998). "Evaluation of Grid-based Data Distribution in the HLA", Proceedings of the 1998 Conference on Simulation Methods and Applications, Orlando FL, November 1-3 1998, pp. 209-215.
2. Danny Cohen and Andreas Kemkes,User-Level Measurement of DDM Scenarios, in Proceedings of the Simulation Interoperability Workshop (SIW), Spring 1997
3. Danny Cohen and Andreas Kemkes, Applying user-level measurements to RTI 1.3 Release 2, in Proceedings of the Simulation Interoperability Workshop (SIW), Fall 1998
4. HLA Data Distribution Management: Design Documents Version 0.7 (November 12, 1997)
5. Petty, M. D. and Mukherjee, A. (1997). "Experimental Comparison of d-Rectangle Intersection Algorithms Applied to HLA Data Distribution", Proceedings of the 1997 Distributed Simulation Symposium, Orlando FL, September 8-12 1997, pp. 13-26.
6. Pratt, D. R. (1999). "Quantifying Interest Partitioning "in a Distributed Model", Proceedings of the Eighth Conference on Computer Generated Forces and Behavioral Representation, Orlando FL, pp. 517-528.
7. Rizik, P et al., Optimal geographic routing space cell size in the FEDEP for prey-centric models, in Proceedings of the Simulation Interoperability Workshop (SIW), Spring 1998
8. Rak, S.J. and Van Hook, D.J., Evaluation of grid-based relevance filtering for multicast group assignment, in in Proceedings of the Distributed Interactive Simulation, 1996
9. Sundir Srinivasan and Paul F. Reynolds, Communications, Data Distribution and other Goodies in the HLA Performance Model, In proceedings of the Winter Simulation conference 1997.
10. Tacic I. and Richard Fujimoto, Synchronized data distribution management in distributed simulation, in Proceedings of the Simulation Interoperability Workshop (SIW), Spring 1997
11. Van Hook, D.J. and James O. Calvin, Data distribution management in RTI 1.3, in Proceedings of the Simulation Interoperability Workshop (SIW), Spring 1998.
12. Wieland F., Hawley L and Blume L, An Empirical study of Data Partitioning and Replication in Parallel Simulation", Proceedings of the %th IEEE Distributed Memory Computing Conference , April 1990.

Distributed, Parallel Simulation of Multiple, Deliberative Agents

A.M.Uhrmacher   K.Gugler

Department of Computer Science

Universität Ulm

D-89069 Ulm

Germany

e-mail: lin@informatik.uni-ulm.de, kgugler@mathematik.uni-ulm.de

Abstract

Multi-agent systems comprise multiple, deliberative agents embedded in and recreating patterns of interactions. Each agent's execution consumes considerable storage and calculation capacities. For testing multi-agent systems, distributed parallel simulation techniques are required that take the dynamic pattern of composition and interaction of multi-agent systems into account. Analyzing the behavior of agents in virtual, dynamic environments necessitates relating the simulation time to the actual execution time of agents. Since the execution time of deliberative components can hardly be foretold, conservative techniques based on lookahead are not applicable. On the other hand, optimistic techniques become very expensive if mobile agents and the creation and deletion of model components are affected by a rollback. The developed simulation layer of JAMES (a Java Based Agent Modeling Environment for Simulation) implements a moderately optimistic strategy which splits simulation and external deliberation into different threads and allows simulation and deliberation to proceed concurrently by utilizing simulation events as synchronization points.

1 Introduction

The definition of agents subsumes a multitude of different facets [17]. Agents are reactive, deliberative, or combine reactive with deliberative capabilities. They should be sufficiently flexible to adapt to changing environments and changing requirements. Reasoning strategies allow them to anticipate the consequences of possible actions and choose the most rational action. Deliberation is typically a time and space consuming operation. Hybrid agents combine deliberation with a reactive behavior pattern to allow timely reactions within a dynamic environment. Besides these "complex" internal processes, multi-agent systems exhibit structural behavior as well [14]. Agents are mobile and solve problems by creating new software components during runtime, moving between locations, and initiating or joining groups of other software components [5].

JAMES, a Java-Based Agent Modeling Environment for Simulation, [15, 16] constitutes a framework which is aimed at supporting experiments with agents under temporal and resource constraints. Its core libraries provide the means for the description of variable structure models and their distributed, parallel execution. For that purpose, JAMES reuses and combines concepts of distributed systems and parallel discrete event simulation with ideas of endomorphy, i.e. models which contain internal models about themselves and their environment [18], and variable structure models, i.e. models whose description entails the possibility to change their own structure and behavior [15, 16]. The focus of this paper will be on the parallel simulation techniques employed.

2 JAMES - A Short Sketch

The model design in JAMES resembles that of parallel DEVS (Discrete Event System Specification) [19], enriched by means to support variable structures. Time triggered automata with the ability to assess and access their own structure are the coarse frame for the description of *BDI* agents whose attitudes comprises beliefs, desires, and intentions [15], and other agent architectures and for testing single modules, e.g. planning or learning components.

As does DEVS, JAMES distinguishes between atomic and coupled models. Testing of agents means rooting mental attitudes within the state of an atomic model, embedding deliberation, reaction and filtering of options within the state transition functions, and transforming the activities of an agent into JAMES constructs. An agent might need some time to decide which action to take, this "reaction" and "deliberation" time is translated into the atomic model's

101

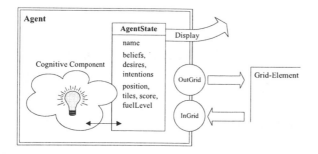

Figure 1. Agents in TILEWORLD

time-advance function. The chosen action of an agent are translated into outputs of the atomic model or into invoking JAMES methods to initiate structural changes, e.g. adding an agent to a location (Figure 1).

Atomic models are able to create new models, to add existing ones within the embedding coupled model. They can delete themselves, and determine their interaction with their environment. A model can initiate its movement from one location to another. It can initiate its move, but for its completion, i.e. for being embedded within the new context, it needs the cooperation of an on-site model. To initiate structural changes elsewhere agents have to turn to communication and negotiation in JAMES. Thus, a movement from one coupled model to another implies that another atomic model complies with the request to add the moving model into the new interaction context. To facilitate modeling, all atomic models are equipped with default methods that allow them to react to requests, e.g. to add models, to create new ones, or to delete themselves. However, these default reactions can be suppressed to decide deliberately what requests shall be executed. The range of structural changes a model can directly execute is restricted to avoid conflicts between concurrent structural changes [16].

Typically, the objective of testing is to analyze how agents cope with knowledge constraints, i.e. incomplete and uncertain knowledge, and with temporal constraints in dynamic and open environments. To test the timeliness of an agent's activities within a virtual world, it becomes necessary to relate the simulation time to the time needed for deliberation.

Some test beds define the simulated time depending on the used deliberation component and the size of the knowledge base [4], others weigh and count instructions which are executed during "deliberation". This presupposes that the deliberation component can be executed in a timed environment, e.g. "Timed Lisp" which simply overloads the standard lisp operators [1]. Most test beds determine the deliberation time as a function of the actually used computation time [3]. Even though in this case noise is induced due to changing work loads, which hampers repeatable test

runs, it is the most flexible and simplistic approach in testing agent architectures and components. Neither does it presuppose a white box implementation nor a specific implementation language. Therefore, we choose this time model to facilitate the testing of different planning systems [10].

3 The Problem

Most test beds for multi-agent systems do not execute their models concurrently. They simply maintain the illusion of simultaneity on a single machine. If only a single deliberative agent is tested in a dynamic environment [1] or the coordination strategies of a moderate number of reactive agents [7], there is no need for a distributed, parallel execution of agents. To efficiently test more than a single deliberative agent, which consumes significant space and computation resources, a concurrent, distributed simulation layer is necessary.

As a first step, we adopted the DEVS parallel simulator in JAMES to exploit the parallelism inherent in the model. As does DEVS, Parallel DEVS [2] associates with each atomic model and each coupled model a simulator and a coordinator, respectively. Thus, the compositional model finds its pendant at the execution level in a hierarchy of *processors*, i.e. *simulators* and *coordinators*, controlled by a so-called *root coordinator*. In this hierarchy, coordinators are associated with coupled models, and simulators with atomic models. The latter form the leafs of the processor tree.

As does Parallel DEVS, JAMES propagates messages, so called *-messages, top down the model tree each time an event is scheduled. Each processor knows how many inputs its associated model will receive at the current time step. It waits for these inputs, which are forwarded by the #-message, to arrive and executes the transition function. Messages indicating the completion of a transition, so called done-messages, report the component's time of next event, and, optionally, structural changes to the coordinator. Each coordinator waits for all its activated components to finish their transition, executes the indicated structural changes, and sends a summary to its own coordinator. Eventually, a done-message reaches the root coordinator. Thereafter, the next simulation step is initiated by the root coordinator.

The problem with this approach is apparent. The time base of JAMES is "quasi continuous" and only events which happen exactly at the same simulation time are processed concurrently. The virtual time an agent needs for generating a plan is determined based on the time it needs for computation. Thus, the event of two or more agents deliberating concurrently will be extremely rare. Not surprisingly, distributing the execution has degraded the performance of most parallel test runs.

The agents' transition functions call the deliberation system, e.g. the planning system. Depending on the time actually needed by the planning system, each agent will determine its time of next event. The time of next event forms a necessary part of the done-message which is sent by the simulator to the coordinator. The problem is that each transition - and thus the simulator and the entire simulation - waits for the planning system to complete. Only thereafter, the time of next event can be determined, and only then a done-message can be sent to the coordinator. Since each coordinator waits for all its components to complete, i.e. for their done-messages, before it sends a done-message to its own coordinator, the entire simulation is blocked. The absurdness is that the simulator waits for the time actually needed for generating the plan to announce its time of next event to its coordinator, rather than for the results. The results will not be needed until the simulation has advanced to the time of next event, which might be in the far future. However, all other events are blocked until the time of next event, the termination of the deliberation, is scheduled, which unfortunately necessitates executing the deliberation.

If the simulator knew this time in advance a planning system could run concurrently with the rest of the simulation until the time at which the results are needed by the simulation, i.e. the time determined as the completion time of the plan. However, this time cannot be predicted. The question is whether it can be guaranteed that the plan generation will take at least a certain amount of time to complete. Unfortunately, as Logan and Theodoropolous summarize their experiences [12], lookaheads are very difficult to determine for deliberative agents. The execution time of deliberative components varies within one and the same scenario drastically - as not only experiences of AI researchers show in general, but our experiences with testing planning systems in particular. We tested two agents equipped with the planning system GraphPlan in the TILEWORLD scenario. In our first experiments, the generation of a plan needed between 2 seconds and 20 hours on a ULTRA 2 [15].

Due to the variance of the deliberation time a conservative strategy based on lookaheads seems questionable. An alternative are optimistic techniques. Optimistic schemes do not strictly avoid causality errors but detect and recover from them. A so called *straggler event* sent by its influencers indicates that a component is ahead of its influencers in time. In response the component has to roll back to the state before the straggler event happened. It annihilates outputs sent, if any, with time stamps later than that of the straggler event and proceeds by re-processing all the input events from the time of the straggler event.

Keeping track of prior states might lead to a storage problem - in JAMES even more so, since not only the state but also the structure of the overall model has to be recorded. Agents move, delete themselves, change their couplings and add new components. These structural events

are subject to rollbacks as any other value changes within a component. Thus, it is crucial to determine a time horizon prior to which information can be discarded [6] and to keep this time horizon close to the current simulation time.

4 Toward a Solution

The basic idea is not to wait until the planner is completed but to create a separate external thread and to return a message which indicates that a deliberation process is under way. Thus, the transition function and the overall simulation can proceed. However, as in other synchronization protocols, e.g. Moving Time Windows [11] and Bounded Time Warp [13], barrier synchronizations are introduced to prevent the simulation from proceeding too far ahead compared to the external processes still running. To prevent cascading rollbacks over several simulation steps the simulation ensures at each step that it is safe to proceed.

At each step the simulator does not only activate the models with imminent events but also those still deliberating. It applies the *real-time-knob* function of the model to the time consumed so far by the deliberation process. This function relates deliberation time to simulation time. If the "thinking" consumed a sufficiently large amount of time to make a completion prior to the current time impossible, the simulator proceeds. Otherwise it waits until it is either safe to proceed or the deliberation is finished. Thus, there is no need to roll back farther than to the last event and a rollback will only require the storage of one state.

For integrating real-time processes into the simulation, the definition of models in JAMES is extended: z describes a port which is filled by an external source and accessed read-only by the model's functions. The $real - time - knob$ relates simulation and deliberation time. Models are equipped with methods that allow starting external programs as separate threads. A transition function invokes an external program by using these methods. In any case, transition and initialization functions will finish without waiting for the results of the external program. Thus, the simulation can continue.

The simulation system shall allow external, internal, and confluent events to take place while an external program is active. If an agent is represented as an atomic model (and not as a coupled model with different specialized components), this enables an agent to react to external events while it is planning or learning.

4.1 Simulator

The simulator of a model is activated by the *-message, which indicates an internal, external, or confluent event.

```
when an input (*, xCount, t) has been received
```

```
am is the associated model
am_old = ∅
inpCount = xCount
outCount = 1
busy_fixed = false
if t = t_finished charge z
if t_start ≠ ∞
  block until
          t_start + real-time-knob(used-time) > t
          ∨¬busy
  busy_fixed = busy
  if ¬busy_fixed then
      (* planner finished just now *)
      t_finished = t_start + real − time − knob(used − time)
      finished_backup = t_finished
      t_start = ∞
      if t_finished ≤ t then rollback = true
  endif
endif
t_min = min(t_next, t_finished)
if ¬rollback ∧ (t = t_min ∨ (t < t_min ∧ xCount > 0))
  s_old = s
  t_old = t_last
  if t = t_min then
      send (λ(z, s)) to parent
      if xCount = 0 then
          s = δ_int(z, s)
      else
          block until inpCount = 0
          s = δ_con(z, s, xb)
      endif
  else
      block until inpCount = 0
      s = δ_ext(z, s, t − t_last, xb)
  endif
  if ¬busy_fixed ∧ busy then
      t_start = t
      busy_fixed = busy
  endif
  am_old = am
  am = ρ(s)
  if t = t_finished then
      t_finished = ∞
      flush(z)
  t_last = t
  t_next = t_last + ta(s)
endif
send (done, min(t_next, t_finished), varStrucRequest(s),
      outCount, busy_fixed, rollback)
        to parent coordinator
end
```

If at the current time the completion of a deliberation process is scheduled, the port z is charged with the results of the deliberation process. A value of t_{start} less than infinity indicates that an external process is running (parallel to the rest of the simulation). In this case, the simulator blocks until the time used for deliberating has reached the current simulation time or until the deliberation is finished. Since the $busy$ flag can be set asynchronously by the deliberation system any time, $busy_{fixed}$ is introduced to ensure a consistent execution. If the deliberation has been finished, the times of last and next event are determined. If the delib-

eration finishes before the time of the *-message the completion marks a straggler event and the variable `rollback` is set to true to initiate a rollback. If the variable `rollback` is true the simulator will return a `done`-message to the coordinator which indicates that a rollback is necessary.

If the deliberation component is still running or no deliberation component is running to begin with the *-handler proceeds as usual. It applies the appropriate state transition function, followed by the model transition function ρ which determines whether a new model structure shall replace the old one. To support a rollback the old state, the old time of last event and the old model structure are recorded. If no internal, external, or confluent event is due and no rollback occurred the simulator has only been checked and it returns its old time of next event with the flag $busy_{fixed}$ still set to true. Whether or not an external thread has been started during a transition function is checked by $¬busy_{fixed} ∧ busy$. The thread controlling the external process must not reset the busy flag if it is finished before this expression has been evaluated. Otherwise the simulator will not notice that a planner had been started. The simulator holds two slots for memorizing the "normal" time of next event (t_{next}) and the completion time of the planner ($t_{finished}$).

The #-handler is responsible for collecting inputs. It remains unchanged by the revised procedure. It collects the inputs and increases the semaphore which will finally kick the *-handler into action.

```
when an input (#, y, t) has been received
  block until inpCount > 0
  xb = xb + y
  inpCount = inpCount − 1
end
```

A new handler is introduced, the `rollback`-handler. If the `rollback`-handler receives the request to perform a rollback from its coordinator it checks whether a rollback was requested by itself. Otherwise, it has to update its associated model's state. If a rollback refers to a time at which the agent started deliberating $t_{start} = t_{last}$ the external thread has to be stopped and the time t_{start} is set to infinity.

If a structural change is affected by a rollback, the old model structure has to be reinstalled (e.g. transition, output, and time advance functions). Afterwards the rollback handler resets the values of the old state.

```
when an input (rollback) has been received
  if rollback then
    rollback = false
  else
    if t_start = t_last then
      stopdeliberation :
        t_start = ∞
        busy_fixed = false
    endif
    if am_old¬am ∧ am_old¬∅
      am = am_old
      am_old = ∅
    endif
    if t_last = finished_backup then
      t_finished = finished_backup
    t_last = t_old
    am = am_old
    s = s_old
    t_next = t_last + ta(s)
    t_min = min(t_next, t_finished)
  endif
  send (done, t_min, outCount, busy_fixed, rollback) to parent
end
```

4.2 Coordinator

We also need a `rollback`-handler at the level of the coordinator - not only to inform its components but also to roll back if a structural change has been executed. But let us first inspect the necessary changes within the *-handler.

```
when an input (*, xCount, t) has been received
  varStruc = ∅
  n_old = ∅
  n is the associated network
  IMM = {d ∈ D | t_next_d = t}
  OM = {d | d ∈ IMM ∧ outCount > 0}
  BM = {d ∈ D | busy_d}
  INF = {d ∈ D | ∃i ∈ OM.i ∈ I_d ∨ (xCount > 0 ∧ d_N ∈ I_d)}
  for each r ∈ INF ∪ IMM ∪ BM
    iCount_r = Σ_{d∈I_r∩OM} outCount_d
    if d_N ∈ I_r then
      iCount_r = iCount_r + xCount
    send (*, iCount_r, t) to r's processor
    actCount := actCount + 1
  end
  block until actCount = 0
  t_old = t_last
  t_last = t
  rollback = ⋁_{d∈D} rollback_d
  busy = ⋁_{d∈D} busy_d
  if ¬rollback then
    if varStruc¬∅ then
      n_old = n
      n = ρ(varStruc2Do)
    endif
  endif
  t_next = minimum{t_next_d}
  outCount = Σ_{{d∈D|d∈I_{d_N} ∧ t_next_d = t_next}} outCount_d
  send (done, t_next, ∅, outCount, busy, rollback)
    to parent
end
```

When a coordinator is activated by a star message no structural changes are pending and no storage of an older version of the network is necessary. In PDEVS, processors are only activated to indicate an internal, external, or confluent event of their associated model. Imminent and influenced components respectively their processors ($IMM \cup INF$) have to be informed. In this version, processors that have a deliberation process running (BM) are activated as well.

Based on the number of imminents which produce outputs (OM) and the existing coupling, the coordinator *-handler calculates the number of inputs each component will receive. Afterwards the coordinator waits for all its activated components to send a done-message. If no rollback has been indicated by any of its components it processes the required structural changes. The old network is stored in case somewhere else in the overall model a causal error will be detected. Delaying the execution of structural changes until all transitions have been completed avoids conflicts between concurrent structural and non-structural changes.

If, within this coupled model, no rollback is necessary the time of next event and the number of outputs to be produced at the next internal or confluent event are determined. Together with the rollback and busy flag, this information is sent to the parent coordinator which proceeds likewise.

```
when (done, t_next, varStrucRequest, outC, b, r)
      has been received from processor p
  block until actCount > 0
  actCount = actCount - 1
  varStruc2Do = varStruc2Do ∪ varStrucRequest
  update information about the sender:
  rollback_p = r
  busy_p = b
  t_next_p = t_next
  outCount_p = outC
end
```

When a done-message is received the done-handler decreases the number of done-messages to be received and updates the information about the receiver (rollback and busy flag). Finally, the time of next event and outputs to be produced are recorded. It adds the received request to change the structure of the network to its *varStruc2Do*. The coordinator executes the requested structural changes only if no rollback is announced within this coordinator.

```
when an input (#, y, t) has been received
  forward outputs (x_i, t) produced by i
      according to Z_{i,j}
    if j = d_N then to parent coordinator
    else to component j
end
```

The #-handler at the coordinator level remains unmodified.

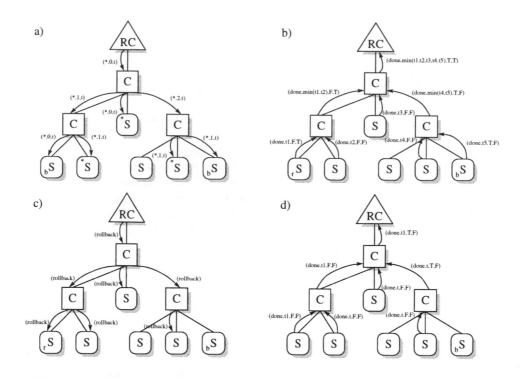

Figure 2. Message passing during rollback: a) An event is announced by propagating *-messages top down. Processors marked with (*) have to process an internal, external, or confluent event while processors marked (b) have a planner running. **b)** The planner of the bottom left model has just finished planning and a rollback becomes necessary. The root-coordinator receives this information through the done messages. **c)** All models that processed an event at t receive a rollback message and restore their old state. **d)** The time of next event is determined by propagating done messages.

```
when an input (rollback) has been received
  if ¬rollback then
    n = n_old
    n_old = ∅
  endif
  for each r ∈ IMM ∪ INF ∪ {d ∈ BM|rollback_d = true}
    send(rollback) to r's processor
      actCount = actCount + 1
    endif
  end
  block until actCount = 0
  t_next = minimum{t_next_d}
  outCount = ∑_{d∈D|d∈I_{d_N} ∧ t_next_d=t_next} outCount_d
  busy = ⋁_{d∈D} busy_d
  send (done, t_next, ∅, outCount, busy, false)
end
```

If a rollback reaches a coupled model it checks whether it is already aware of a rollback. In this case no structural changes have been executed. Otherwise the structural changes executed at the network level have to be undone by installing the old state of the network, i.e. its old components and the couplings which existed among them. Afterwards, the components are informed about the rollback.

After the components completed the rollback operation, the rollback-handler of the coordinator will determine the time of next event, the number of outputs to be produced at the next time step and the busy flag and send its done-message to its own parent coordinator. The rollback flag can be set to false since no successive rollbacks can occur.

4.3 Root Coordinator

The root coordinator controls the simulation by sending *-messages indicating the time of the next event in the abstract simulator. This triggers the processing of events in the processor tree which is eventually confirmed by a done-message from the topmost coordinator.

```
t_next = t_next(topmost coordinator)
repeat until t_next > t_EndOfSimulation ∨ (t_next = ∞ ∧ ¬busy)
  if rollback
    send (rollback) to topmost coordinator
  else
    if busy ∧ t_next = ∞ then
      t_next := estimate_t_next()
    send (*, 0, t_next) to topmost coordinator
```

```
wait for (done,t,outCount,b,r) from topmost coord.
t_next := t    busy := b    rollback := r
```

If a causality error has been detected the root coordinator initiates the execution of the rollback through a `rollback`-message. Otherwise the simulation proceeds as usual. There is another problem the root coordinator has to handle: if there are deliberation processes running and no events are scheduled, i.e. $t_{next} = \infty$ has been returned to the root coordinator. In this case, the root coordinator sends a *-message with an estimated t_{next}, typically a number close to infinity. This will cause the simulator to wait until at least one of the deliberation processes has finished and another event (completion of the process) can be scheduled.

5 Evaluation: Agents in TILEWORLD

Initially, TILEWORLD was developed to test different control, particularly commitment, strategies of IRMA agents [9, 8].

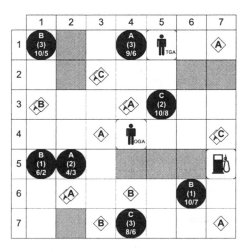

Figure 3. A TILEWORLD **scenario [10]**

TILEWORLD (Figure 3) is a two dimensional grid world with tiles, which can be moved, and holes, which should be filled with tiles. There are obstacles, which impede the movement of agents, and gas stations which allow the refilling of consumed energy. Tiles, holes, and obstacles appear and disappear at certain rates, according to global parameter settings. Thus, the environment displays probabilistic, dynamic behavior.

The effectiveness of an agent is measured in terms of scores that summarize the number and kind of holes filled, and the type of tiles used for filling. TILEWORLD combines a counting problem, how many more tiles of what type does the agent need to fill a particular hole, with route planning in a grid world. This setting puts only few constraints on the

search space and implies a costly deliberation with respect to computing time and memory.

The TILEWORLD scenario we have chosen comprises an 8 by 8 grid, 1000 units of simulation time, and a real-time knob, i.e. factor, of 1. Thus, 1 unit of simulation time should be about 1 second. The grid elements change, e.g. holes and tiles appear and disappear, every 50 time units with a probability of 40%. All agents we tested had a scan range of 5 grid elements, limited, but sufficient fuel, and were planning for two goals simultaneously. Within our implementation of TILEWORLD scanning requires intensive message exchange. The experiments were run on 2 Ultra 2 machines equipped with about 200 MB each. Each experiment consisted of 15 runs.

We first put our algorithm to test using one single agent in the TILEWORLD. The time the simulation runs needed to complete averaged slightly less than 1200 seconds. About 150 of those were due to the scanning activity, and more than 900 were due to planning.

Afterwards, we added another agent to the scenario. For the experiment JAMES distributed the model and the processor tree. The agents and their simulators, including their planners, were running on different machines. Each of the agents was planning an average of more than 900 seconds. The total time used for the simulation averaged about 1450 seconds. About 250 of those were due to the scanning activity of the agents.

Thus, the 900 additional seconds of planning time for the second agent caused almost no additional overhead in simulation time. The overhead caused by the sending of rollback messages turned out to be negligible. However, we did not measure the effort required for saving the state of the model. Not surprisingly, running two agents on a single machine, requires about twice the computation time. The scanning is of course faster but this does not compensate for the loss of efficiency caused by the sequential execution of the planners.

6 Conclusion

The testing of multiple, deliberative agents is space- and time consuming. External modules are plugged into a frame provided by the test bed. The frame provides the interface between agent and agent-architecture to be tested and the virtual environment agents shall be tested in.

Since the performance of agents depends significantly on their timely decisions, a time model is employed to relate the actual or expected execution time of agents to the virtual time of the test environment. One time model is often applied due to its flexibility and simplicity: it clocks the execution of the deliberation component and applies a function to transform the consumed time into simulation time. Thus, only after the generation of a plan the simulation will know at what time to schedule the completion of a deliberation process.

The proposed approach splits simulation and external deliberation into different threads. We allow simulation and deliberation to proceed concurrently by utilizing simulation events as synchronization points. The simulation is delayed to guarantee at each step that no rollback beyond the last state can occur. The simulation proceeds only if the time used by the deliberation process exceeds the current time step in simulation time. Thus, stepwise, the entire simulation and the deliberation processes approach the wallclock and simulation time at which a deliberation component will finally complete its execution. On the way, other agents can start and finish deliberation, models that constitute the environment of an agent can proceed with their dynamics. Looking at performance, one can say that our algorithm simulates several planning agents close to the cost of a single agent, given that a sufficient number of machines are available.

References

[1] S.D. Anderson. Simulation of Multiple Time-Pressured Agents. In *Proc. of the Wintersimulation Conference, WSC'97*, Atlanta, 1997.

[2] A.C. Chow. Parallel DEVS: A Parallel Hierarchical, Modular Modeling Formalism. *SCS - Transactions on Computer Simulation*, 13(2):55–67, 1996.

[3] P. R. Cohen, M. L. Greenberg, D. M. Hart, and A. E. Howe. Trial by Fire: Understanding the Design Requirements for Agents in Complex Environments. *AI Magazine*, 10(3):32–48, 1989.

[4] E. H. Durfee. *Coordination of Distributed Problem Solvers*. Kluwer Academic Publishers, Boston, 1988.

[5] M. R. Genesereth and S. P. Ketchpel. Software Agents. *Communications of the ACM*, 37(7):48–53, 1994.

[6] D. Jefferson and H. Sowizral. Fast Concurrent Simulation Using the Time Warp Mechanism. In *SCS Distributed Simulation Conference*, pages 63–69, 1985.

[7] N. Minar, R. Burkhart, C. Langton, and M. Askenazi. The SWARM Simulation System: A Toolkit for Building Multi-Agent Simulations. http://www.santafe.edu/projects/swarm, June 1996.

[8] M. E. Pollack, D. Joslin, A. Nunes, U. Sigalit, and E. Eithan. Experimental Investigation of An Agent Commitment Strategy. Technical Report 94-31, University of Pittsburg, Department of Computer Science, 1994.

[9] M. E. Pollack and M. Ringuette. Introducing the Tileworld: Experimentally Evaluating Agent Architectures. In *AAAI-90*, pages 183–189, Boston, MA, 1990.

[10] B. Schattenberg. Agentenmodellierung und -evaluierung im Rahmen eines objekt-orientierten, verteilten Simulationssystems. Master's thesis, University of Ulm, Department of Computer Science, 1998.

[11] L. Sokol, D. Briscoe, and A. Wieland. Mtw: A strategy for scheduling discrete simulation events for concurrent execution. In *Proc. of the SCS Western MultiConference on Advances in parallel and Distributed Simulation.*, pages 169–173, 1988.

[12] G. Theodoropoulos and B. Logan. A Framework for the Distributed Simulation of Agent-Based Systems. In H. Szczerbicka, editor, *European Simulation Multi Conference - ESM'99*, pages 58–65. SCS Europe, Ghent, 1999.

[13] S. Turner and M. Xu. Performance Evaluation of the Bounded Time Warp Algorithm. In *Proc. of the 6th Workshop on Parallel and Distributed Simulation*, pages 117–126, 1992.

[14] A.M. Uhrmacher. Concepts of Object- and Agent-Oriented Simulation. *Transactions of the Society of Computer Simulation*, 14(2):59–67, 1997.

[15] A.M. Uhrmacher and B. Schattenberg. Agents in Discrete Event Simulation. In *European Simulation Symposium - ESS'98*, Nottingham, October 1998. SCS.

[16] A.M. Uhrmacher, P. Tyschler, and D. Tyschler. Modeling and Simulation of Mobile Agents. *Future Generation Computer Systems*, (to appear 2000).

[17] M.J. Wooldridge and N. R. Jennings. Intelligent Agents: Theory and Practice. *Knowledge Engineering Review*, 10(2):115–152, 1995.

[18] B. P. Zeigler. *Object-Oriented Simulation with Hierarchical, Modular Models - Intelligent Agents and Endomorphic Systems*. Academic Press, San Diego, 1990.

[19] B.P. Zeigler, H. Praehofer, and Kim T.G. *Theory of Modeling and Simulation*. Academic Press, 1999.

Session 7
Miscellaneous

**Parallelizing a Sequential Logic Simulator using an Optimistic
Framework based on a Global Parallel Heap Event Queue:
An Experience and Performance Report**
S. K. Prasad and N. Junankar

Network Aware Time Management and Event Distribution
G. Riley, R. Fujimoto, and M. H. Ammar

Parallelizing a Sequential Logic Simulator using an Optimistic Framework based on a Global Parallel Heap Event Queue: An Experience and Performance Report

Sushil K. Prasad & Nikhil Junankar
Computer Science Department
Georgia State University, Atlanta
www.cs.gsu.edu/~matskp

Abstract

We have parallelized the Iowa Logic Simulator, a gate-level fine-grained discrete-event simulator, by employing an optimistic algorithm framework based on a global event queue implemented as a parallel heap. The original code and the basic data structures of the serial simulator remained unchanged. Wrapper data structures for the logical processes (gates) and the events are created to allow rollbacks, all the earliest events at each logical processes are stored into the parallel heap, and multiple earliest events are simulated repeatedly by invoking the simulate function of the serial simulator. The parallel heap allowed extraction of hundreds to thousands of earliest events in each queue access. On a bus-based shared-memory multiprocessor, simulation of synthetic circuits with 250,000 gates yielded speedups of 3.3 employing five processors compared to the serial execution time of the Iowa Logic Simulator, and limited the number of rollbacks to within 2,000. The basic steps of parallelization are well-defined and general enough to be employable on other discrete-event simulators.

Keywords: Logic Simulation, Parallelizing Framework, Parallel Heap, Parallel Discrete Event Simulation.

1 Introduction

Logic simulation is one key example of a widely used fine-grained, computation-intensive, discrete-event simulation which has proven to be difficult to effectively parallelize on general-purpose computers. While fine-grained events make it difficult to compensate for the parallel overheads, the large number of events due to the ever-increasing circuit size have generally meant large event-queue access times. The overheads of event independence tests and of deadlock management in traditional conservative schemes, and those of rollbacks and memory-management in optimistic schemes, are additional factors to contend with. The relevant literature is reviewed in Section 6. We undertook the parallelization of an existing logic simulator, the Iowa Logic Simulator of Douglas Jones, using an optimistic protocol and a global event queue. The Iowa Logic Simulator is capable of detailed gate-level simulation. We demonstrate (i) that our optimistic protocol based on a global event queue (parallel heap) effectively controls rollbacks even in large circuits, and efficiently handles and simulates hundreds of thousands of fine-grained events, and these translate into good absolute speedups over the sequential simulator, and (ii) that our optimistic algorithm framework and the parallel heap code can be attached as a "parallelizing engine" to a sequential discrete-event simulator entailing no changes in the simulator's own code or basic data structure. The parallelization steps are general enough to be employable on other existing serial simulators.

This project is the outcome of a series of foundational work. Optimistic protocol of Jefferson [7] is, of course, the beginning. He had advocated simulating earliest multiple events to minimize asynchrony and control rollback frequency. Employing a global event queue as opposed to local queues was shown to be extremely effective in curbing rollbacks and balancing loads [18]. We specifically developed the parallel heap data structure to implement a parallel event queue which can support deletion and insertion of a large number of events concurrently in each queue access [6]. The parallel heap was shown to be the most efficient priority queue on shared-memory machines for large queue sizes of the order of hundreds of thousands to millions [19], obtaining absolute speedups of up to four using six processors. Based on the parallel heap implementing global event queues, Sawant and Prasad implemented three parallel prototype logic simulators: synchronous, conservative, and optimistic. Optimistic simulation of 300,000 events in circuits with 16,000 gates resulted in less than 200 rollbacks. Although the synchronous simulator could complete its simulation cycle twice as fast as the optimistic simulator, it could simulate too few events to be competitive overall. Conservative simulator employed lookahead based on distances between gates, and was not found efficient enough. Optimistic simulator had the best execution time obtaining a relative speedup of two [21]. Despite the low speedups, this work pointed to the potential of global event queue in rollback reduction, potential of a better speedup on larger circuits, and it yielded the first working implementation of an optimistic algorithm framework based on the parallel heap data structure.

The overall approach in parallelizing the Iowa Logic Simulator consisted of (i) identification of the basic components of the serial simulation, (ii) creation of wrapper data structures encapsulating the original data structures implementing events and logic gates and other simulation objects, (iii) changes to event scheduler module to intercept events for their storage in a parallel-heap-based event queue and (iv) integration of the sequential simulator code with the delete-simulate-insert cycle of parallel-heap-based optimistic framework.

On synthetic circuits with 250,000 gates, the parallelized logic simulator obtained absolute speedups of over three while employing five processors as compared to the Iowa Logic Simulator. Rollbacks were limited to a small fraction of the total events simulated. The hardware platform employed was an 8-processor bus-based shared-memory Silicon Graphics multiprocessor, Power Series 4D/280GTX, with 256 MB of main memory.

Section 2 has details on the parallel heap and its performance, and the optimistic framework employing the parallel heap and its performance compared to synchronous and conservative algorithms. Section 3 briefly explains the Iowa Logic Simulator and its modules and capabilities. Section 4 details the parallelization steps of the Iowa Simulator. Section 5 explains the experiments conducted and presents the performance plots. Section 6 briefly surveys the existing literature on parallel logic simulation and on parallelizing serial simulators. Finally, Section 7 presents our conclusions.

2 The Parallel heap and the Optimistic Algorithm Framework

We describe the two main foundational work in this section. The parallel heap code and the optimistic framework code were suitably modified and their capabilities were expanded to handle large circuit simulation in our parallelization effort.

2.1 The Parallel Heap and Its Performance

We provide sketch of the operations of a parallel heap here for an adequate understanding of the optimistic framework and the experiments conducted as reported in the subsequent sections. A parallel heap with node capacity $r \geq 1$ is a complete binary tree such that (i) each node contains

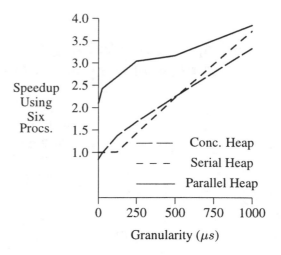

Figure 1. Speedup of Parallel Heap as compared with Concurrent Heap and Serial Heap as a function of granularity (Heap Size $n = 2^{20}$, Node Size, r, of Parallel heap = $8K$)

r items (except for the last node, which may contain fewer items), and (ii) all r items at a node have values less than or equal to the values of the items at its children. When the second constraint holds at a node, the node is said to satisfy the *parallel heap property*. The parallel heap property, when satisfied at all the nodes, ensures that the root node of size r of a parallel heap contains the smallest r items (the r highest priority items).

Deletion of the r earliest items, followed by processing of those items (*think* phase), followed by the insertion of newly produced items constitute the synchronized cycles of delete-think-insert in a parallel heap. The insert- and delete-update processes are carried out in a pipelined fashion from root down to the leaves for overall optimality. Parallel heap is theoretically the first heap-based data structure to have implemented an optimally scalable parallel priority queue on an exclusive-read exclusive-write parallel random access machine model. Its shared-memory implementation was compared with Rao-and-Kumar's concurrent heap [20] and with the conventional serial heap accessed via a lock. The parallel heap outperformed others for fine-to-medium grains achieving speedups of two to four using six processors relative to the best sequential execution times as shown in Figure 1 [19]. Also, the performance of the parallel heap improved with increasing size as shown in Figure 2. Readers are referred to [6] for complete algorithmic details and time complexity analysis, and to [19] for detailed implementation on shared-memory platform and its performance studies.

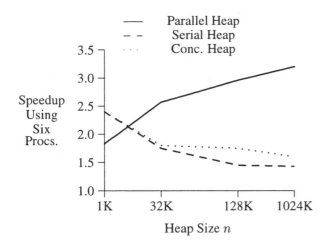

Figure 2. Speedup as a function of heap size (Grain Size= 250 μs and Node Size $r = n/32$).

2.2 An Optimistic Framework based on a Parallel Heap Global Event Queue

The standard optimistic algorithm proposed by Jefferson is easily adapted while employing a global parallel heap event queue. A parallel heap is used to store copies of the earliest events/messages of all logical processes (lps). Each lp contains a sorted list of all the messages received in time-stamp order, and each simulated message is tagged with the state of the lp before its simulation and with all the output messages produced. The saved states are used to restore state after a rollback when a message arrives with a time-stamp less than an lp's local clock. Lazy cancellation is employed to cancel the erroneous output messages. Access to each lp for simulation of a message or to insert output messages in its sorted list is via mutually-exclusive locks.

In each simulation cycle, r earliest messages are extracted from the parallel heap, for some $r \geq 1$ based on the available concurrency, and, assuming p processors, r/p messages are simulated by each processor. The output messages produced are inserted into the destination lps, some of which may cause rollbacks. Anti-messages also result in the annihilation of the corresponding message to be canceled. Among the output messages generated, copies of those which are earliest at their lps are inserted into the parallel heap. The global virtual time (gvt) is conservatively calculated as the time of the earliest message in each cycle, and all the messages before gvt at those lps simulated in a cycle are garbage collected.

A logic simulator employing this optimistic framework was experimentally compared with a conservative logic simulator and a synchronous logic simulator, all based on a global parallel heap [21]. The three simulators were tested on randomly generated network of lps (gates), with each lp's service time assigned randomly between 0 and 15, and in-degree and out-degree of each lp bounded by two. Networks of size up to 16K were simulated, with concurrency factor r varying up to 512. Although the maximum relative speedup of the optimistic simulator was only two, the number of rollbacks in simulating 300,000 messages was just 192 while simulating a network of size 16K and $r = 64$. The other two simulators fared much worse: synchronous needed too many simulation cycles to advance the simulation clock and conservative had large overhead of aggressive independence testing among messages as well as a large preprocessing time to calculate distances among the nearby lps [21].

3 The Iowa Logic Simulator

We chose the Iowa Logic Simulator for our parallelization project both because its source code, albeit in Pascal, was made available to us by Douglas Jones, and because it is a sophisticated gate-level logic simulator capable of handling complex and large circuits. We employed p2c converter of Dave Gillespie to obtain the C version of the Iowa Simulator.

The Iowa Logic Simulator and its Specification Language was developed through the eighties, and has been used for teaching digital logic design. The specification language is powerful enough with abstraction facilities to allow description of large CPUs. Figure 3 shows the basic component of the Iowa Simulator. The Iowa Logic Simulator

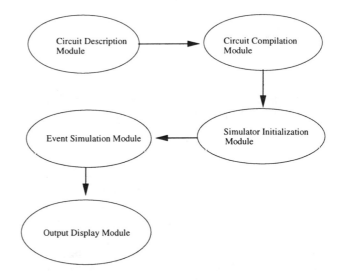

Figure 3. Basic Components of the Iowa Logic Simulator

113

uses a circuit description to interactively request simulated inputs to the circuit, and displays the resulting outputs as waveforms on the terminal screen, emulating a logic analyzer for debugging a digital system. The event queue data structure employs the pairing heap algorithm.

Among the advanced features of this simulator to allow describing large and complex circuits is a sub-circuit mechanism to define a circuit and reuse it multiple times. The simulator supports time delay characteristics for both logic gates and wires. Defaults are obtained from TTL circuits with a gate delay of 10ns and a wire delay of about 1 ns. The kinds of logic components supported include standard logic gates, flip flops, latches, etc. Additional details on Iowa Logic Simulator can be found on its web site at www.cs.uiowa.edu/˜jones/logicsim/.

4 Parallelizing the Iowa Logic Simulator

We now go into the top-level descriptions of the interface functions between the Iowa Simulator and our optimistic framework based on a parallel heap as well as of the necessary wrapper data structures.

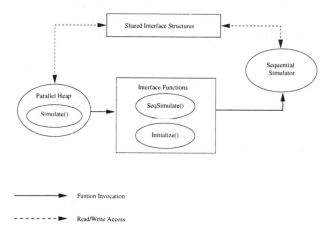

Figure 4. Interface of Optimistic Framework based on Parallel Heap to Iowa Logic Simulator

We provide a few interface functions that act as entry-points to the various services offered by the Iowa Simulator. The code of our optimistic framework acts as a client code which uses these services to simulate the events. The advantage of this approach is that the interface between the optimistic framework code and the Iowa Simulator code becomes very thin. In future, if the Iowa Simulator is to be replaced then only the interface functions are to be rewritten for an easy-integration. We now describe the specification of the interface functions and the shared interface structures as depicted in Figure 4.

4.1 Initialize

The role of this function is to initialize the internal state of the simulator. Normally, there will be an initialization function already implemented in the serial simulator. In such a case, this interface function makes a trivial call to the corresponding function in the simulator. However, if the simulator code is not properly organized then this function is expected to complete (i) setting up the simulator parameters (the maximum simulation clock, the name of circuit description file, the propagation delay of each gate, etc.) and (ii) translating the circuit description file to result in a global data structure such a list of all the gates with the connectivity information between the various gates and connecting wires.

4.2 Integrating the Iowa Simulator Data Structures with the Optimistic Framework's Data Structures

The optimistic framework's Simulate() function accesses the logic gate structure used by the Iowa Simulator to model a logic gate and the event structure which models a simulator event such as input or output change. These two structures are fairly easy to identify in a simulator.

Accessing the gate structure from within the lp structure of the optimistic simulator: In the optimistic framework, a logical process and its characteristics are represented by an lp structure. This structure contains information such as type of the process, its characteristics such as service time (propagation delay), inputs and outputs connections, a sorted queue of events received, etc. However, the information about the gate characteristics now comes from the simulator data structures which are formed by compiling the circuit description file. So, the lp structure acts as a wrapper to the corresponding gate structure in the Iowa Simulator. For this purpose, the new lp structure has an additional field named as *gate∗* which points to the corresponding structure in the Iowa Simulator. Thus, in the Simulate() function of the optimistic framework, all the characteristics of a gate are accessed through this new structure.

Event wrapper structure for the parallel heap: We need to insert all the earliest events at each lp generated by the Iowa Simulator in the parallel heap. In the present implementation, each node in the parallel heap is represented by a *PARHEAP* structure and contains information about an event. To insert a simulator-generated event, we add a reference to that event in the *PARHEAP* structure.

Inserting the power-on initialization events in the parallel heap: In our parallel simulator, we have defined a new function which invokes the appropriate simulator function that performs the power on initialization to generate the initial events. The earliest event at each lp is added to the parallel heap.

4.3 Simulating Events and Directing the Output Events to the Parallel Heap

This function is responsible for actually simulating the events which are deleted from the parallel heap and simulated one by one. The *SEQ_Simulate* function is responsible for simulating the events depending upon the input gate levels and other gate characteristics like propagation delay, etc. As a result of the simulation of an event, a number of events may be generated which are inserted in the parallel heap.

The present architecture of the parallel heap requires that Simulate() function be executed in parallel by many threads. This implies that the *SEQ_Simulate()* function is called in parallel, and, therefore, it should be thread-safe. Care was taken to avoid race-conditions in updating the simulator structures concurrently by using mutually-exclusive locks at each lp.

An important part of implementation of this function is to form an output list of the newly generated events and then pass it back to the caller. For this, a global array of event structures is maintained to store the newly generated events. The Iowa Simulator has a basic function named *schedule()* which has been modified to add the newly created event in this global array. This global array is then inserted in the parallel heap.

5 Performance of the Parallelized Simulator

Since the parallelized simulator was required to be tested with a very large lp networks, a shell script was developed to automate the generation of the test circuits. This script generated combinational circuits in which the logic gates were arranged as a grid array with each logic gate connected to the neighboring logic gates in the grid. Since *nand* gates can implement all other logic gates, each grid point was chosen to be a two-input *nand* gate. In each row i except the last row, the output of a gate at grid position (i, j) feeds (i) into the second input of the subsequent gate at position $(i, j + 1)$ in that row, and (ii) into the first input of the diagonally-across neighboring gate at position $(i + 1, j + 1)$ in the row below. The first input of all the gates in the first row are held at high. Two boolean input vectors are fed, respectively, into the two inputs of the gates in the first column. The outputs of the gates in the last column constitute the output vector of the circuit. The motivation behind choosing this class of circuits was that these are thickly connected

and will simulate more events for a longer time before the outputs stabilize. Also, the input to gates frequently change levels triggering many new events with each clock. This increases the probability of rollbacks. In practical circuits, the events are expected to be fewer, since only part of the circuit gets affected.

The number of rows and columns logic gate were specified as the command-line parameters to the generator script which produced an output file in the Iowa Simulator's circuit description language. The simulation was first tried with about half a million logic gates in the circuit. However, it was found that the SGI multiprocessor got into a lot of secondary page swapping making the simulation extremely slow. Therefore, the results reported were carried out for circuits with 250,000 logic gates.

For the purpose of the performance plots, we report the absolute speedups and rollback frequency by executing the C-version of the Iowa Logic Simulator to obtain the pure sequential time, and then by executing the parallel simulator using three through six processors on a lighted loaded SGI multiprocessor. Although, the multiprocessor has eight CPUs, two CPUs are usually tied up with system tasks. and accurate measurements employing 7 or 8 processors are not obtained.

A range of experiments were conducted to explore the effects of key circuits parameters as well as the two key parameters of the parallel heap, namely, (i) the concurrency factor, r, which is the size of a node of the parallel heap and which indicates how many events are simulated optimistically in parallel in each simulation cycle, and (ii) the number of processors employed in simulation tasks, G, as opposed to those employed for maintaining the parallel heap, M. While using p processors, if $G = p$ then the same set of processors alternate between simulation and maintenance tasks, so $M = p$ as well; else, if $G < p$, then $M = p - G$ processors work exclusively to maintain the parallel heap.

As shown in Figure 5, the best speedup of 3.3 has been obtained while employing 5 processors, with $r = 500$ and $M = 1$. Larger r increases both concurrency as well as rollbacks, as shown in Figure 6, thereby offsetting any speedup gain. Increasing r is expected to gain in speedup if the circuit size is increased further, as inherent concurrency in the circuit should increase causing fewer rollbacks. Rollbacks do not appreciably increase with increasing number of processors as long as the concurrency factor r remains the same (Figure 6).

To see the effect of G and M on speedups and rollbacks, Figures 7 and 8 show these measures for 5 processors. There is a general increase in the speedup as G, the number of processors involved in simulation, increases, but the speedup peeks at $G = 4$ when $M = 1$ processor is involved in maintaining the parallel heap. Even at $G = 3$ corresponding to $M = 2$, speedup is comparable, suggesting

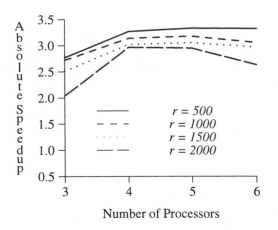

Figure 5. Absolute Speedups Obtained by Parallelized Simulator with No. of Maintenance Processors $M = 1$.

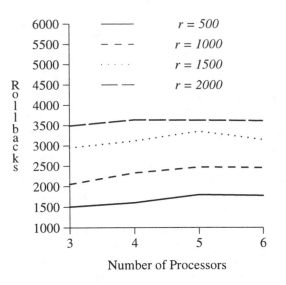

Figure 6. Total Number of Rollbacks Encountered with No. of Maintenance Processors $M = 1$.

that decrease in concurrency in simulation tasks is compensated by the increased concurrency in parallel heap's maintenance. However, further decrease in G clearly cuts into the speedup, because parallel heap is not large enough to exploit increasing number of maintenance processors. Therefore, when both $G = M = 5$, speedup suffers, because $M = p$ processors are not effectively utilized on parallel heap. This observation is consistent with the parallel heap characteristics, which has shown increased speedup with increasing heap size, with significant speedups at million items or more. Currently, the heap size is about 90,000 after the power-on initialization. For a given concurrency factor r, rollbacks increase sharply from $G = 1$ to 2 processors, and then slowly as G is increased further (Fig 8). At $G = 1$, the r earliest messages are simulated serially, so the rollbacks are contributed only by dependency violations across the simulation cycles. However, at $G = 2$ and beyond, an additional source of dependency violations is the inter-cycle asynchrony.

6 Prior Work

For brevity, only representative recent work is cited here, those closely related to the current work. For parallel logic simulation, time-driven algorithms have been shown to be easily parallelizable [10]. This scheme is easily adapted into hardware. The real problem is the wasted effort in simulating the entire circuit in each time step, given that only a very small fraction of the circuit is active on an average (usually less than 1%). Other disadvantages are the specialized nature and the high cost of hardware implementations. An improvement over pure time-stepped algorithm

is to identify and simulate only the active gates in each time step. Because of the techniques such as levelization, this has been shown to be an effective approach to coarser timing grain logic simulation early on [22]. Still, these algorithms can not exploit parallelism available across different time steps – those possible with asynchronous algorithms. A study by Soule [23] concluded that asynchronous conservative algorithms are not competitive with the synchronous algorithm on shared-memory computers. Optimistic simulation seems to be the protocol of choice for asynchronous logic simulation, specially for finer timing grain. This choice is motivated by early studies, both theoretical and empirical, demonstrating the superiority of the optimistic schemes over the conservative methods for general systems. Optimistic schemes have generally performed better as demonstrated by the implementations [13], and by the formal models [1]. Another important advantage of optimistic simulation over conservative ones is that the former can easily handle variable time delays for rising and falling signals through rollbacks, but the latter must enqueue output messages as well to avoid error.

We briefly mention the recent work on parallelizing serial logic simulators. Bajaj et al. [2] have reported a case study in parallelizing a sequential simulation model. Todesco and Meng have reported their 'Symphony' simulation backplane for parallelizing mixed-mode co-simulation of VLSI systems [24]. Krishnaswamy and Banerjee use actor-based optimistic techniques for parallelizing fine-grained circuits [11]. Chen et al. discuss parallelizing switch-level

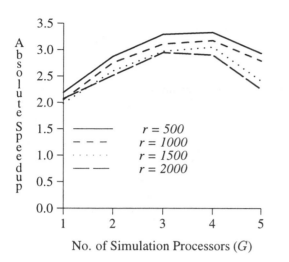

Figure 7. Effect of the Number of Processors Employed for Simulation, G, on the Absolute Speedup Obtained Using a Total of Five Processors.

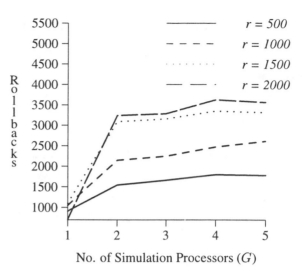

Figure 8. Effect of the Number of Processors Employed for Simulation, G, on the Rollbacks Using A Total of Five Processors.

circuit simulation employing both conservative and optimistic approaches [5]. Hirsch et al. employ component-level partitioning and optimistic protocol to simulate VHDL models on distributed computer [8]. Casas et al. present their 'Shark' switch-level simulator on workstations with a simulation backplane to connect multiple simulators in a distributed environment [3]. Up to 5M transistors have been simulated for logic verification.

A few semi-automatic and automatic parallelization techniques for the broader class of discrete-event simulations have also been proposed. Among several, we mention two: Tsai has presented conversion of simulators in non-C languages to C, and application of optimistic techniques to parallelize them. Overheads of rollbacks and storage management persist [25]. Nicol and Heidelberger propose conservative techniques exploiting lookahead properties for parallelization [15]. Finally, among some recent work on directly developing parallel logic simulators, we mention two: Hsieh et al. propose a relaxation-based timing simulator of MOS circuits on distributed platforms [9]. Chen and Bagrodia implement a parallel switch-level simulator on shared-memory platform using conservative schemes [5].

7   Conclusion and Future Work

This work has demonstrated that the basic framework of our optimistic simulation code based on the parallel heap global event queue is attachable to an existing serial simulator for its parallelization, and that reasonable speedups

are achievable, through grain-packing, even for fine-grained simulations such as logic simulations.

Currently, the circuit compilation time for large circuits is large compared to the circuit simulation time itself, and some effort needs to be directed in speeding up the compilation process. The scalability of the algorithm on larger circuits and more processors remains to be verified; however, better performance is expected both because of larger concurrency in the circuits and increasing parallelism within the parallel heap. The performance of the parallelized simulator needs to be verified also on some benchmark circuits.

We believe that modularity as well as the simplicity of the components in our framework, such as the parallel heap and its delete-simulate-insert cycle to drive the simulation, afford cleaner interfaces between the existing simulator and the framework. A key recent development along this direction has been a much simplified global-queue-based optimistic framework which does away with the traditional message queues at the logical processes and employs just one backup state per lp, without compromising on its efficiency [16]. Additional algorithms have been developed which focus on reducing the state overheads and on extending the parallelizing frameworks to event-based general systems - those without the constraints imposed by the lp-and-message structure [17].

Acknowledgments: We thank Professor Douglas W. Jones for providing us the source code and the user manual of his Iowa Logic Simulator for our parallelization effort. We also thank the graduate assistant Praveen Chelli for duplicating the flowcharts using xfig and for preparing the performance plots using the pictex macros.

References

[1] Bailey, M. L., and Lin, Y. -B. 1993. Synchronization strategies for parallel logic- level simulation. *International Journal on Computer Simulation.* 3, 3, 211-230.

[2] Bajaj, L., R. Bargrodia, and R. Meyer. 1998. Case study: parallelizing a sequential simulation model, *PADS'98 Proceedings of the 12th workshop on Parallel and Distributed Simulation,* Pages 29 - 36.

[3] Casas, J., Yang, H., Khaira, M., Joshi, M., Tetzlaff, T., Otto, S., Seligman, E. 1999. Logic verification of very large circuits using Shark. *Proceedings Twelfth International Conference on VLSI Design.* Goa, India, p.310-17.

[4] Chen, Y.-A., Jha, V., Bagrodia, 1997. R. A multidimensional study on the feasibility of parallel switch-level circuit simulation. *Proceedings. 11th Workshop on Parallel and Distributed Simulation,* Lockenhaus, Austria, p.46-54.

[5] Chen, Y.-A., Bagrodia, R. 1998. Shared memory implementation of a parallel switch-level circuit simulator. *Proceedings. Twelfth Workshop on Parallel and Distributed Simulation PADS '98,* Banff, Canada, p.134-41.

[6] Deo, N., and Prasad, S. 1992. Parallel heap: An optimal parallel priority queue. *Journal of Supercomputing,* 6: 87-98.

[7] Jefferson, D. R. 1985. Virtual Time. *ACM Transactions on Programming Languages and Systems.* 7 (July), 405-425.

[8] Hirsch, H., Chawla, P., Carter, H.W. 1998. Parallel simulation of VHDL-AMS models. *Proceedings of the IEEE 1998 National Aerospace and Electronics Conference. NAECON 1998.* Dayton, p.545-51.

[9] Hsieh, W.-H., Jou, S.-J., Su, C.-C. 1996. Parallel event-driven MOS timing simulator on distributed memory multiprocessors. IEE *Proceedings-Circuits, Devices and Systems,* vol.143, (no.4), p.207-12.

[10] Kravitz, S. A., Byrant, R. E., and Rutenbar, R. A. 1991. Massively parallel switch-level simulation: A feasibility study. *IEEE Transactions on CAD Integrated Circuits and Systems,* 10, 7, 871-894.

[11] Krishnaswamy, V., and Banerjee, P. 1996. Actor based parallel VHDL simulation using Time Warp. *Proceedings. Tenth Workshop on Parallel and Distributed Simulation. PADS 96.* Philadelphia, p.135-42.

[12] Liebrock, L.M., Kennedy, K. 1997. Automatic data distribution for composite grid applications. *Scientific Programming,* vol.6, (no.1), Wiley, p.95-113.

[13] Manjikian, N. and Loucks, W. M. 1993. High performance parallel logic simulation on a network of workstations. *Proceedings of Parallel and Distributed Simulation.* 76-84.

[14] Mueller-Thuns, R. B., Saab, D. G., Damiano, R. F. and Abraham, J. A. 1993. VLSI logic and fault simulation on general purpose parallel computers. *IEEE Transactions on CAD Integrated Circuits and Systems.* 12, 3, 446-460.

[15] Nicol, D. and Heidelberger, P. 1995. On extending parallelism to serial simulators, *PADS'95 Proceedings of the 9th workshop on Parallel and Distributed Simulation,* Pages 60 - 67

[16] Prasad, S. K. 2000. Practical Global-Event-Queue-based Optimistic Simulation Algorithms with One Backup State Vector and Low Rollback Overheads, To appear in *Procs. The First International Conference on Parallel and Distributed Computing, Applications and Technologies (PDCAT'2000),* IEEE, May 22-24, Hong Kong.

[17] Prasad, S. K. 2000. Space-Efficient Algorithms based on Global Event Queues for Parallelization of Existing Discrete Event Simulators, To appear in *Procs. The First International Conference on Parallel and Distributed Computing, Applications and Technologies (PDCAT'2000),* IEEE, May 22-24, Hong Kong.

[18] Prasad, S., and Naqib, B. 1995. Effectiveness of Global Event Queues in Rollback Reduction and Load Balancing. *Proceedings of the 9th Workshop on Parallel and Distributed Simulation,* Lake Placid, NY, pp. 187-190.

[19] Prasad, S., and Sawant, S. 1995. Parallel Heap: A practical priority queue for fine-to-medium-grained applications on small multiprocessors. *Procs. Symp. on Parallel and Distributed Processing,* San Antonio, TX, pp. 328-335.

[20] Rao, V. N., and Kumar, V. 1988. Concurrent access of priority queues. *IEEE Transitions on Computers,* 37, 12 (December) 1657-1665. Parallel analog simulation on distributed memory

[21] Sawant, S. and Prasad, S. K. 1997. An Experimental Comparison Among Shared-Event-Queue-Based Optimistic, Conservative, and Time-Stepped Logic Simulators. *Procs. ISCA 12th Intl. Conf. Computers and Their Applications,* March 13-15, Tempe, AZ, pp. 238-241.

[22] Soule, L., and Gupta, A. 1991. An evaluation of the Chandy-Misra-Byrant algorithm for digital logic simulation. *ACM Transactions on Modeling and Computer Simulation.* 1, (4): 308-47.

[23] Soule, L. 1992. Parallel logic simulation: An evaluation of centralized-time and distributed-time algorithms. CSL-TR-92-527. Stanford University, Stanford, CA.

[24] Todesco, A.R.W., Meng, T.H.-Y. 1996. Symphony: a simulation backplane for parallel mixed-mode co-simulation of VLSI systems. Proceedings of 33rd Design Automation Conference, Las Vegas, p.149-54.

[25] Tsai, J-J. 1994. Automatic Parallelization of Discrete-Event Programs. Ph.D. Diss., College of Computing, Georgia Tech.

Network Aware Time Management and Event Distribution

George F. Riley

Richard Fujimoto

Mostafa H. Ammar

College of Computing

Georgia Institute of Technology

Atlanta, GA 30332

{riley,fujimoto,ammar}@cc.gatech.edu

(404)894-6855, Fax: (404)894-0272

Abstract

In this paper we discuss new synchronization algorithms for Parallel and Distributed Discrete Event Simulations (PDES) which exploit the capabilities and behavior of the underlying communications network. Previous work in this area has assumed the network to be a Black Box *which provides a one-to-one, reliable and in-order message passing paradigm. In our work, we utilize the* Broadcast *capability of the ubiquitous* Ethernet *for synchronization computations, and both unreliable and reliable protocols for message passing, to achieve more efficient communications between the participating systems.*

We describe two new algorithms for computation of a distributed snapshot of global reduction operations on monotonically increasing values. The algorithms require $O(N)$ messages (where N is the number of systems participating in the snapshot) in the normal case. We specifically target the use of this algorithm for distributed discrete event simulations to determine a global lower bound on time-stamp (LBTS), but expect the algorithm has applicability outside the simulation community.

1 Introduction

Distributed applications often require a frequent rendezvous between all participating processes to come to agreement on certain aspects of the distributed computation. For a conservative parallel discrete event simulation, a global concensus on the timestamp of the smallest unprocessed event and the number messages exchanged is a frequent occurrence. Many algorithms exist for distributed consensus agreement. These algorithms typically make some reasonable assumption about the capabilities provided by the underlying communications network, and design the algorithm to work properly given those assumed capabilities A common assumption is the *Black Box* model of network behavior, where messages are injected at one end of a network connection, and reliably come out the other end of the connection at some later time, and possibly out of order.

In actuality, the network can present differing capabilities and reliability guarantees, depending upon how the network is configured and accessed by the application. For example, the ubiquitous *Ethernet* provides, at its lowest level, a simple unreliable in-order datagram service. However, the application can normally request a reliable transport protocol (such as *TCP*), and can also request *Broadcast* service (one-to-all) or *Multicast* service (one-to-many) for individual messages. The performance achieved by the network can vary depending on the services requested by the application, and thus can affect the overall performance of the application. In this paper we show that the capabilities and reliability of the various network models can be exploited in the design of an algorithm, which results in improved performance.

Methods for time management and event message exchange within a parallel discrete event simulation have been examined for some time. Chandy, Misra[1] and Bryant[2] describe the *Null Message Protocol*, in which only the smallest available event at each simulation entity is processed. This protocol assumes there is always an event message available from all peers, and uses a null message as a placeholder when no event message is present. Mattern[3] describes a two pass algorithm for lower bound timestamp computation which is similar in spirit to our method. Mattern's algorithm establishes a consistent cut point in which all messages sent between processors have either been accounted for, or are known to not affect the computation. Chandy's[4] conditional event protocol determines a range of safe events by finding a minimum of all possible events from any peer. Lubachevsky[5] describes a *Bounded Lag* protocol for determining safe events, which takes into account the minimum simulation time delay between any two simulation objects. In the *SPEEDES* simulation engine, Steinman[6] utilizes the *Time Buckets Protocol* in which processes periodically resynchronize to determine a lower bound on events which are safe to process. Time Buckets is also similar to our approach. Nicol[7] describes the *YAWNS* protocol which is also similar to our approach.

The main contributions of our approach are threefold. First we utilize the *Broadcast* capability of an Ethernet network to give an efficient, albeit unreliable, one-to-many message dissemination capability. Secondly, we use knowledge of the inherent message ordering characteristics of the Ethernet to make assumptions about the presence or absence of *Transient Messages*. In traditional time synchronization protocols, a transient message is a message that has not been included in the global concensus because it has not yet been received and processed by the intended receipient. Lastly, we migrate the responsibility of initiating and calculating the concensus to the *slowest running* processor. This results in processors participating in the concensus only when they have no other useful work to perform.

We give two algorithms for computing a *lower bound on time-stamp* (*LBTS*) within a parallel discrete event simulation. For this discussion, we define the *LBTS* to be the minimum timestamp on any message that can possibly be received in the future. The *LBTS* algorithm is a fundamental computation used by conservative synchronization protocols as well as optimistic protocols when computing a *Global Virtual Time* (*GVT*). Our two algorithms assume differing network service models, and we show that the service model assumptions and choices can have a large impact on overall performance. The main contribution of this work is the exploitation of network capabilities (such as broadcast and unreliable event messages) to provide increased performance for large numbers of participating systems.

The remainder of this paper is organized as follows. Section 2 discusses in more detail the network models assumed in our work. Section 3 describes an *LBTS* algorithm which uses broadcast messages for time synchronization, and unreliable datagrams for event messages. Section 4 describes an *LBTS* algorithm which also uses broadcast messages for time synchronization, but uses a reliable transport protocol for event messages. Section 5 describes the experimental methodology used and the hardware platforms on which the experiments were performed, and gives results of the experiments. Finally, Section 6 gives some conclusions and future directions of our work.

2   Network Model

In this section, we discuss the basic behavior of the ubiquitous *Ethernet* network, the programming model used to access the network services, and how these affect the design and performance of our algorithms. We assume that almost all distributed discrete event simulation applications will be executed on a loosely coupled network of workstations connected by an *Ethernet* network. We assume that the programming model allows access to a connection oriented transport protocol such as *TCP*, a connectionless datagram protocol such as *UDP*, and supports both broadcasting and multicasting of data-

grams (although we don't exploit the multicast capability in this work). We also assume that an application programmer can choose any combination of these programming models within a single application.

2.1   Network Reliability Models

As mentioned in the previous section, the performance characteristics and delivery guarantees provided by a given network are not as simplistic as the *Black Box* model. We can, therefore, define the several different models of network behavior. For this discussion, we define *reliable* to mean that any message sent to a single destination will eventually be delivered to that destination. We define *in-order* to mean that all messages received are received in the order they were sent.

The *Reliable In-Order Delivery* (*RIOD*) model assumes that all messages sent between any two entities will arrive correctly, and in the order they were sent. This is the model provided by the *TCP* protocol when using a single connection. The *Reliable Non-Ordered Delivery* (*RNOD*) model also assumes that all messages will be received, but they may be received out of order. This is the model provided by the *TCP* protocol when using multiple connections. The *Unreliable In-Order Delivery* (*UIOD*) model assumes that messages may be lost, but messages which are not lost are delivered in the order they were sent. This is the model provided by the *UDP* protocol when using a single port, and when all communicating systems are on a single shared bus local area network. This model applies to both unicast (one-to-one) *UDP* messages, as well as broadcast (one-to-many) *UDP* messages. Finally, the *Unreliable Non-Ordered Delivery* (*UNOD*) model assumes that messages may be lost and may be received out of order. This is the model provided by the *UDP* protocol when using multiple ports, or when the communicating systems are connected on a wide area network.

3   The *BCUDP* Algorithm

In this section, we describe an algorithm for computing a *lower bound on time-stamp* by utilizing the *Broadcast* capability of the underlying network, and assuming the *UIOD* model for message delivery. The algorithm requires exactly $n + 1$ messages (n is the number of systems participating) in the best case. Experimental data presented later shows that the best case is in fact the typical case. We call this algorithm the *Broadcast UDP* (*BCUDP*) algorithm.

3.1   Assumptions

The algorithm operates under the following assumptions:

1. The underlying communications medium has a *broadcast* capability. In other words, a single system can communicate with all other systems by sending a single network message.

This implies that all of the systems participating in the algorithm are on a single local area subnetwork.

2. Any broadcast message is *NOT* necessarily received by all other systems. Our algorithm is much more efficient, however, if messages are properly received most of the time.

3. Event messages between systems are sent via some unreliable protocol (eg. UDP), and the application can tolerate lost events. Use of unreliable protocols for event message passing has been used within the *Distributed Interactive Simulation* (*DIS*) community, for example when sending real-time state update messages. Our second algorithm addresses the case where event messages are sent using some reliable protocol.

4. The underlying communications medium delivers all messages with the *UIOD* model. This implies that a single socket per process, and single *UDP* port number is used for all communications between processes

3.2 Overview

The algorithm works by designating a *Master* system that will initiate and compute the final *LBTS* value. It does this by sending a broadcast message to all other processors requesting a reply, and collecting replies until all processors have been heard from. The reply messages contain message counts sent to all peers, received message counts, and local simulation time information. After sending a reply, each system stops processing events and stops generating new messages until the *LBTS* computation is complete. If processors did not receive the initial broadcast, or if their reply was lost, the *Master* asks those processors to report again, plus any processor that might have received a transient message, and the process repeats. After all replies have been gathered, the *Master* computes the *LBTS* and informs the other systems of the computed *LBTS* value via a broadcast. The *Master* then designates a new *Master* for the next instantiation of the algorithm. As the algorithm is executed repeatedly during a distributed computation, the *Master* selection will probabilistically be the system with the *slowest* advancing simulation time. Since the algorithm requires the participants to stop generating new event messages, the slowest running simulation is the ideal choice for the *Master*. Other faster running processes will already be blocked with no more safe events to process, and thus will not be impaired by this requirement.

3.3 *BCUDP* Example

In this section we give a simple example to illustrate a typical execution of the algorithm, under three different scenarios. Assume there are four logical processes (LPs) (each on a separate physical processor) denoted LP_0, LP_1, LP_2, and LP_3. The initial *Master* is LP_0. Assume that all LPs start at simulation time T_0, have all determined it is safe to advance to time T_1, send exactly one event message to all other LPs, and advance time to T_1. At that point, all LPs are no longer able to advance simulation time, and must participate in an *LBTS*

computation. Also assume all LPs are trying to advance to simulation time T_2, the time of their next local event. The time of their next local event is called their *Next Event Request* (*NER*) time.

In the first scenario, all LPs receive the initial broadcast from the *Master*, and none of the reply messages are lost. Since LP_0 is the master, it starts the *LBTS* computation by using an *Ethernet* broadcast *Start LBTS* message requesting replies from all peers, and does this at time T_1. Upon receipt of the *Start LBTS* broadcast message, all LPs report to the *Master* (LP_0) their current simulation time (T_1), their *Next Event Request* time (T_2), the count of messages sent to each peer, and the number of messages received. For this example, we assume all event messages have been received properly, so each system reports 1 message sent to each other system, and 3 messages received. The *Master* can simply calculate the *LBTS* as the smallest *Next Event Request* time reported (T_2 in this example). The resultant *LBTS* value is broadcast to all peers, along with an indication of who the next master should be.

In the second scenario, we assume that again all systems receive the initial broadcast, but this time a transient message occurs. LP_0 starts the *LBTS* computation as above and all systems receive the initial broadcast. However, LP_3 has sent a message to LP_1 which has not propagated through the protocol stack and onto the network. All LPs reply, and the *Master* notes that LP_1 has potential transient messages (since more messages were sent to LP_1 than have been received). However, once the *Master* has received the reply from LP_3, the unaccounted for message to LP_1 *must have been either received or lost*. Since the reply by LP_3 was sent after the transient message, the transient message must have also already been sent. Thus, the master can simply broadcast a *Restart LBTS* message, indicating to LP_1 that it should reply again immediately, with no further delay. Once the second reply is received, the *LBTS* can be calculated as above.

In the final scenario, LP_3 does not receive the initial broadcast, and generates transient messages by sending another event to all other LPs after their replies have been generated. Thus the second message from LP_3 to each other peer becomes a transient message. The *Master* notices that LP_3 has not replied (after a suitable timeout period), and requests LP_3 to reply again via a broadcast *Restart LBTS* message. When LP_3 finally replies (after one or more restarts), the *Master* will determine that each system should have received a total of 4 messages, but due to the transients only 3 have been received by LP_1 and LP_2. The *Master* broadcasts a *Round 2 Restart* message, indicating which systems need to reply a second time (in this example it is LP_1 and LP_2). LP_1 and LP_2 will reply again, this time reporting having received 4 messages, and the *LBTS* can be computed by the master as above. If there are still unaccounted for messages after the round 2 reporting, they can be assumed to be lost, due to the message ordering issues described in the previous section. Since all processors in this scenario properly responded to the broadcast, this implies that all event messages sent before the the replies have been either received or lost.

3.4 The *BCUDP* Algorithm

More formally, the *BCUDP* algorithm works as follows:

1. Assume there are k systems participating, designated $S_0, S_1 \ldots S_{k-1}$. The subscript k is known as the *system identifier* (*SID*).

2. Define set R to be the set of systems from which a reply has been received.

3. Define $\mathrm{Rx}[k]$ to be of the total number of messages recieved by system k since the last successful *LBTS* computation.

4. Define $\mathrm{Tx}[k]$ to be the total number of messages sent to system k since the last successful *LBTS* computation.

5. A single system is initially designated the *Master*. A simple way to do this is to assign the first *Master* to be system S_0.

6. When the *Master* system can no longer safely process events, it will initiate an *LBTS* computation by broadcasting a *Start LBTS* (*SLBTS*) message. The *SLBTS* message will contain:

   - The *epoch* for this LBTS computation. The epoch values simply count sequentially by one for each *LBTS* computation. The epoch values allow a system to determine if this request is a duplicate of one already processed.
   - The *SID* for the current *Master*. The replies in step 8 below are unicast directly to the *Master*.

7. The *Master* clears $R = \emptyset$, $\mathrm{Rx}[k] = 0$ $\forall k$ and $\mathrm{Tx}[k] = 0$ $\forall k$.

8. When system S_j receives the *SLBTS* broadcast message, it will respond to the *Master* by sending a *Reply LBTS* (*RLBTS*) message unicast to the *Master*. Note that the *Master* also replies to itself. The replies will consist of:

   - The replier's (*SID*) j.
   - The replier's current simulation time (ST_j).
   - The replier's next event time (NER_j).
   - A count of the total number of event messages received by S_j since the last *LBTS* computation completed (*ThisRx*).
   - An array $\mathrm{MyTx}[k]$ to be an array of the number of messages sent by S_j to each other system k since the last *LBTS* computation completed.
   - An indication of whether this system was unable to continue safely processing events before this *SLBTS* message was received. This is used to determine which S_j will be the next *Master*.

System S_j will stop processing events (and sending event messages to other systems) until the *Done LBTS* message is received (see step 13 below). However, each S_j will continue to poll the message socket, receiving, counting, and enqueing any event new event messages. (These messages are by definition *Transient Messages*, since they were received after the *RLBTS* message was sent, and thus were not accounted for and may affect the NER_j value reported).

9. The *Master* waits for replies from all other systems, or a suitable timeout. The timeout period for the replies is determined heuristically by adapting to the smallest timeout period that still allows all other systems time to reply. Upon receipt of a reply from system S_j, the *Master* will:

   (a) Add j to set R,

   (b) Set $\mathrm{Rx}[j] = \mathrm{ThisRx}$, the received message count reported by j,

   (c) Set $\mathrm{Tx}[i] = \mathrm{Tx}[i] + \mathrm{ThisTx}[i]$ $\forall$ $i = 0 \ldots k - 1$. In other words, add to the count of messages sent to each system the number of messages sent to that system by S_j.

   (d) Store the reported simulation time ST_j.

   (e) Store the reported next event time NER_j.

10. If all systems have replied, there are three possible cases:

   (a) $\mathrm{Tx}[i] = \mathrm{Rx}[i]$ $\forall$ $i = 0 \ldots k - 1$. In other words, there are no transient messages. The *LBTS* is the calculated as the smallest NER_j, plus the lookahead value. Proceed to step 13.

   (b) At least one system has *Transient Messages* or *lost* messages. Note that at this point in the algorithm it is not possible to distinguish between the two possibilities. We simply know that there are some messages which have been sent but have not been received. For each S_j that has missing messages ($\mathrm{Tx}[j] \neq \mathrm{Rx}[j]$), remove j from set R, subtract out the transmit counts from step 9c above, set a local flag indicating round 2 is in progress, and restart the computation (step 11).

   (c) At least one system has lost messages. After the second round of replies have been received, any unaccounted for messages are lost and can be ignored. This is because all systems have replied, and no system sends new messages after a reply. With the *UIOD* model, all messages sent before the reply have also been received or lost. The *LBTS* is the calculated as the smallest NER_j, plus the lookahead value. Proceed to step 13.

11. If some systems have not replied, after a suitable timeout period the *Master* will will broadcast a *Restart LBTS (RstLBTS)* message containing:

    (a) The *epoch* for this LBTS computation.

    (b) A copy of set R indicating which systems need not reply (those systems *not* in set R should reply).

12. Upon receipt of the *RstLBTS* message, any system S_j will check if j is in set R. If j is in set R, S_j just ignores the *RstLBTS*. If not, S_j sends a new *RLBTS* message as in step 8. Return to step 9.

13. When a valid *LBTS* has been calculated, the *Master* will broadcast a *Done LBTS (DLBTS)* message, with the following information:

    - The value of the computed *LBTS*.

    - The epoch for this *LBTS*.

    - An indication of the *SID* of the *Master* for the next iteration. The next *Master* will be chosen at random among those systems that reported they were not yet ready for the current *LBTS* computation. The rationale for this is that the *slowest* system will be the best choice to decide when the next *LBTS* should start.

14. Upon receipt of the *DLBTS* message, all systems will note the calculated *LBTS* and resume processing events. Should any system not receive the *DLBTS* message, it will be stuck until the next *SLBTS* is processed. (Note: As an efficiency enhancement, we suggest that the current *LBTS* value be included with all event messages, so any system which missed the *DLBTS* can still determine the *LBTS* value when it receives an event message.)

15. The newly appointed *Master* will respond to the old *Master* with a *Master Accept LBTS (MaLBTS)* message, indicating it has received the *DLBTS* message and recognizes it is responsible for the next *SLBTS*. If it is not received in a reasonable time period, the old *Master* will resend the previous *DLBTS* message (unicast directly to the new *Master*) and repeat this step.

3.5 *BCUDP* Correctness Proof

In this section we outline a proof that the above algorithm gives a *consistent cut*. For this discussion, we define a *consistent cut* to be a point in time where we can be certain that no message sent by any system prior to the *consistent cut* will be received by any other system after the *consistent cut*.

Define set R as above, to be the set of all systems from which a reply has been received. The focus of the proof is to show that at any point in time, we are assured to have a *consistent cut* between all systems in R. As more and more systems reply, the cut remains consistent between those replying

systems, until the set R contains all systems. Define an *incremental consistent cut* to be a consistent cut among systems presently in set R. Also define S_m to be the *Master* system.

1. The initial set R is empty, which by definition is an *incremental consistent cut*.

2. The *Master* S_m initiates an *LBTS* computation and immediately adds itself to set R. By definition, system S_m has processed any messages sent to itself, so at this point set R contains an *incremental consistent cut* set of exactly one system.

3. The *Master* receives a reply from some system S_j. S_j is added to set R. By assumption 4, any message sent by S_j to any other system will have been received (or lost) prior to S_j sending the reply. In other words, any messages sent by S_j prior to S_j sending the reply is either already received or lost by all other systems. Thus we have an *incremental consistent cut* with the newly added S_j. Note that systems in set R may still be receiving messages from systems *NOT* in set R, perhaps due to those systems having lost the original *SLBTS* broadcast, or not having processed it yet. However, this does not violate our definition of the *incremental consistent cut* as above.

4. If not all replies have been received, return to step 3

5. At this point, set R contains all systems, and the *incremental consistent cut* is now a *complete consistent cut* for all systems. This implies only that all systems in set R (all participants at this point) are now guaranteed to have received all messages that are going to be received. This does *not* guarantee that the reported simulation time values were correct when reported, only that they are correct *now*.

6. Since some systems may have have reported incorrect values for the local minima (due to *Transient Messages*), the round 2 processing of the algorithm collects new minima from those systems which experienced *Transient Messages* during round 1 (as determined by the reported message counts). The round 2 processing simply allows all systems a chance to report revised minima as determined by the *consistent cut* of set R at the end of round 1.

4 The BCTCP Algorithm

In this section, we describe an algorithm for computing a *lower bound on time-stamp* by utilizing the *Broadcast* capability of the underlying network, and assuming *RIOD* model for event messages, and applying the observations made previously about message ordering using the *sockets* network programming abstraction. We call this algorithm the *Broadcast TCP (BCTCP)* algorithm.

4.1 Assumptions

The algorithm operates under the same assumptions as the *BCUDP* algorithm (given in section 3.1), excepting assumptions 3 and 4, which are revised below:

3. Event messages between systems are sent via some reliable protocol (eg. TCP), and all event messages will be delivered to the intended receiver.

4. The underlying communications medium delivers messages with the *RIOD* model when using a single socket, and the *RNOD* model when using multiple sockets.

4.2 Overview

The *BCTCP* algorithm works identically to the *BCUDP* algorithm, except in the handling of *Transient Messages*. With *BCUDP* we were able to assume that unaccounted for messages at the end of round 1 were lost and could be ignored, but with the *RIOD* model used for *BCTCP* we must assume that the messages will eventually be delivered. When processing a round 2 *RstLBTS* message, all peers must wait until all expected messages have been received before replying. An outline of a correctness proof is given in [8], but omitted here for brevity.

4.3 The *BCTCP* Algorithm

More formally, the *BCTCP* algorithm works the same as *BCUDP* excepting the handling of step 12, which is replaced below:

12. Upon receipt of the *RstLBTS* message, each system S_j will check if j is in set R. If j is in set R, S_j just ignores the *RstLBTS*. If not, and if the round 2 flag in the *RstLBTS* is *NOT* set, S_j will respond immediately with a *RLBTS* message, as in step 8. If the round 2 flag is set, S_j must wait for all transient messages to be received. The *RstLBTS* message contains an array $(TotTx[k])$ which notifies each system of the total number of messages that should be received before proceeding. Once all messages have been received, send the *RLBTS* message as above. Return to step 9.

5 Experiments and Results

In this section, we describe the environment we used to implement and test the algorithms described in the previous sections. The hardware used is a collection of 48 Intel Pentium-II 300Mhz systems each with 512Mb main memory and two processors. The systems are connected with a 100BT *Ethernet* network (100 Mbps). Each system runs the Intel Solaris operating system, version 5.5.1.

The software used for testing was a simple airport simulation. The program models 480 airports,

and 48,000 airplanes. Airplanes travel between airports with a travel time uniformly distributed between 30 and 360 minutes. When arriving at an airport, they remain on the ground for a time interval uniformly distributed between 10 and 60 minutes. The simulation was run on a varying number of systems between 1 and 48. As more systems were used, the overall size of the simulation remained the same (when running on 2 systems, each system managed 240 airports and 24,000 planes initially). This test simulation is very fine grained, with little CPU processing per event, and thus the *LBTS* computation time and the message transmission times will dominate the overall performance.

For a baseline, the airport simulation was first implemented and tested using the *RTIKIT* software developed at Georgia Tech. The *RTIKIT* uses *TCP* sockets (the *RIOD* model) for all communication, and a classical butterfly barrier[9] for *LBTS* calculations. The RTIKIT implementation is described in [10]. We refer to the *RTIKIT* version as *Base1*.

Then both of our new algorithms were implemented and tested for overall performance using the same airport simulation. Three performance metrics were used:

1. Elapsed time. The overall running time of the system, in wall-clock seconds.

2. Time spent per *LBTS* calculation. The total time spent calculating new *LBTS* values was tracked, and divided by the number of *LBTS* calculations made.

3. Reliability metrics, specifically the number of lost event messages and the number of *LBTS* computations that were successful on the first try.

All tests were performed on dedicated systems, with no other user jobs running (normal operating system daemons were present and running). No network traffic was present other than that generated by our tests.

5.1 Results

The results of these experiments are shown in the graphs above. All graphs in this section have the number of systems used for this simulation on the X-Axis, with the various performance metrics on the Y-Axis, and separate curves for each of the implementations.

Figure 1 shows the overall elapsed time of the simulation runs, for systems counts of 1, 2, 4, 6, 8, 12, 16, 24, 32, and 48. (Note. The metrics for the one system case is identical in all cases, since no network activity is needed and no *LBTS* computations are used, and thus the *LBTS* algorithm and the network event passing mechanisms are not used). The results show substantial reduction in overall running time, with algorithm *BCUDP* being the best.

Another way to measure the efficiency of the *LBTS* computation algorithm is to measure the average time spent calculating the *LBTS*. Figure 2

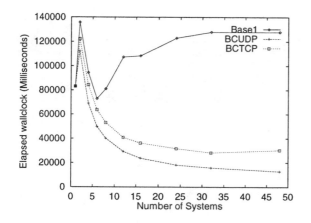

Figure 1. Elapsed Running Time

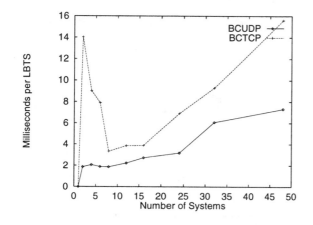

Figure 2. Milliseconds per LBTS

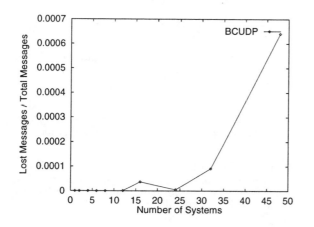

Figure 3. Fraction of Lost Event Messages

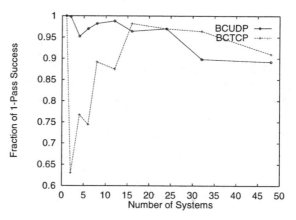

Figure 4. Fraction of Successful One-Pass

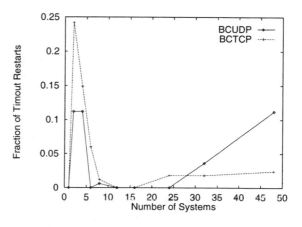

Figure 5. Fraction of Timeout Restarts

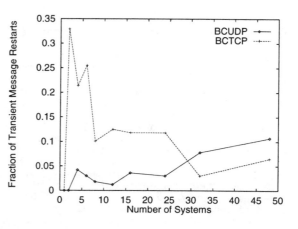

Figure 6. Fraction of Transient Restarts

shows the amount of wall-clock time spent on average performing each *LBTS* computation for algorithms *BCUDP* and *BCTCP*. (Note. The *LBTS* computation times were not available for the baseline runs). Intuitively we expect *BCUDP* to be slightly better (less time spent) since the *BCUDP* algorithm never waits for transient messages in round 2, where the *BCTCP* algorithm does. Figure 2 shows that the times spent in *LBTS* computations is fairly high for the *BCTCP* algorithm with small numbers of processors, we suspect due to the timeout value being too low in this case (note the large number of restarts due to timeouts in figure 5). For processor counts between 8 and 32 the time spent processing *LBTS* computations is roughly comparable between our two algorithms, with *BCUDP* slightly better as expected.

We also measured the amount of *unreliability* exhibited by the *UIOD* network models assumed by our algorithms. Specifically, we measured the number of lost event messages when using *BCUDP* and the number of successful *one pass LBTS* computations. A successful *one pass LBTS* computation indicates that the *SLBTS* broadcast message was received properly by all peers, the *RLBTS* was received properly by the *Master* from all peers, there were no *Transient Messages*, and the *DLBTS* message was received successfully by all peers. Figure 3 shows the fraction of event messages which were lost when using the *BCUDP* algorithm (for our simulation there were over 1 million event messages transmitted). We note that less than 0.0007 of all event messages were lost, even when 48 systems were used. Figure 4 shows the fraction of all *LBTS* computations that were successful in one pass. A further breakdown of the reasons for one pass failures is shown in figures 5 (restarted due to lost *SLBTS* or lost *RLBTS* message) and 6 (restarted due to *Transient Messages*). For the most part, we see that most of the multiple pass *LBTS* computations are due to transient messages, excepting the *BCTCP* algorithm when using a small number of processors (less than 8). Again we believe the large number of timeout restarts are due to the timeout value being too small in this case.

6 Conclusions and Future Directions

The performance results show conclusively that careful attention to and exploitation of the underlying network model can give a substantial improvement in overall performance. Simply choosing the *RIOD* model of network behavior and counting on reliable, in-order delivery of all communications is not always the best choice. Distributed algorithms should be designed with the simplest and most efficient network model in mind, and optimized to work well in the *expected* case. Both of our algorithms, *BCUDP* and *BCTCP* are optimized to perform well in the case where all messages arrive correctly, even when using the *UIOD* network model. When unusual events occur, such as lost or delayed network messages, the algorithms expend extra time handling these events and may not perform as well. However, if the *expected* case occurs often enough, and the unusual events occur infrequently enough, the algorithms perform well.

For future research, we intend to examine how to combine the *LBTS* algorithm and the message retransmission request mechanism, to give way to an apparent *RIOD* model when in fact using the *UIOD* model provided by *UDP* sockets. Since the *Master* system is able to collect a complete record of message counts to and from every pair of systems, the *Master* can determine which systems have lost messages and need retransmissions. Again, the expected case will be where no messages are lost, resulting in little additional overhead most of the time.

References

[1] K. Chandy and J. Misra, "Asynchronous distributed simulation via a sequence of parallel computations," in *Communications of the ACM*, vol. 24, November 1981.

[2] R. E. Bryant, "Simulation of packet communications architecture computer systems," in *MIT-LCS-TR-188*, 1977.

[3] F. Mattern, "Efficient algorithms for distributed snapshots and global virtual time approximation," in *Journal of Parallel and Distributed Computing*, 1993.

[4] K. M. Chandy and R. Sherman, "The conditional event approach to distributed simulation," in *Proceedings of the SCS Multiconference on Distributed Simulation*, 1989.

[5] B. D. Lubachevsky, "Efficient distributed event-driven simulations of multiple-loop networks," *Communications of the Association for Computing Machinery*, vol. 32, no. 1, pp. 111–123, 1989.

[6] J. Steinmann, "Speedes: Synchronous parallel enviornment for emulation and discrete event simulation," *Advances in Parallel and Distributed Simulation, SCS Simulation Series*, vol. 23, pp. 95–103, 1991.

[7] D. M. Nicol, "The cost of conservative synchronization in parallel discrete event simulations," *Journal of the Association for Computing Machinery*, vol. 40, no. 2, pp. 304–333, 1993.

[8] G. F. Riley, R. M. Fujimoto, and M. A. Ammar, "Network aware time management and event distribution," Feb 2000. Technical Report GIT-CC-00-11.

[9] D. E. Brooks, "The butterfly barrier," *The International Journal of Parallel Programming*, vol. 14, pp. 295–307, 1986.

[10] R. M. Fujimoto and P. Hoare, "HLA RTI performance in high speed lan environments," in *Proceedings of the Fall Simulation Interoperability Workshop*, 1998.

Session 8
Work-in-progress

Session 9
Load balancing

**Locality-Preserving Load-Balancing Mechanisms
for Synchronous Simulations on Shared-Memory Multiprocessors**
V.-Y. Vee and W.-J. Hsu

**Load Balancing for Conservative Simulation
on Shared Memory Multiprocessor Systems**
B. P. Gan, Y. H. Low, S. Jain, S. J. Turner, W. Cai, W. J. Hsu, and S. Y. Huang

**Model Structure and Load Balancing
in Optimistic Parallel Discrete Event Simulation**
T. K. Som and R. G. Sargent

Locality-Preserving Load-Balancing Mechanisms for Synchronous Simulations on Shared-Memory Multiprocessors

Voon-Yee Vee   Wen-Jing Hsu

Centre for Advanced Information Systems, SAS
Nanyang Technological University
Nanyang Avenue, Singapore 639798
Email: vyvee@singnet.com.sg, hsu@ntu.edu.sg

Abstract

Many synchronous algorithms have been proposed for parallel and discrete simulations. However, the actual performance of these algorithms have been far from ideal, especially when event granularity is small. Barring the case of low parallelism in the given simulation models, one of the main reasons of low speedups is in the uneven load distribution among processors. We present several new locality-preserving load balancing mechanisms for synchronous simulations on shared-memory multiprocessors. We show both theoretically and empirically that some of these mechanisms incur very low overhead. The results confirm that one of the new mechanisms is indeed more efficient and scalable than common existing approaches.

1 Introduction

Many algorithms have been proposed for parallel and distributed simulation, see, e.g. [5, 8, 20]. Synchronous simulation algorithms constitute an important class of these algorithms. Examples include time-stepped simulations [1, 6], the bounded lag algorithm [13, 14], the safe time algorithm [3], and the conditional event approach [4].

The simulation model is usually decomposed into a number of N submodels, each called a *logical process* (LP), and is simulated on P physical processors. In this paper, we concentrate on the performance issue of synchronous simulations with sufficient *parallel slackness* [16], i.e. $N \gg P$. The simulation advances in a series of iterative steps or cycles, where all LPs (and effectively all physical processors) synchronize at the transition between cycles. Synchronous algorithms presume that messages sent among the LPs will only be processed by the receiving LPs in subsequent cycles. When the simulation is to be executed on shared-memory multiprocessors, it is important to preserve the temporal and spatial localities associated with the set of state variables of each LP.

The cache effect has been largely ignored by many traditional approaches such as the popular randomized work-stealing mechanism. If no attempt is made to preserve localities, however, the high cache misses can incur large overhead as the cache misses cause the processors to stall and wait for data transfer from memory to the processor's cache. The potential benefits of load balancing can be undermined by the adverse effect of nonlocal accesses, which is especially true for simulations with fine grain LPs.

We will present new locality-preserving load-balancing mechanisms for synchronous simulations on shared-memory multiprocessors. By exploiting the properties of synchronous simulations, we have derived a spectrum of schemes (*cf.* Section 3) for an idle processor to find work with minimal overhead. We have analyzed the mechanisms theoretically and shown that some of the more efficient versions incur little overhead. The efficiency is also verified empirically with synchronous simulations implemented with Cilk-5 [2, 15], a C-based multithreaded runtime system developed at MIT. We refer to [9, 18] for descriptions of related works.

2 Locality-Preserving Load-Balancing Mechanisms

Figure 1 illustrates the pattern of a typical synchronous simulation, where all physical processors synchronize at the transition of cycles. Each LP is generally associated with a set of local variables which may be updated during a cycle. It is therefore desirable to arrange the LPs to be processed by the same processor[1] as much as possible so that the variables can be cached locally.

---

[1]The terms processors and physical processors will be used synonymously.

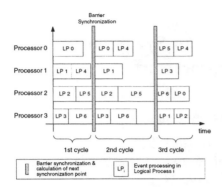

Figure 1: The pattern of typical synchronous simulations. A synchronous simulation comprises a number of cycles (or iterations) where all processors synchronize at the transition of cycles

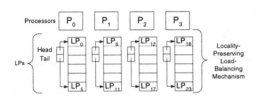

Figure 2: The conceptual configuration of the locality-preserving load-balancing mechanisms

2.1 Skeleton of the mechanism

The philosophy behind our mechanism is to assure high probabilities for LPs to be processed by the same processors. Figure 2 illustrates the conceptual configuration of our mechanism.

The set of LPs is partitioned into P *pools* $\Pi_0, \Pi_1, \ldots, \Pi_{P-1}$, where P denotes the number of processors. Each pool Π_i is assigned to one processor p_i initially. Ideally, the set of LPs is partitioned such that the workload is well-balanced among all P processors. However, the partitioning of the LPs is itself a hard problem. (Specifically, its related decision problem is NP-hard [10].) Furthermore, the workload of each LP may be quite dynamic. Therefore, except for special cases, no known algorithms can guarantee good load balance among the processors. Here, we will assume that the set of LPs has been somehow partitioned into P pools.

At the beginning of each cycle, each processor p_i is a *worker* and attempts to grab an LP from Π_i, the pool of LPs assigned to p_i. It will then process the work associated with the LP for the current cycle.

When Π_i becomes empty, the processor p_i becomes a *thief* that will *steal* LPs from the other processors. A thief p_i performs the following **StealLP** operation whenever it looks for an LP to process:

Step 1. Decide (i.e. select) a candidate victim p_j (from whom to steal an LP). Return failure if there is no more LP to process in the current cycle.
Step 2. If Π_j is non-empty, then steal an LP from Π_j and return.
Step 3. Repeat Step 1.

In summary, a thief selects a *victim* processor p_j and attempts to steal an LP from Π_j. The victim is selected by a thief according to a *victim selection scheme*. The thief repeats the attempt until it steals an LP successfully, or until it discovers that no more work remains in the current cycle.

Intuitively this work stealing strategy could balance the workload among the processors. It could also preserve localities because an LP is likely to be processed by the same processor. Clearly, for efficient realization of the mechanism, the following aspects must be tackled properly:

- *Synchronization in sharing LPs.* I.e., the interactions among the workers, thieves and victims in grabbing LPs. We adopt a simplified version of the efficient THE protocol [7] for this purpose.

- *Victim selection.* The schemes followed by the thieves to choose candidate victims. We will carefully examine this issue and present schemes optimized for synchronous computations in Section 3.

3 Victim Selection Schemes

To achieve load balancing, many relied on randomized work stealing. For instance, in the Cilk-5 runtime system, to steal a thread, a thief selects a victim randomly. For synchronous simulations, however, it is possible to achieve better victim selections by exploiting certain properties of such algorithms. Specifically, all synchronous simulations share an important property: *the number of LPs yet to be processed decreases monotonically in any cycle.* The pool of each processor is filled up at the beginning of each cycle. As the simulation progresses, *the size of each pool decreases monotonically* until the end of the cycle. This knowledge allows us to achieve better victim selections. For instance, *if a thief already knows that a victim has an empty pool, then it need not visit the victim again.*

3.1 Schemes optimized for synchronous simulations

Ideally, a thief should select a victim which itself is a worker rather than a thief, because the latter has run out of work. For ease of discussion, we will refer to a victim with a non-empty pool as a *live* victim (i.e. the processor is a worker) or being *alive*, and refer to a victim with an empty pool as a *deceased* victim (i.e. the processor has turned into

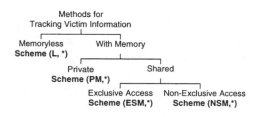

Figure 3: Victim selection schemes classified according to methods for tracking the victim information

a thief and will never become alive again until the next cycle).

When a thief p_i looks for a victim, it relies on some status information to select its candidates. With perfect up-to-date information, a thief need only select once to find work successfully. In reality, depending on the mechanism for updating the status information, a thief may have to select a few candidate victims before landing on a non-deceased victim. We will call a victim p_j a *potential victim* of a thief p_i if p_j is known by p_i to be still alive. A thief always chooses candidate victims from its potential victims. The exact meaning of the *potential victim* will become clear when we discuss the representation of the victim information in the next section.

We will examine the following two crucial aspects of our victim selection schemes:

- *How is the victim information being tracked and updated?* A few methods for tracking the victim information are presented in Section 3.2.

- *How can the victim information be utilized in selecting a victim?* Two such methods will be introduced in Section 3.3.

Notational remarks

In the rest of the paper, we denote a victim selection scheme in terms of two parameters as **Scheme** (α, β). This means that the given scheme adopts method α for tracking the victim information and method β for selecting candidate victims.

Furthermore, a parameter with a value of * (wildcard) can be substituted by any value. For example, **Scheme** $(\alpha, *)$ refers to any victim selection scheme that adopts method α for tracking the victim information.

3.2 Methods for tracking victim information

The relationship among the four methods to be introduced in this section is illustrated in Figure 3.

3.2.1 Memoryless schemes vs schemes with memory

A victim selection scheme can either be *memoryless* or *with memory*. In a *memoryless scheme*, denoted as **Scheme** (**L**,*), a thief does *not* refer to the victim information to decide the victim to select. In this scheme, even a thief has found a victim deceased, it may still visit the same victim again within the same cycle.

In a *scheme with memory*, a thief will refer to the victim information to decide the victim to select. Unlike a memoryless scheme, a thief may avoid some deceased victims with a scheme with memory.

We first present an efficient data structure for recording the victim information before further elaborating the schemes with memory.

3.2.2 Encoding victim status information

We use a P-bit variable $(b_0 b_1 \ldots b_{P-1})_2$ called the *encoding vector* to record the information of potential victims. The encoding vector that is referenced by processor p_i will be denoted by v_i. Each bit b_j of v_i is defined as follows:

$$b_j = \begin{cases} 0, & \text{if victim } p_j \text{ is known by } p_i \text{ to be deceased} \\ 1, & \text{if victim } p_j \text{ is known by } p_i \text{ to be alive} \\ & \text{(i.e. a potential victim)} \end{cases}$$

where P denotes the number of processors. All bits of the encoding vector are initialized to 1's since each processor is associated with some work at the beginning of each cycle. This representation of the victim information with an encoding vector clearly incurs minimal overhead in space.

3.2.3 Various schemes with memory

Memory schemes can be classified into two types: (a) schemes with *private memory* (or *private encoding vectors*), and (b) schemes with *shared memory* (or *shared encoding vectors*). A private-memory scheme, denoted as **Scheme** (**PM**,*), maintains a total of P encoding vectors for P processors. Each encoding vector v_i is assigned to one processor p_i initially, and will only be accessed and updated by p_i. Since no victim information is being shared, each encoding vector can be cached locally and exclusively. Although each thief can avoid the deceased victims it has found in a cycle, it cannot always avoid the deceased victims found by other thieves because no victim information is shared among the thieves.

In contrast to a private-memory scheme, a *shared-memory scheme* maintains only one global encoding vector. The global encoding vector is a shared resource which can be accessed and updated by all processors. The encoding vector v_i of each processor p_i thus refers to the global encoding vector. The processors may need to synchronize to update the global encoding vector with any of the following methods:

(1) In the *exclusive version of a shared-memory scheme*, denoted as **Scheme (ESM,*)**, *at most one processor is allowed to perform the StealLP operation or to update the encoding vector at any moment* by resorting to a lock.

(2) In the *non-exclusive version of a shared-memory scheme*, denoted as **Scheme (NSM,*)**, *any number of processors is allowed to update the encoding vector* without resorting to any lock. Unlike the exclusive version, this version does not incur any lock contention. This version is therefore expected to outperform the exclusive version.

Note that, with the non-exclusive version, *data races* can occur when more than one processor updates the encoding variable simultaneously. Figure 4 illustrates the possible outcomes when two processors update the same variable. In this scenario, processors p_0 and p_1 attempt to set bit 0 and bit 1 of the encoding vector respectively from 1 to 0. With the likelihood of data races, only one winning value may eventually be set afterwards.

Nevertheless, the non-exclusive version is still *correct* in the sense that *all* live victims will still be considered by all thieves. The reason being that, regardless of the outcome of the data races, all live victims will still be reflected as such in the encoding vector. This is easily verified by noting the bits of the encoding vector that are not modified by any processor remain unmodified even with data races.

3.2.4 Update of victim information

Consider the encoding vector v_i that is assigned to processor p_i. To maximize the efficiency of locating a live victim, it is desirable to keep v_i as up-to-date as possible. In particular, v_i should be updated in the following situations:

(1) *When p_i runs out of LPs and becomes a thief.* v_i should be updated so that p_i will not select itself as a candidate victim. More importantly, the update is observed by other processors if a shared-memory scheme is adopted.

(2) *When p_i fails to steal an LP from a victim p_j.* In this case p_i should update v_i so that p_j is no longer a potential victim of p_i[2]. The update is performed in Step 3 of the StealLP operation.

3.2.5 Detecting end of cycle

When there is no more LPs that need to be processed in a cycle, a thief will always fail to steal an LP. In a scheme

with memory, this causes all thieves to run out of potential victims eventually. Therefore, a thief can tell the end of a cycle by simply checking if there is potential victim left.

However, in a memoryless scheme, no thief will run out of potential victims. To facilitate detection for memoryless schemes, we implement a memoryless scheme **Scheme (L,β)** similar to its non-exclusive shared-memory counterpart **Scheme (NSM,β)**[3]. The only difference is that, while the processors in the former scheme still update the shared encoding vector v and use it to check for the end of a cycle, they select a candidate victim from *all* other victims *without* relying on v.

3.3 Methods for selecting candidate victims

We have described four methods for tracking the victim information in the previous section. In this section, we will present two methods for selecting candidate victims based on the encoding vectors.

In a *random* scheme, denoted as **Scheme (*,R)**, a thief p_i selects a candidate victim from its potential victims randomly and uniformly. In other words, if there are m potential victims, each potential victim has an equal chance of $\frac{1}{m}$ to be selected as the candidate by the thief.

The candidate victim of a thief p_i can be decided efficiently with the following steps. Each processor is assigned with a unique physical ID, while each potential victim is assigned with a unique logical ID ranging between 0 and $(m-1)$.

Step 1. Determine m, the number of potential victims of p_i. This is equal to the number of 1-bits of v_i (i.e. $\sum_0^{P-1} b_j$ where b_j is j-th bit of v_i).
Step 2. Determine the logical ID of the candidate victim by selecting an integer i randomly from the range $0 \leq i \leq m-1$.
Step 3. Map the logical ID of the candidate victim to its physical ID.

A candidate victim can be decided even more efficiently if we *precompute for each thief its (deterministic) candidate victim for every possible value of the encoding vector.* We will examine one of such schemes, namely the *successor* scheme here.

In the *successor* scheme, denoted as **Scheme (*,S)**, the processors are logically connected to form a ring. Let $p_0, p_1, \ldots, p_{P-1}$ denote P processors. A total of P edges are in the ring, where each edge is of the form $(p_i, p_{(i+1) \bmod P})$, i.e., from p_i to $p_{(i+1) \bmod P}$, for $i =$

---

[2]With **Scheme (NSM,*)**, p_j may still be a p_i's potential victim if there is data race.

[3]The non-exclusive shared-memory method has been chosen because it is the most efficient among the methods proposed in Section 3.2.3, as will be verified theoretically in Section 3.4 and experimentally in Section 4.

Case 1			Case 2			Case 3		
p_0	p_1	v_i	p_0	p_1	v_i	p_0	p_1	v_i
read v_i		1111_2	read v_i		1111_2		read v_i	1111_2
write v_i		0111_2		read v_i	1111_2	read v_i		1111_2
	read v_i	0111_2	write v_i		0111_2		write v_i	1011_2
	write v_i	0011_2		write v_i	1011_2	write v_i		0111_2

Figure 4: An illustration of data races when updating the encoding vector v_i. p_0 and p_1 attempt to set bit 0 and bit 1 of v_i respectively from 1 to 0. The encoding vector is updated correctly only in Case 1.

$0, 1, 2, \ldots, P - 1$. We call $p_{(i+1) \bmod P}$ the immediate successor of p_i.

In **Scheme (*,S)**, a thief p_i decides its candidate victim by visiting its successors along the edges emanating from itself. The first successor that is a potential victim of p_i will be selected as the candidate victim. Formally, let $v_i = (b_0 b_1 \ldots b_{P-1})_2$ denote the encoding vector of a thief p_i. The candidate victim p_j for p_i is given by $j = \min\{k > i : b_{k \bmod P} = 1\} \bmod P$ and is undefined (i.e. end of the current cycle) if $b_k = 0$ for all $0 \leq k \leq P - 1$. If we precompute for each thief the candidate victim for every possible value of the encoding vector, a thief takes only $\Theta(1)$ time to look up a table for the candidate victim.

The lookup tables for the random scheme and the successor scheme can be prohibitively large if P is large. It is easy to show that each table occupies $\Theta(P2^P)$ space, which is exponential to P. For large P, we can apply an efficient technique described in [11] to reduce the size of the lookup tables. In particular, each table requires only $\Theta(P)$ space.

All the schemes that can be obtained by combining the methods introduced are tabulated in Table 1.

3.4 Time complexity

The time complexity of each victim selection scheme is summarized in Table 2. Refer to [18] for detailed analysis. The time complexity analysis suggests that the best method for tracking the victim information is the non-exclusive shared-memory method (i.e. SN method).

4 Comparisons of Victim Selection Schemes

To evaluate various victim selection schemes, the following simulation models have been developed as test cases:

(1) Super-Ping Simulation. The topology of the networks is illustrated in Figure 5(a). A total of 1000 LPs are simulated in our experiment.
(2) A simple yet typical manufacturing model as illustrated in Figure 5(b) [3, 12].

The experimental results are summarized in Figure 6. They are consistent with our theoretical analysis.

5 Applications to Synchronous Simulations

We have implemented several programs that make use of synchronous simulation algorithms to evaluate the proposed locality-preserving load-balancing mechanisms. All the programs are developed by using Cilk-5 [2, 15], a C-based multithreaded runtime system developed in MIT.

We have implemented a few programs (the *original versions*) relying on Cilk's native work scheduler for load balancing and implemented others (the *improved versions*) by using our load-balancing mechanism incorporating **Scheme (NSM,S)**. Although the Cilk scheduler ensures generally good workload balance among the processors, the system makes no attempt to control the processor that will process a given LP. Expectedly, the original version incurs high cache misses and each processor spends a significant portion of time to wait for the cache content to be validated. The improved version shows marked improvements.

Time-stepped simulation of AGV systems

We have developed a simulation program to model the movement of AGVs (*Automated Guided Vehicles*) [19]. The simulation progresses in a time-stepped fashion where the simulation model is first decomposed into a number of components and a constant time step $\triangle$ is applied to progress the simulation.

Some experimental results are presented in Figure 7. In a simulation with 150 AGVs, we obtained a speedup of about 6.5 using 8 processors, with 1,000 floating operations per AGV move. However, the original version (using Cilk's work-stealing mechanism) manages to provide a speedup of only about 2.4 with the same configuration.

PDES with the safe time algorithm

We have also implemented several simulation applications based on the safe time algorithm [3], a synchronous simulation algorithm, and tested with superping simulation, manu-

		Methods for tracking victim information			
		Memoryless: **Scheme (L,*)**	With Memory: **Scheme (-M,*)**		
			Private-Memory: **Scheme (PM,*)**	Shared-Memory: **Scheme (-SM,*)**	
				Exclusive: **Scheme (ESM,*)**	Non-exclusive: **Scheme (NSM,*)**
Methods for selecting candidate victim	Random: **Scheme (*,R)**	**Scheme (L,R)**	**Scheme (PM,R)**	**Scheme (ESM,R)**	**Scheme (NSM,R)**
	Successor: **Scheme (*,S)**	**Scheme (L,S)**	**Scheme (PM,S)**	**Scheme (ESM,S)**	**Scheme (NSM,S)**

Table 1: Possible schemes resulting from using various methods for tracking the victim information and for deciding candidate victims. Note that **Scheme (L,S)** is not meaningful in the context of our paper due to its limited capability in load balancing.

Victim selection schemes	Time complexity (per one StealLP operation)	
	Without interference	With interference
Scheme (L,R)	$O(P\tau_R)$†	
Scheme (PM,β)	$O((1 + \frac{P^2}{n})\tau_\beta)$	
Scheme (ESM,β)	$O((1 + \frac{P}{n})\tau_\beta)$	$O(P(1 + \frac{P}{n})\tau_\beta)$
Scheme (NSM,β)		$O((1 + \frac{P^2}{n})\tau_\beta)$

The parameters:
- P: total number of physical processors
- n: total number of StealLP operations in the given cycle
- τ_β: the overhead incurred by method β in deciding a candidate victim

† An expected time bound.
Note: all time complexities are amortized bounds, except for **Scheme (L,R)** which shows an expected time complexity.

Table 2: A summary of various victim selection schemes

facturing simulation and torus interconnection network simulation.

Figure 8 shows clearly that the improved version of the safetime algorithm does outperform the original version in all the experiments we have carried out.

6 Conclusion and Future Work

We have presented several efficient locality-preserving load-balancing mechanisms for synchronous simulations on shared-memory multiprocessors. We have also analyzed two aspects of the mechanism—the interaction among the processors and the victim selection schemes—and showed that some of the new mechanisms are indeed very efficient.

The mechanisms have been tested with several applications with synchronous computation. Our empirical studies confirm that, with the most efficient version of these mechanisms, the time taken for a processor to grab a job is indeed quite short, and furthermore, it scales well with more number of processors. For future work, we plan to evaluate our mechanisms by comparing them with a few more existing load-balancing mechanisms.

References

[1] V. C. Barbosa. *An Introduction to Distributed Algorithms*. The MIT Press, 1996.

[2] R. D. Blumofe, C. F. Joerg, B. C. Kuszmaul, C. E. Leiserson, K. H. Randall, and Y. Zhou. Cilk: an efficient multithreaded runtime system. In *Proceedings of the 5th ACM SIGPLAN Symposium on Principles and Practice of Parallel Programming*, pages 207–216, Honolulu, Hawaii, July 1995. ACM Press, New York.

[3] W. Cai, E. Letertre, and S. J. Turner. Dag consistent parallel simulation: a predictable and robust conservative algorithm. In *Proceedings of 11th Workshop on Parallel and Distributed Simulation (PADS'97)*, pages 178–181, Lockenhaus, Austria, June 10–13, 1997.

[4] K. M. Chandy and R. Sherman. The conditional event approach to distributed simulation. *Proceedings of the SCS Multiconference on Distributed Simulation*, 21(2):93–99, Mar. 28–31, 1989.

[5] A. Ferscha. Parallel and distributed simulation of discrete event systems. In *Handbook of Parallel and Distributed Computing*. McGraw-Hill, 1995.

[6] P. A. Fishwick. *Simulation Model Design and Execution: Building Digital Worlds*, chapter 9, pages 333–369. Prentice-Hall, 1995.

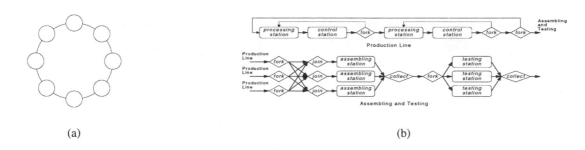

(a)   (b)

Figure 5: (a) A super-ping model and (b) a simplified manufacturing model.

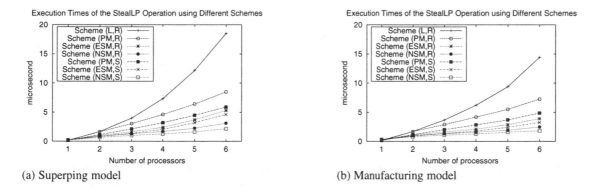

(a) Superping model   (b) Manufacturing model

Figure 6: Execution times of the StealLP operation for (a) a super-ping and (b) a simplified manufacturing simulation. The models are simulated with the safetime algorithm [3], a synchronous simulation algorithm, on a 6-processor 250Mhz UltraSPARC Enterprise 3500 Sun SMP. The figures are measured using Sun's high-resolution clock. Each data point is averaged from more than 100,000 samples.

[7] M. Frigo, C. E. Leiserson, and K. H. Randall. The implementation of the Cilk-5 multithreaded language. In *1998 ACM SIGPLAN Conference on Programming Language Design and Implementation (PLDI'98)*, pages 212–223, Montreal, Canada, June 17–19, 1998.

[8] R. M. Fujimoto. Parallel discrete event simulation. *Commun. ACM*, 33(10):30–53, Oct. 1990.

[9] R. M. Fujimoto. *Parallel and Distributed Simulation Systems*. John Wiley & Sons, 2000.

[10] M. R. Garey and D. S. Johnson. *Computers and Intractability: A Guide to the Theory of NP-Completeness*. W. H. Freeman and Company, New York, 1979.

[11] C. E. Leiserson, H. Prokop, and K. H. Randall. Using de Bruijn sequences to index a 1 in a computer word. Extended abstract submitted for publication. Available on the Internet from http://supertech.lcs.mit.edu/cilk/.

[12] C.-C. Lim, Y.-H. Low, W. Cai, W. J. Hsu, S. Y. Huang, and S. J. Turner. An empirical comparison of runtime systems for conservative parallel simulation. In *2nd Workshop on Runtime Systems for Parallel Programming (RTSPP'98)*, Orlando, Florida, Mar. 30, 1998.

[13] B. D. Lubachevsky. Bounded lag distributed event simulation. *Proceedings of the SCS Multiconference on Distributed Simulation*, 19(3):183–190, Feb. 3–5, 1988.

[14] B. D. Lubachevsky. Efficient distributed event-driven simulations of multiple-loop networks. *Commun. ACM*, 32(1):111–123, Jan. 1989.

[15] K. H. Randall. *Cilk: Efficient Multithreaded Computing*. PhD thesis, Department of Electrical Engineering and Computer Science, Massachusetts Institute of Technology, June 1998.

[16] L. G. Valiant. A bridging model for parallel computation. *Commun. ACM*, 33(8):103–111, Aug. 1990.

[17] V.-Y. Vee and W.-J. Hsu. Locality-perserving mechanism for synchronous simulation algorithms. Technical Report CAIS-TR-99-24, Centre for Advanced Information Systems, Nanyang Technological University, Singapore, Aug. 1999.

[18] V.-Y. Vee and W.-J. Hsu. Locality-preserving load-balancing mechanisms for synchronous simulations on shared-memory multiprocessors. Technical Report CAIS-TR-00-29, Centre for Advanced Information Systems, Nanyang Technological University, Singapore, Mar. 2000.

[19] V.-Y. Vee, R. Ye, S. S. Niranjan, and W.-J. Hsu. Meeting challenges of container port operations for the next millennium. Report for Supercomputer Programming Contest (CrayQuest'99), Singapore, Oct. 1999. Gold Award Winner.

[20] A. J. Wing. Discrete event simulation in parallel. In L. Kronsjö and D. Shumsheruddin, editors, *Advances in Parallel Algorithms*, Advanced Topics in Computer Science Series, chapter 7, pages 179–226. Blackwell Scientific Publications, 1992.

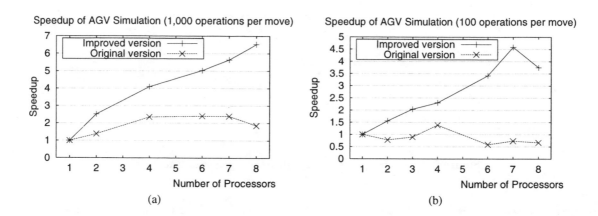

(a)   (b)

Figure 7: The speedups obtained for AGV simulations with a 250MHz SGI Origin 2000 multiprocessor. The dip of performance beyond 8 processors is believed to be caused by heavy usage of the shared system. We obtain superlinear speedups in some simulation cases. This is due to the fact that the sequential simulation engine spends extra time to maintain a larger global event list, while the parallel simulation engine uses an individual message list for each LP.

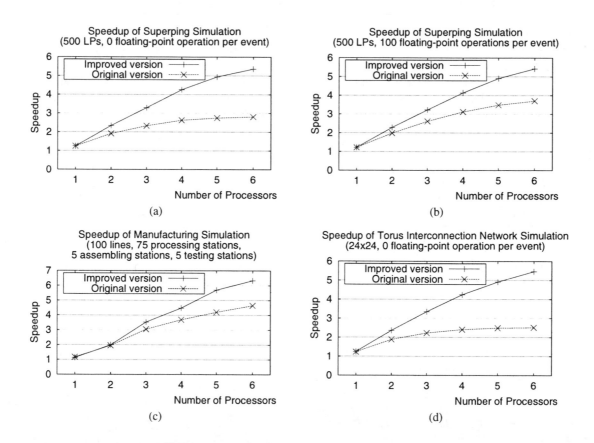

(a)   (b)

(c)   (d)

Figure 8: The speedups obtained for superping, manufacturing and torus interconnection network simulations. The experimental results are collected with a 6 processor 250Mhz UltraSPARC Enterprise 3500 Sun SMP. The topologies of the superping simulation and manufacturing simulation are given in Figure 5.

Load Balancing for Conservative Simulation on Shared Memory Multiprocessor Systems

Boon Ping Gan, Yoke Hean Low,
Sanjay Jain
Gintic Institute of
Manufacturing Technology
71 Nanyang Drive
Singapore 638075
{bpgan,yllow,sjain}@gintic.gov.sg

Stephen J. Turner, Wentong Cai, Wen Jing Hsu,
Shell Ying Huang
School of Applied Science
Nanyang Technological University
Nanyang Avenue
Singapore 639798
{assjturner, aswtcai, hsu, assyhuang}@ntu.edu.sg

Abstract

Load balancing is a crucial factor in achieving good performance for parallel discrete event simulations. In this paper, we present a load balancing scheme that combines both static partitioning and dynamic load balancing. The static partitioning scheme maps simulation objects to logical processes before simulation starts while the dynamic load balancing scheme attempts to balance the load during runtime. The static scheme involves two steps. First, the simulation objects that contribute to small lookahead are merged together by using a merging algorithm. Then a partitioning algorithm is applied. The merging is needed to ensure a consistent performance for our dynamic scheme. Our dynamic scheme is tailor-made for an asynchronous simulation protocol that does not rely on null messages. The performance study on a supply-chain simulation shows that the partitioning algorithm and dynamic load balancing are important in achieving good performance.

1. Introduction

Load balancing is an important ingredient to achieving good performance for parallel simulation. In general, it can be done either statically or dynamically. The static approach assigns logical processes to processors before the simulation starts. The logical processes then stay at the same processor till the end of the simulation. The approach will not be able to respond to load variation during runtime. Furthermore, an accurate load estimation strategy is required in order to apply the scheme effectively. The alternative approach, the dynamic scheme, does not have these drawbacks. Logical processes are migrated from one processor to another in response to system load variations.

Both static and dynamic load balancing schemes have been applied to parallel simulation. The general observation is that a static load balancing scheme alone is not enough to achieve good performance due to the dynamic nature of the simulation models. Relying on the operating system to dynamically balance the system load is also not enough since this system does not try to balance the simulation time advancement of logical processes (LPs), which is crucial in parallel simulation as shown in [10],[12]. Thus, several customised dynamic load balancing schemes have been proposed for various parallel simulation protocols [7],[8],[10],[12],[18].

A CMB-SMP protocol, an extension to the conservative asynchronous simulation protocol by Chandy, Misra, and Bryant [1],[2],[3], was proposed in [20]. It is an efficient protocol that is customised for shared memory multiprocessor systems. To improve performance, simulation objects were partitioned to form LPs with the objective of achieving load balancing and maximum lookahead (between LPs). These LPs are then mapped to the processor and stay at the same processor throughout the simulation. This particular approach does not guarantee good performance, especially when the model exhibits dynamic behaviour. The dynamic nature of the model makes load estimation difficult and in turn restricts the performance of the parallel simulation. We therefore extend the protocol by proposing a simple, yet effective dynamic load balancing scheme that tackles the dynamic behaviour of simulation models. The dynamic scheme has to be coupled with a merging algorithm that eliminates small lookahead cycles during static partitioning to guarantee a consistent performance. We have observed that small lookahead cycles restrain LPs from advancing their simulation times and offset the benefits gained by using dynamic load balancing.

A supply-chain simulation was used to evaluate our proposed load balancing schemes. It involves modelling of

139

the flow of material and information through multiple stages of manufacturing, transportation and distribution until the final product reaches the customer [19]. This modelling can be used to study different strategies that can help in planning of replenishments of incoming inventory, planning of operations at each manufacturing stage and so on. For example, striking a balance between inventory level and service level[1] is crucial to the electronics industry, in which the product life-cycle is short. Keeping a high inventory level for short life-cycle products might put companies at risk. But a low inventory level might degrade a company's service level. Due to the inherent complexity of modelling multiple factories, this application is a good candidate for parallel simulation.

The rest of the paper is organised as follows. Section 2 presents related works on load balancing for parallel simulation. A brief overview of the supply-chain simulation model is presented in Section 3. Then the CMB-SMP protocol is briefly described and the proposed load balancing schemes are presented in Section 4. Section 5 presents the experimental results. The study is concluded in Section 6.

2. Related Works

Even though load balancing is a well-studied area for parallel and distributed systems, the work that has been done for parallel simulations is limited. Most of the load balancing schemes proposed for parallel simulation are focused on optimistic simulation protocols. These load balancing schemes are mostly dynamic load balancing strategies [5],[7],[8],[12],[18] because of the protocol's dynamic nature. Some of these load balancing schemes are designed specifically for certain classes of applications, such as logic simulation in [7], while others are designed for general parallel simulation applications [5],[8],[18]. Some schemes are proposed for a time sharing environment in which the parallel simulation applications are contending for processing resources with other non-parallel applications [5],[8], while others assume exclusive use of the processing resources [7],[12],[18]. Some of the schemes are also integrated with the underlying time warp mechanism, for example, dynamic load balancing was integrated with a flow control algorithm to reduce the number of rollbacks and number of anti-messages in [18].

Several load balancing schemes were also proposed to improve the performance of parallel simulation based on conservative protocols [4],[10],[16], in particular the CMB protocol. In both [4] and [10], the schemes attempt not only to balance the load for a distributed memory system, but also to minimise the number of null messages sent between logical processes. The only difference is that the

optimisation is done statically in [4], while it is done dynamically in [10]. A scheme targeted for shared memory systems was proposed in [16]. It balances the load dynamically by allowing processors to acquire a task[2] from a centralised queue whenever the processor is idle. In this respect, the approach is very similar to our dynamic scheme. The differences between the two schemes will be analysed in a later section.

3. Simulation Models

A supply-chain model is used to evaluate the proposed partitioning strategies in this study. It models an electronics industry in which multiple wafer fabrication factories are supplying wafers to a single assembly & test (A&T) factory. The A&T factory receives orders from customers and schedules the lot releases based on these orders. A lot can only be released into the A&T process if there are raw materials (wafers) available in the inventory. At the wafer fabrication side, the lot releases are governed by its own forecasted demand. The lot release rate is adjusted periodically based on the forecasted demand of the period, inventory level of the A&T factory, and the current work-in-progress.

In the supply-chain simulation, a detailed modelling of the manufacturing process is done for each factory. The flow of products from the first step till the last step of its manufacturing process is modelled. This includes the modelling of contention for resources, such as machines and operators, and stochastic events, such as machine failure and lot/part scrap.

The models that are used in this work are based on some real world examples. The wafer fabrication models were obtained from the Sematech's Modeling Data Standard (MDS) project [9]. There are a total of six example data models that model manufacturing processes of wafer products such as memory and ASIC. The A&T model was obtained from an industrial project. Each product in the A&T is mapped to a particular wafer product from the wafer fabrication factory based on their volume release rate. Multiple wafer fabrication factories are needed in order to fulfil the release rate of the A&T factory. A detailed discussion on the simulation model can be found in [19].

4. The Load Balancing Schemes

4.1 The CMB-SMP protocol

The CMB-SMP protocol is an extension to the conservative asynchronous simulation protocol by Chandy, Misra, and Bryant (CMB) [1],[2],[3]. It is

---

[1] Service level is defined as the percentage of orders that can be delivered before or on the product due date.

[2] A task is defined as a collection of logical processes that are highly dependent on each other in [16].

specifically designed for shared memory multiprocessor systems. It eliminates the need for sending null messages by using the concept of safetime. Safetime is defined as the next earliest timestamp of an event that the LP will receive from its upstream LPs. Thus, an LP can only safely simulate events with timestamp less than or equal to the safetime to adhere to the causality constraint. The safetime is computed using the equation below:

$$safetime_i = \mathbf{min}\{simul\_time_j + lookahead_{j,i} \mid LP_j \in \text{set of}$$
$$\text{upstream LPs of } LP_i\},$$

where $safetime_i$ is the safetime of LP_i, $simul\_time_j$ is the local simulation time of LP_j, and $lookahead_{j,i}$ is the lookahead from LP_j to LP_i. Lookahead is defined as the minimum (simulation) time interval between event arrival, from a source LP to a destination LP.

This safetime computation is only initiated when an LP has simulated all the events with timestamp less than the safetime. Events at the safetime are not processed to ensure repeatability of the simulation. Before a new safetime computation can be initiated, the local simulation time of the LP needs to be set to the safetime to ensure that the simulation is deadlock free. During the computation, an LP will keep on polling the upstream LP that constrains its progress until the safetime advances. Figure 1 outlines the CMB-SMP protocol. The outline assumes that the simulation time can be read and written using an atomic operation. Further description and proof of correctness of the protocol can be found in [20].

4.2 The Static Scheme

Allowing a one-to-one mapping between simulation objects[3] and logical processes could incur a heavy overhead for parallel simulation. To reduce this overhead, partitioning schemes are needed to group multiple simulation objects to form logical processes (LP) prior to the simulation. Three objective functions can be used for the partitioning scheme: minimising load imbalances, minimising inter-processor communications, or maximising lookaheads. Since our CMB-SMP protocol is applied on shared memory systems, inter-processor communications will not be a major issue. Balancing the load of LPs and maximising lookaheads are more crucial. By balancing the load, it helps to ensure that all LPs make (simulation time) progress at similar pace, and reduces the time wasted on polling of upstream LPs for safetime update. Doing just load balancing might not be enough since the final partition might affect the parallelism of the model with small lookahead values between LPs. Thus, by maximising lookahead, it helps to better exploit the model's parallelism.

---

[3] In this context, the simulation objects are the resources within the simulation model, such as machines and operators of the supply-chain model.

```
for each LP_i do
// 1) Swapping buffers and merging events
  for each inBuff_ji, where j is set of
  upstream LPs do
   lock inBuffLock_ji
   swap inBuff_ji with old_inBuff_ji
   unlock inBuffLock_ji
   for each event, e_g, in inBuff_ji do
    local_eventlist_i.ordered_insert(e_g)
   endfor
  endfor

// 2) Safetime computation - spin on the
// simulation time of constraining LP
 safetime_i = min(simul_time_j + lookahead_{j,i})
   where j is set of upstream LPs

// 3) Simulating up to safetime
 while (top_event_i.timestamp < safetime_i) do
  e_top = local_eventlist_i.pop()
  simul_time_i = e_top.timestamp
  generated_events = simulate(e_top)

// 4) Insertion of generated events
  for each generated_events, e_g, do
   if (external_event(e_g))
    lock inBuffLock_ik
    old_inBuff_ik.push(e_g)
     where k is the receiving LP
    unlock inBuffLock_ik
   else
    local_eventlist_i.ordered_insert(e_g)
   endif
  endfor
 endwhile

// 5) Update virtual time to safetime
  simul_time_i = safetime_i
endfor
```

Figure 1 The CMB-SMP protocol

```
for product P, where P=1,…,n and n is
number of products
 Let R be the process route used by P
 for every step in R that uses obj_i
  obj_i.wg = obj_i.wg + (n*(release_rate(P)/T)
  where obj_i.wg is the weight of the
  simulation object i, release_rate(P) is
  the release rate of P, T is the total
  release rate
 endfor
endfor
```

Figure 2 Algorithm to Compute Node Weight

Existing partitioning packages, such as Metis [14] and Scotch [15], have proven to be capable of generating good partitions. Thus, we adopted these packages without any modification in our static partitioning schemes. The packages share the same objectives of minimising load imbalances and inter-process communications. Since our objective functions do not involve minimising inter-process communications, modifications were done to the input of these algorithms.

The Metis and Scotch partitioning algorithms take undirected graphs as their input. In our context, the simulation objects will be mapped to the nodes of the given graph, and the edges represent the interaction between the simulation objects. Each node will have an associated weight, whereby the load is estimated by referring to the volume release rate of the products. Figure 2 shows the algorithm for estimating the node weight [13]. Other than the node weight, each edge has an associated edge weight. This weight is taken as the inverse of lookahead values. By doing so, the effect of minimising the edge weight (inter-process communication) will be the maximisation of lookahead values. With this, we achieve our primary goal of minimising load imbalances and maximising lookaheads.

Through experiments, we have found that the partitions generated fail to eliminate small lookahead cycles occasionally (which is affecting the performance of our dynamic scheme significantly as will be discussed in the experimental section). This might be due to the trade off between the two objective functions, namely minimizing load imbalances and maximizing lookahead values. In order to eliminate this problem, a merging algorithm is applied to the input graph, to eliminate small lookahead values, before the partitioning algorithms are initiated.

The merging algorithm needs a lookahead value to serve as the threshold, which is called the cut-off lookahead hereafter. All the edges with lookahead values less than this cut-off will be eliminated by merging the simulation objects involved. Specifying an absolute lookahead value as the cut-off might not be correct. A small lookahead value might not be small in one model as compared to another and vice versa. In fact, it is the lookahead distribution that is important in selecting the right cut-off. Thus, a cumulative frequency of lookahead values is first generated by using the following equations:

Let *sampInv* be the **sampling interval**
Let *lookaheads* be the **set of lookahead values**
Let $inv_i = sampInv * i$ be the end of the i-th interval

$$cumulFreq(inv_i) = \sum_{j=1}^{i} freq(inv_j) \text{ for } i = 1,2,3,...,k$$

$$\text{where } k = \frac{max(lookaheads)}{sampInv}$$

$$freq(inv_i) = \frac{\text{no of times } lookaheads \text{ value falls in } (inv_{i-1}, inv_i)}{l}$$

$$\text{where } l = sizeof(lookaheads)$$

By having the cumulative frequency of lookahead values, a cut-off lookahead value can be determined by specifying a cut-off frequency. Figure 3 shows the outline of the merging algorithm. The cut-off frequency, *cf*, in the figure is a user supplied value. This value is independent of the model's meaning of lookahead values. With this value, there is no longer the need of specifying an absolute lookahead value as the cut-off point. In this study, we set the cut-off frequency at 10% and the sampling interval as 1.0. The process of determining the cut-off lookahead through this cut-off frequency is automated in our simulator as outlined in Figure 3.

```
Compute freq(invᵢ) for i=1,2,3,…,k
Compute culmulFreq(invᵢ) for i=1,2,3,…,k
Let cf be the cutoff frequency
Let cf_la be the cutoff lookahead value
while (i ≤ k AND cumulFreq(invᵢ) < cf)
  i = i + 1
  cf_la = invᵢ
endwhile
for all edges weighted with
  lookahead values ≤ cf_la do
  merge the simulation objects involved
endfor
```

Figure 3 Outline of the Merging Algorithm

To summarise, our static partitioning strategy involves two levels of partitioning. At the first level, the merging algorithm is applied to eliminate small lookahead cycles, in which simulation objects that are connected by small lookahead links are merged into the same partition. Then, the partitioning package is initiated to map the remaining simulation objects to LPs at the second level. During runtime, each LP is assigned to a thread (a one-to-one mapping) and stays with the thread till the end of the simulation. A thread is bound to a processor (a one-to-one mapping) such that no thread migration is allowed. By disabling migration, cache locality can be improved.

4.3 The Dynamic Scheme

The static schemes discussed in Section 4.2 will not be effective on simulation models that exhibit dynamic behaviour. This is especially true in a feedback control system such as our supply-chain model. The release rate of products is adjusted at the wafer fabrication factories during runtime according to the factory's forecasted demand, work-in-progress, and current inventory level of the assembly and test factory. This variation in release rate invalidates the load estimation that was done by the static partitioning scheme. Also, queuing of lots changes the arrival rate of lots to machines, which again invalidates the load estimation. Some form of correction needs to be performed during runtime in order to eliminate the problem of load imbalances created by the inaccurate load estimation. A simple, yet effective dynamic load balancing scheme was developed for this purpose.

The dynamic load balancing that we discuss here is customised for the CMB-SMP protocol. It takes advantage of the shared memory architecture by having a centralised pool from which idling threads grab LPs. The scheme works together with the static partitioning strategy that was discussed in the previous section. Static partitioning is first used to map simulation objects to LPs. These LPs are then dynamically scheduled to threads using the dynamic strategy. In this context, an LP is no longer bound to a thread as in the case when only the static partitioning is applied. Any thread in the system can simulate any LP. As a result, the number of LPs generated must always be larger than the number of threads (to keep every thread busy) in order to apply the dynamic scheme effectively. To avoid the operating system from scheduling the threads dynamically, each thread is bound to a single processor in the proposed scheme.

```
for each thread Tk do
 while (not end of simulation) do
// 0) Grab an LP from the centralised pool
  LPi = Tk.get_nextLP()

// 1) Swapping buffers and merging events

// 2) Safetime computation - without
//    spinning on the simulation time of
//    constraining LP

     [ 1) and 2) refer to Figure 1 ]

// 2a) Get next LP if safetime does not
//     progress
  if (safetimei == old_safetimei)
   Tk.yield_LP()
   continue
  else
   old_safetimei = safetimei
  endif

// 3) Simulating up to safetime

// 4) Insertion of generated events

// 5) Update virtual time to safetime
   [ 3), 4) and 5) refer to Figure 1 ]
 endwhile
endfor
```

Figure 4 Outline of CMB-SMP Protocol with Dynamic Load Balancing

In our dynamic scheme, LPs with a lower simulation time are given higher priority to be scheduled. But this introduces a potential deadlock into the system since it is possible that a higher priority LP is constrained by a lower priority LP that never gets a chance to run. To resolve this problem, two centralised pools, called active pool and passive pool, were used. Processors will grab LPs from the active pool and return LPs to the passive pool. When all the LPs in the active pool are consumed, the two pools

will be swapped. The swapping is done by the first processor that attempts to grab from an empty active pool.

Once a processor grabs an LP, the LP will be simulated until no further safetime progress is obtained in the safetime computation. This is to ensure that enough work is done to offset the overhead spent in doing dynamic load balancing. An LP that cannot make any further progress will be returned to the passive pool. A new LP is then grabbed from the active pool. Since the active and passive pools are resources accessed by multiple threads, they must be accessed within critical sections. The critical sections are implemented using spin-locks due to the short locking duration. Figure 4 shows the outline of our CMB-SMP protocol with the integration of the dynamic load balancing scheme. It is an extension to our CMB-SMP protocol in Figure 1. In the figure, the *get_nextLP()* has the responsibility of grabbing an LP from the active pool. The *yield_LP()* is used to return LPs to the passive pool.

Our load balancing scheme is similar to the CCT scheme proposed in [16]. The differences lie in the way static partitioning is done, the way LPs are scheduled, and the simulation protocol itself. In our scheme, other than partitioning simulation objects to form LPs, a merging algorithm is employed to eliminate small lookahead cycles. This is crucial to our dynamic load balancing scheme as will be shown in Section 5.2. Furthermore, our scheme allows only one thread/processor to simulate the simulation objects within an LP at any one point in time. This avoids the need for a locking mechanism in order to simulate the simulation objects within an LP.

On the simulation protocol, CCT and the scheme proposed here arc targeted for a different extension of the CMB protocol. The extended CMB protocol in CCT still has the concept of null message associated with it. How far an LP can progress in terms of simulation time is still based on the incoming messages. In comparison, the progress in LP's simulation time is not dependent on incoming messages with our CMB-SMP protocol. The extent to which an LP can progress its simulation time is constrained by the safetime imposed by its upstream LPs.

5. Experimental Results

In this section, we present the experimental results of our study. The results will be presented to show the importance of applying the partitioning algorithm as compared to random partitioning, the importance of the merging algorithm to the dynamic load balancing scheme and the importance of dynamic load balancing in achieving good performance. No detailed comparison of the static partitioning algorithms, namely Metis and Scotch, will be done in this paper since our experimental results have shown that neither of them exhibits an obvious performance advantage over the other. Thus, we use the Metis partitioning algorithm to perform most of the experiments in this paper. The performance metric used in this study is speedup. Speedup is taken as the ratio of the sequential execution time to the parallel execution time. The sequential execution time is obtained from our own implementation of a sequential simulator.

All the experiments were performed on a 4-CPU Sun Enterprise 3000 (250 MHz UltraSparc2) shared memory system. A multithreaded package, the *ActiveThread* library [11], is used as the underlying runtime library for the parallel simulator. The source code of the simulation program is compiled by the GNU g++ compiler (version 2.7.2.1). Table 1 shows the summary information of the six supply-chain models. Each supply-chain model consists of one A&T factory and multiple identical wafer fabrication factories.

Supply-chain model	1	2	3	4	5	6
No. of wafer fabs Factories	3	5	3	15	6	10

Table 1 Summary Information on the Supply-chain Model

Supply-chain model	1	2	3	4	5	6
Critical Path Speedup	3.75	6.10	5.08	3.45	4.43	6.20

Table 2 Critical Path Speedup of the Supply-chain Model

Before the experiments were performed, the parallelism of each supply-chain model was first estimated. A critical path analyser [17] was used for this purpose. It gives the best possible speedup that a model can achieve when a conservative simulation protocol is used (independent of partitioning algorithm). Table 2 shows the results of this performance prediction, whereby the critical path speedup of the six supply-chain models fall in the range of 3.45 to 6.20. Apparently, the inherent parallelism of the models is quite limited.

5.1 The Importance of the Partitioning Algorithms

First, we would like to show the importance of the partitioning algorithms as compared to a random partitioning scheme[4]. To see a significant difference in performance between the two strategies, a scalability study was performed with 8, 16, 32, and 64 processors. But due to the unavailability of hardware with this number of processors, the CMB protocol performance analyser was used for this purpose. The performance analyser is

---

[4] A random partitioning scheme randomly assigns simulation objects to LPs

integrated to the sequential simulation engine such that a simulation of the parallel simulation is done while the sequential simulation is running. The accuracy of the analyser was verified through comparisons of the predicted and actual results on our 4-processor system. Note that the performance analyser does not take locking overheads into consideration since the overheads are negligible. More details on the analyser are in [6],[17].

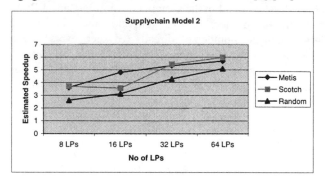

Figure 5 Scalability Study with Metis, Scotch, and Random Partitioning Strategy

Figure 5 compares the predicted scalability of parallel simulation with Metis, Scotch, and the random partitioning scheme. Only supply-chain 2 is used for this comparison since it is one of the models with higher critical path speedup (6.10) as shown in Table 2. It is obvious from Figure 5 that the random partitioning scheme does not perform as well as Metis and Scotch. This shows the importance of applying certain partitioning algorithm, such as Metis and Scotch, in order to achieve good performance with parallel simulation. Another observation from Figure 5 is that the estimated performance achieved by Metis and Scotch does not differ much in most of the cases. Due to this observation, we used Metis for the rest of the experiments in this paper.

5.2 The Importance of the Merging Algorithm

Experiments in Section 5.2 and 5.3 were done with actual parallel simulation runs on 4 processors. Figure 6 shows the speedup achieved with our dynamic load balancing scheme for varying number of LPs. As can be seen, the speedup achieved by the dynamic scheme is not consistent with different number of LPs. In some cases, the speedup even drops below 1 (64 LPs with supply-chain model 1). Careful examination of the final LPs connectivity graph reveals that small lookahead cycles exist among LPs for those cases with bad performance. These small lookahead cycles constrain the simulation time progress of the LPs. LPs are repeatedly being grabbed by threads but only a small number of events can be simulated. The actual work done by each grab is not enough to offset the overhead incurred for the grabbing operation. Thus, poor speedup was achieved.

To eliminate this problem, the merging algorithm described in Section 4.2 is applied before the partitioning algorithm is initiated. Figure 7 shows the actual speedup achieved with this merging algorithm being turned on. It is obvious from the graph that the performance of the dynamic load balancing becomes more consistent. For example, the slowdown for supply-chain model 1 with 64 LPs has now gone to the speedup range (approximately 2.7 from the figure). As such, our merging algorithm is effective in eliminating small lookahead cycles. This also suggests that small lookahead cycles are a major obstacle to achieving good speedup in parallel simulation.

Another interesting point to note from the figure is that, in general, better speedup is achieved with a larger number of LPs. This is understandable since with more LPs, each LPs' granularity will be finer. This eases the dynamic load balancing strategy in performing its job. Furthermore, a higher number of LPs allows for better exploitation of the model parallelism.

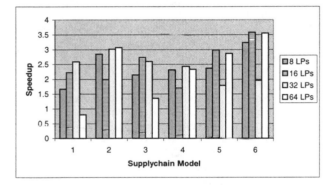

Figure 6 Speedup of Dynamic Scheme without LP Merging

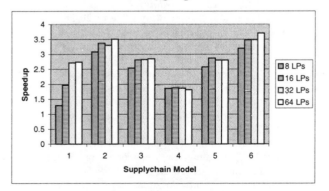

Figure 7 Speedup of Dynamic Scheme with LP Merging

5.3 The Importance of Dynamic Load Balancing

Figure 8 compares the performance of parallel simulation that runs with and without dynamic load balancing. Obviously, the performance with dynamic load balancing produces a much better speedup as compared to the case where only the static scheme is employed. This is mainly due to the dynamic behaviour of the feedback control system of the simulation model that we mentioned earlier. With dynamic load balancing, the errors caused by the inaccurate load estimation are corrected during runtime. Hence, consistently good performance is observed when dynamic load balancing is invoked. This also confirms that dynamic load balancing is needed for models that exhibit dynamic behaviour during the simulation.

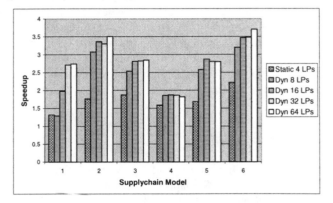

Figure 8 Comparing Speedup with and without Dynamic Load Balancing

6. Conclusions

In this paper, both static partitioning and dynamic load balancing strategies were studied. We proposed a static partitioning strategy that attempts to minimise load imbalances while maximising lookahead values. The static partitioning packages, Metis and Scotch, were used to achieve these objective functions. The scalability study based on a performance analyser has shown that it is indeed important to apply a partitioning algorithm instead of using a random partitioning strategy. The predicted speedup number is consistently better for experiments that were done with Metis or Scotch partitioning packages.

Experimental results of the proposed dynamic load balancing scheme have shown that the scheme is sensitive towards small lookahead cycles. With the help of a merging algorithm to eliminate small lookahead cycles, we are able to achieve consistent performance with the proposed dynamic scheme. Comparing parallel simulations that were done with and without dynamic load balancing, it is obvious that parallel simulations with dynamic load balancing achieve better performance. The speedup achieved goes as high as 3.7 (on 4 processors) in some cases. This is a respectable speedup considering the fine event granularity of the model (less than 100 microseconds based on the clock speed of 250 MHz).

Even though the dynamic scheme performs extremely well on our 4-processor SMP system, we would like to further investigate its performance on a larger system. We believe some form of fine tuning is required to enhance cache locality and reduce the conflicts in accessing the centralised pool.

One last point that we would like to make is that it is very difficult to determine an optimal number of LPs that one should use when dynamic load balancing is applied. We believe this optimal value varies with different model characteristics and different model sizes. Unless the model characteristics can be defined clearly with certain metrics, trying to determine the interrelationship between the number of LPs and model characteristics will be difficult. Thus, we did not attempt to find an optimal number of LPs for our dynamic load balancing scheme in this study. We believe that by obtaining consistent performance with a varying number of LPs, obtaining the optimal number of LPs for dynamic load balancing is no longer an important issue.

Acknowledgements

This research is supported by National Science and Technology Board, Singapore, under the project: Parallel And Distributed Simulation of Virtual Factory Implementation. It is a collaborative project between Gintic Institute of Manufacturing Technology, Singapore and the School of Applied Science in Nanyang Technological University, Singapore. The project is located at the Centre for Advanced Information Systems at Nanyang Technological University, Singapore. The authors would like to acknowledge the contribution of Dr. Lim Chu Cheow to this project.

References

[1]   R.E. Bryant, "Simulation of Packet Communications Architecture Computer Systems", *MIT-LCS-TR-188*, Massachusetts Institute of Technology, 1977.

[2]   K.M. Chandy and J. Misra, "Distributed simulation: A Case Study in Design and Verification of Distributed Programs", *IEEE Trans. On Software Engineering*, SE-5, 1979, pp 440-452.

[3]   K.M. Chandy and J. Misra, "Asynchronous Distributed Simulation via a Sequence of Parallel Computations", *Communications of the ACM*, vol 24, 1981, pp 198-205.

[4]   A. Boukerche and C. Tropper, "A Static Partitioning and Mapping Algorithm for Conservative Parallel Simulations", In *Proceedings of the 8th Workshop on PADS*, Edinburgh, Scotland, July 1994, pp 164-172.

[5]   R. Schlagenhaft, M. Ruhwandl, C. Sporrer, and H. Bauer., "Dynamic Load Balancing of a Multi-Cluster Simulator on a Network of Workstations", In *Proceedings of the 9th Workshop on PADS*, Lake Placid, New York, June 1995, pp 175-180.

[6]   Y.C. Wong, S.Y. Hwang, and Y.B. Lin. A Parallelism Analyser for Conservative Parallel Simulation. *IEEE Trans. on Parallel and Distributed Systems*, vol 6, pages 628-638, 1995.

[7]   H. Avril and C. Tropper, "The Dynamic Load Balancing of Clustered Time Warp for Logic Simulation", In *Proceedings of the 10th Workshop on PADS*, Philadelphia, Pennsylvania, May 1996, pp 20-27.

[8]   C. Carothers and R. Fujimoto, "Background Execution of Time Warp Programs", In *Proceedings of the 10th Workshop on PADS*, Philadelphia, Pennsylvania, May 1996, pp 12-19.

[9]   Sematech. Modeling Data Standards, version 1.0. Technical report, Sematech, Inc. Austin, TX78741.

[10] A. Boukerche and S.K. Das, "Dynamic Load Balancing Strategies for Conservative Parallel Simulations", In *Proceedings of the 11th Workshop on PADS*, Lockenhaus, Austria, June 1997, pp 20-28.

[11] B. Weissman, *Active threads manual*, International Computer Science Institute, Berkeley, CA94704, Technical Report TR-97-037, 1997.

[12] E. Deelman and B.K. Szymanski, "Dynamic Load Balancing in Parallel Discrete Event Simulation for Spatially Explicit Problems", In *Proceedings of the 12th Workshop on PADS*, Banff, Alberta, Canada, May 1998, pp 46-53.

[13] C.C. Lim, Y.H. Low, B.P. Gan, S.J. Turner, S. Jain, W. Cai, W.J. Hsu, and S.Y. Huang, "A Parallel Discrete-Event Simulation of Wafer Fabrication Processes", *3rd High Performance Computing (HPC) Asia*, Singapore, Sep 1998, pp. 1180-1189.

[14] G. Karypis, "Metis: Family of multilevel partitioning algorithms", *http://www-users.cs.umn.edu/karypis/metis*, University of Minnesota, Minneapolis, 1998.

[15] F. Pellegrini, "Scotch: Static mapping and graph partitioning package.", *http://www.labri.u-bordeaux.fr/Equipe/ALiENor/membre/pelegin/scotch*, LaBRI, Université Bordeaux-1, 1998

[16] Z. Xiao, B. Unger, R. Simmonds, J. Cleary, "Scheduling Critical Channels in Conservative Parallel Discrete Event Simulation", In *Proceedings of the 13th Workshop on PADS*, Atlanta, Georgia, May 1999, pp 20-28.

[17] C.C. Lim, Y.H. Low, B.P. Gan, S. Jain, W. Cai, S.Y. Huang, and W.J. Hsu, "Performance Prediction Tools for Parallel Discrete Event Simulation", In *Proceedings of the 13th Workshop on PADS*, Atlanta, Georgia, May 1999.

[18] M. Choe and C. Tropper, "On Learning Algorithms and Balancing Loads in Time Warp", In *Proceedings of the 13th Workshop on PADS*, Atlanta, Georgia, May 1999, pp. 101-108.

[19] S. Jain, C.C. Lim, B.P. Gan, and Y.H. Low, "Criticality of Detailed Modeling in Semiconductor Supply Chain Simulation", In *Proceedings of 1999 Winter Simulation Conference*, Phoenix, Arizona, Dec 1999.

[20] B.P. Gan and S.J. Turner, "An Asynchronous Protocol for Virtual Factory Simulation on Shared Memory Multiprocessor Systems", *Journal of Operational Research Society, Special Issue on Progress in Simulation Research*, 2000.

Model Structure and Load Balancing in Optimistic Parallel Discrete Event Simulation

Tapas K. Som* and Robert G. Sargent
Simulation Research Group
Department of Electrical Engineering and Computer Science
Syracuse University
Syracuse, NY 13244
E-mail: tsom@us.ibm.com   rsargent@syr.edu

Abstract

The concept of strong groups is introduced to describe the structure of simulation models. It is shown that logical processes within strong groups process at approximately the same rate and that different strong groups can progress at different rates. An algorithm based on the rates of the strong groups is presented to balance the load among the physical processors and for flow control.

Keywords - Parallel simulation, optimistic protocols, simulation model structure, load balancing, flow control.

1 Introduction

Load balancing in optimistic parallel discrete event simulation (PDES) [4] can have a significant impact on the run time performance by reducing the mismatch in the rate of progress between different logical processes (LPs). Limited research has been conducted on load balancing; see [2,3,5,8] and the references contained within these. Balanced loading is often achieved and maintained by periodically remapping LPs to processors so that the 'load' (estimated as the computation which has not been rolled back) on each processor is (approximately) equalized/balanced. Model structure is usually not considered a relevant factor in determining this mapping and is therefore ignored.

In this paper we show that model structure is an important factor that should be considered when determining the mapping to achieve a balanced load across processors.

We view the simulation model as a collection of strong groups. Each strong group is a collection of LPs that strongly affect each other's progress. We look at the nature of interaction between these strong groups and show that the interaction among strong groups may lead to i) a flow balancing problem, ii) a non-optimal use of cpu resources, and iii) excessive rollbacks. We show that LPs within the same strong group progress at approximately the same rate and present an algorithm for load balancing using the rate of progress of each strong group. Load balancing using this algorithm alleviates the above three problems.

The remainder of this paper is organized as follows. In Section 2 we briefly describe the structural framework used in this paper. In Section 3 we discuss how the progress of one LP is related to the progress of other LPs within the same strong group. In Section 4 we take a close look at the current load balancing technique. Section 5 presents a load balancing algorithm for simulation models with multiple strong groups and illustrates the algorithm with an example. Section 6 presents the summary and conclusions.

2 Simulation Model Structures and Strong Groups

In this section we examine the notion of strong groups, a collection of LPs that strongly affect each other's progress. First, we introduce the notion of *interconnection graph* which is a convenient graphical representation of simulation models.

For every simulation model one can construct a unique directed graph. A node in this directed graph corresponds to an LP in the simulation model, and an arc from a node L_i to another node L_j indicates that L_i can schedule an event in L_j's event queue. The directed graph corresponding to a simulation model will be referred to as the interconnection graph for that model. Figures 1 (a) and (b) show a queueing model and its interconnection graph.

It is obvious that an LP L_i can affect the progress of another LP L_j (directly) if there is an arc from

---

*Currently with IBM.

L_i to L_j, or (indirectly) if there is a path from L_i to L_j in the interconnection graph. For example, in Figure 1 (b) L_1 can directly affect L_2's progress and can indirectly affect L_3's progress.

An interconnection graph can have one or more strongly connected components (SCCs)[1]. See Figure 1 (c). It is obvious that LPs belonging to the same SCC can affect each others progress since by definition there is always either an arc or a path between any two LPs within the same SCC.

It is possible that an LP L_i schedules an event in LP L_j's input queue only infrequently. The arc between L_i, and L_j can then be considered as an *weak link* in the interconnection graph. Other arcs can be considered as *strong links*. One can remove all such weak links from an interconnection graph (e.g., if the arc from L_3 to L_2 in Figure 1 (b) is a weak link, it can be removed), and this removal will split some of the SCC's into multiple SCCs (e.g., C_2 now splits into two SCCs, SG_2 and SG_2' each containing one LP, see Figure 1 (d)). The resulting SCCs after the removel of weak links will be considered as the *strong groups* (SGs) of the simulation model. Note that a strong group is always a part of some SCC.

An interaction graph can also be viewed as a feed forward graph of its SCCs or strong groups (feed forward graphs are directed graphs without cycles). For example, the queuing model in Figure 1 (a) can be viewed as a feed forward graph $C_1 \rightarrow C_2 \rightarrow C_3 \rightarrow C_4$ before the removal of the arc $L_3 \rightarrow L_2$ (Figure 1 (c)) or as $SG_1 \rightarrow SG_2 \rightarrow SG_2' \rightarrow SG_3 \rightarrow SG_4$ (Figure 1 (d)) after the removal of the weak link $L_3 \rightarrow L_2$.

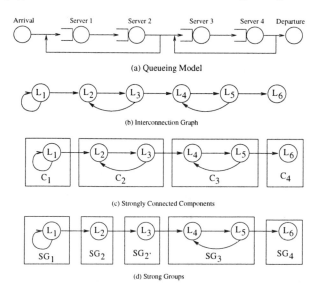

Figure 1: Queueing Model, Interconnection Graph, SCCs, and SGs.

3 Viewing SGs as a Single Entity

In this section we show that progress of LPs within the same strong group remain close to each other during a PDES run. As a consequence, with the passage of time during a PDES run the rate of progress of LPs within the same strong group tends to converge to one single value. One can therefore realistically view a strong group as a single entity which has a meaningful rate of progress and can talk about interaction among strong groups. We start by examinining how interacting LPs control each other's progress. Specifically, we examine what happens when one LP sends a message to another LP. We shall use the *Local Virtual Time (lvt)* (defined as the timestamp of the last processed input message in the input queue of an LP) as a measure of an LP's progress.

3.1 LPs within the Same SCC Cannot Race Ahead of Each Other

We make the following assumption:

A.1 The difference between the timestamp of an input message and the timestamp of the output message (this difference is referred to as time stamp increment) caused by this input message is bounded above. We shall denote this bound by B. Note that for most steady state simulations, e.g., steady state queuing simulations, B is always finite.

Notations:

- $lvt(L_i)$ denotes the *lvt* of L_i.

- $d(L_i, L_j)$ denotes the difference $lvt(L_i)$ - $lvt(L_j)$, i.e., $d(L_i, L_j)$ denotes how far L_i has progressed ahead of L_j.

Suppose L_2 can schedule events in L_1's input queue. Consider a scenario (see Figure 2) when L_2 sends a message M to L_1. (Note that we are using the terms messages and events synonymously in this discussion.) This message will have a timestamp of t_M $<= lvt(L_2) + B$. If $lvt(L_1)$ is larger than $lvt(L_2) +$ B, i.e., $d(L_1, L_2) = lvt(L_1)$ - $lvt(L_2) > $ B, then $lvt(L_l)$ $> t_M$ and M will immediately cause a rollback at L_1 reducing the difference between $lvt(L_1)$ and $lvt(L_2)$. I.e., every time L_2 sends a message to L_1, $d(L_1, L_2)$ becomes $<=$ B. Therefore, $d(L_1, L_2)$ can grow larger than B only during the interval between two consecutive messages sent by L_2 to L_1. If this interval is bounded, $d(L_1, L_2)$ can grow larger than B only by a finite amount, say "delta". I.e., $d(L_1, L_2)$ will be bounded above by B + delta. If L_2 sends messages to L_1 only infrequently (i.e., $L_2 \rightarrow L_1$ is a weak link)

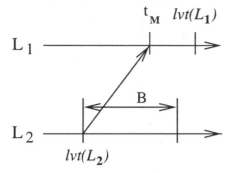

Figure 2: Scenario.

then the interval between two consecutive messages will be high and "delta" will have a large value. On the other hand if messages are sent frequently "delta" will be small.

We started this discussion by assuming that L_2 can schedule events in the input queue of L_1. In practice one can relax this requirement by requiring only that L_2 and L_1 belong to the same SCC. When L_1 and L_2 belong to the same SCC there exists a sequence of logical processes $L_2, L_p, L_q, \ldots, L_i, L_1, L_j, \ldots, L_s, L_2$ such that L_2 can schedule an event in (the input queue of) L_p, L_p can schedule an event in L_q, $\ldots$, and L_s can schedule an event in L_2. Consider the subsequence $L_2, \ldots, L_1$. Following the argument presented above, $d(L_p, L_2)$, $d(L_q, L_p)$, $\ldots$, and $d(L_1, L_i)$ will be bounded above and therefore $d(L_1, L_2)$ will also be bounded above (the value of this bound will depend on the length of the path $L_2, L_p, L_q, \ldots, L_i, L_1$). Similarly, it can be argued (consider the subsequence $L_1, L_j, \ldots, L_s, L_2$) that $d(L_2, L_1)$ will also be bounded above. Consequently, we can conclude that neither L_2 or L_1 can progress unboundedly ahead of each other. Since L_1 and L_2 are two arbitrary LPs within the same SCC, we can make the following general observation:

O1 The difference in progress of LPs within the same SCC is bounded.

It is clear from the preceding discussion that the bound mentioned in the observation **O1** above depends on how frequently LPs within a SCC interact with each other. If the interactions are infrequent i.e., if the SCC has a lot of weak links then the bound is likely to be high. On the other hand if the SCC has no weak links then the bound will be low. Recalling that a strong group is an SCC after all the weak links have been removed we can make the following observation:

O2 Progress of LPs within the same strong group remain close to each other.

3.2 Interaction among Strong Groups

Recall that strong groups form a feed forward graph when weak links are ignored. Consider two strong groups SG_i and SG_j with an arc from SG_i to SG_j. This arc implies that there is an LP L_i in SG_i which can schedule events in the input queue of an LP L_j in SG_j. Following the logic in Subsection 3.1, L_j's lvt cannot be larger than L_i's lvt by more than B + delta, i.e., L_j cannot race ahead of L_i. Since progress of LPs within the same strong group are close to each other we can rephrase the above as: SG_j *cannot race ahead of* SG_i. Whether or not SG_i can race ahead of SG_j temporarily or permanently depends on whether or not there is a weak link from SG_j to SG_i. (There cannot be any strong link from SG_j to SG_i, otherwise SG_i and SG_j will be a single strong group). We study these two cases separately.

3.2.1 No Weak Link from SG_j to SG_i

It follows that there is nothing inherent in the model structure to constrain SG_i from racing ahead of SG_j. Consequently, L_i may race ahead of L_j and L_j's input queue may be swamped by the messages received from L_i, causing severe flow control problems. Even in cases where large memory may keep the flow control problem managable, the use of cpu resources is less than optimal since the completion time of a PDES run to a given Global Virtual Time will be determined by the progress of its slowest LP.

3.2.2 One or More Weak Links from SG_j to SG_i

Messages are passed along weak links only infrequently. During the (long) interval when no messages have passed along the weak links from SG_j to SG_i, it is possible for SG_i to race far ahead of SG_j (since SG_i is not constrained by any inherent structural property of the model). When finally a message from SG_j arrives at SG_i it sets off a chain of rollbacks which brings lvt of all LPs within SG_i to a level lower than the timestamp of the arriving message.

To summarize, *strong groups are not restrained by inherent structural properties to progress at the same rate (only LPs within the same strong group do so)*. This unequal rate of progress may cause: (i) a flow balancing problem, (ii) a longer completion time of a PDES run, and (iii) chains of rollbacks. It is therefore important to equalize the rate of progress of strong groups during a PDES run.

4 A Close Look at Utilization Based Load Balancing

In this section we take a closer look at utilization based load balancing and examine why utilization based load balancing does not equalize the rate of progress of strong groups. We first discuss the notion of utilization.

4.1 Utilization

During a PDES run an LP usually generates both useful and erroneous computation. Computations that are rolled back are erroneous, those which are not rolled back are useful. This notion can be formalized as utilization. Suppose, a PDES run started at time 0 and is observed till time T_1. Suppose during the interval $[T, T_1]$, $0 < T < T_1$, the cpu time used by an LP L for computation that has not been rolled back is T_u. Then the utilization of L over the interval $[T, T_1]$ is defined as $T_u/(T_1 - T)$. It is obvious that utilization is always $<= 1$. Utilization is a measure of the amount of processing power (1 processor = 1 unit of procesing power) required to sustain the useful rate of computation achieved by L in a specified interval during a given PDES run. The amount of erroneous computation may vary from run to run (for the same LP) or during different intervals within the same PDES run depending on run time parameters, e.g., LP to processor assignments. Consequently, utilization of an LP may vary from run to run or during different intervals within the same run.

4.2 Utilization Based Dynamic Load Balancing

Utilization may also be viewed as the "load" imposed on a processor in a given interval by the useful computation done by an LP during a PDES run. The load balancing scheme reported in [8] is based on balancing aggregate utilization across processors. At periodic intervals the utilization of individual LPs and the "load" on each processor (i.e., sum of utilization of LPs assigned to that processor) are recomputed. If the load is not balanced, LPs from overloaded processors are migrated to lightly loaded processors to balance the load. The effect of this migration is to change an LP's access to processing power. As an example, in Figure 3 LP_2 is migrated from Processor 2 to Processor 1 equalizing the load (load is 0.2 for Processor 1 and 0.8 for Processor 2 before migration and is 0.5 on each processor after migration). The notation being used is L_i(utilization of L_i).

As can be seen from Figure 3 the net effect of the utilization based load balancing is to: (i) lower the share of processing power for LPs with low utilization (a characterisric of LPs experiencing a lot of rollbacks)

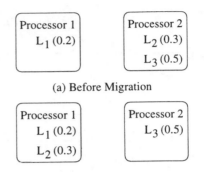

(a) Before Migration

(b) After Migration

Figure 3: Migration Example.

by forcing them to share a processor with other LPs (L_1 is forced to share Processor 1 with L_2 now), and (ii) increase the share of processing power for LPs with high utilization (a characteristic of LPs doing a lot of computation and experiencing few roll backs) by letting them share a processor with fewer LPs (L_3 does not share Processor 2 with any other LP after migration). This enables L_1 to slowdown and L_3 to speed up.

4.3 Strong Groups and Utilization Based Load Balancing

Migration of LPs from overloaded processors to underloaded processors has the effect of equalizing the rate of progress of LPs as explained above and is triggered through the following sequence of events: (i) rollbacks at faster moving LPs are caused by some slower moving LPs, (ii) these rollbacks are reflected as lower utilization of the corresponding LPs and consequently as lower loads on the corresponding processors, and (iii) migration is triggered to equalize the load on processors.

Unfortunately when the faster moving LPs and slower moving LPs belong to different strong groups, there may not be any rollback or the rollback may be severely delayed. Consider for example the scenario described in Subsections 3.2.1 and 3.2.2. If there is no weak link from SG_j to SG_i a slower moving L_j will never cause any rollback (directly or indirectly through a rollback tree) at L_i. Consequently, no migration will be triggered. Thus SG_i will keep progressing faster than SG_j causing either an overflow problem and/or inefficient utilization of cpu power as discussed earlier. If there is a weak link, the rollback may occur only after SG_i has progressed far ahead of SG_j. Penalties for these delayed rollbacks are high since the effect of erroneous computation are allowed to spread considerably. Another problem associated with delayed rollback is highly distorted values of utilization.

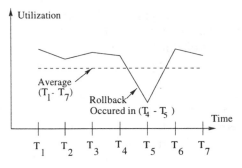

Figure 4: Periodic Computations.

Utilization is computed using data from the current period only. For example (see Figure 4), utilization at time T_i is computed using data during the time period $[T_{i-1}, T_i]$. Except for the period containing the severe rollback the computed utilization shows a strong positive bias. For the period containing the severe rollback the computed utilization has a strong negative bias. Consequently, the load balancing is based on distorted values of utilization and may not be effective in equalizing the rate of progress of LPs.

5 Load Balancing in Models with Multiple Strong Groups

In this section we present an utilization based load balancing algorithm for models with multiple strong groups. We first explain the basic ideas behind the algorithm.

5.1 Basic Ideas behind the Algorithm

The utilization based approach of load balancing can be easily modified to equalize progress of all LPs in models with multiple strong groups. We start by noting that a two way relationship exists between utilization and LP to processor mapping. One can use the observed utilization values to change the LP to processor mapping that achieves a balanced loading across processors. This relationship is used in the dynamic load balancing described in Subsection 4.2. On the other hand one can also change the LP to processor mapping to alter the observed utilization values. Consider for example the simulation model and its mapping as shown in Figure 5. Suppose the observed utilization values are 0.1, 0.4, 0.3, and 0.2 for LPs L_1, L_2, L_3, and L_4, respectively. The mapping shown in Figure 5(b) is obviously balanced. If one wishes to reduce the utilization of L_3, L_1 can be moved from processor 1 to processor 2. This will force L_3 to share processing power with an additional LP (in this case L_1) and lower L_3's utilization. Suppose we target to lower L_3's utilization to 0.1 without changing the

utilizations of $L_1(0.1)$, $L_2(0.4)$, and $L_4(0.2)$. If we *assume* that the observed utilization values after the new mapping (L_2 to processor 1 and the remainder to processor 2) are proportional to the target utilization values ($L_1(0.1)$, $L_2(0.4)$, $L_3(0.1)$, and $L_4(0.2)$), then the new mapping is also a balanced mapping. Based on the above assumption, the remapping can be guided by the target utilization values and our desire to retain a balanced loading.

The question we have not yet addressed is how to compute the target utilizations based on our primary goal of equalizing the rate of progress for all strong groups within a simulation model. Equal rates of progress can be achieved by slowing down the faster moving strong groups relative to the slower moving strong groups. We first examine the relationship between utilization and rate of progress. Recall that utilization is the amount of processing power required to sustain the computation of events that are not rolled back. We assume that for a given LP the average cpu time required to process one event does not change and the average change in *lvt* per processed event is also unchanged (both are reasonable assumptions over short intervals). The rate of change of *lvt* for a given LP is therefore proportional to utilization. It follows that if one wishes to reduce the rate of progress of a given LP by a factor of k one must target to reduce its utilization by factor of k from the currently observed utilization. Since all LPs within a given strong group have approximately the same rate of progress, to reduce the rate of progress of a strong group by a factor of k, the utilization of all LPs within this strong group must be targeted to be reduced by a factor of k. We also note that the faster a strong group is (relative to other strong groups), the higher will be its k and the target utilization values will be sharply lower than the observed utilization values.

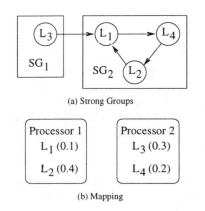

(a) Strong Groups

(b) Mapping

Figure 5: Strong Graphs and Mapping.

A revised balanced LP to processor mapping can be found by using these target utilization values. The net effect will be to slow down the faster moving strong groups and to speed up the slower moving strong groups. This happens because of the twofold effect of using target utilization on LP to processor mapping: (i) Processors having higher number of faster moving LPs appear to be lightly loaded when target utilization values are used to compute load on a processor. This is because as noted earlier target utilization values for faster moving LPs are lower because of high k values. Therefore, additional LPs are migrated to such processors forcing the faster LPs to share processing power with additional LPs. This will slow down the faster moving LPs. (ii) Processors having a large number of slower moving LPs appear to be (relatively) heavily loaded for similar reasons. LPs are migrated away from such processors allowing the remainder LPs a larger share of processing power.

Note that we need not necessarily achieve the target utilization values after a new mapping. As long as the observed utilization values after the remapping are proportional to the target values, the rates of progress of all strong groups have (approximately) equalized and we have a balanced loading. If the rates of progress are still unequal we can go through one more iteration of computing target utilizations and remapping.

We can now formally state the steps of the algorithm.

1. Identify the strong groups from the interaction graph and find the rate of progress of each strong group.

2. Compute the target utilization values. The target utilization value for an LP in a strong group SG_i is: (currently observed utilization x rate of progress of the slowest strong group / rate of progress of SG_i).

3. Change the LP to Processor Mapping to achieve a balanced loading based on the target utilization values.

5.2 An Example

In this subsection we present a simple example to show how the above algorithm works. A simulation model of a queueing network is used which does not have any weak links (to keep things simple). A PDES simulator is used to illustrate and demonstate the effect of the algorithm.

The PDES simulator is based on the Time Warp[6,7] protocol and will be referred to as TWOSS (Time Warp Operating System Simulator). A brief description of TWOSS is given in [9]. A simulation of a PDES run using TWOSS requires specifying two sets

of parameters. The first set of parameters (simulation model parameters) defines the simulation model, e.g., branching probabilty and timestamp increments. The second set of parameters (the simulator parameters) define the run time environment of the PDES run, e.g., cpu time required to process individual events (computation grain), message communication times, and the overhead to send an antimessage.

Our example simulation model is a tandem server queuing shown in Figure 6(a) with feedbacks at servers 2, 4, and 6. The interarrival and service times are exponentially distributed. There are no weak links. The model can be viewed as a collection of six strong groups (see Figure 6 (b)). The branching probabilities assumed for this model are shown in Table 1. A probability of p for L_i to L_j in this table implies that a customer after leaving a server or arrival process represented by L_i joins the queue of another server or departure process represented by the logical process L_j with probability p; e.g., a customer leaving L_1 joins the input queue of L_2 with probability 0.65. Other parameters, e.g., the means of the exponential interarrival (IA) or service times, are also shown in this table. The computation grains were sampled from an uniform distribution U[0.9g - 1.1g], where g is the mean computation grain shown in Table 1. The communication time between every pair of LPs was assumed constant (0.1 time unit) when the LPs are on separate processors. For LPs on the same processor, this time is assumed to be 0. The time to generate one antimessage was also assumed to be constant (0.05 time units).

We illustrate each step of the algorithm by explain-

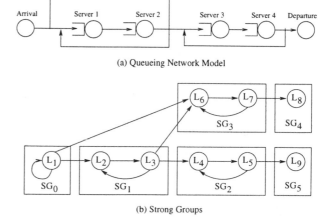

(a) Queueing Network Model

(b) Strong Groups

Figure 6: Queueing Network Model Example.

Table 1: Parameter Values of the Model for the Experiment.

Physical Process	Logical Process	To: Branching Probability	Mean IA or Service Time	g
Arrival	L_1	$L_2 : 0.65, L_6 : 0.35$	0.5	0.1
Server 1	L_2	$L_3 : 1.00$	0.1	0.2
Server 2	L_3	$L_2 : 0.50, L_4 : 0.25, L_6 : 0.25$	0.1	0.1
Server 3	L_4	$L_5 : 1.00$	0.1	1.2
Server 4	L_5	$L_4 : 0.50, L_9 : 50$	0.1	0.1
Server 5	L_6	$L_7 : 1.00$	0.1	0.8
Server 6	L_7	$L_6 : 0.50, L_8 : 0.50$	0.1	0.1
Departure	L_8	-	-	0.001
Departure	L_9	-	-	0.001

Table 2: Results from the Experiment.

Logical Process	Strong Group	Relative Rate of Progress (k)	Observed Utilization	Targeted Utilization	Observed Utilization After Remapping
L_1	SG_0	3.48	0.200	0.0575	0.066
L_2	SG_1	3.48	0.530	0.1523	0.174
L_3			0.270	0.0776	0.087
L_4	SG_2	1.0	0.350	0.3500	0.512
L_5			0.028	0.0280	0.042
L_6	SG_3	1.0	0.550	0.5500	0.695
L_7			0.069	0.0690	0.087

ing how each step is carried out for this example. Since the computation required by LPs L_8 and L_9 in our model is trival we shall ignore strong groups SG_4 and SG_5 in all subsequent discussions.

We start with the following LP to processor assignments: $L_1, L_2, L_3 \rightarrow P_1$ and $L_4, L_5, L_6, L_7 \rightarrow P_2$, where P_1 and P_2 are processors. This mapping is a balanced loading based on observed utilization values but does not equalize the rate of progress of different strong groups. Observed utilization values are shown in column 4 of Table 2.

Steps of The Algorithm:

1. Identify the strong groups from the interaction graph.

There are four(4) strong groups (Figure 6(b)) after ignoring SG_4 and SG_5.

2. Compute the target utilization values for each strong group.

The rate of progress for each strong group is computed using the data generated by TWOSS. The rate of progress for SG_1 was estimated using the lvt of L_2. (Recall that all LPs within a strong group progress at

approximately equal rate. Therefore, we could have chosen either L_2 or L_3 with equal validity). Similarly, lvt of L_6 and L_4 were used for computing the rates of progress for SG_2 and SG_3, repectively. The rate of progress for SG_0 was based on lvt of L_1 (there is no other LP in SG_0). SG_3 was found to be the slowest strong group. The relative rates of progress of the other strong groups with respect to SG_3 (i.e., the rate of progress if SG_3's rate of progress is taken as one) are: SG_2: 1.0; SG_1: 3.48; SG_0: 3.48. Therefore, the k values (presented in column 3 of Table 2) for the different strong groups are: SG_0: 3.48 SG_1: 3.48; SG_2: 1.0; SG_3: 1.0. The targeted utilization values computed using these k values are shown in column 5 of Table 2. (These values are obtained by dividing the values in column 4 by the values in column 3.)

3. Change the LP to Processor Mapping based on target utilization values.

Load computation based on the target utilization values show P_1 to be severely underloaded. (P_1's target load would be 0.0575 + 0.1523 + 0.0776.) A revised balanced LP to processor mapping based on the targeted utilization values is $L_1, L_5, L_6 \to P_1$ and $L_2, L_3, L_4, L_7 \to P_2$. Results from TWOSS showed that the rate of progress of all LPs were approximately equal with this revised process to processor assignment. Note that the observed utilizations (column 6 of Table 2) are close to the targeted utilizations. More interesting, however, is the fact that the utilization for LPs belonging to the slowest strong groups (i.e., L_4, L_5, L_6, and L_7) have gone up after remapping. The effect of this is to speed up the slowest components of the simulation, reduce the number of rollbacks, and achieve a faster completion time of the PDES run.

5.3 Some Comments about the Algorithm

Note that this algorithm requires no directive from the programmer regarding how to slow down the faster strong groups as in some other approaches, e.g., preferential allocation of processor cycles, idle spinning of processors, or a sliding window approach. These approaches require the programmer to specify conditions under which the lowest time stamped message available to a processor is delayed by prespecified amounts, decided apriori by the programmer. This entails the risk of delaying "good work" while the intention is just to avoid "bad work." The algorithm presented above does not suffer from this weakness.

The algorithm presented in this paper works by reducing the stratification in LP to processor mapping. Consider again the example presented above. Orginally SG_0 and SG_1 are assigned to P_1 and SG_3 and SG_4 are assigned to P_2. Because of the explaintion given in Subsection 3.2, it is possible for SG_0 to race ahead of SG_1 and SG_3, and for SG_1 to race ahead of SG_2. The present mapping is stratified - faster and slower strong groups are mapped to different processors (strata). However, load computation based on target utilization identifies the processor (P_1) hosting SG_0 and SG_1 as underloaded forcing some of the slower LPs from the other processor (P_2) to the under loaded processor. This reduces the stratification.

Note that the algorithm presented in this paper only addresses the macro level structural features. The interaction among LPs within the same strong group can be viewed as micro level structural features and is not addressed in this paper. Knowledge about micro level structural features can also be utilized to reduce rollbacks. An algorithm that exploits microlevel features to reduce rollback can be found in [10].

6 Summary and Conclusions

In this paper we investigated the effect of model structure on load balancing during optimistic PDES runs. We introduced the notion of strong groups which forms the basis of a model structure. We showed that LPs within a strong group progress at the same rate, but different strong groups can progress at different rates. It was pointed out that unequal rate of progress of strong groups may lead to (i) memory overflow, (ii) excessive rollbacks, and (iii) inefficient use of cpu resources. An algorithm to equalize the rate of progress of strong groups was presented. Future research should include a detail evaluation of the presented algorithm and an investigation of handling simulation models whose model structures change during run time.

References

[1] C. Berge. *Graphs and Hypergraph*, North-Holland, Amsterdam, 1976.

[2] M. Choe and C. Tropper. On Learning Algorithms and Balancing Loads in Time Warp. In: *Proc. 13th Workshop on Par. and Distr. Sim.*, 101-108, 1999.

[3] E. Deelman and B. Szymanski. Dynamic Load Balancing in Parallel Discrete Event Simulation for Spatially Explicit Problems. In: *Proc. 12th Workshop on Parallel and Distr. Sim.*, 46-53, 1998.

[4] R.M. Fujimoto. Parallel Discrete Event Simulation. *Comm. of the ACM*, 33 (10), 30-53, 1990.

[5] D. Glazer and C. Tropper. On Process Migration and Load Balancing in Time Warp. *IEEE Trans. on Parallel and Distr. Comp.*, 4 (3), 318-327, 1993.

[6] D. Jefferson. Virtual Time. *ACM Trans. on Prog. Lang. and Systems*, 7 (3), 404-425, 1985.

[7] D. Jefferson and H. Sowizral. Fast Concurrent Simulation Using the Time Warp Mechanism, Part II, Global Control. Tech. Report, Rand Corp., 1983.

[8] P.L. Reiher and D. Jefferson. Dynamic Load Management in the Time Warp Operating System. *Trans. Soc. for Comp. Sim.*, 7 (2), 91-120, 1990.

[9] T.K. Som. Allocation of Processing Power in Optimistic Parallel Discrete Event Simulation, Ph.D. Dissertation, Syracuse University, 1992.

[10] T.K. Som and R.G. Sargent. A New Process to Processor Assignment Criterion for Reducing Rollbacks in Optimistic Simulation. *J. of Parallel and Distributed Computing*, 18 (4), 509-515, 1993.

Session 10
Scheduling

Pre-Sampling as an Approach for Exploiting Temporal Uncertainty
M. L. Loper and R. M. Fujimoto

An Empirical Study of Conservative Scheduling
H. Y. Song, R. A. Meyer, and R. Bagrodia

Grain Sensitive Event Scheduling in Time Warp Parallel Discrete Event Simulation
F. Quaglia and V. Cortellessa

Pre-Sampling as an Approach for Exploiting Temporal Uncertainty

Margaret L. Loper and Richard M. Fujimoto
College of Computing
Georgia Institute of Technology
Atlanta, Georgia 30332-0280
{margaret, fujimoto}@cc.gatech.edu

Abstract

In this paper we describe an approach to exploit temporal uncertainty in parallel and distributed simulation by utilizing time intervals rather than precise time stamps. Unlike previously published work that propose new message ordering semantics, our approach is based on conservative, time stamp order execution and enhancing the lookahead of the simulation by pre-drawing random numbers from a distribution that models temporal uncertainty. The advantages of this approach are that it allows time intervals to be exploited using a conventional Time Stamp Order (TSO) delivery mechanism, and it offers the modeler greater statistical control over the assigned time stamps. An implementation of this approach is described and initial performance measurements are presented.

1. Introduction

Federated simulation systems represent perhaps the most widespread application of parallel and distributed simulation technology to date. Fueled by the substantial cost savings realized through model reuse and the observation that no one system can meet the requirements of all simulations in the U.S. Department of Defense, the High Level Architecture (HLA) effort is perhaps the most well known exploitation of this technology [1].

Many federated simulations require time management mechanisms (synchronization algorithms) to ensure before and after relationships are correctly modeled by the simulation. The traditional approach to time management used by the parallel simulation community, and adopted by the HLA, is to assign a precise time stamp to each event, and ensure that events are processed in time stamp order. Though widely used, assigning a specific time stamp to an event ignores the fact that there is almost always uncertainty concerning when an event occurs. One can immediately think of many examples illustrating this temporal uncertainty. For example:

- The time a moving vehicle comes into range of a sensor depends on factors such as the speed the vehicle is traveling and the sensitivity of the sensor, which in turn depend on environmental conditions and other factors that cannot be known with complete certainty.
- The think time required by human operators in issuing orders in a military simulation cannot be determined with complete certainty.
- Job service times such as the amount of time for a bank teller to serve a customer cannot be known with complete certainty.

It is clear that temporal uncertainty is ubiquitous in simulation modeling, stemming from the fact that simulations are only an approximation of the real world. The goal of the approach described here is to exploit this uncertainty to enhance the performance of parallel simulations.

The context for the work described here is in federating existing simulations (which use precise timestamps). Specifically, Runtime Infrastructure (RTI) software is used to interconnect the simulations. Each simulator (federate in HLA terminology) processes its internal events using precise time stamps. Messages sent to other federates are assigned a time interval indicating a range in times when the event could occur. The interface between the simulator and RTI assigns a precise time stamp within this interval by drawing a random number. This value is used as the precise time stamp for the out-going message. The message is then delivered to the destination simulator using a time stamp order (TSO) delivery mechanism.

This approach is doomed to fail if the application has poor lookahead. To address this problem, the random number generator is sampled *in advance*, prior to when the time stamps are needed, and these pre-sampled values are used to improve the lookahead of the simulation. The advantages of this approach are it allows time stamp intervals to be exploited using a conventional TSO delivery mechanism and it offers the modeler greater statistical control over the precise time stamps assigned to messages.

The next section reviews motivation for the pre-sampling approach, including a description of time intervals. Related work in pre-sampling and the interval-based time management mechanisms is then described. The semantics of the pre-sampling mechanism is covered next, as well as a distributed algorithm to realize it. Finally, experimental results are presented to evaluate the impact of pre-sampling in zero lookahead simulations in terms of execution speed.

2. Motivation

Existing conservative and optimistic synchronization mechanisms have significant disadvantages, especially in the context of federated simulation systems. Specifically:

- Conservative synchronization protocols degenerate to serial execution of events[1] if the application contains zero lookahead. Moreover, even if the lookahead is not zero, it is well known that parallel and distributed simulations will yield poor performance if the lookahead is small [2]. This is particularly problematic for military simulations, especially process-oriented models, where simulators typically schedule events "as they occur" in the model, e.g., when a tank moved to a new position, an update message is sent with time stamp equal to the tank's current position. This results in zero lookahead simulations. This fact is reinforced by the immediate demand by the DoD simulation community for the HLA to support zero lookahead as soon as the baseline definition of the HLA was announced [3].

- Optimistic synchronization approaches offer a solution to the zero lookahead problem, but require that each federate provide a rollback capability. This requires substantial re-

engineering of existing simulations to introduce state saving calls. Further, optimistic synchronization introduces a substantial amount of complexity as well as a host of other issues. One must have the ability to roll back arbitrary computations, e.g., I/O calls, memory allocation (to avoid memory leaks if the memory allocation is rolled back), and execution errors (e.g., floating point exceptions or illegal memory references such as errant pointer references must be caught before they irreversibly modify memory that has not been checkpointed [4]), to mention a few. While technical solutions exist for many of these problems, they significantly complicate the task of federating an existing sequential simulation.

New algorithms for realizing time stamp order event processing which use semantics *other than* time stamp order have been proposed [5] to provide a practical time management mechanism for federated simulations. This work is based on time intervals, which have been studied as a means for specifying temporal or other types of uncertainty in simulation applications [6] [7]. Prior work in time intervals does not address issues concerning model execution on parallel and distributed computing platforms, however. Rather it addresses issues concerning the rationale, assignment, and manipulation of intervals within the model.

In [7] the rationale for using intervals as a temporal representation includes allowing significant imprecision in absolute times (some temporal knowledge is strictly relative), supporting the uncertainty of information (often the exact relationship between two event times is not known), and providing a mechanism for varying the grain of reasoning. It is these characteristics that we exploit in our approach to representing temporal uncertainty.

Our work differs from that proposed in [5] (see next section for description of this work) because our approach is based on using time intervals to enhance the lookahead of the simulation. For the reader interested in time intervals, see [7] [8] or [9] for a discussion of the definition of intervals. This paper will focus on concurrent execution of the federated simulation system once the intervals have been defined.

---

[1] that is, except in the special case of events containing *exactly* the same time stamp.

3. Related Work

3.1. FCFS Queueing Network

Nicol proposed using detailed simulation-specific information to compute lookahead in stochastic FCFS queueing network models [10]. In the simplest but most common type of stochastic simulation, the service time of every job at a queue is drawn from a common distribution and the branching destination is chosen from a common distribution. Nicol notes that these quantities could be drawn at any time and it can be advantageous to select a job's service time and branching destination before the job arrives in order to improve lookahead. This observation led him to an organization, which associates with every queue, a future list of jobs that have not yet arrived. A job's service time and branching destination are determined when it joins the future list. Additional jobs are appended to the future list in a manner that preserves the statistical integrity of the simulation. In our approach, we exploit an idea similar to Nicol, but in the context of time intervals.

3.2. Approximate Time Causal Order

Recently, new ordering semantics have been proposed that exploit temporal uncertainty in the simulation model to relax time stamp order. Specifically, approximate time causal (ATC) order assumes each event is assigned a time interval to indicate when the event *could* occur and define a partial ordering among events [11]. In ATC, each event X is assigned a time interval [E(X), L(X)] where E(X) < L(X). E(X) denotes the earliest point in simulation time that the event may occur, and L(X) the latest. Time intervals are assigned to the event by the simulation model, typically based on uncertainty regarding when the event occurs. If the time intervals of two events do not overlap, then the event with the earlier time interval must be processed before the one with the later time interval (e.g., events X and Z in Figure 1).

If the two events have overlapping intervals and there is a causal relationship between these events, as defined by Lamport's "happens before" relationship [12], the two events must also be processed in causal order [13] [14]. For example, in Figure 2 the "fire" event happens before the "target hit," so the fire event must be processed by the observer before the target hit event. Two events with overlapping time intervals

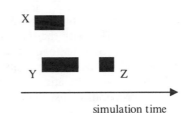

Figure 1. Time intervals for events X, Y, and Z. X and Y are concurrent events (X || Y) while X precedes Z (X~>Z) in ATC-order.

but no causal relationship between them may be processed in any order, e.g., events X and Y in Figure 1.

Results from the ATC experiments [11] show that time intervals offer excellent potential for synchronizing distributed simulations, especially federated simulation systems. However, in order to implement ATC in the HLA RTI, changes to the delivery mechanisms and HLA Interface Specification [15] will be required. In other words, existing TSO mechanisms in the RTI can not be used with this approach to implementing ATC. The approach described here using pre-sampling

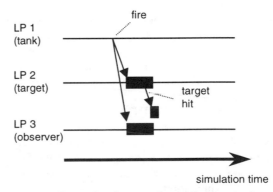

Figure 2. Example of approximate time causal order of events.

implements ATC order, but can be realized over existing RTIs (e.g., HLA RTIs) that provide time stamp order message delivery.

4. Approach

There are two approaches for implementing time intervals on top of the HLA RTI. One approach would have the interface between the federate and RTI assign an interval to each event equal to the federate_lookahead (L) + interval_size (INT). The timestamp for the event could then be selected as the upper end of the interval or L + INT. In other words, the interval could be thought as of additional lookahead for the federate. This approach is straight forward, but could interfere with the semantics of the simulation. Since the timestamp of events would always be at the end of the interval, this approach could tend to bias the simulation outcome. In contrast, using a probability distribution to assign timestamps inside the interval gives the modeler more control and flexibility in how timestamps are assigned. This leads to the second approach for implementing intervals on top of the RTI, pre-sampling.

The key idea behind pre-sampling is that the sender assigns an interval to each message. The interface between the federate and RTI assigns a precise time stamp within that interval pre-sampled from a random number generator. Both the sender and receivers use the precise time stamp for the message, which also ensures consistent time stamp assignment if the event is distributed to multiple destinations. Using this approach, the federation can be executed as a conventional TSO simulation, where pre-sampling the random number generator enhances lookahead and thus improves performance.

This approach is illustrated as follows. Suppose the federate has a lookahead of L without pre-sampling and is at simulation time T, as shown in Figure 3. If we know in advance that the time interval used by the federate is size INT and time stamps within this interval follow some probability distribution, we can sample the random number generator in interval [0, INT] to generate a value. If the random number generator yields a value R, then this implies the next message generated by the federate must have a time stamp of at least $T+L+R$. The larger the lookahead, the better the performance of the TSO simulation.

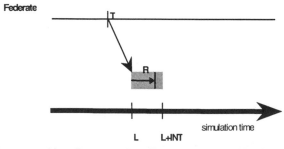

Figure 3. How Pre-sampling Enhances Lookahead.

There are several complications with this approach. Obviously, one must know the time interval size and probability distribution in advance in order to pre-sample the random number generator.

Further, suppose the federate decided to send two messages rather than one after its next time advance, as shown in Figure 4. Then the lookahead would be the minimum of the two random number generator samples (R and R'). What if the federate generated

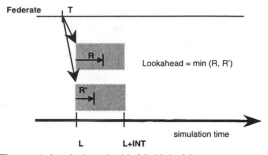

Figure 4. Lookahead with Multiple Messages.

three? There needs to be some bound on the number of messages the federate will generate over its next time increment in order to correctly set the lookahead. Further, if this bound is high, the increased lookahead one can gain from this approach will be limited because the resulting lookahead will in general decrease as more random number generator samples are required.

We assume all events sent between federates utilize the same time interval size and probability distribution to select the precise time stamp within the interval. We also define a parameter, M, to indicate the maximum number of messages the federate can produce over a unit of simulation time advance. The federation must specify M in advance of the execution (although M could change during the execution) and adhere to this constraint throughout the execution. Violation of this constraint may result in a lookahead violation.

5. Pre-Sampling Algorithm

In this section, we will define both the pre-sampling algorithm and how it is used by a federate. Before describing the algorithm, we define the following parameters:

DT   a simulation time period; this can be set arbitrarily by the federate

M   the maximum number of messages the federate can produce over the next DT units of simulation time advance

S_i i^{th} pre-sample of the random number generator

$S_{min.}$ minimum of the M values of S_i

INT   a time interval from which samples are chosen; this can be set arbitrarily by the federate

5.1. The Algorithm

The pre-sampling algorithm has two parts: pre-sampling the random number generator to set lookahead and intercepting messages to replace timestamps.

The *first part of the algorithm* has three functions: pre-sample the random number generator to generate time values (S_i), find the minimum of the pre-sampled value (S_{min}), and set Lookahead.

Sampling a uniform probability distribution generates the values S_i. The values are then multiplied by the interval size so that all values are in the range [0→INT]. The values are stored in a circular queue in the order they were generated. During initialization, all M values are generated and S_{min} is computed. Subsequently, when a sampled value is needed, it is selected from the front of the queue, and a new random number is sampled and placed at the end. Therefore, the queue always contains M pre-sampled values. The enhanced lookahead is recomputed once all the new values have been generated for the simulation time period.

Lookahead is computed from the minimum of the M pre-sampled random numbers (S_i) and the simulation time period as:

$$L_i = L_i' + \min\{S_{min}, DT\}$$

Where L_i' is the lookahead of federate i without using time intervals. Suppose the federate is currently at simulation time T. In the worst case, the federate will generate all M messages without advancing simulation time, so the minimum time stamp of any message it will produce among these M messages is $T + L_i' + \min\{S_1, S_2, \ldots S_M\}$. However, once this has occurred, the federate is constrained to advance DT time units before it can generate any additional messages. Once it has advanced DT units, it is possible the federate could generate a message with time stamp $T + L_i' + DT$ since we have not pre-sampled the M+1st message. This is the reason DT is included in the lookahead equation.

The *second part of the algorithm* involves "intercepting" a message before it reaches the RTI and replacing the timestamp with one that includes the pre-sampled random number. To compute the new timestamp, we must first place an interval around the original time stamp. We define the leading edge of the interval as:

$$TS_N = TS - (INT/2)$$

Ideally, we want to define the new time stamp by adding the pre-sampled value to the beginning of the interval. However, if the beginning of the interval is less than the current simulation time (i.e., $TS_N < T$), then the interval has a starting edge in the past. And if the pre-sampled value (S_i) happens to be 0, then the new timestamp will not be valid because $TS' < T$. Therefore, the pre-sampled value is added to the maximum of T and TS_N and the new timestamp (TS') is defined as:

$$TS' = \max\{TS_N, T\} + S_i$$

5.2. Federate Implementation

A useful feature of this approach is its simplicity. A federation does not have to use a specialized RTI, nor do federates have to make major code modifications to use pre-sampling. Instead, pre-sampling can be implemented using the existing HLA TSO mechanisms.

A typical processing cycle for a federate includes an initialization phase, a time advance phase, and a processing phase. To implement pre-sampling, the federate requires two new functions: one function generates/regenerates the pre-sampled values and sets lookahead and the second function intercepts the outgoing message and attaches the new time stamp. The first function is included in the initialization phase to generate the pre-sampled values and also in the processing phase to regenerate the values and set lookahead. The second function is only included in the processing phase to intercept outgoing timestamps. Therefore, code changes to implement pre-sampling is localized and fairly transparent to the federate.

6. Experiments

An implementation of the pre-sampling algorithm described above was developed in order to compare its performance with the ATC-order mechanism [11]. An RTI, called BRTI that implements variable lookahead and the ATC-RTI that implements ATC order were developed using version 2.3 of the RTI-

Kit software package [16]. RTI-Kit is a collection of libraries implementing key mechanisms that are required to realize distributed simulation RTIs, especially RTIs based on the High Level Architecture. The RTI-Kit libraries are designed so they can be used separately, or together to enhance existing RTIs, or to develop new ones. The ATC-RTI uses RTI-Kit's MCAST library that provides group communications facilities, and the TM-Kit library that implements time management functions. The version of RTI-Kit used in this study is built over version 2.0 of the Fast Message software package developed at the University of Illinois [17]. Other implementations of RTI-Kit are built over TCP/IP, and over shared memory in SMP environments, but were not used in this study.

6.1. Experimental Environment

A cluster of eight Sun Ultrasparc-1 workstations interconnected by a low latency Myrinet switch were used for these experiments. The workstations run Solaris version 5.5. LANai Version 4.1 Myrinet cards with 640 MBit/second communication links are used. Myrinet switches provide point-to-point switched interconnection between workstations, and feature cut-through message routing to reduce message latency [18].

6.2. Applications

We are particularly interested in simulations with zero lookahead, because it is well known that conservative simulation techniques fail for this important class of applications. Both of the simulations used in this study are well-known benchmarks widely used in the parallel discrete event simulation community.

The first benchmark is the PHOLD synthetic workload program [19]. A single logical process is mapped to each federate, and LPs do not send messages to themselves. Thus, there are no local events, i.e., each event processed by a federate was generated on a different processor. The target time stamp is selected from a uniform distribution with mean 1.0, and the destination federate is selected from a uniform distribution. The minimum time stamp increment is zero, resulting in a zero lookahead simulation.

The second application is a queueing network (QNET), configured in a toroid topology. This simulation does *not* attempt to exploit lookahead. A textbook approach to realizing this simulation was used that includes both job arrival and job departure events. Each departure event schedules an arrival event at another queue with time stamp equal to the current simulation time of the LP scheduling the event, i.e., messages sent between LPs all contain zero lookahead. Service times are selected from an exponential distribution, and jobs are serviced in first-come-first-serve order. Each federate models a rectangular portion of the queueing network.

It is well known that certain classes of queueing network simulations can be optimized to exploit properties of the queues to improve their lookahead. This approach was intentionally *not* used here, because such optimizations lead to fragile code that is highly dependent on specific aspects of the model. Such techniques are generally difficult to apply in large, complex models. Rather, the experiments performed here were intended to evaluate the effectiveness of pre-sampling in federating simulations in distributed computing environments without rewriting the models to exploit lookahead.

6.3. Execution Speed

The experiments described in [5] were repeated for both ATC-order and pre-sampling for both the PHOLD and QNET applications. The PHOLD simulation uses one logical process per federate, and one federate on each of the eight processors with a job population of 256. The queueing network simulation (QNET) modeled 256 (16 by 16) queues and assumed fixed population of 256 jobs, or one job per queue.

As mentioned previously, all messages sent between federates use the same interval size and all simulations have zero lookahead. The pre-sampling experiments varied three parameters: INT, M, and DT. The data shown in Figures 5 and 6 are for DT = 0.1, INT = 0.5, and a variable M.

In Figures 5 and 6, the performance of the simulation is plotted relative to the distributed simulation using precise time stamps (and ATC-order) for the PHOLD and QNET benchmarks, respectively. As can be seen, pre-sampling provides speed up over the distributed simulation that uses precise timestamps. The speed up varies with the value of M. As M decreases, we see better speed up since there are fewer random number samples to select from. Therefore, there is a better chance of having a large S_{min}, which gives a larger lookahead and increases performance. However, M must be greater than 4 for this benchmark.

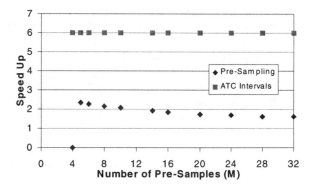

Figure 5. Speed Up of PHOLD simulation for the Pre-Sampling and ATC algorithms.

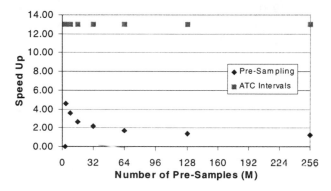

Figure 6. Speed Up of QNET simulation for the Pre-Sampling and ATC algorithms.

Also in Figures 5 and 6, we see the speed up of the pre-sampling approach compared to the ATC-order approach. The ATC experiments were run using the same interval size and federation message population. The ATC approach outperforms pre-sampling. This is because the increased parallclism using enhanced lookahead obtained by pre-sampling is not as large as that exploited by ATC.

6.4. Discussion

The experiments described above were also run with larger values of DT. We found that the results did change, but only slightly. Therefore, the selection of DT was arbitrary. The experiments were also run varying the interval size. We found that we got better speed with larger intervals as M decreased. The reason was due to fewer random number samples of larger values. This increased the lookahead and improved the over-all speed up of the simulation.

7. Conclusions

In this paper, we described a method of exploiting time stamp intervals using pre-sampling of random numbers to enhance lookahead. An advantage to exploiting temporal uncertainty in this manner is that it can be used on a conventional RTI using the existing RTI interface; no specialized time management algorithms are needed. Instead, two new functions are called by the federate to generate the pre-sampled values and replace the time stamp assigned to the outgoing message with one that includes the pre-sampled value. Another important advantage is that pre-sampling allows probability distributions to be used to define assigned time stamps. This offers the modeler greater flexibility and statistical control over the assigned time stamps.

The pre-sampling approach is relatively simple to implement, but requires several assumptions in order to realize the solution. These assumptions include fixed sized time intervals, the same distribution for all messages, and knowledge concerning the number of messages the simulation will produce in the "near-future" (M) before advancing simulation time.

Pre-sampling does give performance improvement over a simulation that uses precise timestamps; however, lookahead enhancement is small if many random number samples are required.

8. Acknowledgements

We thank the anonymous referees for their comments on this paper. Funding for this research was provided under the DARPA Advanced Simulation Technology Thrust (ASTT) program, contract MDA972-97-C-0017.

9. References

1. Kaminski, P., *USD(A&T) Policy Letter on DoD HLA for Simulations*, . 1996, Under Secretary of Defense for Acquisition and Technology (USD(A&T): Washington, D.C.

2. Fujimoto, R.M., *Performance Measurements of Distributed Simulation Strategies.* Transactions of the Society for Computer Simulation, 1989. **6**(2): p. 89-132.

3. Fujimoto, R., M. *Zero Lookahead and Repeatability in the High Level Architecture.* in *Proceedings of the Spring Simulation Interoperability Workshop.* 1997. Orlando, FL.

4. Nicol, D.M. and X. Liu. *The Dark Side of Risk.* in *Proceedings of the 11th Workshop on Parallel and Distributed Simulation.* 1997.

5. Fujimoto, R.M. *Exploiting Temporal Uncertainty in Parallel and Distributed Simulations.* in *Proceedings of the 13th Workshop on Parallel and Distributed Simulation.* 1999.

6. Nance, R.E., *The Time and State Relationships in Simulation Modeling.* Communications of the ACM, 1981. **24**(4): p. 173-179.

7. Allen, J.F., *Maintaining Knowledge about Temporal Intervals.* Communications of the ACM, 1983. **26**(11): p. 832-843.

8. Dutta, S. *An Event Based Fuzzy Temporal Logic.* in *Proceedings of the 18th IEEE International Symposium on Multiple-Valued Logic.* 1988. Palma de Mallorca, Spain.

9. Diehl, C. and C. Jard. *Interval Approximations and Message Causality in Distributed Systems.* in *Proceedings of the 9th Annual Symposium on Theoretical Aspects of Computer Science (STACS '92).* 1992: Springer.

10. Nicol, D., *Parallel Discrete-Event Simulation of FCFS Stochastic Queueing Networks.* SIGPLAN Notices, 1988. **23**(9): p. 124-137.

11. Fujimoto, R.M., *Approximate Time Causal Order,* . 1999, College of Computing, Georgia Institute of Technology: Atlanta, GA.

12. Lamport, L., *Time, Clocks, and the Ordering of Events in a Distributed System.* Communications of the ACM, 1978. **21**(7): p. 558-565.

13. Birman, K., A. Schiper, and P. Stephenson, *Lightweight Causal and Atomic Group Multicast.* ACM Transaction on Computer Systems, 1991. **9**(3): p. 272-314.

14. Raynal, M. and M. Singhal, *Logical Time: Capturing Causality in Distributed Systems.* IEEE Computer, 1996. **29**(2): p. 49-56.

15. Office, D.M.a.S., *High Level Architecture Interface Specification, Version 1.3,* . 1998: Washington, D.C.

16. Fujimoto, R.M. and P. Hoare. *HLA RTI Performance in High Speed LAN Environments.* in *Proceedings of the Fall Simulation Interoperability Workshop.* 1998. Orlando, FL.

17. Pakin, S., *Fast Message (FM) 2.0 Users Documentation,* . 1997, Department of Computer Science, University of Illinois: Urbana, IL.

18. Boden, N., *Myrinet: A Gigabit Per Second Local Area Network.* IEEE Micro, 1995. **15**(1): p. 29-36.

19. Fujimoto, R.M. *Performance of Time Warp Under Synthetic Workloads.* in *Proceedings of the SCS Multiconference on Distributed Simulation.* 1990.

An Empirical Study of Conservative Scheduling

Ha Yoon Song, Richard A. Meyer and Rajive Bagrodia
UCLA Computer Science Department
Los Angeles, CA 90095
{hayoon,meyerr,rajive}@cs.ucla.edu

Abstract

It is well known that the critical path provides an absolute lower bound on the execution time of a conservative parallel discrete event simulation. It stands to reason that optimal execution time can only be achieved by immediately executing each event on the critical path. However, dynamically identifying the critical event is difficult, if not impossible. In this paper, we examine several heuristics that might help to determine the critical event, and conduct a performance study to determine the effectiveness of using these heuristics for preferential scheduling.

1. Introduction

Ultimately, performance is the most important issue in parallel processing in general and parallel simulation in particular. There are two widely used families of parallel simulation algorithms: conservative [1] and optimistic [2]. Conservative techniques are so called because they only execute events that are known to be safe, while optimistic algorithms execute any available events, but must roll back to prior states should an already executed event be identified as incorrect. Numerous studies have been undertaken to identify the various sources of overhead in optimistic simulations and to elaborate on their impact [3] [4] [5] [6] [7]. Similar studies of conservative algorithms [8] [9] are not as extensive, perhaps because they appear to have fewer sources of overhead that are amenable to detailed investigations of the sort that are ideal for graduate theses! It is well known that lookahead properties of a model have a considerable influence on performance with conservative algorithms and these characteristics have been the focus of intense scrutiny by the PADS community [10] [11]. However, the scheduling policy used by a processor to schedule simulation objects (commonly called logical processes or LPs) when several of them are assigned to a processor can also have a

significant impact on its performance; and this factor does not appear to have been studied as extensively. The goal of this paper is to investigate the impact of alternative scheduling policies on the performance of conservative algorithms.

In general, the execution time of a model is constrained by its critical path (the longest chain of causally dependent events). In certain cases, optimistic algorithms with lazy cancellation and a little luck can beat the critical path [12] [13] [14]. The overhead of state saving and the resulting relatively poor cache and memory behavior usually prevent this from being realized in practice, but a great deal of work has been done in scheduling of optimistic algorithms to try to achieve this goal [15] [16] [17] [18]. Intuitively, an optimal scheduling algorithm for a conservative simulation will schedule events on the critical path before any others. Unfortunately, dynamically identifying which event or LP might be on the critical path is, for all practical purposes, impossible. However, there appear to be useful heuristics for predicting which LP is likely to be on the critical path. For example, if each blocked LP assumes that its next event is on the critical path, its predecessor on the critical path must be the LP from which it is currently awaiting input. In a Chandy-Misra [19] style deadlock avoidance algorithm (a.k.a. null message algorithm), the awaited input may be the null message that will allow the LP to advance its "safe" time to the point that it can execute its next event. Thus, the "critical" parent of an LP may be the one with the smallest lookahead, rather than the one with the earliest safe message. If many LPs are waiting on the same predecessor, it could be that the predecessor is on the critical path, and scheduling priority can be given to that LP. This paper presents a performance study comparing several scheduling algorithms, including ones based on the preceding idea.

The remainder of this paper is organized as follows. Section 2 describes the null message algorithm currently in use, and related work in the area. Section 3 will outline an analytical approach for measuring the overhead of conservative simulation, and introduce a scheduling heuristic derived from the model. Section 4 includes a

---

This work was funded in part by the Defense Advanced Research Projects Agency (DARPA) under contract AAB07-97-C-D321, as a part of the Global Mobile Information Systems (GloMo) program.

discussion of scheduling heuristics and implementation issues. Section 5 will present a detailed performance study comparing the scheduling heuristics with the default scheduling policy. Section 6 will summarize the results and give pointers for future research.

2. Conservative protocols

A PDES model is composed of a set of logical processes that are connected in a (possibly dynamic) topology. For LP L, we define the following [20]:

- $SourceSet_L$: the set of LPs which send messages to L

- $DestSet_L$: the set of LPs to which L sends messages

- EOT_L (Earliest Output Time): the earliest time at which L might send a message to any LP in $DestSet_L$.

- EIT_L (Earliest Input Time, a.k.a. "safe time"): the earliest time at which this LP might receive a message, calculated as $min(EOT_S: S \in SourceSet_L)$. Any events with timestamp earlier than EIT_L are safe to process.

- $Lookahead_L$: the difference between EIT and EOT. Lookahead is the degree to which an object can predict its future messages.

We have implemented a null message algorithm based on the Chandy-Misra deadlock avoidance algorithm. Whenever an LP updates its EOT, it must send the new value to each LP in its DestSet. This is done (transparently to the user) using null messages. Upon receiving a null message, the recipient LP might be able to update its EIT and one or more messages might become safe to process. LPs with large lookahead will be able to send large values of EOT to their neighbors, advancing the EIT of those LPs to the point that several events may become safe to process, thus increasing the parallelism available to the conservative algorithm.

An LP with safe messages (or a null message) will be placed in the scheduling queue, which by default is implemented as an unsorted queue. Each LP in turn processes all of its null messages and all of its safe events before being placed in a waiting queue. This scheduling system has been shown to outperform global event list methods on a single processor in some cases, because it reduces the number of context switches between events. The next section provides the motivation for evaluating alternative scheduling policies.

3. Conservative overhead

The primary overhead of a conservative algorithm is the blocking time of an LP between the (physical) time a message arrives at the corresponding processor, and that later time when the message is deemed safe to process.

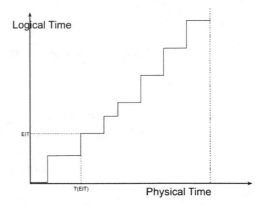

Figure 1. Time progression of an LP

Figure 1 shows the manner in which logical time of an LP advances as a function of physical time (wall clock time). The EIT of an LP L advances in discrete steps as it receives new EOT messages from members of $SourceSet_L$. Let the EIT of a given LP be x; we use $T(x)$ to refer to the physical time of the last "EIT update," when the EIT was advanced to x. We define the rate of EIT advancement of an LP as $x/T(x)$. All things being equal, improving the rate of EIT advancement of an LP will tend to improve execution time of the model. In general, several LPs are usually mapped onto each physical processor and the scheduling policy can have some impact on the EIT advancement rate.

3.1. Critical parent

The EIT of an LP is determined by its source LP with the smallest EOT, and can only be advanced upon receipt of an updated EOT from that source. That source LP is called the "critical parent." (This is the same concept as the critical channel defined in [8]. However, they use the knowledge to delay scheduling of the child LP until an update arrives on the critical channel. We try to preferentially schedule the critical parent itself.)

The concept of the critical parent is related to the idea of the critical path. If we assume that the next event at an LP is on the critical path, then the critical parent is the one blocking execution of the critical event. The critical parent will vary during the execution, possibly each time the EIT is updated, but at any specific time, it is easily identified. Because this LP is delaying execution of the presumed critical path, it should be preferentially scheduled. Of course, each LP may have a different critical parent, and only one LP per processor can be scheduled at a time. So for purposes of scheduling, one of the critical parents on each processor is designated the "critical LP," and is scheduled first. The next section discusses a number of heuristics to select the critical parent for preferential scheduling.

166

4. Scheduling algorithms

Scheduling based on minimum EOT feels intuitively like a good heuristic. For example, an LP that sends no messages will have an infinite EOT and will be scheduled last (subject to buffer overflow controls). Other heuristics could be considered as well. At each EIT update, both a new earliest safe event may be discovered, and a new EOT may be calculated. EIT is easier to calculate than EOT, because it doesn't depend on the state of the LP. It can be calculated simply be examining the source set. In models with fairly uniform lookahead, EIT and EOT will be approximately equidistant, so EIT might be an effective approximation of EOT. Both global event list and most optimistic algorithms schedule the earliest event first – the sequential algorithm by definition, the optimistic because the earliest event is the least likely to require rollback – so it is also valuable to consider the earliest event as a scheduling key.

The null message algorithm has been shown to work well using an unsorted scheduling queue. Each LP in turn executes all its safe events (subject to throttling and memory constraints), and all queue operations have O(1) complexity. To put any of the aforementioned scheduling heuristics into use requires that the LP queue be sorted, and the benefit of the scheduling must outweigh the cost of the sorting. Among the multiple varieties [21] of sorting algorithms, the most commonly used in discrete event simulation is the splay tree [22], which has $O(\log_n)$ insertion time and O(1) removal time. We will also consider a partially sorted list with O(1) insertion and removal time called a *bipartition queue*. During insertion, the value of the new element is compared with those of the head and the tail of the queue. If closer to the value of the head, it is inserted at the beginning, else at the end. This queue insertion method has the property of pushing all "sink" LPs to the back (if EOT is used as a sort key), and inserting all other objects at the front. The experiments in the next section compare multiple scheduling policies using both the splay tree and the bipartition queue.

5. Experiments and results

The benchmark program used for most of the experiments is a closed queuing network of FIFO servers (CQNF). A detailed wireless network model was used for one experiment. Two CQNF configurations were used. The first, CQNF-Tandem, is a set of tandem queues – five singly linked FIFO queues and a router – as shown in Figure 2. The router forwards jobs with uniform probability to any of the other tandem queues. The job service times are taken from a Poisson process with exponential distribution and a mean time of 100. Each tandem queue is initially assigned 96 jobs. We use FIFO queues because they have predictable lookahead

properties, and are therefore useful for conservative simulation. The tandem queue configuration has been studied previously [23], so comparisons can be made with previous results. The singly linked chain of objects effectively adds computation grain, but makes determination of the critical parent trivial for the majority of objects, so a second model is needed.

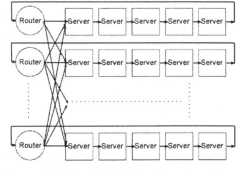

Figure 2. The CQNF-Tandem topology

The second configuration, CQNF-Grid, pictured in Figure 3, is based on PHOLD [24]. Each processor gets a 9x9 grid of LPs, with each LP forwarding messages with equal probability to any neighbor within its geometric "reach."[1] The published PHOLD model uses infinite servers, but we substituted FIFO queues to better control the lookahead in the model. The grid configuration also allows the connectivity to be controlled. Less speedup is expected of the grid topology for three reasons: 1) less computation (five queues in tandem act like one queue with high computation), 2) greater connectivity, and 3) fewer events in the system, eight per LP.

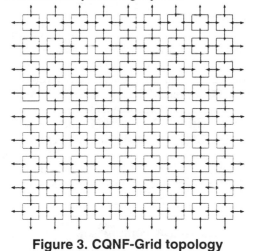

Figure 3. CQNF-Grid topology

The applications were programmed using the PARSEC simulation language [20]. PARSEC uses an unsorted queue for scheduling LPs in its conservative algorithms.

---

[1] Reach is a parameter of the model that represents the radius of a circle centered at an LP. If the radius length is 1, as in Figure 3, the LP is connected to its north, south, east, and west neighbors. At 1.5, it can also reach its diagonal neighbors.

(Multiple *events* at a given LP are stored in a splay tree.) LPs are placed in the scheduling queue when they receive any message, real or null. LPs receiving null messages (including piggyback null messages) are scheduled even if they don't have any safe messages, so that they can calculate a new EOT. The run time system of the simulator was modified to replace the unsorted queue with a splay tree or a bipartition queue. PARSEC uses a hybrid null message algorithm in which EOT is aggressively piggybacked on regular messages, but explicit null messages are delayed to reduce overhead. This implementation was not changed for these experiments, although more aggressive strategies are under study. Three different LP attributes were used to sort the LPs: EOT, EIT, and event time, where event time refers to the timestamp of its earliest future event.

The experiments being presented fall into six groups. First is a set of experiments where perfect knowledge of lookahead is assumed. The second set compares the splay tree as a queue mechanism with the bipartition queue. The third set reexamines the three heuristics in the face of variable knowledge of lookahead. Cases of uniformly poor, average, or good lookahead are tested. If the performance of models with poor lookahead can be significantly improved, it could broadly increase the applicability of conservative techniques. The fourth set of experiments tests whether these heuristics can help in cases of large computation granularity, or whether the granularity overwhelms the scheduling benefits. The fifth set of experiments examines varying levels of connectivity. The final experiment compares the heuristics using a real world example – a wireless network model.

Two metrics are used to present the impact of the scheduling policy: execution time of the model and the number of inter-processor null messages. Unless otherwise stated, the experiments were run on a Sun SPARC 1000 server with eight processors and 512MB main memory. Some experiments were run on a ten CPU SGI Origin with 256MB memory per node (a node includes two CPUs). Experiments are repeated at least five times for a given set of parameters. The average and standard deviation are calculated. The minimum value inside the 95% confidence interval is presented in the graphs.

5.1. Basic scheduling comparison

Figure 4 graphs the change in the execution time of the CQNF-Tandem benchmark when using each of the three heuristics, compared with using the unsorted queue. The experiment used 192 total LPs. All three keys generally outperform the unsorted queue, yielding as much as a 15% improvement. Note that with the total number of LPs in the model fixed, the number of LPs per processor decreases inversely with the number of processors. With

more than three processors, the scheduling benefit starts covering the scheduling queue overhead. The performance benefit of the various heuristics varies a great deal. To some extent, the graph tends to exaggerate the appearance of variability because of the small scale, but there are other factors at play. Only the tests on two, four, and eight processors are fully balanced, because a tandem queue and its router (six LPs in all) are always assigned to a single processor. The scheduling heuristics perform best in the most balanced cases, four and eight processors. On the other cases, particularly the unbalanced five CPU test, the greater overhead in the system is the blocking time due to idleness, and the extra overhead of scheduling leads to little benefit.

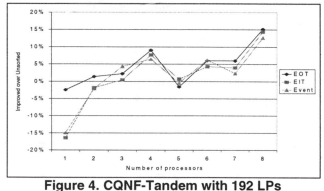

Figure 4. CQNF-Tandem with 192 LPs

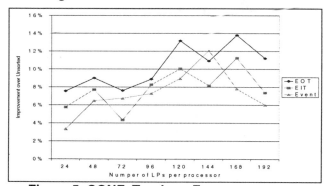

Figure 5. CQNF–Tandem: Four processors, variable number of LPs

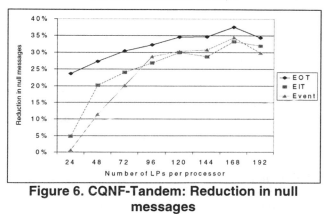

Figure 6. CQNF-Tandem: Reduction in null messages

168

Figure 5 shows the results of an experiment where the number of processors is held at four, but the number of LPs per processor was varied. LPs are added by adding new tandem queues (six LPs at a time). All of the routers are completely connected to the other tandem queues, so the communication density also increases. All three heuristics outperform the unsorted queue, and generally improve with the number of LPs. Figure 6 shows the reduction in the number of inter-processor null messages resulting from the use of the heuristics. Each of the scheduling heuristics leads to a significant reduction in the null message traffic, especially as the number of LPs is increased. Since the number of null messages increases with the square of the number of tandem queues, there is greater opportunity for improvement in the larger test cases.

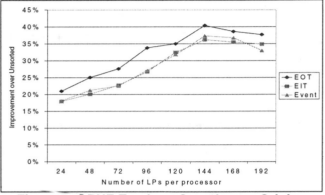

Figure 7. CQNF-Tandem: Speedup on Origin

Figure 7 shows the results of the experiment in Figure 5 when run on an SGI Origin 2000. The Origin is a scalable cache-coherent NUMA machine with relatively slow inter-processor memory latency. This causes remote null messages to be relatively more expensive than on the SPARC 1000. The moderate reductions in null messages are matched by the performance improvement achieved on the Origin. This result rather convincingly demonstrates that the cost of null message delivery is the limiting factor in the performance of the null message algorithm on the Origin.

5.2. Splay tree versus bipartition queue

Given that EOT appears to be the best scheduling heuristic, we would like to determine how aggressive we should be in sorting the LP queue. The splay tree implementation used in the previous experiments has O(log n) insertion time. A simpler mechanism is the bipartition queue described in Section 4, with O(1) insertion. This insertion technique has the nice property that it will insert "sink" LPs at the back, because they have infinite EOT, thus delaying their execution until nothing else is enabled.

Figures 8 and 9 show the results of repeating the experiments in Figures 4 and 5, measuring the performance of the bipartition queue relative to that of the splay tree. Neither queuing mechanism shows any consistent advantage over the other in execution time. Since the bipartition queue has lower overhead, it can be concluded that the splay tree probably does a slightly better job of scheduling.

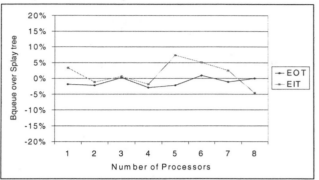

Figure 8. CQNF-Tandem: Splay Tree versus Bipartition Queue

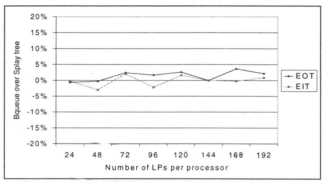

Figure 9. CQNF-Tandem: Splay Tree versus Bipartition Queue, four Processors, variable number of LPs

5.3. Lookahead experiments

In general, if the lookahead in a model is good, the conservative performance will also be good. As the lookahead improves, the number of safe events per LP will increase, and the scheduling overhead is reduced as each LP is able to execute many events consecutively. A desirable quality for a conservative scheduling heuristic is that it improves the performance in the face of poor lookahead. The experiments in this section use the CQNF-Grid topology with a reach of 1.5, giving a branching factor of eight.

Figure 10 shows the results of an experiment in which the job service time for the next event was pre-computed, but only a fixed fraction of that time was specified as available lookahead. EOT again outperformed the other heuristics, and provided the largest benefit when the lookahead was poor.

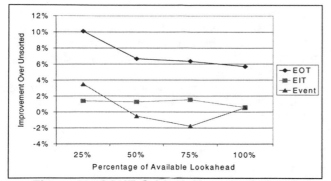

Figure 10. CQNF-Grid: Uniform lookahead

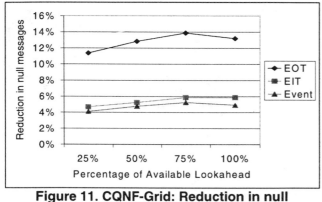

Figure 11. CQNF-Grid: Reduction in null messages

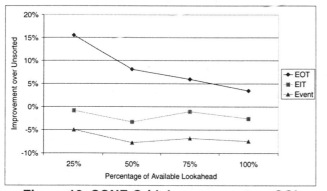

Figure 12. CQNF-Grid: Improvement on SGI Origin

Figure 11 shows the reduction in remote null messages corresponding to this experiment, and Figure 12 shows the performance improvement on the SGI Origin. In the CQNF-Grid experiments, the reduction in null messages is less than in the CQNF-Tandem configuration. The corresponding performance improvement on the Origin is also reduced, in fact degrades as lookahead gets better, because the null message reduction is not enough to generate improvement

5.4. Granularity

The experiments in this section are used to determine whether the benefits of heuristic scheduling hold up in the face of increased computation granularity. It is often the case that large computation granularity can overwhelm the overhead of any synchronization protocol, making them all look the same. In certain situations, though, you might expect to see an increase in parallelism result from a scheduling decision. Consider Figure 13, for example. Events B and C are on node P1, while event A, which depends on C, is scheduled on node P2. If event C is scheduled before B, as in part a), the total execution time is reduced.

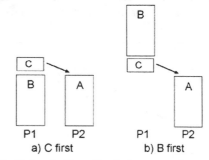

Figure 13. Scheduling Decisions and parallelism

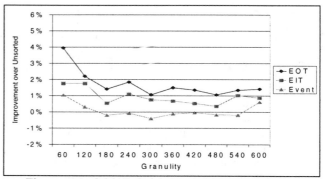

Figure 14. CQNF-Grid: Variable granularity

Experiments were run using the CQNF-Grid topology on four processors of the SPARC 1000 with various levels of uniform event granularity. An event consists of a call to a random number function and a single message, and takes approximately 60µs on the SPARC 1000. We increase the granularity to ten times that amount by using spin loops. Figure 13 shows what happens over a range of grain sizes. The benefits of the heuristic scheduling quickly degrade to negligible values. It is easy to contrive a case like that in the Figure 13 when there are few LPs. If there are many, each processor will typically have enough safe events to keep busy. Also, the scenario described can only occur with large variation in grain sizes.

5.5. Connectivity

To determine whether the sorting heuristics are impacted by connectivity, the reach was varied from one to five. Increasing the communication density should not decrease the amount of available parallelism, because the number of jobs in the system is unchanged, but it definitely leads to higher overhead in the null message protocol, making it more difficult to achieve that potential parallelism. A single LP with poor lookahead may effectively block dozens of LPs on several processors.

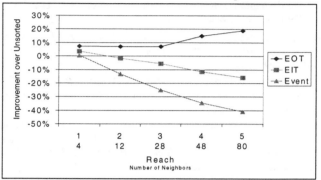

Figure 15. CQNF-Grid: Variable connectivity

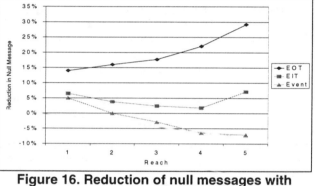

Figure 16. Reduction of null messages with variable connectivity

Figure 15 shows that the performance of the EOT heuristic improves with connectivity, while the others quickly degrade. Figure 16 shows the corresponding reduction in null messages, and it is clear that EOT based scheduling is having a significant impact. The other heuristics are having little effect, so as the number of connections increases, the overhead of the scheduling cost becomes less justified.

5.6. Wireless Network Simulation

Although synthetic benchmarks are easily controlled to test for specific conditions, the ultimate test is to apply these scheduling heuristics to a practical application. GloMoSim [25] is a wireless network simulation wherein each LP represents all the mobile nodes within a geographical region. GloMoSim adapts the standard ISO/OSI protocol stack to the wireless domain. For this experiment, 2000 network nodes are spread over an 800m x 800m region. The region is partitioned into a 4x4 grid, with each grid square represented by four LPs, one at each of the four lowest layers of the protocol stack. The

experiments were run on the Origin 2000. The results given in Section 5.1 suggest that more improvement should be expected from heuristic scheduling on the Origin than on the older SPARC 1000.

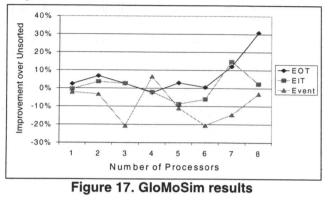

Figure 17. GloMoSim results

Figure 17 shows the performance results. As documented in [26], GloMoSim has poor lookahead, and sees relatively little performance improvement from the heuristic scheduling, except on eight CPUs. With 16 grid squares, only the two, four, and eight CPU tests are balanced.

6. Conclusion

The optimal scheduling strategy for a parallel discrete event simulation is to schedule events on the critical path first (assigning independent overlapping events to other processors). Based on both intuition and analysis, it has been proposed that EOT might be used to guess which LP is next on the critical path. The LP with the minimum EOT might not have the critical event, but it is "critical" in the sense that it is limiting the progress of all its descendents, and should therefore be preferentially scheduled. EOT-based scheduling was compared in a series of experiments with two simpler to calculate heuristics and an unsorted queue.

The experimental results confirm our intuition that using the EOT of an LP for preferential scheduling is the best strategy. Similar performance improvement was shown for both a partially sorted queue, and a fully sorted splay tree. Interestingly, the benefits of the new scheduling strategy were most visible for models that tend to exhibit poor performance with conservative algorithms: e.g., models with poor lookahead, lower computation granularity, and greater connectivity. Our results show a consistent and significant reduction in explicit null messages sent between processors, usually a major overhead in the null message protocol. We hypothesize that a large enough reduction in null messages will make up for the additional queuing cost, and that the benefit gained will be more noticeable on newer machines such as the Origin 2000 with its relatively slow communication. Experiments confirm this hypothesis.

Additional study is necessary to determine whether a more aggressive scheduling strategy can further improve performance. The experiments in this paper used a non-preemptive scheduler. Each LP was allowed to process all of its safe messages, although it may no longer have the lowest heuristic value after processing an event. A preemptive strategy might prove beneficial, despite the increased context switching cost. Another issue is how aggressive an LP should be about sending null messages. In PARSEC, an LP might not immediately send null messages to all of its descendants. The runtime system first tries to piggyback EOT on any regular messages that it sends, and delays sending explicit null messages. The scheduling strategies discussed here might produce greater gains with a more aggressive strategy.

References

[1] Chandy, K. and J. Misra, *Asynchronous Distributed Simulation via a Sequence of Parallel Computations.* Communications of the ACM, 1981. **24**(4): p. 198-206.

[2] Jefferson, D., *Virtual time.* ACM Transactions on Programming Languages on Systems, 1985. **7**(3): p. 404-425.

[3] Cortellessa, V. and G. Iazeolla, *Performance analysis of optimistic parallel simulations with limited rolled back events.* Simulation Practice and Theory, 1999. **7**(4): p. 325-47.

[4] Balsamo, M.S. and C. Manconi, *Rollback overhead reduction methods for time warp distributed simulation.* Simulation Practice and Theory, 1998. **6**(8): p. 689-702.

[5] Ferscha, A. and J. Luthi. *Estimating rollback overhead for optimism control in Time Warp.* in *28th Annual Simulation Symposium.* 1995. Phoenix, AZ, USA.

[6] Palaniswamy, A. and P. Wilsey. *An analytical comparison of periodic checkpointing and incremental state saving.* in *The 7th Workshop on Parallel and Distributed Simulation.* 1993. San Diego, CA, USA.

[7] Hwang, S. and Y. Lin, *On checkpointing in Time Warp parallel simulation.* Information Science and Engineering, 1992. **8**(4): p. 587-602.

[8] Xiao, Z., *et al. Scheduling critical channels in conservative parallel discrete event simulation.* in *Proceedings of the 13th Workshop on Parallel and Distributed Simulation.* 1999. Atlanta, GA: IEEE Computer Society Press.

[9] Naroska, E. and U. Schwiegelshohn. *A new scheduling method for parallel discrete-event simulation.* in *Euro-Par '96 Parallel Processing. Second International Euro-Par Conference.* 1996. Lyon, France.

[10] Lin, Y., E. Lazowska, and J. Baer. *Conservative parallel simulation for systems with no lookahead prediction.* in *Distributed Simulation. The SCS Multiconference.* 1990. San Diego, CA, USA.

[11] Preiss, B. and W. Loucks. *The impact of lookahead on the performance of conservative distributed simulation.* in *Modeling and Simulation. Proceedings of the 1990 European Simulation Multiconference.* 1990. Nuremberg, West Germany.

[12] Gunter, M. *Understanding supercritical speedup.* in *8th Workshop on Parallel and Distributed Simulation.* 1994. Edinburgh, UK.

[13] Srinivasan, S. and P.F. Reynolds, Jr. *Super-criticality revisited.* in *9th Workshop on Parallel and Distributed Simulation.* 1995. Lake Placid, NY, USA.

[14] Jefferson, D. and P. Reiher. *Supercritical speedup.* in *24th Annual Simulation Symposium.* 1991. New Orleans, LA, USA: IEEE Computer Society Press.

[15] Palaniswamy, A. and P. Wilsey. *Scheduling Time Warp processes using adaptive control techniques.* in *1994 Winter Simulation Conference.* 1994. Lake Buena Vista, FL, USA.

[16] Panesar, K.S. and R.M. Fujimoto. *Adaptive flow control in Time Warp.* in *11th Workshop on Parallel and Distributed Simulation.* 1997. Lockenhaus, Austria.

[17] Som, T.K. and R.G. Sargent. *A probabilistic event scheduling policy for optimistic parallel discrete event simulation.* in *12th Workshop on Parallel and Distributed Simulation.* 1998. Banff, Alberta, Canada.

[18] Roenngren, R. and R. Ayani. *Service Oriented Scheduling in Time Warp.* in *Winter Simulation Conference.* 1994.

[19] Chandy, K. and J. Misra, *Distributed Simulation: a case study in design and verification of distributed programs.* IEEE Transactions on Software Engineering, 1979. **5**(5): p. 440-52.

[20] Bagrodia, R., *et al.*, *Parsec: a parallel simulation environment for complex systems.* Computer, 1998. **31**(10): p. 77-85.

[21] Roenngren, R. and R. Ayani, *A Comparative Study of Parallel and Sequential Priority Queue Algorithms.* ACM TOMACS, 1997. **7**(2): p. 157-209.

[22] Sleator, D. and R. Tarjan, *Self-adjusting binary search trees.* Journal of the Association for Computing Machinery, 1985. **32**(3): p. 652-86.

[23] Jha, V. and R. Bagrodia. *A performance evaluation methodology for parallel simulation protocols.* in *Proceedings of the 10th Workshop on Parallel and Distributed Simulation.* 1996. Philadelphia, PA, USA: IEEE Computer Society Press.

[24] Fujimoto, R. *Performance of time warp under synthetic workloads.* in *Distributed Simulation, SCS Multiconference.* 1990. San Diego, CA, USA.

[25] Zeng, X., R. Bagrodia, and M. Gerla. *GloMoSim: a library for parallel simulation of large-scale wireless networks.* in *Proceedings of the 12th Workshop on Parallel and Distributed Simulation.* 1998. Banff, Alberta, Canada: IEEE Computer Society Press.

[26] Meyer, R.A. and R.L. Bagrodia. *Improving lookahead in parallel wireless network simulation.* in *Proceedings of MASCOTS '98: 6th International Symposium on Modeling, Analysis and Simulation of Computer and Telecommunication Systems.* 1998. Montreal, Quebec, Canada: IEEE Computer Society Press.

Grain Sensitive Event Scheduling in Time Warp
Parallel Discrete Event Simulation

Francesco Quaglia
Dipartimento di Informatica e Sistemistica
Università di Roma "La Sapienza"
Via Salaria 113, 00198 Roma, Italy
quaglia@dis.uniroma1.it

Vittorio Cortellessa
Dipartimento di Informatica Sistemi e Produzione
Università di Roma "Tor Vergata"
Via di Tor Vergata, 00133 Roma, Italy
cortelle@info.uniroma2.it

Abstract

Several scheduling algorithms have been proposed to determine the next event to be executed on a processor in a Time Warp parallel discrete event simulation. However, none of them is specifically designed for simulations where the execution time (or granularity) for different types of events has large variance. In this paper we present a grain sensitive scheduling algorithm which addresses this problem. In our solution, the scheduling decision depends on both timestamp and granularity values with the aim at giving higher priority to small grain events even if their timestamp is not the lowest one (i.e. the closest one to the commitment horizon of the simulation). This implicitly limits the optimism of the execution of large grain events that, if rolled back, would produce large waste of CPU time. The algorithm is adaptive in that it relies on the dynamic recalculation of the length of a simulated time window within which the timestamp of any good candidate event for the scheduling falls in. If the window length is set to zero, then the algorithm behaves like the standard Lowest-Timestamp-First (LTF) scheduling algorithm. Simulation results of a classical benchmark in several different configurations are reported for a performance comparison with LTF. These results demonstrate the effectiveness of our algorithm.

1 Introduction

In a parallel discrete event simulator, each part of the simulated system is modeled by a distinct *logical process* (LP) which is basically a sequential discrete event simulator having its own simulation clock, namely *Local Virtual Time* (LVT), its own event list and its own state variables [4]. The execution of any simulation event at an LP usually modifies its state and possibly produces new events to be executed at later simulated time. The notification of new events among distinct LPs takes place through the exchange of messages carrying the content and the occurrence time, namely *timestamp*, of the event. Synchronization mechanisms are used to ensure a timestamp ordered execution of events at each LP, which is a sufficient condition for the correctness of simulation results.

In Time Warp synchronization [7], the simulation progress of any LP is "optimistic" in that the LP executes its events as soon as they are available, without the guaranty of no timestamp order violation. If a timestamp order violation is detected, then a rollback procedure is executed for recovering the LP state to its value prior the violation. While rolling back, the LP "cancels" the events produced during the rolled back part of the simulation; the event cancellation possibly leads other LPs to rollback.

It is widely recognized that one of the essential factors having an impact on the performance of Time Warp synchronization is the scheduling algorithm for the selection of the next event to be executed on a processor. We recall that the need for a scheduling algorithm arises as for simulations of large and/or complex systems it is extremely likely that any processor is responsible for the execution of more than one LP and several LPs hosted by the same processor may simultaneously have at least one non-executed event in their event lists.

Currently the term "good" for a scheduling algorithm is interpreted as the capability of the algorithm to allow fast completion of the simulation by producing a low amount of rollback (i.e. a low amount of rolled back events), which typically means low rollback frequency and short rollback length. However, this perspective becomes inadequate when dealing with Time Warp simulations having high variance of the event granularity, that is, high variance of the event execution time; this is typical of several real world simulations, such as battlefield simulations or simulations of mobile communication systems. In this context, the term "good" should be interpreted as the capability of the scheduling algorithm to allow fast completion by producing a low amount of rollback and also by guaranteeing that the majority of the rolled back events are fine grain ones. The combination of these two features will allow a reduction of the waste of CPU time due to rolled back events, compared to scheduling algorithms which attempt only to reduce the amount of rollback without taking granularity features into account.

In this paper we present a scheduling algorithm, namely Grain Sensitive (GS), specifically designed for simulations with high variance of the event granularity. In this aspect GS differs from all previous scheduling algorithms. Actually our solution is a modification of the Lowest-Timestamp-First algorithm (LTF) [8] which is recognized as a standard solution for the scheduling problem. LTF always schedules for the execution the non-executed event with the minimum timestamp, say e, under the implicit assumption that it has the lowest probability to be rolled back in the future of the simulation execution (this is because it is the closest one to the commitment horizon). Instead, GS delays the scheduling of e each time there is a non-executed event e' (of an LP distinct from the owner of e) such that: (i) the granularity of e is larger than that of e' and (ii) the distance between the timestamps of e and e' is within a Scheduling Window (SW). The rationale behind this solution is as follows. If SW is selected appropriately, then e and e' will have about the same probability to be eventually rolled back if scheduled for the execution, therefore:

(a) scheduling e' prior to e is likely to not increase the amount of rollback of the simulation;

(b) delaying the execution of e might decrease the probability that e will be eventually rolled back (this is the classical positive throttling effect [1, 2, 19]); as e has large granularity, we get a reduction of the probability that large grain events are rolled back, thus keeping low the waste of CPU time.

The combination of features in points (a) and (b) leads GS to be a "good" algorithm when dealing with simulations having high variance of the event granularity. The key problem to address in order to ensure features in points (a) and (b) is the selection of an adequate size for the scheduling window SW. Too large values for SW may lead feature in point (a) to be not ensured as e' will actually have higher probability than e to be eventually rolled back (this will possibly degrade performance due to an increase in the amount of rollback of the simulation). On the other hand, too small values for SW may lead feature in point (b) to be not ensured as there is low probability to produce the throttling effect on e, even if e has very large granularity (this will not reduce the waste of CPU time compared to the classical LTF algorithm). To tackle this problem GS is adaptive in that it relies on the dynamic recalculation of SW based on the monitoring of the real waste of CPU time which is a measure of both the amount of rollback of the simulation and the average granularity of the rolled back events. As an extreme, adaptiveness may lead the value zero to be selected for SW; if this occurs then GS behaves like LTF. This outlines the generality of GS, which has the capability to produce at least the same performance of a standard algorithm.

We report simulation results of a classical benchmark in several different configurations demonstrating the effectiveness of our solution. These results show that GS provides performance improvements in every case considered.

The remainder of the paper is organized as follows. In Section 2 we report a brief overview of existing scheduling algorithms. GS is described in Section 3 together with the technique for the adaptive selection of SW. The performance data are reported in Section 4.

2 Background

The standard solution for the scheduling problem is the Lowest-Timestamp-First algorithm (LTF) [8] which always schedules as next event to be executed on a processor the one with the minimum timestamp. LTF implicitly assumes that the event with the minimum timestamp has the lowest probability to be rolled back in the future of the simulation execution as it is the closest one to the Global-Virtual-Time (i.e. the commitment horizon) of the simulation ([1]). If this presumption reveals true, as in most simulations, then LTF keeps low the amount of rollback, thus producing good performance. Another scheduling algorithm, namely Lowest-Local-Virtual-Time-First (LLVTF) [10], gives higher priority to LPs having lower simulation clocks (i.e. lower LVTs). In particular, LLVTF chooses for the execution the non-executed event of the LP with the lowest LVT value. As the LVT of the LP moves up to the event timestamp upon the execution, the objective of this scheduling algorithm is to reduce the probability for any LP to remain back in simulated time, thus reducing the probability for any LP to induce a timestamp order violation in any other LP involved in the simulation. In [9] an Adaptive Control based scheduling algorithm (AC) has been presented. In this solution, statistics on the past behavior of an LP are collected to establish the "useful work" of the LP (computed as the frequency of committed events of the LP); higher priority is assigned to events of the LPs having higher values of their useful work. The model for the useful work developed by the authors assumes that all the events have the same granularity. A rather different solution, namely Service Oriented scheduling (SO), is presented in [15]. The idea behind this solution is to try to produce and deliver as soon as possible events not yet produced that will have the lower timestamps. This is done in order to deliver promptly those events to the recipient LPs, thus reducing the probability of timestamp order violations. Such an approach needs the capability of the LPs to predict the timestamps of events that have not yet been produced. SO gives the highest scheduling priority to the event whose execution will produce the event with the minimum predicted timestamp. A Probabilistic scheduling algorithm (P) has been presented in [17]. The consideration at the basis of this algorithm is that low amount of rollback can be obtained if the event scheduled for the execution is the one with the minimum real probability to be rolled back in the future; this event may be different from that with the minimum timestamp. In this solution statistics on the past behavior of the LPs are maintained in order to estimate the probability for the next event of any LP to be not rolled back in the future. The event of the LP associated with the highest estimated probability value is scheduled for the execution. Finally, in [14] a State Based scheduling algorithm (SB) has been presented. In this algorithm, the schedul-

---

[1] The definition of Global-Virtual-Time will be provided in Section 3.1 while describing the basic ideas underlying the GS algorithm.

ing priority of any LP is computed using state information related to the LPs in its immediate predecessor set. Specifically, higher priority is assigned to the LPs, if any, whose next event could be rolled back only conditional a rollback occurs on an LP in their immediate predecessor sets. If no such an LP is detected at the scheduling time, then SB acts as the classical LTF.

None of the previous algorithms is designed to maximize the performance for the case of simulations with high variance of the event granularity. This is because the event granularity either is not taken into account at all, or is assumed to have no variance like for the case of AC. However there exist several important classes of simulations in which the execution of different types of events actually takes very different amounts of CPU time. Examples are simulations of battlefields and of mobile communication systems. The GS scheduling algorithm we present in this paper copes with high event granularity variance, thus being well suited for previous classes of simulations.

3 Grain Sensitive Scheduling

This section describes the GS scheduling algorithm. We proceed along the following line. We first provide the basic ideas underlying the algorithm. Then we describe the algorithm structure into details and present the solution for the adaptive tuning of the scheduling window SW. Finally we discuss the relation between GS and classical throttling algorithms.

3.1 Basic Ideas

Consider the example shown in Figure 1 involving three LPs, namely LP_1, LP_2 and LP_3. Assume that these three LPs are hosted by the same processor P and no other LP is hosted by P. Suppose the event list of LP_1 contains two non-executed events a and b, the event list of LP_2 contains one non-executed event c and the event list of LP_3 contains two non-executed events d and e. The timestamps associated with these events are those shown in Figure 1. Furthermore, suppose the width of the rectangular box associated with a simulation event is representative of the event granularity. We denote the granularity of an event x as $G(x)$. In our example, the event a has granularity $G(a)$ which is four times the granularity $G(c)$ of the event c.

The correctness criterion the simulation relies on requires that each LP must execute its events in the order of their timestamps ([2]). We call the set of non-executed events that could be scheduled without violating the correctness criterion as the *Scheduling Candidates* set, denoted as SC. The set SC contains for any LP the non-executed event with the lowest timestamp. Furthermore, we denote as $min(SC)$ the event $e \in SC$ having the minimum timestamp value. If several events have the minimum timestamp value then $min(SC)$ denotes whichever of those events. For the example in Figure 1 we have $SC = \{a, c, d\}$ and $min(SC) = a$.

[2] Recall that timestamp ordered execution suffices, but is not a necessary condition, to guarantee the correctness of simulation results. It is the criterion usually adopted in practice.

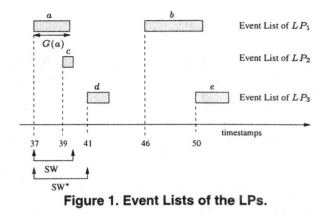

Figure 1. Event Lists of the LPs.

In the classical LTF scheduling algorithm the selection of an event in SC for the execution exploits the timestamp distance from the Global-Virtual-Time (GVT). The GVT of a Time Warp simulation is defined as the minimum of the LVTs of all LPs and the timestamps of events not yet executed. It represents the commitment horizon of the simulation as no LP will ever rollback to a simulated time before GVT. The relevance of the GVT for the scheduling problem arises as it is widely recognized that the difference between the timestamp of a non-executed event e, denoted as $ts(e)$, and the current GVT of the simulation is representative of the likelihood for e to be eventually rolled back if currently scheduled for the execution. Specifically, the less the value of the difference $ts(e) - GVT$, the lower the probability that e will be rolled back in the future of the simulation execution. Starting from this presumption, which is actually verified in most simulations, the LTF algorithm always selects for the execution the event with the minimum timestamp among those in SC. This is done in order to maximize the probability to execute productive simulation work, that is, simulation events that are not eventually rolled back. For the example in Figure 1, LTF would select for the execution the event a.

However, it is relevant to point out that the minimization of the number of rolled back events implies the minimization of the waste of time only in the case all the events of the simulation have the same granularity. This is not true for the case of events with distinct granularity values. The GS scheduling algorithm tackles exactly this problem. Let us now describe the two basic ideas underlying GS.

IDEA-1. If the timestamp of an event $e \in SC$ distinct from $min(SC)$ is not so different from the timestamp of $min(SC)$, then $min(SC)$ and e are likely to have about the same probability to be eventually rolled back as they have about the same distance from the GVT of the simulation (i.e. $ts(e) - GVT \simeq ts(min(SC)) - GVT$). Specifically, we get that there may exist a simulated time interval $I(SW)$ defined as follows:

$$I(SW) = [ts(min(SC)), ts(min(SC)) + SW] \quad (1)$$

such that all the events in SC with timestamp within $I(SW)$

have about the same probability as $min(SC)$ to be eventually rolled back if currently scheduled for the execution. All these events are good candidates for the scheduling as the execution of any of them is likely to not decrease the probability to perform productive simulation work compared to that resulting from LTF scheduling.

As pointed out before, we refer to SW as *scheduling window*. The value of SW adequate for a given simulation (i.e. guaranteeing that all the events with timestamp within $I(SW)$ actually have about the same probability to be eventually rolled back if currently scheduled for the execution) depends on features proper of the simulation, such as number of LPs, how they interact, etc.. Each simulation has its adequate SW value which could also change in the lifetime of the simulation. For the example in Figure 1, we get that if at the time the scheduling decision must be taken the adequate value for SW is 3 simulated time units, then both a and c are good candidates for the scheduling.

The relevance of IDEA-1 for the scheduling problem is as follows. Having a set of events considered as good candidates for the execution increases the flexibility of the scheduling decision so that the decision can be aimed at improving the performance by exploiting granularity features of the good candidate events.

IDEA-2. The second idea is related to the classical notion of throttling in Time Warp synchronization. Specifically, given a non-executed event e, we have that the probability for e to be eventually rolled back if executed at real time t is higher than, or at least equal to, the probability to be eventually rolled back if executed at real time $t + \Delta t$. This is because:

$$[ts(e) - GVT]_t \geq [ts(e) - GVT]_{t+\Delta t} \qquad (2)$$

In other words, as the GVT value does not decrease in real time, the difference between the timestamp of the event e and the GVT does not increase in real time (i.e. the distance of the event from the commitment horizon of the simulation does not increase); therefore the probability for the event e to be eventually rolled back is likely to decrease if its execution is delayed.

The relevance of IDEA-2 for the scheduling problem is as follows. If we can delay the execution of an event e which has very large granularity without increasing the whole amount of rollback, compared to the classical LTF scheduling algorithm, then we can get an increase in the performance.

Both IDEA-1 and IDEA-2 form the basis of the GS scheduling algorithm presented in the next subsection.

3.2 The Scheduling Algorithm

Let us assume at a given real time instant t a scheduling decision must be taken on processor P. Also, assume that SW* is the adequate value of the scheduling window at real time t. According to IDEA-1, SW* determines a set of Good Candidate events for the scheduling, namely GC,

containing at least $min(SC)$. GC is formally defined as:

$$GC = \{e \in SC \mid ts(e) \in I(\text{SW}^*)\} \qquad (3)$$

Let us denote as $P_r(e, t)$ the probability for the event $e \in GC$ to be eventually rolled back if scheduled for the execution at real time t. Adequacy of the scheduling window SW* implies that, for any pair of events e and e' belonging to GC, $P_r(e, t) \simeq P_r(e', t)$. We approximate these probability values with $P_r(t)$ representing the probability for any event belonging to GC to be eventually rolled back if scheduled for the execution at real time t.

We can now build the following simple model $M(e, t)$ for the waste of CPU time associated with the scheduling of the event e belonging to GC for the execution at real time t:

$$M(e, t) = P_r(t)G(e) \qquad (4)$$

where $G(e)$ is the granularity of e. Note that this model neglects the effects any scheduling action will produce on the progress of the simulation. It takes into account only the waste of CPU time predictable at time t as a function of the granularity of the events considered as good candidates for the scheduling. In this aspect, it shares the same limitation of the scheduling algorithms discussed in Section 2, except the one in [15], as these algorithms do not take any future effect of the outcome of the current scheduling decision into account ([3]).

The rationale behind the GS algorithm is to schedule for the execution at time t the event e belonging to GC which minimizes the value of the function in (4). This simply implies the scheduling of the event $e \in GC$ with the lowest granularity value. Compared to LTF, this scheduling decision will produce the following two positive effects each time the scheduled event e has not the minimum timestamp in the set GC:

- the waste of CPU time due to the outcome of the scheduling decision at time t is reduced; this is because LTF would schedule for the execution $min(SC)$ with granularity $G(min(SC)) > G(e)$, therefore $M(min(SC), t) > M(e, t)$. In other words, the waste of CPU time produced by the scheduling decision according to the model in expression (4) is larger for LTF than for GS;

- a throttling effect is produced on $min(SC)$ whose execution is delayed from real time t to real time $t + \Delta t$; if $min(SC)$ has large granularity then we get a reduction of the probability that large grain events are rolled back, thus producing a further reduction of the waste of CPU time compared to LTF.

The first effect is a direct effect due to the minimization of the model for the waste of CPU time in (4). The second

---

[3]In the algorithm in [15] the effects of the scheduling decision on the progress of the simulation are taken into account at some extent. This is because the scheduling decision relies on (predicted) timestamp values of future events not yet produced.

```
GS Scheduling:
1 if SC ≠ ∅
2 then
3       <select the adequate value for the scheduling window SW*>
4       <compute the set GC = {e | (e ∈ SC) ∧ (ts(e) ∈ I(SW*))}>
5       <compute the set β = {e | (e ∈ GC) ∧ (∀e' ∈ GC :
          M(e, t) ≤ M(e', t))}>
6       <from among all the events in β select for execution the
          event with the minimum timestamp>
7 else <no action>
```

Figure 2. The GS Scheduling Algorithm.

effect is an indirect effect due to the delay induced for the execution of large grain events.

Considering the example in Figure 1, if we assume the adequate scheduling window is $SW^* = 4$ then GS favors the fine grain event c compared to the larger grain one a.

In Figure 2, the GS scheduling algorithm is shown. Although not discussed before, there may exist several events in GC, with the same granularity value, minimizing the cost model in (4) (see Line 5 of the algorithm). If this occurs, GS schedules from among these events the one with the minimum timestamp (see Line 6), following the classical policy underlying LTF.

The key problem in order to guarantee the feasibility of the model in (4) underlying the algorithm is how to select the adequate value SW^* for the scheduling window. This issue will be tackled in the following subsection. It is important to note that if the selected value for SW^* is zero, then the GS scheduling algorithm behaves similarly to the classical LTF algorithm. In this case the major difference is that if GC contains several events, then GS gives the highest priority to the event belonging to GC with the lowest granularity value, while LTF randomly selects in GC the event which must be executed. This slightly different behavior of GS will possibly favor the performance, as compared to LTF, by producing throttling on large grain events. The similarity in the behaviors of GS and LTF when the value of SW^* is set to zero will be exploited in the technique for the adaptive recalculation of the value of SW^*.

Finally, we recall that the event granularity could be either deterministic or of a random nature. In the second case, an estimation system for predicting the expected granularity of the events in GC should be coupled with the GS algorithm.

3.3 Adaptive Tuning of the Scheduling Window

We base the adaptive selection of the value of the adequate scheduling window SW^* on the monitoring of the average waste of CPU time per event, namely WT. From a mathematical point of view WT is defined as the following product of two quantities:

$$WT = P_r \bar{G} \tag{5}$$

The former quantity, namely P_r, is the ratio between the number of rolled back events and the total number of executed simulation events (committed plus rolled back). P_r expresses the probability for whichever executed event to be

eventually rolled back, it is therefore representative of the amount of rollback of the simulation ([4]). The latter quantity, namely $\bar{G}$, is the average granularity of the executed events (committed plus rolled back). If we denote with EX the set of the executed events, then $\bar{G}$ is expressed as:

$$\bar{G} = \frac{\sum_{e \in EX} G(e)}{|EX|} \tag{6}$$

The LTF scheduling algorithm produces some values for P_r and $\bar{G}$. The objective of the GS algorithm is to produce a probability value P_r similar to that produced by LTF (this should be the outcome of IDEA-1) and an average granularity value $\bar{G}$ lower than that produced by LTF (this should be the outcome of IDEA-2) as under GS the set of executed events EX should contain less rolled back large grain events due to the throttling effect on them. This points out the adequacy of WT as expressive parameter of the performance of GS, as compared to LTF, since it accounts for the two quantities directly affected by the scheduling decision performed by GS. Specifically, the difference of the WT value produced by GS with a given scheduling window, compared to that produced by LTF, is a direct measure of how effectively are IDEA-1 and IDEA-2 supported with that scheduling window. This is the consideration at the basis of the adaptive tuning of SW^* presented below. Before entering the details of the adaptive tuning, it is important to remark that the average waste of CPU time which should be reduced by GS, compared to LTF, is the average waste of CPU time on all the processors. This is because the reduction of WT on a single processor does not necessarily lead to performance improvements. For this reason, adaptiveness must be such that the same value for SW^* has to be adopted on all the processors in order to monitor the real impact of its variations on the performance.

We consider the execution of the simulation as divided into observation periods. Each period consists of N committed/rolled-back events. The value of N should be chosen in the way to ensure statistical data on WT collected in any period to be meaningful (suggestions to solve this problem have been already pointed out in other studies [16]). Furthermore, we assume there exists a master processor MP which gathers statistical data related to WT collected on the remote processors and adaptively computes the new value for SW^*. This value is then notified to the slave processors. The interaction between MP and the slave processors is as follows. When the observation period expires at MP, it sends a `statistic_request` message to the slave processors. Upon the receipt of this message, any slave processor replies with a `collected_statistic` message whose payload is the locally observed WT value since the last request sent by MP was processed. When all the replies are received by MP, it computes the observed WT value of the simulation in the current observation period as the average of the WT values on all the processors.

---

[4]The quantity $1 - P_r$ is widely known as the efficiency of the simulation.

It then selects the new value for SW* and notifies it to the slave processors through an `SW_notification` message. The new value is adopted for the next observation period. Note that the simulation is not frozen while the interaction between MP and the slave processors takes place.

The adaptive selection of the value of SW* performed by MP is as follows. At the beginning of the simulation execution the value SW* = 0 is selected and notified to all the slave processors. This means that during the first period GS behaves like LTF. At the end of the successive observation periods, the value of SW* is increased by a quantity δ if the observed WT of the simulation did not increase. If latter quantity increases, then SW* is decreased by 2δ (in the case SW* is less than 2δ, it is set to zero). The step for the increase is δ, the step for the decrease is 2δ; this difference is in order to quickly move the adequate scheduling window SW* towards the value zero (i.e. to quickly move the behavior of GS towards the one of LTF) when successive increments of the value of WT are observed. This adaptive solution aims at keeping the value of SW* as large as possible while still guaranteeing the feasibility of IDEA-1 (i.e. while still producing no relevant increase in the amount of rollback, expressed by P_r, as compared to LTF scheduling). This is done in order to increase the expected cardinality of the good candidates set GC at the time the scheduling decision must be taken. This should actually lead to high flexibility of the scheduling decision as a function of the granularity of the events in GC, thus producing throttling on very large grain ones, which is the final outcome of IDEA-2. If too large values for SW* are selected then IDEA-1 could become infeasible thus originating an increase of P_r (i.e. an increase in the amount of rollback). If such an increase is poor and is still balanced by the gain from the throttling effect on large grain events, then SW* is further increased. Otherwise, it is decreased.

Concerning the selection of the value for δ, preliminary performance results have shown that low values for δ, compared to the average timestamp increment of the simulation, usually produce the best performance results. As a general rule for the selection of δ we suggest the following expression:

$$\delta = \frac{\bar{T}}{10} \qquad (7)$$

where $\bar{T}$ represents the average timestamp increment of the simulation.

Finally, we note that, from a "philosophical" point of view, our approach for the adaptive tuning of SW* borrows from adaptive techniques for choosing the checkpointing protocol parameters in Time Warp simulations, for example the frequency of periodic checkpoints, such as the ones in [3, 11, 12].

3.4 Relation with Classical Throttling Algorithms

A number of throttling algorithms (e.g. [1, 2, 19]) have been proposed to associate with a non-executed event e an adequate execution delay in order to get good balance between the gain from the reduction of the probability for e

to be eventually rolled back and the loss from the limitation of the optimism of the execution. Typically in these algorithms the delay is computed once the event e has been already scheduled for the execution, therefore the throttling is actuated at a higher level compared to that of the scheduling algorithm. This makes these algorithms different from our solution where the throttling on large grain events is actuated exactly at the level of the scheduling algorithm.

Although we have no empirical evidence yet, we argue that these two distinct types of throttling, being actuated at distinct levels, could be used in conjunction in order to further improve the performance.

4 Performance Data

In this section experimental results are reported to compare the performance achievable by using the GS scheduling algorithm to the one of the classical LTF algorithm. Before showing the results of the comparative analysis, we describe the main features of the used hardware/software architecture, present the selected benchmark and introduce the performance parameters we have measured.

As hardware architecture we used a cluster of machines (Pentium II 300 MHz - 128 Mbytes RAM) connected via fast switched Ethernet. The number of machines in the cluster is four. Inter-processor communication relies on message passing supported by PVM [20]. Our software is such that event cancellation is aggressive (i.e. antievents are sent as soon as the LP rolls back [6]) and fossil collection is executed periodically.

We tested the performance of the scheduling algorithms using the synthetic benchmark known as PHOLD model, originally presented in [5]. It consists of a fixed number of LPs and of a constant number of jobs circulating among the LPs (that is referred to as job population). Both the routing of jobs among the LPs and the timestamp increments are taken from some stochastic distributions. We have chosen this benchmark for two main reasons: (i) its parameters (e.g. event execution time and state saving cost) can be easily modified, (ii) it usually shows rollback behavior similar to many other synthetic benchmarks and to several real world models. In addition, it is important to remark that it is one of the most used benchmarks for testing the performance of both scheduling algorithms [14, 17] and checkpointing techniques [11, 13, 16, 18, 21].

The PHOLD model we considered is composed of 64 homogeneous LPs. Two different distributions were used for the timestamp increments: an exponential distribution with mean 1 simulated time unit and an uniform distribution in the interval [0,2] simulated time units. There are four hot spot LPs to which 30% of all the jobs are routed. The remaining percentage of jobs are equally likely to be routed to any LP. The spots randomly move among the LPs in the course of the simulation. In each simulation there are two distinct event types (i.e. two distinct job types), say *light* and *heavy*. Any light event takes about 200 microseconds to process and the effect of its execution is the production of a new light event. A heavy event takes a time which is about

10 times the one of a light event; its execution produces a new heavy event. This simulation model has resemblances to the model considered in [18] for testing the performance of a checkpointing technique specifically designed for simulations with high event granularity variance. It nicely approximates simulations of mobile communication systems. In this context, light events model position updates while heavy ones model resource allocation/utilization, which is typically more costly to simulate. Two distinct job populations were considered: one job per LP and 10 jobs per LP. In both cases 50% of all the jobs are light, 50% are heavy; they are randomly assigned to the LPs at the simulation starting. State saving is performed after the execution of each event; its cost has been fixed at about 15 microseconds.

The four configurations of the benchmark were run using all the 4 machines of the cluster. Each machine hosts the same number of LPs (no other user load runs on any machine). For the GS algorithm, the recalculation of the value of the adequate scheduling window SW* is executed each 5000 events (i.e. the observation period at the master processor is fixed at 5000 committed/rolled-back events).

We report measures related to the following parameters:

- the *amount of rollback* (AR), that is, the ratio between the number of rolled back events and the total number of executed events (committed plus rolled back); this parameter corresponds exactly to the probability value P_r in expression (5); it indicates how good is a given scheduling algorithm from the point of view of the rollback originated during the simulation execution;

- the *average granularity* of the executed (committed plus rolled back) events (AG); this parameter corresponds exactly to the average granularity value $\bar{G}$ defined in expression (6); it represents a metric for the granularity of the rolled back events; specifically, the larger the granularity of the rolled back events the larger the value of AG;

- the *event rate* (ER), that is, the number of committed events per second; this parameter indicates how fast is the simulation execution with a given scheduling algorithm, it is therefore representative of the achieved performance.

For the GS algorithm we report also the observed value of the average scheduling window length (ASW). For each configuration of the benchmark we report the average observed values of previous parameters, computed over 20 runs that were all done with different seeds for the random number generation. At least 2×10^6 committed events were simulated in each run. The results for the case of exponential timestamp increment are reported in Table 1 and in Table 2. Those for the case of uniform distribution are reported in Table 3 and in Table 4. The values for AG are reported in microseconds, those for ASW in simulated time units.

The obtained data show that the amount of rollback AR under GS remains quite close to that obtained with LTF. The maximum difference is about 10%; it is observed for the case of exponential timestamp increment with a job population of 10 jobs per LP. This is achieved with values of ASW that in no case are much smaller (e.g. one order of magnitude or more) than the average timestamp increment of the simulation. Specifically, for the case of exponential timestamp increments, the observed values of ASW are in the order of 1/4, or 1/5 the average timestamp increment; for the case of uniform timestamp increments those values are in the order of 1/3, or 1/4 the average timestamp increment. This points out the feasibility of IDEA-1 since non-minimal scheduling window lengths can be actually used for increasing the flexibility of the scheduling decision as a function of the event granularity, without producing relevant negative effects from the point of view of the rollback originated in the simulation execution. We note that for both exponential and uniform timestamp increments, simulations with 1 job per LP show values of ASW higher than those with 10 jobs per LP. This behavior is an expected one when considering that large job populations originate high density of events in the simulated time. In this cases, the flexibility of the scheduling decision is actually increased even with small scheduling window lengths (i.e. the set of good candidate events GC in (3) is likely to have large cardinality even with small scheduling windows).

Table 1. Exp. Timest. Incr. - 1 Job per LP

Algorithm	AR	AG	ER	ASW
LTF	0.174	1104	1241	-
GS	0.177	1029	1309	0.28

Table 2. Exp. Timest. Incr. - 10 Jobs per LP

Algorithm	AR	AG	ER	ASW
LTF	0.110	1088	1539	-
GS	0.123	915	1637	0.19

The second point outlined by the results is a strong reduction of the values of AG when GS is adopted. Specifically, we get that the values of AG under GS are lower, between 6% and 16%, compared to those under LTF. This points out the real gain achievable through the throttling effect underlying IDEA-2, which strongly reduces the number of large grain events that are eventually rolled back.

When combining the results for AR and AG (i.e. when multiplying them, see expression (5)) we get that GS actually originates a reduction of the waste of CPU time between 4% and 10%. This allows GS to provide higher values for ER (between 3% and 8%), thus leading to faster execution of the simulation. The performance gain is achieved for all the four tested configurations, thus pointing out that GS could actually represent an adequate solution in simulations with high event granularity variance.

5 Summary

In this paper we have presented a scheduling algorithm for the selection of the next LP to be run on a processor in a

179

Table 3. Unif. Timest. Incr. - 1 Job per LP

Algorithm	AR	AG	ER	ASW
LTF	0.128	1112	1260	-
GS	0.135	1017	1299	0.34

Table 4. Unif. Timest. Incr. - 10 Jobs per LP

Algorithm	AR	AG	ER	ASW
LTF	0.083	1123	1452	-
GS	0.091	949	1565	0.22

Time Warp simulation which is well suited for simulations with high variance of the event granularity. In our solution, the scheduling decision is a function of both timestamps and granularity values of the simulation events. The algorithm aims at reducing the average granularity of the rolled back events without increasing the whole amount of rollback of the simulation. The combination of these two features will possibly reduce the waste of CPU time due to rolled back events, thus yielding faster execution of the simulation.

We have tested the performance of the algorithm using a classical benchmark in different configurations. The obtained data point out that our solution allows faster simulation execution (up to 8%) in every considered configuration compared to the classical Lowest-Timestamp-First algorithm.

Acknowledgments. The authors thank the anonymous referees for helpful comments which have improved the content and the presentation of the paper. A special thank goes to Paolo Molinari for his help in the implementation of the simulation code.

References

[1] A. Ferscha, "Probabilistic Adaptive Direct Optimism Control in Time Warp", *Proc. 9th Workshop on Parallel and Distributed Simulation (PADS'95)*, pp.120-129, June 1995.

[2] A. Ferscha and J. Luthi, "Estimating Rollback Overhead for Optimism Control in Time Warp", *Proc. 28th Annual Simulation Symposium*, pp.2-12, April 1995.

[3] J. Fleischmann and P.A. Wilsey, "Comparative Analysis of Periodic State Saving Techniques in Time Warp Simulators", *Proc. 9th Workshop on Parallel and Distributed Simulation (PADS'95)*, pp.50-58, June 1995.

[4] R.M. Fujimoto, "Parallel Discrete Event Simulation", *Communications of ACM*, Vol.33, No.10, 1990, pp.30-53.

[5] R.M. Fujimoto, "Performance of Time Warp Under Synthetic Workloads", *Proc. Multiconf. Distributed Simulation*, Vol.22, No.1, January 1990.

[6] A. Gafni, "Space Management and Cancellation Mechanisms for Time Warp", *Tech. Rep. TR-85-341*, University of Southern California, Los Angeles (Ca,USA).

[7] D. Jefferson, "Virtual Time", *ACM Transactions on Programming Languages and Systems*, Vol.7, No.3, 1985, pp.404-425.

[8] Y.B. Lin and E.D. Lazowska, "Processor Scheduling for Time Warp Parallel Simulation", *Advances in Parallel and Distributed Simulation*, pp.11-14, 1991.

[9] A.C. Palaniswamy and P.A. Wilsey, "Scheduling Time Warp Processes Using Adaptive Control Techniques", *Proc. 1994 Winter Simulation Conference*, pp.731-738, December 1994.

[10] B.R. Preiss, W.M. Loucks and D. MAcIntyre, "Effects of the Checkpoint Interval on Time and Space in Time Warp", *ACM Transactions on Modeling and Computer Simulation*, Vol.4, No.3, 1994, pp.223-253.

[11] F. Quaglia, "Event History Based Sparse State Saving in Time Warp", *Proc. 12th Workshop on Parallel and Distributed Simulation (PADS'98)*, pp.72-79, May 1998.

[12] F. Quaglia, "Combining Periodic and Probabilistic Checkpointing in Optimistic Simulation", *Proc. 13th Workshop on Parallel and Distributed Simulation (PADS'99)*, pp.109-116, May 1999.

[13] F. Quaglia, "Fast-Software-Checkpointing in Optimistic Simulation: Embedding State Saving into the Event Routine Instructions", *Proc. 13th Workshop on Parallel and Distributed Simulation (PADS'99)*, pp.118-125, May 1999.

[14] F. Quaglia, "A State-Based Scheduling Algorithm for Time Warp Synchronization", *Proc. 33rd Annual Simulation Symposium*, April 2000.

[15] R. Ronngren and R. Ayani, "Service Oriented Scheduling in Time Warp", *Proc. 1994 Winter Simulation Conference*, pp.1340-1346, December 1994.

[16] R. Ronngren and R. Ayani, "Adaptive Checkpointing in Time Warp", *Proc. 8th Workshop on Parallel and Distributed Simulation (PADS'94)*, pp.110-117, May 1994.

[17] T.K. Som and R.G. Sargent, "A Probabilistic Event Scheduling Policy for Optimistic Parallel Discrete Event Simulation", *Proc. 12th Workshop on Parallel and Distributed Simulation (PADS'98)*, pp.56-63, May 1998.

[18] S. Skold and R. Ronngren, "Event Sensitive State Saving in Time Warp Parallel Discrete Event Simulations", *Proc. 1996 Winter Simulation Conference*, December 1996.

[19] S. Srinivasan and P.F. Reynolds Jr., "Elastic Time", *ACM Transactions on Modeling and Computer Simulation*, Vol.8, No.2, 1998, pp.103-139.

[20] V.S. Sunderam, "A Framework for Parallel Distributed Computing", *Concurrency: Practice and Experience*, Vol.2, No.4, 1990.

[21] D. West and K. Panesar, "Automatic Incremental State Saving", *Proc. 10th Workshop on Parallel and Distributed Simulation (PADS'96)*, pp.78-85, May 1996.

Author Index

Steering Committee
R. L. Bagrodia
UCLA, USA
D. I. Bruce
DERA, UK
A. S. Elmaghraby
Univ of Louisville, USA
A. Ferscha
Univ of Vienna, Austria
R. M. Fujimoto (Honorary)
Georgia Inst. of Tech, USA
B. W. Unger
Univ of Calgary, Canada
F. P. Wieland
The MITRE Corp, USA
General Co-Chairs
R. L. Bagrodia and E. Deelman
UCLA, USA
Program Chair
P. A. Wilsey
Univ of Cincinnati, USA
Program Committee Members[†]
A. Boukerche
Univ of North Texas, USA
D. I. Bruce
DERA, UK
W. Cai
Nanyang Tech Univ, Singapore
C. D. Carothers
Rensselaer Polytechnic, USA
J. G. Cleary
U. of Waikato, New Zealand
S. R. Das
Univ of Cincinnati, USA
A. Ferscha
Univ of Vienna, Austria
P. A. Fishwick
Univ of Florida, USA
R. M. Fujimoto
Georgia Inst. of Tech, USA
D. M. Nicol
Dartmouth College, USA
C. D. Pham
Univ of Lyons, France
F. Quaglia
Univ of Rome, Italy
B. R. Ronngren
Royal Inst. of Tech., Sweden
M. Takai
UCLA, USA
C. Tropper
McGill Univ, Canada
S. J. Turner
Univ of Exeter, UK
B. W. Unger
Univ of Calgary, Canada
F. P. Wieland
The MITRE Corp., USA

CALL FOR PAPERS

15th Workshop on Parallel and Distributed Simulation
PADS 2001

May 15-18 2001, Lake Arrowhead, California, USA

Sponsors: ACM Special Interest Group on Simulation (SIGSIM)[†], IEEE Computer Society Technical Committee on Simulation (IEEE-TCSIM)[†], and Society for Computer Simulation (SCS)[†].

Topics: PADS provides a forum for presenting recent results in parallel and distributed simulation. The scope of the conference includes, but is not limited to:

- Algorithms and methods for parallel simulation (e.g. synchronization, scheduling, memory management, load balancing, partitioning and allocation.)
- Models of parallel simulation (e.g. stochastic, Markovian, process algebraic, temporal logic.)
- Methodology for parallel simulation. (e.g. system modeling for parallel simulation, specification, adapting sequential methodologies, parallelizing existing simulations.)
- Parallel simulation languages and models (e.g. language and implementation issues, models of parallel simulation, execution environments, libraries.)
- Performance of parallel simulation (e.g. theoretical and empirical studies, prediction and analysis, cost models, benchmarks, comparative studies.)
- Application of parallel simulation (e.g. computer architecture, VLSI, telecommunication networks, manufacturing, dynamic systems, biological/social systems, parallel and distributed computing.)
- Web based distributed simulation (e.g. multimedia and real time applications, fault tolerance, implementation issues, use of Java, CORBA.)
- Distributed Interactive Simulation (e.g. synchronization in multi-user distributed simulation, virtual reality environments, HLA, interoperability.)

Schedule: Send submissions to the program chair by **October 13, 2000** for hardcopy or by **October 1, 2000** for electronic submission. Notification of acceptance will be made by **December 20, 2000**. Camera ready copy is due **February 28, 2001**.

Submissions: Papers must be written in English and should not exceed 5000 words. Papers must be unpublished and must not be submitted for publication elsewhere. Authors are encouraged to submit their papers in electronic form (Postscript only.) Guidelines for electronic are available on the World-Wide Web at the URL given below. Paper may also be submitted in hardcopy form in which case **six** copies are required. Each submission must be accompanied by the following information: a short abstract, a complete list of authors and their affiliations, a contact person for correspondence, post and email addresses.

All submissions will be reviewed using a double-blind review process, i.e., the identity of authors, and referees will not be revealed to each other. To ensure blind reviewing, authors' names and affiliations should not appear in the paper, bibliographic references should be modified so as not to reveal the identities of the authors.

General Co-Chairs:		**Program Chair:**
Rajive Bagrodia	Ewa Deelman	Philip A. Wilsey
3531F Boelter Hall	3532C Boelter Hall	Experimental Computing Lab
Dept. of Computer Science, UCLA		Dept of ECECS, PO Box 210030
Los Angeles, CA 90095-1596		Cincinnati, OH 45221-0030
Fax: +1 310 794-5056		voice: +1 513 556-4779
voice: +1 310 825-0956	+1 310 825-2091	fax: +1 513 556-7326
email: rajive@cs.ucla.edu	deelman@cs.ucla.edu	email: philip.wilsey@ieee.org

Online Information: Up-to-date information about PADS 2001 can be obtained from: **http://ececs.uc.edu/~paw/pads2001** . Please send email to **pads@ani.univie.ac.at** with subject: **subscribe** for inclusion in the PADS electronic mailing list.

[†]approval pending

Notes

Notes

Notes

Notes

Notes

Notes

IEEE
COMPUTER
SOCIETY

Press Activities Board

IEEE Computer Society Publications

The world-renowned IEEE Computer Society publishes, promotes, and distributes a wide variety of authoritative computer science and engineering texts. These books are available from most retail outlets. Visit the Online Catalog, *http://computer.org*, for a list of products.

IEEE Computer Society Proceedings

The IEEE Computer Society also produces and actively promotes the proceedings of more than 141 acclaimed international conferences each year in multimedia formats that include hard and softcover books, CD-ROMs, videos, and on-line publications.

For information on the IEEE Computer Society proceedings, send e-mail to *cs.books@computer.org* or write to Proceedings, IEEE Computer Society, P.O. Box 3014, 10662 Los Vaqueros Circle, Los Alamitos, CA 90720-1314. Telephone +1 714-821-8380. FAX +1 714-761-1784.

Additional information regarding the Computer Society, conferences and proceedings, CD-ROMs, videos, and books can also be accessed from our web site at *http://computer.org/cspress*

Revised 9 November 1999